System Dynamics in Economic and Financial Models

WILEY

SERIES IN FINANCIAL ECONOMICS
AND QUANTITATIVE ANALYSIS

Further titles in preparation
Proposals will be welcomed by the Series Editor

System Dynamics in Economic and Financial Models

Edited by

Christiaan Heij, Hans Schumacher, Bernard Hanzon
and Kees Praagman

JOHN WILEY & SONS

Chichester • New York • Weinheim • Brisbane • Singapore • Toronto

330.015195
5995

Other Wiley Editorial Offices

John Wiley & Sons, Inc., 605 Third Avenue,
New York, NY 10158-0012, USA

WILEY-VCH Verlag GmbH, Pappelallee 3,
D-69469 Weinheim, Germany

Jacaranda Wiley Ltd, 33 Park Road, Milton,
Queensland 4064, Australia

John Wiley & Sons (Asia) Pte Ltd, 2 Clementi Loop #02-01,
Jin Xing Distripark, Singapore 129809

John Wiley & Sons (Canada) Ltd, 22 Worcester Road,
Rexdale, Ontario M9W 1LI, Canada

Library of Congress Cataloging-in-Publication Data

System dynamics in economic and financial models / edited by C. Heij ... [et al.].
    p.   cm. — (Series in financial economics and quantitative analysis)
    ISBN 0-471-96934-6 (alk. paper)
    1. Econometric models.   2. Finance — Mathematical models.
  3. Statics and dynamics (Social sciences)   I. Heij, C.   II. Series.
  HB141.S973   1997
  330'.01'5195 – dc21   97–17075
                                                                              CIP

British Library Cataloguing in Publication Data

A catalogue record for this book is available from the British Library

ISBN 0-471-96934-6

Typeset in 10/12pt Times from the author's disks by Keytec Typesetting Ltd, Bridport, Dorset.
Printed and bound in Great Britain by Biddles Ltd, Guildford and King's Lynn.
This book is printed on acid-free paper responsibly manufactured from sustainable forestation,
for which at least two trees are planted for each one used for paper production.

Contents

List of Contributors

M. BASSEVILLE
IRISA/CNRS, Rennes, France

M. BEEBY
London School of Economics, UK

H.J. BIERENS
Department of Economics, The Pennsylvania State University, USA

J. BREITUNG
Institute of Statistics and Econometrics, Humboldt University, Berlin, Germany

W.A. BROCK
Department of Economics, University of Wisconsin, USA

M. CAMPBELL
Post-Orthodox Economics, London, UK

M.H.A. DAVIS
Tokyo-Mitsubishi International plc, London, UK

M. DEISTLER
Institute of Econometrics, Operations Research and System Theory, Technical University of Vienna, Austria

E.J. DOCKNER
Department of Business Administration, University of Vienna, Austria

J.C. ENGWERDA
Department of Economics, Tilburg University, The Netherlands

G. FEICHTINGER
Institute of Econometrics, Operations Research and System Theory, Technical University of Vienna, Austria

P.H.B.F. FRANSES
Econometric Institute, Erasmus University Rotterdam, The Netherlands

M. FUNKE
Department of Economics, Hamburg University, Germany

S.G. HALL
The Management School, Imperial College of Science, Technology and Medicine, London, UK

A.C. HARVEY
Faculty of Economics and Politics, University of Cambridge, UK

C.H. HOMMES
Department of Economics, University of Amsterdam, The Netherlands

T. KLOEK
Econometric Institute, Erasmus University Rotterdam, The Netherlands

S.J. KOOPMAN
Department of Statistics, London School of Economics and Politics, UK

H. LÜTKEPOHL
Institute of Statistics and Econometrics, Humboldt University, Berlin, Germany

A.H.Q.M. MERKIES
Faculty of Economics and Econometrics, Free University Amsterdam, The Netherlands

J.M. MORALEDA
Tinbergen Institute, Erasmus University Rotterdam, The Netherlands

H. NIJMEIJER
Department of Applied Mathematics, University of Twente, The Netherlands

M. OOMS
Econometric Institute, Erasmus University Rotterdam, The Netherlands

P. ORMEROD
Post-Orthodox Economics, Richmond, UK

F.C. PALM
Department of Economics, Maastricht University, The Netherlands

D.J. PEDREGAL
Institute of Environmental and Biological Sciences, Lancaster University, UK

D.S.G. POLLOCK
Department of Economics, Queen Mary and Westfield College, University of London, UK

A. PRSKAWETZ
Institute of Econometrics, Operations Research and System Theory, Technical University of Vienna, Austria

I.J. STEYN
Faculty of Economics and Econometrics, Free University Amsterdam, The Netherlands

F. TAKENS
Department of Mathematics, University of Groningen, The Netherlands

T. TERÄSVIRTA
Department of Economic Statistics, Stockholm School of Economics, Sweden

R. TSCHERNIG
Institute of Statistics and Econometrics, Humboldt University, Berlin, Germany

D. VAN DIJK
Tinbergen Institute, Erasmus University Rotterdam, The Netherlands

A.C.F. VORST
Econometric Institute, Erasmus University Rotterdam, The Netherlands

M. WAGNER
Institute of Econometrics, Operations Research and System Theory, Technical University of Vienna, Austria

P.C. YOUNG
Institute of Environmental and Biological Sciences, Lancaster University, UK

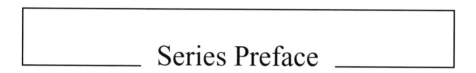

Series Preface

This series aims to publish books which give authoritative accounts of major new topics in financial economics and general quantitative analysis. The coverage of the series includes both macro and micro economics and its aim is to be of interest to practitioners and policy-makers as well as the wider academic community.

The development of new techniques and ideas in econometrics has been rapid in recent years and these developments are now being applied to a wide range of areas and markets. Our hope is that this series will provide a rapid and effective means of communicating these ideas to a wide international audience and that in turn this will contribute to the growth of knowledge, the exchange of scientific information and techniques and the development of cooperation in the field of economics.

Stephen Hall
London Business School, UK and
Imperial College, UK

Editors' Preface

This book discusses a variety of viewpoints around the central theme of dynamic models in economics and finance. It consists of eleven chapters written by distinguished authors with backgrounds ranging from econometrics and quantitative finance to systems and control. The main purpose of the book is to promote the exchange of ideas between these related fields. Therefore every chapter is followed by comments, expressing alternative and sometimes contrasting points of view. These discussions clarify the similarities and differences between the various approaches. The book starts with a brief introduction to the general theme of the volume.

Most of the authors and discussants were present at a workshop on 'Dynamic models in economics and finance', held in 1995 at the castle of Oud Poelgeest in Oegstgeest, the Netherlands. We thank all authors and discussants for their contributions, for their enthusiasm, and for their patience in dealing with our sometimes tight guidelines and time schedules. Through their efforts the contributors show a genuine interest in communicating their ideas to a broader audience. Furthermore we thank the European Research Network on System Identification (ERNSI, EU-SCIENCE project SC1*-CT920779) and the Dutch Institute of Systems and Control (DISC) for their support.

Christiaan Heij
Erasmus University Rotterdam
Hans Schumacher
CWI, Amsterdam, and Tilburg University
Bernard Hanzon
Free University Amsterdam
Kees Praagman
University of Groningen

Introduction

C. HEIJ, J.M. SCHUMACHER, B. HANZON
AND C. PRAAGMAN

1 THE PURPOSES OF THIS BOOK

This volume is devoted to the dynamic modelling of economic data. In eleven chapters a survey is given of the variety of approaches in this research area. Dynamic models in economics already have a rich tradition, and the field is still full of activity. New developments are spurred by the general availability of considerable computational power allowing the analysis of a large variety of complex models, by the abundance of data in particular in financial applications, and by developments in neighbouring fields of research such as economic and financial theory and the theory of dynamical systems. The richness of the field of dynamic modelling has allowed the development of a number of disparate approaches. In this volume we bring together viewpoints from different angles and aim for an exchange between these viewpoints. So the reader will find in this book not only expository chapters written by leading specialists but also comment sections written by discussants representing other vantage points. In this way we hope to contribute to the fertility of the research area of dynamic economic modelling, which we believe depends critically on the continuing debate between researchers with differing backgrounds, in spite of the drive towards hyperspecialization that is all too often visible in today's scientific world.

The fact that there is such a wide variety of models for dynamic economic phenomena does not come as a surprise, of course. First, the particular application field is of importance; even within the broad areas of macroeconomics, microeconomics, and finance, there are many differences between subfields. Second, there are various theoretical developments which are incorporated, in one way or another, into empirical research; one may think of the Lucas critique of macroeconometric modelling and the no-arbitrage theories of mathematical finance, or of the advances that have been made in the understanding of chaotic behaviour in non-linear dynamical systems. Third, a crucial consideration concerns the purposes of the model. It makes a difference whether a model is required to produce short-term forecasts, or that it should increase our under- standing of the mechanisms that play a role in a certain context, or that the model is to serve as a basis for the development of policies that can be expected to have a major effect on the dynamics under consideration. So there are justifiable differences between modelling procedures, and the choice between different procedures can often not be made on the basis of statistical arguments alone.

Having said this, we must add that no sharp dividing lines can be drawn between the approaches that are applied to the dynamic modelling of economic phenomena. It is important to understand the mutual relations between them, not only to arrive at a correct appraisal of different methodologies for a given problem but also for the benefit of further development. Crossing the boundaries of scientific disciplines and overcoming the barriers of specialization can pave the way for substantial progress. Just as the chapters in this book serve to outline modelling alternatives under various circumstances, the comments sections are intended to provide feedback between approaches and to contribute to the coherence of the field.

2 SOME OF THE BACKGROUND

2.1 Economic Dynamic Modelling

Dynamic models are used in economic analysis in different ways. Some models are formulated as an aid in theoretical discussions, to give a sharply defined meaning to ideas and to demonstrate relations by calculation. Such models make it possible to establish relations between assumptions and conclusions with an exactness that could not be obtained from a purely verbal discussion. However, only these relations are made more exact; the conclusions themselves cannot be stronger than the assumptions on which they are based. For reasons of tracta- bility the model assumptions are usually rather schematic, which means that the conclusions will also be schematic. When used in this way, models thus fulfil a rhetorical purpose; in a sense they take the place of metaphors in the economic debate of an earlier age. This observation is not meant as a criticism of such use of models, since it is not reasonable to expect that the relation between inflation and unemployment can be discussed with the same exactness as, say, the relation between air pressure and the boiling temperature of water. The replacement of metaphors by models does imply that, for participants in the economic debate, mathematical talents have gained importance relative to literary talents.

Another use of dynamic models in economics lies in forecasting and policy analysis. When models are used in such a way, reasonable plausibility of model assumptions is usually not considered enough, and statistical methods of estimation and testing are called in. This implies that forecasting models must be formulated in terms of observable variables, a restriction which need not be imposed on models used in economic theory. On the other hand, requirements of analytical tractability can be less severe. A theoretical model is typically small, whereas an econometric model might be large. Econometric models have been large indeed, especially in the 1960s, and such models are still in use. Academic interest in large econometric models has waned, however, due to several developments in the 1970s, among them the well-known Lucas (1976) critique, and this has gone some way in bringing econometric models and theoretical models more closely together. In the present volume, which emphasizes econometric model building and confrontation with data, models are nevertheless typically small and are often formulated with an eye towards economic theory.

An area in which theoretical research and econometric work have been particularly close is that of finance. The theoretical development here has been fairly spectacular over the past decades. Traditionally, econometric and mathematical models in finance have been applied to the problem of portfolio selection, leading from the mean-variance analysis of Markowitz (1959) to the dynamic programming solution of Merton (1969, 1971). The 'price of risk' lost its elusiveness with the paper of Sharpe (1964) on capital asset pricing. Likewise, the pricing of derivative securities was brought into the realm of mathematical analysis by the paper of Black and Scholes (1973) on option pricing. In both asset pricing models and in the pricing of derivatives there have been important developments since these early papers, including empirical and numerical work. Also in portfolio selection there is an ongoing development, stimulated by the availability of new financial instruments and by the needs of institutions such as insurance companies and pension funds, which have called for the development of special models for asset/liability management.

2.2 System Dynamics

The study of dynamical systems has flourished for a long time and still keeps renewing itself. Since Newton studied the motion of the planets, differential equations have been the main tool of the trade, with difference equations as a close associate. The study of closed systems with no external influences has long been dominant, but systems with exogenous variables have also been the subject of extensive study.

Traditionally, the theory of dynamical systems is concerned with the behaviour of solutions of closed systems of differential or difference equations, especially the dependence of this behaviour on parameters. Highlights include the work on celestial mechanics by Poincaré (1892), the stability theory of Lyapunov (1947) developed at the end of the nineteenth century, and the asymptotic theory of Birkhoff (1927). A new turn in the development of dynamical systems was initiated by the work of Lorenz (1963) and Smale (1967) on chaotic dynamical systems and the corresponding limits to predictability. It has become clear that simple deterministic models may exhibit characteristics that are usually associated with stochastic disturbances. The study of time series has been influenced by the introduction of the concepts of Lyapunov exponents and correlation dimension, which can be used as measures of chaos and of serial correlation.

In economics, the development of the theory of chaotic dynamical systems has revived the classical debate on the exogenous or endogenous explanation of economic fluctuations. While Slutzky (1937) and Frisch (1933) asserted that an economic system is stable by itself and will fluctuate only under the influence of external shocks, Kaldor (1940), Hicks (1950), and Goodwin (1951) claimed that the fluctuations are caused by non-linear economic laws. Irregularity and unpredictability even at short time scales is typical of financial time series, so that applications of chaos in finance suggest themselves; see, for instance, Mosevich (1994).

The variational calculus, which together with planetary motion has been among the first application fields of differential equations, took a new form in the 1950s with the work of Pontryagin *et al.* (1962) on the Maximum Principle and of Bellman (1957) on Dynamic Programming. In contrast to the classical formulation, the new setting emphasizes the presence of exogenous ('control') variables. Optimal control theory has become a basic theoretical tool in macroeconomics and finance, as evidenced, for instance, in the books by Blanchard and Fischer (1989) and Merton (1990). In fact, the use of dynamic optimization arguments in macroeconomics was already foreshadowed in a paper by Ramsey (1928).

A duality link between linear-quadratic optimal control and filtering of Gaussian processes was discovered by Kalman around 1960. This led to the development of the Kalman filter (Kalman (1960); Kalman and Bucy (1961)), which now is part of the standard toolbox of statistical time series analysis. It also marked the birth of a new mathematical discipline that became known as mathematical systems theory. This area differs from the classical theory of dynamical systems by its emphasis on the distinction between state variables, input variables, and output variables.

One of the problems that mathematical systems theory has addressed is the one of constructing a model (in state-space or equivalent form) based on measured input–output data. To compare models of different state space dimensions, an information-theoretic criterion was developed by Akaike (1972, 1974); for further developments see, for instance, Ljung (1987). Depending on the intended application, other ways of comparing models may be appropriate, and in the context of control applications several schemes have been proposed such as balanced truncation and Hankel norm approximation (Glover, 1984, 1989). Parameterization and approximation issues for linear systems are further discussed in Hannan and Deistler (1988). Model order selection remains a sensitive topic, however, as is also clear from several contributions to the present volume.

2.3 Econometrics

The development of techniques for the dynamic modelling of economic phenomena and the emergence of econometrics as a scientific discipline have been closely related processes. Business cycle analysis has been the subject of early contributions, notably the work of Tinbergen (1937, 1939). The sharply formulated criticism of this work by Keynes (1939) identified a range of 'puzzles' (in the terminology of T.S. Kuhn) and in this way contributed to the further development of econometrics.

In spite of the resolution of many technical problems, some of the debates from the early days of econometrics are still very much alive. This holds, for instance, for the relation between economic theory and econometrics. The claims made by economic theory are usually not sufficiently specific to make them testable as such, that is, without the introduction of additional assumptions. With this in mind one may even doubt the relevance of econometric modelling to the economic debate. In response to this, the econometrician may nevertheless attempt to come up with models in which somehow the more basic economic relations are represented separately from the minor fluctuations that unavoidably will also be found in empirical data. The theory of cointegration provides one possible form of doing this, as is shown by several examples in this volume.

Keynes and Tinbergen differed on the role of stochastics in the modelling of economic phenomena. Of course, the use of stochastic models has become standard in econometrics, despite Keynes' objections; but there are still important differences in the way that stochastic elements are incorporated. Haavelmo (1944, p. 52) wrote: 'Observable economic variables do not satisfy exact relations. Therefore we have, for the purpose of application, to add some stochastical elements, to bridge the gap between the theory and the facts.' This would suggest that the stochastic element can be brought into a model as an output error; however, many models have stochastic elements in the dynamic equations themselves or have errors placed on explanatory variables. As noted above, it has become clear from the theory of dynamical systems that even the erratic behaviour that is typical for so many economic time series need not necessarily be explained in terms of stochastic influences, but may also be due to non-linear dynamics.

The model that was used by Tinbergen in his work for the League of Nations was already fairly large (more than thirty equations). Especially during the 1960s, macroeconometric models grew in size to impressive constructs of several hundreds of equations. There has been a clear decline in the popularity of such large models, however, especially in academic circles. Several reasons may be given for this. The forecasting performance of the large models has often been not quite as good as their builders expected, and in some cases better results could be obtained from much smaller time series models. From a theoretical point of view, the Lucas (1976) critique implied that the models of the 1960s could not be trusted as a basis for policy formation. It may be added that the world entered into a more turbulent phase in the 1970s and this also made it less attractive to build models based on the assumption of long-term stability of economic relations. Smaller models which allow some flexibility towards non-stationarities have drawn considerable interest in recent years.

New directions in econometric modelling have also been brought about by developments in the area of finance. There is an obvious need for dynamic models in this area; moreover, there is a large supply of data, the availability of computing power to handle such data is still increasing quickly, and there is a well-established theory which can be used to guide empirical research. The circumstances may seem ideal, but that impression may be misleading. In particular, the relation between theory and data is highly non-trivial and there is a need for a development of proper concepts of model accuracy.

Whereas in its early days econometrics paid attention mostly to optimal estimation within postulated models, currently much more attention is devoted to the phases that come before and after estimation, that is, the specification of the model and the diagnostic testing and evaluation of estimated models. A more or less standard theory has been developed for the linear case, in particular regression analysis for cross-section data and ARMA modelling in time series analysis. Most recent activities concentrate on models that are needed because of specific deviations from these prototype models, such as non-stationarity, structural breaks, and non-linearities. Well-known examples of modelling methodologies designed to cope with such deviations include common trends and cointegration, stochastic volatility and ARCH modelling, transition models, and neural nets. The main focus lies with relatively simple statistical models that give rise to a tractable statistical theory and to implementations of testing and estimation procedures that are easy to apply.

3 OUTLINE OF THE BOOK

The main purpose of this volume is to compare different approaches to dynamic modelling in economics and finance, rather than to give an encyclopedic survey of time series modelling or to delve into the latest technical results. As editors of the volume, our aim has therefore been to present a range of possible modelling strategies and to confront these strategies with each other. We have placed less emphasis on completeness in a technical sense. We have specifically asked the authors of chapters to concentrate on motivation and central concepts, to present core results rather than technical details, and to illustrate their approaches by an empirical example. They were also asked not to enter into specialized technicalities but rather to provide a representative reference list for readers who are interested in further details. The discussants were asked to complement the papers by presenting alternative views.

We have divided the chapters into three groups. The chapters in Section 1 are concerned with the uncovering of non-linear structure in data, whereas those in Section 2 deal with specific non-linear models. The chapters in Section 3 discuss trends and non-stationarity.

The book starts with a chapter by Brock and Hommes on chaotic dynamics in financial markets. Based on assumptions concerning types of traders, the authors develop a non-linear model for stock prices. The chaotic behaviour that is obtained from the model is then compared with empirical data. In the following chapter by Dockner, Prskawetz, and Feichtinger, the authors are also looking for non-linear dynamics behind financial data, but they use a black-box approach rather than the white-box approach of Brock and Hommes. Both chapters suggest that there is evidence against the efficient market hypothesis in some cases. Ormerod and Campbell present a third search for non-linear structure, this time applied to macroeconomic data rather than financial data. Their conclusion is that for practical purposes the business cycle must be considered as inherently unpredictable. Not surprisingly, the discussants tend to disagree with this conclusion, but in their reply the authors maintain that an inspection of the forecasting performance of the macroeconometric models that have been developed in the past decades already provides ample support for their claim.

It is often plausible that certain peculiarities of data can be explained by a switching between several regimes or modes of operation. Teräsvirta presents a model that is capable of performing a smooth transition between two modes. Although the modes themselves are taken to be linear, the presence of the transition leads to a global model that is non-linear. Teräsvirta uses the model to illustrate that tests of causality may be sensitive to the specification of dynamics, so that, for instance, a causality relation that is rejected in a linear dynamic model may be accepted in a non-linear model. Moraleda and Vorst present an empirical test of relations predicted by mathematical finance. Even though the no-arbitrage assumption appears to provide an exceptionally sound basis for drawing conclusions, it turns out that the relation between theory and data is a complicated one and holds plenty of pitfalls. A key question that emerges from the discussion of the chapter is in what sense one should understand the robustness of the conclusions of the theory towards modelling imperfections. The final contribution to Section 2 is by Young and Pedregal, who present a method which they call 'data-based mechanistic modelling'. In a sense the method is a compromise between white-box and black-box modelling; the data analysis is undertaken without imposing much prior structure, but still the methodology is aimed at obtaining relations that may express real mechanisms. Among the issues raised in the discussion is the remark that, for instance, in the choice of variables the method still applies some pre-imposed structure.

In the third part of the volume we turn to the analysis of trends and non-stationarity. The concept of cointegration in non-stationary multivariate time series has in recent years emerged as one way of separating, in a way that is susceptible to statistical treatment, major economic relationships from short-term fluctuations. A problem that has been mentioned above, namely the sensitivity of testing procedures to dynamic specifications, also plays a role here. Bierens argues in his contribution that this problem can at least partly be overcome by the use of non-parametric methods. An example of the use of statistical cointegration analysis to provide evidence in an economic debate (in this case the monetarist/Keynesian discussion) is given in the chapter by Funke, Hall, and Beeby. In their analysis they incorporate structural change as well. The chapter by Harvey and Koopman presents a method that is aimed at explicit representation of trends as well as seasonals in a time series model, in order to capture the stylized facts of the system under study, which may involve cointegration or other effects. An alternative is to use relatively unstructured vector autoregressive models, possibly extended with moving-average terms for parsimony or perhaps with non-linear terms to get, for instance, conditional heteroscedasticity. This approach is advocated by Lütkepohl and Breitung. In their setting, a link with economic theory is established via identifying restrictions needed to determine impulse responses. The final chapter by Pollock considers trends in a univariate context. The detrending of time series has been a traditional source of debate, and Pollock reviews the positions.

Although we have found it useful to divide this volume into three parts, one should not attach too much weight to the grouping of the chapters, since there are several interconnections between the parts. Regarding applications, the chapters by Brock and Hommes, by Dockner, Prskawetz, and Feichtinger, and by Moraleda and Vorst deal with finance, whereas those of Young and Pedregal, Funke, Hall, and Beeby, and Teräsvirta are geared towards drawing conclusions in macroeconomic debates. Structural change is a common theme in the contributions of Brock and Hommes, Teräsvirta, and Funke, Hall, and Beeby. Established econometric methods are criticized, from different points of view, in the chapters of Bierens, Pollock, and Ormerod and Campbell.

REFERENCES

Akaike, H. (1972) Information theory and an extension of the maximum likelihood principle. In B.N. Petrov and F. Csaki (eds.), *Proc. 2nd Int. Symp. Information Theory*. Akademiai Kiado, Budapest, pp. 267–81.

Akaike, H. (1974) A new look at the statistical model identification. *IEEE Trans. Automat. Contr.* **AC-19**, 716–23.

Bellman, R. (1957) *Dynamic Programming*. Princeton University Press, Princeton, NJ.

Birkhoff, G.D. (1927) *Dynamical Systems*. American Mathematical Society Publications, Providence, RI.

Black, F. and Scholes, M. (1973) The pricing of options and corporate liabilities. *Journal of Political Economy*, 637–54.

Blanchard, O.J. and Fischer, S. (1989) *Lectures on Macroeconomics*. MIT Press, Cambridge, MA.

Brockwell, P.J. and Davis, R.A. (1991) *Time Series: Theory and Methods*. Springer, New York.

Box, G.E.P. and Jenkins, G.M. (1970) *Time Series Analysis, Forecasting and Control*. Holden-Day, San Francisco.

Frisch, R. (1933) Propagation problems and impulse problems in dynamic economics. In *Economic Essays in Honor of Gustav Cassel*. George Allen and Unwin, London.

Glover, K. (1984) All optimal Hankel-norm approximations of linear multivariable systems and their $\mathscr{L}_\infty$-error bounds. *Int. J. Control* **39**, 1115–93.

Glover, K. (1989) Tutorial on Hankel-norm approximation. In J.C. Willems (ed.), *From Data to Model*. Springer, New York.

Goodwin, R.M. (1951) The nonlinear accelerator and the persistence of business cycles. *Econometrica* **19**, 1–17.

Granger, C.W.J. (ed.) (1990) *Modelling Economic Series*. Clarendon Press, Oxford.

Haavelmo, T. (1944) The probability approach in econometrics. Supplement to *Econometrica* **12**.

Hannan, E.J. and Deistler, M. (1988) *The Statistical Theory of Linear Systems*. Wiley, New York.

Hendry, D.F. and Morgan, M.S. (1995) *The Foundations of Econometric Analysis*. Cambridge University Press, Cambridge.

Hicks, J.R. (1950) *A Contribution to the Theory of the Trade Cycle*. Clarendon Press, Oxford.

Kaldor, N. (1940) A model of the trade cycle. *Economic Journal* **50**, 78–92.

Kalman, R.E. (1960) A new approach to linear filtering and prediction problems. *Trans. ASME (J. Basic Engineering)* **82D**, 35–45. Reprinted in T. Kailath (ed.), *Linear Least Squares Estimation*. Dowden, Hutchinson, and Ross, Stroudsburg, PA, 1977, pp. 254–64.

Kalman, R.E. and Bucy, R.S. (1961) New results in linear filtering and prediction theory. *Trans. ASME (J. Basic Engineering)* **83D**, 95–108. Reprinted in A. Ephremides and J.B. Thomas (eds.), *Random Processes, Part I: Multiplicity Theory and Canonical Decompositions*. Dowden, Hutchinson, and Ross, Stroudsburg, PA, 1973, pp. 181–94.

Keynes, J.M. (1939) The statistical testing of business cycle theories. *Economic Journal* **49**, 558–68.

Leamer, E.E. (1978) *Specification Searches: Ad-Hoc Inference with Non-Experimental Data*. Wiley, New York.

Ljung, L. (1987) *System Identification: Theory for the User*. Prentice Hall, Englewood Cliffs, NJ.

Lorenz, E.N. (1963) Deterministic non-periodic flows. *J. Atmos. Sci.* **20**, 282–91.

Lucas, R.E. (1976) Econometric policy evaluation: a critique. In K. Brunner and A.M. Meltzer (eds.), *The Phillips Curve and Labor Markets.* Carnegie-Rochester Conferences on Public Policy, vol. 1, North-Holland, Amsterdam, pp. 19–46.

Lütkepohl, H. (1993) *Introduction to Multiple Time Series Analysis* (2nd edn). Springer, Berlin.

Lyapunov, A.M. (1947) *Problème Général de la Stabilité du Mouvement.* Annals of Mathematics Studies, vol. 17, Princeton University Press, Princeton. (Reproduction of the French translation (1907) of a memoir in Russian of 1892.)

Markowitz, H.M. (1959) *Portfolio Selection: Efficient Diversification of Investments.* Wiley, New York.

Merton, R.C. (1969) Lifetime portfolio selection under uncertainty: the continuous-time case. *Rev. Econ. Stat.* **51**, 247–59.

Merton, R.C. (1971) Optimum consumption and portfolio rules in a continuous-time model. *J. Econ. Theory* **3**, 373–413.

Merton, R.C. (1990) *Continuous-Time Finance.* Blackwell, Oxford.

Mosevich, J. (1994) Chaos theory. In J. Lederman and R.A. Klein (eds), *Global Asset Allocation.* Wiley, New York, pp. 247–63.

Nijmeijer, H. and Schumacher, J.M. (eds) (1989) *Three Decades of Mathematical System Theory.* Springer, Berlin.

Ott, E. (1993) *Chaos in Dynamical Systems.* Cambridge University Press, Cambridge.

Poincaré, H. (1892) *Les Méthodes Nouvelles de la Mécanique Céleste.* Gauthier-Villars, Paris. (Reprinted by Dover, New York, 1957.)

Pontryagin, L.S., Boltyanskii, V.G., Gamkrelidze, R.V. and Mishchenko, E.F. (1962) *The Mathematical Theory of Optimal Processes.* Wiley, New York.

Ramsey, F. (1928) A mathematical theory of saving. *Economic Journal* **38**, 543–59. Reprinted in J. Stiglitz and H. Uzawa (eds), *Readings in the Modern Theory of Economic Growth.* MIT Press, Cambridge, MA, 1969.

Sharpe, W.F. (1964) Capital asset prices: a theory of market equilibrium under conditions of risk. *J. Finance* **19**, 425–42.

Slutzky, E. (1937) The summation of random causes as the source of cyclic processes. *Econometrica* **5**, 105–46.

Smale, S. (1967) Differential dynamical systems. *Bull. Am. Math. Soc.* **73**, 747–817.

Tinbergen, J. (1937) *An Econometric Approach to Business Cycle Problems.* Hermann, Paris.

Tinbergen, J. (1939) *Statistical Testing of Business Cycle Theories. Vol. I: A Method and its Application to Investment Activity. Vol. II: Business Cycles in the United States of America.* League of Nations, Geneva.

SECTION 1
Non-linear Dynamics in Economic and Financial Models

1

Models of Complexity in Economics and Finance

W.A. BROCK AND C.H. HOMMES

1.1 INTRODUCTION

There are two contrasting viewpoints concerning the explanation of observed fluctuations in economic and financial markets. According to the first (*Neoclassical*) view the main source of fluctuations is to be found in *exogenous*, random shocks to fundamentals. In the absence of shocks, prices and other variables would converge to a steady-state (growth) path, completely determined by fundamentals. According to the second (*Keynesian*) view a *significant* part of observed fluctuations is caused by *non-linear* economic laws. Even in the absence of any external shocks, non-linear market laws can generate endogenous business fluctuations. The neoclassical view is intimately related to the concept of *rational* expectations, whereas *animal spirits* or *market psychology* have been an important Keynesian theme.

In finance the two different viewpoints lead to opposite views concerning the efficiency of financial markets. In the *efficient market hypothesis* (EMH) the current price already contains all information and past prices cannot help in predicting future prices. Parametric stochastic processes have been used in the empirical literature that are consistent with the EMH. Examples include random walk processes, GARCH processes and the like. In contrast, Keynes already argued that stock prices are not only determined by fundamentals but, in addition, market psychology and investors' animal spirits influence financial markets significantly. In the Keynesian view, simple technical trading rules, such as extrapolation of a trend, may help predict future price changes. In fact,

System Dynamics in Economic and Financial Models. Edited by C. Heij, J.M. Schumacher, B. Hanzon and C. Praagman © 1997 John Wiley & Sons Ltd

recently Brock, Lakonishok and LeBaron (1992) have indeed shown that simple technical trading rules, such as moving average and trading range break, when used in predicting the Dow Jones Index consistently outperform several popular stochastic finance models, such as the random walk and the GARCH model.

The discovery of chaotic, seemingly random dynamical behaviour in simple deterministic models sheds important new light on this debate. A simple deterministic financial market model with a strange attractor may generate erratic, seemingly unpredictable stock price fluctuations very similar to a random walk. Prices moving on a strange attractor may be very difficult to predict and chaos may thus be consistent with a weak form of the EMH. Intermittent chaotic time series, characterized by irregular switching between a stable phase of low volatility and an unstable phase of high volatility, may explain the well-known GARCH effects frequently observed in financial data.

At this point, let us briefly review the state of the art concerning chaos in economics and finance. It has been shown that simple non-linear general equilibrium models, satisfying the currently dominating assumptions in economic theory (i.e. utility- or profit-maximizing agents, rational, self-fulfilling expectations and market clearing), can generate chaotic equilibrium dynamics. For the popular overlapping generations (OLG) model this has been shown by Benhabib and Day (1982) and Grandmont (1985) and in optimal growth models by Boldrin and Montrucchio (1986), as, for example, surveyed in Boldrin and Woodford (1990) and Nishimura and Sorger (1996). In all these examples the dynamics can be reduced to a one-dimensional non-linear difference equation. Only very recently there have been some two-dimensional generalizations, for example an OLG economy with production (Medio and Negroni (1996), and De Vilder (1995)). In higher-dimensional models, chaos may arise with much less nonlinearity than in the one-dimensional case. For example, in the one-dimensional OLG model a strong income effect is needed to generate chaotic equilibrium cycles, whereas in the two-dimensional OLG model with production, chaos may arise even when the two goods, current leisure and future consumption, are gross substitutes.

The (chaotic) time series generated by these models all seem to be clearly different from actual (macro) economic data. Apparently, the models are still 'too simple to be true'. In fact, there is little empirical evidence for low-dimensional chaos in (macro) economic data. But as Brock and Sayers (1988, p. 78) emphasize, 'the methods we utilized may be too weak to detect chaos if it exists'. The main reason is that macroeconomic time series are too short and probably too noisy to detect chaos, even if it were present. For surveys on testing for chaos in economics and finance; see, for example, Brock (1986) and Brock, Hsieh and LeBaron (1991).

Daily or weekly financial series are much longer than (macro) economic series and a number of papers have looked for deterministic chaos in financial time series. For example, Scheinkman and LeBaron (1989) present some evidence for a strange attractor with fractal (correlation) dimension of about 6. They are very careful in their claim however: 'the data are not incompatible with a theory where some of the variation in weekly returns could come from nonlinearities as opposed to randomness and are not compatible with a theory that predicts that the returns are generated by IID random variables' (p. 332). The most optimistic claims for chaos in financial data seem to be due to Barnett and Chen (1988) in their Divisia monetary aggregates series (about 800 observations) for which they find low correlation dimension of about 1.5. However, Ramsey, Sayers and Rothman (1990) have emphasized that estimates of the correlation dimension may be strongly downward biased in short (say, 1000 or less observations) data sets. LeBaron (1994) reviews evidence for out-of-sample short-term predictability using non-linear prediction methods that would work well if (noisy) chaotic dynamics (or other 'established' sources of dynamics) were present in returns. There is some evidence for short-term predictability provided *one conditions on certain events such as near-past volatility.* In summary, it seems to be fair to say that there is no convincing evidence for a low-dimensional chaotic explanation of economic or financial data. One should add, however, that the chaos tests are sensitive to noise and series length. On the other hand, by now it is also a mathematical fact that in two- and higher-dimensional models weak non-linearities may already lead to bifurcation routes to chaos (e.g. Palis and Takens (1993)). Hence, there seems to be a 'chaos model-data paradox' in economics: chaos is hard to find in economic and financial data, but is easily generated by economic equilbrium models under increasingly plausible assumptions.

There is evidence of patterns in financial data that seems inconsistent with simple versions of the EMH, especially in high-frequency data. See, for example, the work of the Olsen group as in Guillaume *et al.* (1994) and Dacorogna *et al.* (1995). 'Financial psychologists' like DeBondt and Thaler (1985) (see also the papers in Thaler (1994, part V)) have also emphasized the role of quasi-rational, overreacting and biased traders in financial markets. Furthermore, the large amount of trading volume and the persistence of this trading volume that is observed in real markets suggests that heterogeneous beliefs must play a key role in generating these observed patterns in financial data. Some evidence, for example on trading rule profits, suggests that some periods may be consistent with the EMH and certain other periods may not be. It thus seems useful to investigate possible routes of departure from the EMH. This chapter contributes to the task of building analytic frameworks that can help shed light on financial economic forces that may cause the market to move towards or move away from the equilibrium predicted by the EMH. We develop a class of heterogeneous belief models that nest the usual rational expectations models (e.g. EMH) and are econometrically tractable. Beliefs are expressed as beliefs about deviations from the EMH fundamental. The models should help identify periods where the rewards to possessing rational expectations are relatively large or relatively small. This kind of analysis may suggest periods when one would expect larger departures from rational expectations than other periods.

Recently several structural non-linear financial market models have been introduced. A number of these emphasize heterogeneity in expectation formation, with two or more groups of traders having different expectations about future prices. Two typical investor types are the fundamentalists, expecting prices to return to their fundamental value, and the chartist or technical analysts, using simple technical trading rules and extrapolating trends in past prices (e.g. Day and Huang (1990), DeGrauwe, DeWachter and Embrechts (1993) and Lux (1995)). In the 'artificial economic life' literature an evolutionary dynamics in an 'ocean' of traders using different expectations has been introduced (e.g. Arthur *et al.* (1996) or the review of LeBaron (1995)). Most of this work is computationally oriented with a large number of different predictors. Brock (1993, 1995) and Brock and LeBaron (1996) have started to build a theoretical framework and analyse simple versions of these adaptive belief systems. Brock and Hommes (1995) investigate a simple demand–supply cobweb type model with rational versus naive expectations and show how an adaptive belief system may lead to market instability and chaos, when rational expectations are more costly than naive expectations.

In this chapter we introduce a tractable form of evolutionary dynamics which we call *Adaptive Belief Systems* into the present value asset pricing theory. Asset traders migrate across different beliefs or predictors of the future value of a risky asset according to a 'fitness' or 'performance' measure based upon how these beliefs perform in the generation of trading profits. Agents switch between fundamentalists' beliefs and simple technical trading rules. Predictor choice is *rational* in the sense that, at each date, most agents choose the predictor generating the highest weighted sum of net past profits. One may say that the market is thus driven by *rational animal spirits*. We show how an increase in the 'intensity of choice' to switch predictors can lead to emergence of complicated dynamics for asset returns, where an irregular switching occurs between phases where the market is close to the fundamental solution and phases where traders become excited and extrapolate trends by simple technical analysis. These dynamics suggest complicated dynamics for volatility and volume as well.

In our model not all agents are perfectly rational. We emphasize, though, that our traders are also not completely 'irrational', but in fact boundedly rational. In periods where prices are close to fundamentals, most agents will be fundamentalists, but when prices move away from fundamentals, most agents will abandon fundamentalist beliefs and, for example, use a simple trend predictor to extrapolate an observed price trend. Predictors with highest performance will dominate the evolutionary dynamics. If the evolution takes place on a strange attractor, simple technical trading rules need not be 'systematically wrong' and such expectations may become self-fulfilling and consistent with actual observations (cf. Grandmont (1994), Hommes (1991, 1996), Sorger (1996)).

This chapter may be seen as a first step to uncover classes of adaptive learning dynamics which are consistent with the main stylized facts of returns, volatility of returns and volume. We state these stylized facts immediately so the reader can see what we are seeking. If p_t is the price of a financial asset at date t, define returns ('continuously compounded') to be $r_t \equiv \ln(p_t) - \ln(p_{t-1})$. Then (1) the autocorrelation function (ACF) of individual security returns is approximately zero at all leads and lags; (2) the ACF of most measures of high-frequency data volatility and volume (detrended) is positive and dies off as the lag increases; (3) the cross-autocorrelation function between volume measures and volatility measures is contemporaneously positive with rapid falloff with leads and lags. We investigate whether our simple evolutionary dynamics can match some of these stylized facts, in particular, whether the evolutionary dynamics can converge to a strange attractor, with price fluctuations 'similar' to a random walk (e.g. with slowly decaying ACF) and chaotic returns with close to zero ACF.

The plan of the chapter is as follows. In Section 1.2 we set up a mean variance framework in the present discounted value asset pricing model with one risk-free and one risky asset. We add adaptive heterogeneous beliefs to the model and develop a general evolutionary theory for this mean variance setting. Section 1.3 presents two typical examples of 'few' belief type adaptive systems, one example with two and another with four predictors. One type will be fundamentalist, who believe that prices will return to their EMH fundamental value. Other simple belief types will typically be trend extrapolators and upward- or downward-biased beliefs. We also present a first 'calibration' of the four-belief type model to monthly IBM data.[1] In Section 1.4 we sketch how one might use the theory advanced here to help structure empirical work in *testing* for the presence of 'extra endogenous dynamics' in stock returns, above and beyond the 'conventional dynamics' stressed in current financial work. In particular, we show how one might set up a nested testing situation for the presence of boundedly rational traders, with the 'standard', GARCH(1,1) model as the fundamental returns process. Both the calibration and the nested testing exercise are, at best, an outline of what kind of empirical work might be suggested by the theoretical work presented here. Finally, Section 1.5 concludes and briefly discusses some future lines of research.

1.2 ADAPTIVE BELIEFS IN THE SIMPLE MEAN VARIANCE FRAMEWORK

Consider an asset pricing model with one risky asset and one risk-free asset. The risk-free asset is perfectly elastically supplied at gross return R. Let p_t, denote the price (ex dividend) per share of the risky asset. Let $\{y_t\}$ denote the stochastic process of dividends of the risky asset. For illustration and because of space limitations, we shall assume that $\{y_t\}$ is independently and identically distributed

(IID), but the analysis can be carried out for more general dividend processes. The dynamics of wealth is

$$\mathbf{W}_{t+1} = RW_t + (\mathbf{p}_{t+1} + \mathbf{y}_{t+1} - Rp_t)z_t \tag{1}$$

where bold type denotes random variables and z_t is the number of shares of the asset purchased at date t. Write E_t, V_t for the conditional expectation and conditional variance operators. These are based on a publicly available information set, which we here take to be past prices and past dividends. Let E_{ht}, V_{ht} denote the 'beliefs' of investor type h about these conditional expectation and conditional variance. Note that the choice variable z_t in equation (1) is multiplied by the *excess returns per share*, $p_{t+1} + y_{t+1} - Rp_t$, so that the conditional variance of wealth is z_t^2 times the conditional variance of excess returns per share. Furthermore, the conditional variance of excess returns per share is just the conditional variance of $p_{t+1} + y_{t+1}$, because p_t is part of the information set at date t. Beliefs about the conditional variance of excess returns are assumed to be a constant, σ^2, and the same for all traders. Each investor type is a myopic mean variance maximizer, maximizing expected risk adjusted wealth, so demand for shares z_{ht}, by type h, solves

$$\text{Max } \{ E_{ht}\mathbf{W}_{t+1} - (a/2)V_{ht}(\mathbf{W}_{t+1}) \} \tag{2}$$

i.e.

$$z_{ht} = E_{ht}(\mathbf{p}_{t+1} + \mathbf{y}_{t+1} - Rp_t)/a\sigma^2 \tag{3}$$

where a denotes the risk aversion, which is assumed to be equal for all traders. Write z_{st} for the supply of shares per investor and n_{ht} for the fraction of traders of type h. Equilibrium of supply and demand at date t implies

$$\sum n_{ht} \{ E_{ht}(\mathbf{p}_{t+1} + \mathbf{y}_{t+1} - Rp_t)/a\sigma^2 \} = z_{st} \tag{4}$$

In the case of homogeneous expectations, i.e. when there is only one type h, equilibration of supply and demand yields the pricing equation

$$Rp_t = E_{ht}(\mathbf{p}_{t+1} + \mathbf{y}_{t+1}) - a\sigma^2 z_{st} \tag{5a}$$

Given a sequence of information sets $\mathbb{F}_t$ equation (5a) defines a notion of *fundamental solution* by letting E_{ht}, V_{ht} denote conditional mean and variance upon $\mathbb{F}_t$. Furthermore, in order to obtain a benchmark notion of 'fundamental solution' put $\mathbb{F}_t = \{p_t, p_{t-1}, \ldots; y_t, y_{t-1}, \ldots\}$. In the special case of zero supply of outside shares, i.e. $z_{st} = 0$ for all t, equation (5a) becomes

$$Rp_t = E\{\mathbf{p}_{t+1} + \mathbf{y}_{t+1}|\mathbb{F}_t\} = E\{\mathbf{p}_{t+1}|\mathbb{F}_t\} + \bar{y} \tag{5b}$$

Recall that $\{\mathbf{y}_t\}$ is IID, so $E\{\mathbf{y}_{t+1}|\mathbb{F}_t\} = \bar{y}$ is a constant. The 'fundamental' solution $\mathbf{p}_t^* = \bar{p}$ then must satisfy

$$R\overline{p} = \overline{p} + \overline{y} \tag{6}$$

Typically equation (5b) has infinitely many solutions but only the constant solution $\overline{p} = \overline{y}/(R-1)$ satisfies the 'no bubbles' condition

$$\lim_{t\to\infty} (Ep_t/R^t) = 0$$

To improve tractability, we will work in the space of deviations from the benchmark fundamental. Let $x_t = p_t - \overline{p}$ denote deviation from the fundamental solution.

We now introduce heterogeneous beliefs and study the equilibrium dynamical system. In the case of zero supply of outside shares and heterogeneous beliefs, equation (4) becomes

$$Rp_t = \sum n_{ht} E_{ht}(\mathbf{p}_{t+1} + \mathbf{y}_{t+1}) \tag{7}$$

It seems plausible that more of the disagreement among investors will be about the future *price* rather than the future earnings, because the future earnings are determined by the fortunes of the company whereas the future prices depend upon how the market reacts to those future earnings. The market reaction adds an additional layer of complexity to the forecasting problem. Note that Thaler (1994) discusses work by De Bondt and Thaler that documents strong disagreement, overreactions, and biases among securities analysts in forecasting *earnings* which one might argue would be easier to agree upon than future prices. Assume

Assumption 1 All beliefs $E_{ht}\{\mathbf{p}_{t+1} + \mathbf{y}_{t+1}\}$ are of the form

$$E_{ht}\{\mathbf{p}_{t+1} + \mathbf{y}_{t+1}|\mathbb{F}_t\} = E_{ht}\{\mathbf{p}^*_{t+1} + \mathbf{y}_{t+1}|\mathbb{F}_t\} + f_{ht}(x_{t-1}, \ldots, x_{t-L}), \tag{8}$$

where f_{ht} is a *deterministic* function of past deviations from the fundamental solution and $\{p^*_t\}$ denotes the fundamental solution process.

There can be many beliefs about departures from the baseline fundamental solution, $\overline{p}$, that are not captured by Assumption 1, but it gives us a useful start. Using Assumption 1 write the equilibrium equation (7) in the form of deviations,

$$Rx_t = \sum n_{ht} f_h(x_{t-1}, \ldots, x_{t-L}) \equiv \sum n_{ht} f_{ht} \tag{9a}$$

At this stage we shall be very general about the beliefs $\{f_{ht}\}$ which we have expressed in the form of deviations from the fundamental solution $\{p^*_t\} \equiv \{\overline{p}\}$. Note how we are developing the special case of IID $\{\mathbf{y}_t\}$ and zero supply of outside shares to position ourselves for treatment of more general cases. In these more general cases, we may deal with a large class of $\{\mathbf{y}_t\}$ processes, even non-stationary ones, by working in the space of *deviations from the fundamental*.

This device allows us to dramatically widen the applicability of stationary dynamical systems analysis to financial modelling.

Recall that all traders are assumed to have common, constant conditional variances $\sigma^2 = V_{ht}(R_{t+1})$, on excess returns $R_{t+1} = p_{t+1} + y_{t+1} - Rp_t$. Let $\rho_{ht} = E_{ht}(R_{t+1})$ and consider the goal function

$$\text{Max}_z \{E_{ht}R_{t+1}z - (a/2)z^2 V_{ht}(R_{t+1})\} = \text{Max}_z \{\rho_{ht}z - (a/2)z^2\sigma^2\} \quad (10)$$

Since equation (10) is equivalent to the objective (2) up to a constant, the optimum choice of shares of risky asset is the same. Let $z(\rho_{ht})$ solve equation (10), and let $\rho_t = E_t R_{t+1}$ denote rational expectations. Note here that rational expectors take into account the impact of the non-rational expectations traders. That is, $E_t R_{t+1}$ is the *actual* conditional expectation of the *actual* equilibrium stochastic process based upon information at time t. Note that, in deviations form, $\rho_t \equiv E_t R_{t+1} = E_t x_{t+1} - Rx_t$. This brings us to the issue of precise mathematical formulation of the class of deviations $\{x_t\}$ that we shall consider. Digress for a moment to consider the case where all expectations are rational. In this case the equilibrium equation (9a) can be written as

$$Rx_t = E\{x_{t+1}|\mathbb{F}_t\}, \qquad \mathbb{F}_t = \{y_t, y_{t-1}, \dots; p_t, p_{t-1}, \dots\} \quad (9b)$$

Hence *any* stochastic process $\{x_t\}$ that is measureable w.r.t. the sequence of sigma algebras generated by the information sets $\{\mathbb{F}_t\}$ qualifies as a solution of equation (9b). Any solution of (9b) that is not the zero solution is called a 'bubble' solution. If $R > 1$ the requirement that a solution $\{x_t\}$ be almost certainly bounded implies that it is the zero solution.

Turn now to the adaptation of beliefs, i.e. the dynamics of the fractions n_{ht}. First, lagging equation (9a) one period, rewrite market equilibrium as

$$Rx_t = \sum n_{h,t-1}f_h(x_{t-1}, \dots, x_{t-L}) \equiv \sum n_{h,t-1}f_{ht} \quad (9c)$$

where $n_{h,t-1}$ denotes the fraction of type h at the beginning of period t, before the equilibrium price x_t has been observed. Define

$$\pi_{h,t} = \pi(\rho_t, \rho_{ht}) = \rho_t z(\rho_{ht}) - (a/2)[z(\rho_{ht})]^2\sigma^2 \quad (11)$$

The first term in the RHS of equation (11) denotes realized profits for type h, whereas the second term captures risk adjustment. In this chapter, we concentrate on the case without risk adjustment, i.e. where the second term in equation (11) is dropped. As the 'fitness function' or the 'performance measure', we take

$$U_{ht} = \pi_{h,t} + \eta U_{h,t-1} \quad (12)$$

that is, predictor performance is measured by a weighted sum of (non-risk adjusted) realized profits. For $\eta = 1$ memory is infinite and all past profits get equal weight; for $\eta = 0$ only last periods profit feeds into the fitness measure.

Now write type h beliefs $\rho_{ht} = E_{ht} R_{t+1} = f_{ht} - Rx_t$ in deviation form. Let the updated fractions $n_{h,t}$ be given by the discrete choice probabilities (see Anderson, de Palma and Thisse (1993) for an extensive discussion of discrete choice modelling and Brock and Hommes (1995) for using discrete choice models in adaptive belief systems)

$$n_{h,t} = \exp\left[\beta U_{h,t-1}\right]/Z_t \qquad Z_t \equiv \sum_h \exp\left[\beta U_{h,t-1}\right] \qquad (13)$$

We call the equilibrium dynamics defined by equations (9c) and (13) an *Adaptive Belief System*. The timing of updating of beliefs in equation (13) is important. We can only allow the fitness function that goes into the RHS of equation (13) to depend upon ρ's dated $t - 1$ and further in the past in order to ensure that $n_{h,t}$ depends only upon x's dated t and further in the past. The parameter β is called the *intensity of choice* and measures the degree of rationality among traders, i.e. how fast traders switch to 'better' predictors. Note that if $\beta \to \infty$, then equation (13) places all mass on the 'best' predictor.

In Brock and Hommes (1997) we show for the risk-adjusted case that, if memory is infinite, i.e. $\eta = 1$, and costs for rational expectations are zero, then all deterministic deviations $\{x_t\}$ converge to zero as $t \to \infty$. This result may be seen as an efficient market hypothesis (EMH) for the heterogeneous adaptive beliefs asset pricing model. To put it another way, Thaler's overreacting investors and/or securities analysts would be driven out of the market in an infinite memory world where rational expectations are costlessly available. But since it is argued by Thaler and others that such investors are present and impact actual markets (cf. Thaler (1994) and his references), it behoves us to study what kind of relaxations of the assumptions in the above theorem can lead to survival of 'boundedly rational' traders in equilibrium. This will be the subject of Section 1.3.

1.3 SOME ADAPTIVE BELIEF SYSTEMS

In this section two typical examples of the asset pricing with a few belief types are discussed, one with two and one with four types. Brock and Hommes (1996) contains a more systematic investigation of the role of simple belief types in deviations from fundamentals and primary and secondary bifurcations in possible routes to complexity. All beliefs will be of the simple form

$$f_{ht} = g_h x_{t-1} + b_h \qquad (14)$$

where g_h is the *trend* and b_h is the *bias* of agent h. These simple predictors could be viewed as the simplest idealization of De Bondt and Thaler's overreacting securities analysts or overreacting investors (cf. Thaler (1994, Part Five)). In the special case $g_h = b_h = 0$, equation (14) reduces to *fundamentalists*, believing that prices return to their fundamental value. Fundamentalists do have all past prices and dividends in their information set, but they do *not* know the fractions $n_{h,t}$ of the other belief types, and act as if all agents were fundamentalists. The parameter values we select below are for illustrative purposes only. They are not meant to be realistic parameter values for actual financial data.

Rewriting equation (3) in deviations form yields the demand for shares by type h:

$$z_{h,t-1} = E_{h,t-1}(x_t - Rx_{t-1})/(a\sigma^2) = (f_{h,t-1} - Rx_{t-1})/(a\sigma^2) \qquad (15)$$

We focus on the polar case with zero memory, i.e. $\eta = 0$, and no risk adjustment, i.e. the second term in equation (11) is dropped, so that the fitness measure reduces to last periods' realized profit $\pi_{h,t-1} = \rho_{t-1}z_{h,t-1}$, which for predictor type h in equation (14) becomes

$$\pi_{h,t-1} = \frac{1}{a\sigma^2}(x_t - Rx_{t-1})(g_h x_{t-2} + b_h - Rx_{t-1}) \qquad (16)$$

1.3.1 Two Belief Types: Fundamentalists versus Trend

As a typical two-belief type example, consider the case where type 1 are fundamentalists, believing that prices return to their fundamental solution $x_t = 0$ (corresponding to the fundamental $p_t^* = \bar{p}$), whereas type 2 are pure trend chasers, with $f_{2t} = gx_{t-1}$ (so there is no bias, i.e. $b = 0$). The adaptive belief system (9a–13) becomes

$$Rx_t = n_{2,t-1} gx_{t-1} \qquad (17a)$$

$$n_{1t} = \exp\left[\beta\left(\frac{1}{a\sigma^2} Rx_{t-1}(Rx_{t-1} - x_t) - C\right)\right] \Big/ Z_t \qquad (17b)$$

$$n_{2t} = \exp\left[\beta\left(\frac{1}{a\sigma^2}(x_t - Rx_{t-1})(gx_{t-2} - Rx_{t-1})\right)\right] \Big/ Z_t \qquad (17c)$$

It will be convenient to work with the difference in fractions:

$$m_t \equiv n_{1t} - n_{2t} = \operatorname{Tanh}\left(\frac{\beta}{2}[-Dgx_{t-2}(x_t - Rx_{t-1}) - C]\right) \qquad (17d)$$

where $D = 1/(a\sigma^2)$. Here $C \geqslant 0$ is the cost of obtaining access to the belief system type 1. This cost C may be positive because 'training' costs must be borne to obtain enough 'understanding' of how markets work in order to believe that they should price according to the EMH fundamental.

The adaptive belief system (17) is a third-order difference equation or, equivalently, a three-dimensional system. Asset price dynamics exhibit the following properties (see Brock and Hommes (1996) for details and proofs):

Proposition 1 (fundamentalists versus trend extrapolators)

D1. For $0 < g < R$, the fundamental steady state $E_1 = (0, \text{Tanh}(-(\beta C/2)))$ is the unique, globally stable steady state.

D2. For $g > 2R$, there exist three steady states: the (unstable) fundamental steady state E_1 and two additional non-fundamental steady states $E_2 = (x^*, m^*)$ and $E_3 = (-x^*, m^*)$, where $m^* = 1 - 2R/g$.

D3. Let $R < g < 2R$ and assume that costs $C > 0$. There exist $0 < \beta^* < \beta^{**}$, with

    (a) For $0 \leqslant \beta < \beta^*$ the fundamental steady state is globally stable;

    (b) At $\beta = \beta^*$ a pitchfork bifurcation occurs in which two additional non-fundamental steady states are created;

    (c) For $\beta^* < \beta < \beta^{**}$ the fundamental steady state is unstable and both non-fundamental steady states are stable;

    (d) At $\beta = \beta^{**}$ a Hopf-bifurcation of the non-fundamental steady states;

    (e) For $\beta > \beta^{**}$ all three steady states are unstable.

D4. Let $\beta = +\infty$, $C > 0$ and $R < g < R^2$. The unstable manifold $W(E_1)$ of the fundamental steady state is bounded; all orbits converge to the locally unstable (saddle point) fundamental steady state.

Hence, when the trend chasers extrapolate only weakly ($0 < g < R$), the fundamental steady state E_1 is globally stable. If costs $C = 0$ half of the traders are of type 1 and half are of type 2 for any β. This makes sense because the difference in profits is zero at $x = 0$. Now if $C > 0$, we see that the mass on type 1 decreases to zero as β (or C) increases to $+\infty$. This makes economic sense. There is no point in paying any cost in a steady state for a trading strategy that yields no extra profit in that steady state. As intensity of choice β increases, the mass on the most profitable strategy in net terms increases. When the trend chasers extrapolate very strongly ($g > 2R$) there are two additional non-fundamental steady states E_2 and E_3, even when there are no information costs.

The case of strongly extrapolating trend chasers ($R < g < 2R$) and positive information costs for the fundamentalists is the most interesting. As the intensity of choice β increases, the fundamental steady state becomes unstable in a *pitchfork* bifurcation, and two additional (stable) non-fundamental steady states are created. As β further increases, the two non-fundamental steady states also become unstable in a Hopf bifurcation. Immediately after this secondary bifurcation, the model has two attracting invariant circles around the two (unstable) non-fundamental steady states E_2 and E_3 with periodic or quasi-periodic dynamics (see the attractors in Figure 1.1(a) and (b)).

An important question is whether, as the intensity of choice β further increases, the invariant circles break into strange attractors as in the cobweb model with rational versus naive expectations in Brock and Hommes (1995). Property D4 above suggests that for $R < g < R^2$, when the intensity of choice to switch predictors is large but finite, all orbits remain bounded and for β large the

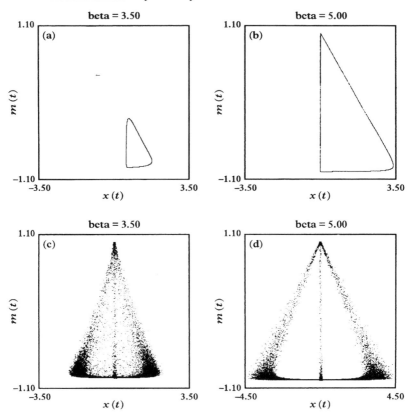

Figure 1.1 Trend versus fundamentalists: $g = 1.2$, $D = (1/a\sigma^2) = 1.0$, $C = 1.0$ and $R = 1.1$. Attractors ((a), (b)) and noisy attractors ((c), (d)) (with dynamic noise ε_t, with uniform distribution over the interval $[-0.05, 0.05]$, added to equation (17a)). (a) Attracting invariant circle around the positive unstable non-fundamental steady state; there is a second attracting invariant circle (not shown) around the negative unstable non-fundamental steady state. (b) Both attractors (only one is shown) have moved close to the stable manifold $x \equiv 0$ of the fundamental steady state $E = (0, \text{Tanh}(-\beta C/2))$. ((c), (d)) Noisy attractors

system must be close to having a *homoclinic point*, a notion already introduced by Poincaré.

Let us briefly recall the definition of this important concept, which is one of the key features of a chaotic system. Let p be a saddle point steady state (or periodic saddle). A point q is called a homoclinic point if $q \neq p$ is an intersection point between the stable and the unstable manifolds of p. From property D4 it follows in fact that for $R < g < R^2$ and $\beta = +\infty$ there exist homoclinic points; therefore, also for β large but finite one may expect (transversal) homoclinic points. It is well known that homoclinic orbits imply very complicated dynamical behaviour and possibly the existence of strange attractors for a large set of parameter values. However, because our system is three-dimensional, applying recent homoclinic bifurcation theory (Palis and Takens (1993)), as was done in Brock and Hommes (1995) for the two-dimensional cobweb adaptive belief system with rational versus naive expectations, is much more delicate. The attractor in Figure 1.1(b), suggests that the system is already close to having a homoclinic orbit; the stable manifold $W^s(E_1)$ contains the vertical segment $x = 0$, whereas the unstable manifold $W^u(E_1)$ moves to the right and then 'folds back' close to the stable manifold.

Figure 1.1 shows attractors in the (x_t, m_t) plane, with and without noise, for different β-values. Figure 1.2 shows some corresponding time series. The asset price fluctuations are characterized by a switching between an unstable phase of an upward or downward trend and a stable phase of close to fundamental price fluctuations. In the noise free case, this switching seems to be fairly regular. In the presence of small noise however, the switching becomes highly irregular and unpredictable.

1.3.2 Four Belief Types: Fundamentalists versus Trend versus Bias

Next consider an example with four belief types. As before, type 1 are fundamentalists. Belief parameters for the other three types are: $g_2 = 0.9$, $b_2 = 0.2$; $g_3 = 0.9$, $b_3 = -0.2$; $g_4 = 1.01$ and $b_4 = 0$. Hence, type 2 is a trend with upward bias, type 3 a trend with downward bias and type 4 a pure trend chaser. This example exhibits some typical features observed in many other examples as well. With four predictors, the adaptive equilibrium dynamics (9a–13) is:

$$Rx_t = \sum_{j=1}^{4} n_{j,t-1}(g_j x_{t-1} + b_j) \tag{18a}$$

$$n_{j,t} = \exp\left(\frac{\beta}{a\sigma^2}(g_j x_{t-2} + b_j - Rx_{t-1})(x_t - Rx_{t-1})\right) \Big/ Z_t, \qquad j = 1, 2, 3, 4 \tag{18b}$$

System (18) is equivalent to a third-order difference equation in x_t. The following holds (see Brock and Hommes (1996)):

Proposition 2 With the parameters as above, the fundamental $x^* = 0$, $n_j^* = 1/4$, is a steady state of system (18). This fundamental steady state is stable for $0 < \beta < 50$ and unstable for $\beta > 50$. At $\beta = 50$, a Hopf bifurcation occurs.

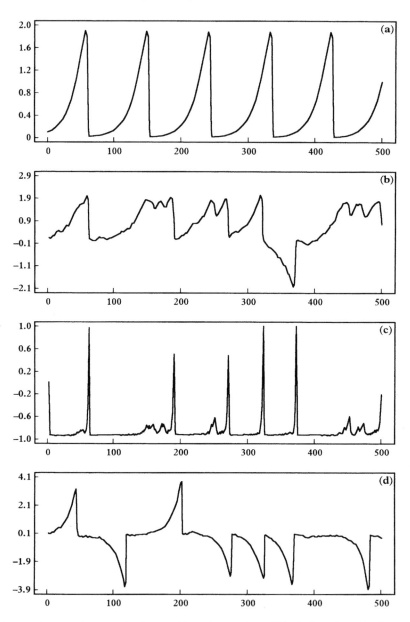

Figure 1.2 Trend versus fundamentalists: time series of (deviations from fundamental) prices: (a) $\beta = 3.6$ without noise; (b) $\beta = 3.5$, with dynamic noise ε_t, uniformly distributed over the interval $[-0.05, 0.05]$, added to equation (17a)); (c) difference in fractions corresponding to noisy price series in (b); (d) $\beta = 5$, with dynamic noise ε_t

Figure 1.3 shows some attractors projected into the (x_t, x_{t-1}) plane for different values of the intensity of choice β. For low values of the intensity of adaptation the fundamental steady state is stable. As β increases, the steady state becomes unstable due to a Hopf bifurcation and an 'invariant circle' with

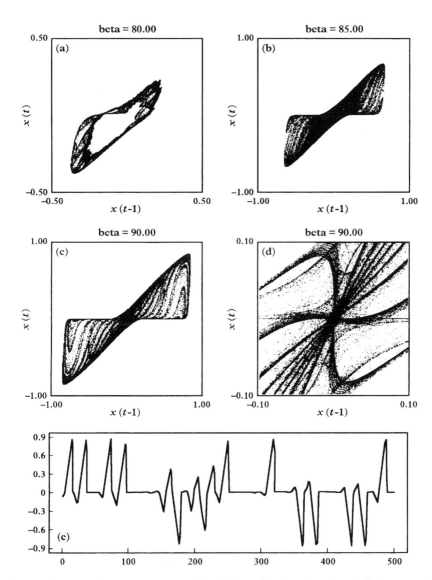

Figure 1.3 (a)–(d) Strange attractors for different β-values, in a four-belief type model with $R = 1.01$ and belief parameters as in the text. (e) Chaotic time series of deviations from fundamental, for $\beta = 90.5$

quasi-periodic dynamics arises. As β further increases, the invariant circle breaks up into a strange attractor with a fractal structure (Figures 1.3(a)–(d)). Figure 1.3(e) shows a chaotic series of deviations from the fundamental. Chaos is characterized by an irregular switching between a stable phase with prices close to the fundamental and an unstable phase of an upward or downward trend where most agents are of type 2 respectively type 3. This irregular switching is triggered by a rational choice between the four predictors.

For a very high intensity of choice (say, $\beta > 120$), at some point almost all traders become fundamentalists, driving prices back to their fundamental steady state. However, the fundamental steady state is locally unstable. The simulations suggest (see, for example, Figure 1.3(c) and the enlargement 1.3(d)) that, as in the two predictor example, for high values of the intensity of choice, the system is close to having a homoclinic intersection between the stable and unstable manifolds of the fundamental steady state.

Our results imply that in a four-type world, even when there are no costs, fundamentalists cannot drive out trend chasers and biased beliefs, when the intensity of adaptation is high. Hence, the market can protect biased or trend traders from their own folly if they are part of a group of traders whose biases are 'balanced' in the sense that they average out to zero over the set of types. Centralized market institutions can make it difficult for unbiased traders to prey on a set of biased traders provided they remain 'balanced' at zero. Of course, in a pit trading situation, unbiased traders could learn which types are biased and simply take the opposite side of the trade. This is an example where a centralized trading institution like the New York Stock Exchange could 'protect' biased traders, whereas in a pit trading institution, they could be eliminated.

1.3.3 A Calibration Exercise

Do the strange attractors in our simple adaptive belief system explain a 'significant' part of observed fluctuations in real asset markets? In order to get some insight into this problem, we 'calibrate' a (noisy) chaotic time series of the four-belief type model, to ten years of monthly IBM-data. Figure 1.4 shows linearly detrended logs of IBM common stock prices[2] (i.e. $\ln(p_t)$ minus a linear trend), returns (i.e. $\ln(p_t) - \ln(p_{t-1})$) and squared returns, from January 1980 to December 1989. Figure 1.5 shows the autocorrelation function (ACF) plots of these IBM series; all ACFs are displayed with 'Bartlett 5% significance bands' (e.g. Box et al. (1994, pp. 32–4)). The ACF of linearly detrended logs of IBM prices is slowly decaying with positive significant lags 1–7; the ACFs of returns and squared returns are both close to zero, with only the first lag significant. These patterns are not uncommon for monthly data of individual stocks.

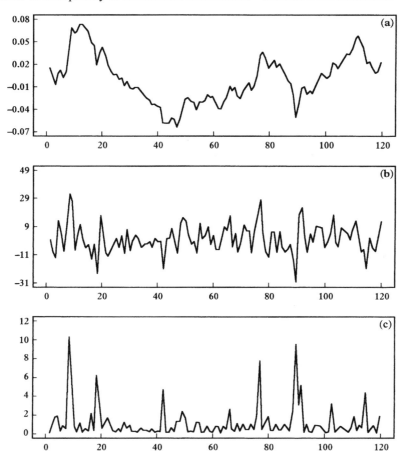

Figure 1.4 (a) linearly detrended logs of monthly IBM-prices; (b) monthly IBM returns; (c) monthly IBM squared returns

Figure 1.6 shows a chaotic time series of the deviation x_t from the fundamental, excess returns $R_t = x_t - Rx_{t-1}$ and squared returns R_t^2, all of the same length as the corresponding IBM series (120 observations). Figure 1. 7 shows the corresponding ACFs. The ACF of deviations x_t from the fundamental is slowly decaying with positive significant lags 1–4; the ACFs of returns R_t is significant only at the first lag, whereas the ACF of squared returns has no significant lags. Similar patterns of the ACFs have been observed for other initial states, neighbouring parameters and also for longer chaotic series. Note that in Figure 1.6 we chose an initial state[3] such that the chaotic series starts with an upward trend, followed by a downward trend, a stable phase of close to

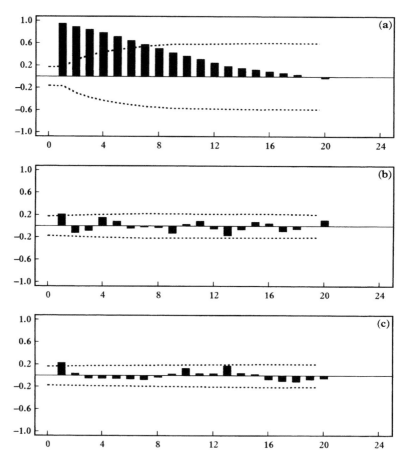

Figure 1.5 Autocorrelation functions with Bartlett 5% significance bands: (a) for linearly detrended logs of monthly IBM prices; (b) for monthly IBM returns; (c) for monthly IBM squared returns

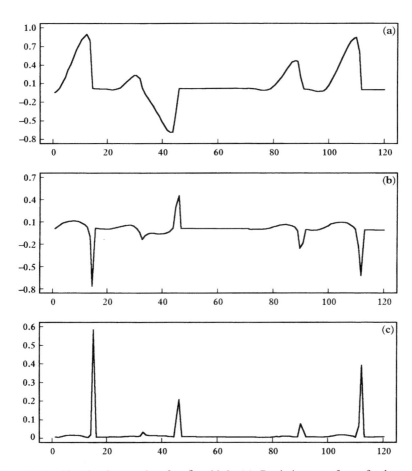

Figure 1.6 Chaotic time series for $\beta = 90.5$. (a) Deviations x_t from fundamental; (b) returns $R_t = x_t - Rx_{t-1}$; (c) squared returns R_t^2

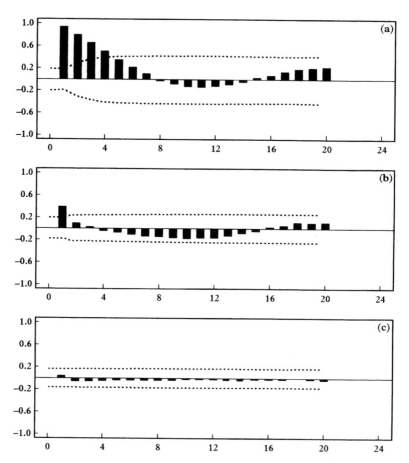

Figure 1.7 Autocorrelation functions with Bartlett 5% significance bands: (a) for deviations x_t from fundamental; (b) for returns $R_t = x_t - Rx_{t-1}$; (c) for squared returns R_t^2

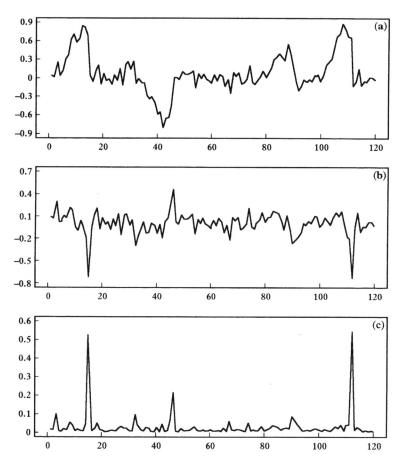

Figure 1.8 Noisy chaotic time series for $\beta = 90.5$. (a) Noisy deviations from fundamental, i.e. $x_t + \varepsilon_t$, $\varepsilon_t \sim N(0, \sigma^2)$, $\sigma = 0.1$; (b) noisy returns $R_t + \varepsilon_t$; (c) noisy squared returns $(R_t + \varepsilon_t)^2$

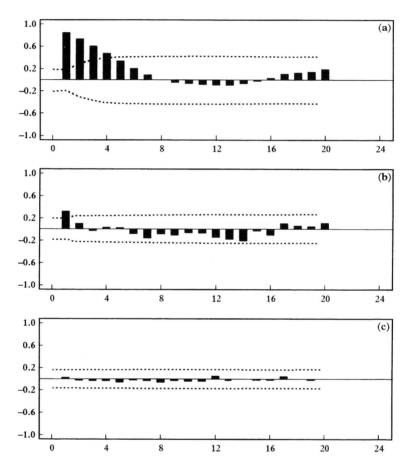

Figure 1.9 Autocorrelation functions with Bartlett 5% significance bands: (a) for noisy deviations from fundamental; (b) for noisy returns $R_t + \varepsilon_t$; (c) for noisy squared returns $(R_t + \varepsilon_t)^2$

fundamental prices and finally two upward trends at the end of the 120 periods. This pattern has been chosen in order to mimic the behaviour of the IBM log price series. For other chaotic series, the pattern may, of course, be different, since along the strange attractor, exactly the switching between the different phases is highly unpredictable.[4] However, in the chaotic adaptive belief system the 'IBM pattern' apparently can occur with positive probability, triggered by a 'rational' choice between the four predictors.

Figure 1.8 shows noisy chaotic deviations from the fundamental, i.e. $x_t + \varepsilon_t$, with $\varepsilon_t \sim N(0, \sigma^2)$ and $\sigma^2 = 0.01$, noisy returns $R_t + \varepsilon_t$ and noisy squared returns $(R_t + \varepsilon_t)^2$. The variance of the deterministic deviation x_t is about 0.09, so that the signal-to-noise ratio in this example is 9. Figure 1.9 shows that the ACFs of the noisy series are similar to the noise-free case.

Readers may judge for themselves how well the noisy chaotic model matches the stylized facts of the data, by comparing Figure 1.4 with Figure 1.8 and Figure 1.5 with Figure 1.9. It seems that prices and returns in our simple four-belief type financial market exhibit some of the stylized facts. In particular, we find decaying ACFs of prices and close to zero ACFs of returns. Noisy chaotic squared returns also seem to be similar to monthly IBM squared returns. The strange attractors show little persistence in volatility, however. The adaptive belief system thus does not produce (G)ARCH effects, at least not in its simplest form as discussed here. In monthly data like the IBM prices (G)ARCH effects are also not too strong, and less strong than in high-frequency data.

1.4 AN EMPIRICAL EXERCISE SUGGESTED BY THE EVOLUTIONARY THEORY

In this section we sketch a possible strategy, using the theory developed in previous sections, to set up an econometric test for the presence of 'extra endogenous dynamics' in stock returns above and beyond the 'conventional dynamics' stressed in current financial work. See Altug and Labadie (1994) for work that stresses the interaction of movements in financial returns and movements in macroeconomic aggregates. See Grossman (1989) for work that stresses movements in financial returns due to asymmetric information among traders and the role of the price system in communicating information to traders. In these models traders receive signals (measurements with error) on a 'latent' fundamental that is not observed by the econometrician. See Brock and LeBaron (1996) for a start on unification of work that stresses information with evolutive dynamics based upon fitness measures. The spirit of this chapter is to see how far one can go in testing for the presence of non-fundamental traders in financial markets in using *only* returns data.

It was suggested by Brock and Hommes (1995) that it should be possible to extend the deterministic heterogeneous adaptive belief system (where one of the belief systems is rational expectations) into a stochastic set-up and nest the Rosen, Murphy and Scheinkman (1994) 'RMS' model within this extended set-up. More precisely, if n_1 of the agents are RMS rational expectations types and n_2 are some backward-looking type, then, holding the n_1 fixed, one could set up a linear quadratic general equilibrium model with heterogeneous beliefs. One could then estimate it along the lines of Anderson *et al.* (1995) and set up a test of the null hypothesis, $H_0: n_2 = 0$ and test H_2 by the usual 'nest it, test it' method. Baak (1996) and Chavas (1995) have carried out a similar research strategy and have adduced evidence for the presence of some backward-looking agents in agricultural data sets. We outline a similar project here for financial data that is stimulated by the theoretical findings for trend chasers that were developed in previous sections.

The results on dynamics with trend chasers suggest that, perhaps in the 'real' world, certain patterns in returns may 'excite' a mass of investors to extrapolate such patterns of deviations from a commonly shared idea of fundamental value. An example might be a positive run of two or three (or more) consecutive periods of positive returns, or the symmetric opposite of this pattern. But a positive measure mass of deviant beliefs from the fundamental may attract an 'opposite' mass which would profit by taking a position that deviates away from the fundamental. The appearance of this counter-mass should generate extra volatility in returns that would be added to the amount of volatility one would expect from a fundamental which is estimated from data on earnings. Of course, calculation and estimation of a 'serious' fundamental is beyond our data resources. Therefore we propose a 'first-cut' procedure here. Recall the pricing equation (5a) in Section 1.2,

$$Rp_t = E_t(p_{t+1} + y_{t+1}) - ah_t z_t \tag{19}$$

where a is the risk-aversion parameter, h_t is conditional variance of $v_{t+1} \equiv p_{t+1} + y_{t+1}$, E_t is conditional mean, p_t, y_t are ex-dividend price and dividends at date t, and z_t is supply of shares per investor. Here conditional expectation and conditional variance are conditional on past prices, past dividends and past supplies of shares per trader.

Before continuing further, let us briefly discuss how one solves equation (19) for a fundamental solution. If one assumes that $\{y_t\}$, $\{z_t\}$ are finite-order Markov processes, then under regularity conditions, a fixed-point argument may be developed to produce a unique fundamental solution $p_t^* = P(y_t, z_t)$. The assumed stationarity of the solution that one seeks avoids the class of 'non-fundamental' solutions, e.g. bubble solutions. See Stokey and Lucas (1989) for a general treatment of this kind of theory. Consider the equilibrium excess returns generated by the fundamental solution p_t^*, i.e. consider

$$R^*_{t+1}/p^*_t = (p^*_{t+1} + y_{t+1} - Rp^*_t)/p^*_t \tag{20}$$

If no restrictions are placed on $\{y_t\}$ and $\{z_t\}$, then the set of $\{R^*_{t+1}/p^*_t\}$ that one can generate by equation (20) will be too large to be useful in empirical work. Empirical work on earnings and dividends can be used to restrict $\{y_t\}$. It is much more difficult to discover how to use observational data to usefully restrict the $\{z_t\}$ process, representing net supply of shares per trader to the community of traders that is being modelled. In the case of a closed community of traders, that are trading only contracts written between each other, z_t is zero for all t. In the case of a stock such as IBM, the process $\{z_t\}$ represents not only the shares outstanding of IBM per trader but also a netting out of sources of supply and demand for IBM shares that are 'outside' the community of traders that is being modelled. In view of the simple purpose of this section, to show how use of the theory *can help guide empirical work*, we shall focus on drastic simplifications of many features of reality, and concentrate on the case with zero supply of outside shares.

Return to equation (19). Here is an example where the fundamental solution is easy to calculate. Let the dividend process be given by the random walk with martingale difference sequence errors

$$y_{t+1} = \mu + y_t + \varepsilon_{t+1} \qquad E_t\varepsilon_{t+1} = 0,\ t = 1, 2, \ldots \tag{21}$$

For the special case where the variance of the errors $\{\varepsilon_t\}$ is a constant $\equiv h$, by equating coefficients, it follows that the fundamental solution of equation (19) is

$$p^*_t = P(y_t) = A_0 + A_1 y_t \qquad A_0 = [\mu R/r - ahz]/r$$

$$A_1 = 1/(R-1) \equiv 1/r \tag{22}$$

We shall drop the asterisk superscript whenever it is clear that we are talking about the fundamental solution of equation (19). Note that if $z = 0$, solution (22) holds for *any* martingale difference sequence (MDS) process $\{\varepsilon_t\}$ for dividends. In particular, the conditional variance does *not* have to be constant. Define excess returns per share by

$$R_{t+1} \equiv v_{t+1} - Rp_t = v_{t+1} - E_t v_{t+1} + E_t v_{t+1} - Rp_t = v_{t+1} - E_t v_{t+1}$$

$$= (1 + A_1)\varepsilon_{t+1} \tag{23}$$

Note how excess returns per share, R_{t+1}, is just the market's prediction error in equilibrium. Before going further, let us discuss dealing with actual data. Financial researchers typically work with continuously compounded returns

$$\ln(v_{t+1}/p_t) = \ln[(v_{t+1}/p_t - R) + R] \cong (1/R)(v_{t+1}/p_t - R) + \ln(R)$$

$$\cong (v_{t+1}/p_t - 1) \tag{24}$$

for $R \cong 1$. For high-frequency data we have $R \cong 1$ and also the data are adjusted for dividend payouts, so researchers typically replace equation (24) by

$$r_{t+1} \equiv \ln(p_{t+1}/p_t) \cong R_{t+1}/p_t \qquad (24')$$

and the daily IBM data that we study here is given in the form of equation (24').

Return now to theory. Let v_{t+1}^f denote the 'fundamental solution' generated by equations (22) and (23). Now introduce 'bounded rationality' by type j having expectations $E_j v_{t+1} = E_t v_{t+1}^f + f_{jt}$ and let there be fractions n_{jt} of type j believers at date t. Here f_{jt} denotes the deviation in type j's beliefs from the fundamental at time t. The pricing equilibrium equation, with zero supply z of outside shares, is

$$Rp_t = E_t v_{t+1}^f + \sum n_{jt} f_{jt} \equiv E_t v_{t+1}^f + \overline{f}_t \qquad (25)$$

Let us set up a test of H_0: $\overline{f}_t = 0$ for all t. This hypothesis is true when, for example, all traders have fundamental beliefs, i.e. all traders have $f_{jt} = 0$, or the set of non-fundamental traders is 'balanced', i.e. $\overline{f}_t = 0$. Let the alternative H_a be: There exist some time t such that $\overline{f}_t$ is not zero.

The econometric problem is to use available data to set up an econometric test for the presence of non-fundamental traders. The spirit of this chapter is to see how far one can go in such testing using *only* returns data. In order to set up an econometric test, we have to specify an econometrically tractible model to play the role of the 'base line' fundamental. A popular class of parametric time series models that is consistent with parametric versions of the EMH is the GARCH(1,1)-M class defined by

$$r_{a,t+1} = a_0 + a_1 h_t^{1/2} + h_t^{1/2} N_{t+1} \qquad \{N_t\} \text{ IIDN}(0, 1)$$

$$h_t = b_0 + b_1 \eta_t^2 + b_2 h_{t-1} \qquad (26)$$

$$\eta_t = r_t - a_0 - a_1 h_{t-1}^{1/2} \qquad (27)$$

The notation $\{r_{a,t+1}\}$ is meant to suggest that equation (26) is an *approximation* to the true process. See Bollerslev (1986) and Bollerslev, Engle and Nelson (1994) for a large literature on fitting this type of model to financial data. Note that $E_t r_{a,t+1} = a_0 + a_1 h_t^{1/2}$ in equation (26), and using the equilibrium equation (19), also $E_t r_{a,t+1} = E_t\{R_{t+1}\}/p_t = ah_t z_t/p_t$. Since the 'M-part' $a_0 + a_1 h_t^{1/2}$ in equation (26) is statistically small, we shall concentrate on the case $a_0 = a_1 = 0$, which is consistent with $z_t = 0$ for all t.

In order to implement the testing procedure suggested here, we need to find a process $\{\varepsilon_{t+1}\}$, for the innovations in the $\{y_t\}$ process (21), so that the equilibrium fundamental returns process $\{r_{t+1}^*\} = \{R_{t+1}^*/p_t^*\}$, generated by equation (19) with $z_t = 0$ for all t, is a GARCH(1,1) process of the form (26) and (27), with $a_0 = a_1 = 0$. Use equations (23) and (26) to write

$$R^*_{t+1}/p^*_t = (1 + A_1)\varepsilon_{t+1}/(A_0 + A_1 y_t) = h_t^{1/2} N_{t+1} \equiv r_{a,t+1} \qquad (28)$$

i.e.

$$\varepsilon_{t+1} = h_t^{1/2} N_{t+1}(A_0 + A_1 y_t)/(1 + A_1) \qquad (29)$$

It is easy to check that $\{\varepsilon_{t+1}\}$ given by equation (29) is a Martingale Difference Sequence w.r.t. past prices and dividends. Furthermore, $\{\varepsilon_{t+1}\}$ generates the 'target' process $\{r_{a,t+1}\}$ when $\{\varepsilon_{t+1}\}$ is inserted into equation (21) and $\{y_{t+1}\}$ is inserted into equation (19), with z_t set equal to zero for all t.

Next, for testing purposes, we wish to nest the special model which generates equation (26), within the general model (25). We shall estimate both the special model and the general model and test whether the extra parameters implied by the general model are 'significant'. Equations (23), (25) and (26) imply[5]

$$R_{t+1} \equiv v_{t+1} - Rp_t = p^*_t r_{a,t+1} + (\overline{f}_{t+1}/R - \overline{f}_t) \qquad (30)$$

The extra parameters that we shall test for 'significance' appear in the term $\overline{f}_{t+1}/R - \overline{f}_t$. Let n_{1t} be the fraction of traders with $f_{1t} = 0$ and lump all others into n_{2t}. Equations (24'), (28) and (30) suggest considering the model

$$r_{t+1} = \{h_t^{1/2} N_{t+1} p^*_t + n_{2,t+1} f_{2,t+1}/R - n_{2t} f_{2t}\}/p_t \qquad \{N_t\} \text{ IIDN}(0,1) \quad (31a)$$

$$h_t = b_0 + b_1 \eta_t^2 + b_2 h_{t-1} \qquad (31b)$$

Our theoretical work above suggests that the fraction of type 2 traders will increase when profits to the fundamental traders have been less than profits to the type 2 traders in the recent past. Let the type 2 traders put f_{2t} proportional to r_{t-1} so their demand at date t increases when returns have increased in the near past. Equation (17d) suggests setting the term $n_{2t} f_{2t} = [(1 - m_t)/2] f_{2t}$, $m_t = \text{Tanh}[(\beta/2) d\pi_{t-1}]$, where $d\pi_t$ is the difference in profits in strategy 1 ($f_{1t} = 0$, since it is the fundamental strategy), and strategy 2. By experimenting with the form of f_{2t} one can 'tune' the term $(\overline{f}_{t+1}/R - \overline{f}_t)$ to increase when events of investigative interest such as short runs in returns, either positive runs or negative runs, occur. One can do this 'tuning' by parameterizing f_{2t} in terms of past returns and implementing a likelihood ratio test that the 'extra' parameters in the term $(\overline{f}_{t+1}/R - \overline{f}_t)$ are statistically significant.

In a preliminary version of this empirical exercise on daily IBM data[6] the results were not very good, since the estimated standard errors of the coefficients were rather unstable. GARCH-M was also estimated but GARCH-M did not improve much on GARCH. By comparing the sample log likelihood of the GARCH(1,1) model and a version of the GARCH(1,1)-M with biased traders model, the null hypothesis that the extra parameters in the term $(\overline{f}_{t+1}/R - \overline{f}_t)$ were all zero was marginally rejected. However, technical problems allowed execution of a likelihood ratio exercise that was only an approximation to the representation in equation (31a).

Thus, we see that there may be some evidence against the 'standard' GARCH(1,1) model in favour of the alternative. However, there were also some first-order autocorrelations in the returns data. Hence, the rejection of the null could be due to this first-order autocorrelation which was not present in the fundamental process $\{r_{a,t+1}\}$. The rejection could also be due to misspecification of the fundamental and the approximation we made to equation (31a).

The presence of first-order autocorrelation raises the issue whether we could design a $\{z_t\}$ process and a $\{y_t\}$ process that had some credibility in the financial literature and solve equation (19) to produce an AR(1) returns process with GARCH(1,1) errors for the model returns $\{r_t\}$ that match the AR(1) with GARCH(1,1) errors which were estimated on the actual returns data. Then one could carry out the process above where one tested the AR(1) with GARCH(1,1) errors as the 'fundamental' null hypothesis against an alternative with beliefs which deviated from this benchmark fundamental. We believe this kind of exercise would be very indicative, but it is beyond the scope of this chapter.

If one studies the form of the alternative for this particular example, we believe it is trying to capture evidence of 'excitement' in beliefs caused by short runs in returns of either sign. This suggests that it may be worth while to scour the trading literature (technical and fundamental, as well as the work of 'finance psychologists' like Werner De Bondt and Richard Thaler) to find pattern sequences (such as runs perhaps) that such literature believes 'excites' at least some subset of traders. This search would allow us to frame and test alternatives using a framework much like that set up above.

Of course, any parsimoniously parameterized stochastic process is, at best, an approximation to the true stochastic data-generating process of the returns on any asset such as IBM stock. Hence, one would always expect such a model to be rejected in large-sample situations such as daily data. However, the *direction* of the rejection as well as a measure of the *economic* magnitude of the rejection may be instructive. The very preliminary work presented here suggests rejection in the direction of a type of trader whose presence is stimulated by positive or negative runs in returns measured relative to GARCH(1,1). It is beyond the scope of this chapter to consider the economic magnitude of the rejection or explore further the space of alternative null hypotheses which are consistent with versions of the efficient markets hypothesis that may be consistent with the data analysed here.

In any event, the character of the evidence adduced by Brock, Lakonishok and LeBaron (1992) against several classes of models, including AR models and GARCH models, indicates that our approach may be on the right track. That is, the fact that these models underpredict volatility and returns following buy signals shows that endogenous dynamics may be temporarily pushing returns above and keeping volatility below base-line.

1.5 CONCLUSIONS

We have set out a general framework for adaptive belief systems in asset pricing theory. Fluctuations in prices and returns are driven by an evolutionary dynamics between traders with different expectations about future prices. In each period, traders revise their beliefs according to a 'fitness measure', such as past realized profits. In particular, we have focused on the evolutionary dynamics with only a few (i.e. two, three or four) different trader types. As the intensity of choice to switch predictors becomes high, complicated asset price fluctuations arise, with prices and returns moving on a strange attractor. Chaos is characterized by an irregular switching between upward or downward trends and close to the fundamental price fluctuations. Asset price fluctuations are driven by a rational choice of prediction rules by the traders (*rational animal spirits*).

We have conducted two empirical exercises to investigate whether our very simple structural non-linear model can match some stylized facts observed in actual stock market data. First, we calibrated a chaotic time series of the four-belief type model to monthly IBM data. It seems that the strange attractors exhibit some of these stylized facts, e.g. with slowly decaying ACFs of prices and close to zero ACFs of returns. However, unlike most financial high-frequency series, the strange attractors in our simple adaptive belief systems show little persistence in volatility. There may be several ways to extend the adaptive belief models:

(1) Let adaptation of beliefs occur on a slower time scale than the high-frequency trading.
(2) Increase the memory in the performance measure (i.e. take $\eta > 0$, instead of our focus on $\eta = 0$).
(3) Let predictor choice be based on a different performance measure, e.g. risk-adjusted profits.
(4) Consider 'large type limits', where the number of trader types is much larger than four or even goes to infinity.
(5) Add weakly correlated noise (e.g. correlated noisy dividends or outside shares) and investigate how this weak correlation is amplified by the dynamics.
(6) Consider the case of asynchronous adjustment, where traders update their belief strategies according to some asynchronous adjustment rule rather than all adjusting synchronously as was done here.

We leave it for future work to see whether these possible extensions lead to stylized facts closer to actual data, and especially to more persistence in volatility.

Second, we sketched a possible strategy for econometric testing, using *only* returns data, to see whether one might adduce some evidence consistent with the presence of evolutive endogenous dynamics of the type studied here. The second empirical exercise was different in spirit from the first calibration type exercise. It investigated whether the benchmark fundamental stochastic GARCH-(1,1) model is valid or whether 'non-fundamental' traders are present in the market.

We stress that the variance of the fluctuations in the fundamental may be large relative to fluctuations induced by the presence of endogenous dynamics, if any. A more serious empirical attempt to adduce evidence for (or against) the presence of 'extra endogenous' dynamics due to shifting evolutive dynamics would use *both* volume and price (returns) data. Purposive agent and bootstrap based methods as in Brock, Lakonishok and LeBaron (1992) are going to be required to adduce any convincing evidence for the presence of 'extra' dynamics above and beyond the 'base line' fundamental. Investigating the impulse responses to difference price and volume shocks, as discussed in the empirical work in Gallant, Rossi and Tauchen (1993), would also be needed to adduce evidence of what kind of forces may be playing a role in determining movements in returns. Our empirical exercise suggests that there may be non-fundamental traders, but much more work is needed to arrive at definite conclusions.

ACKNOWLEDGEMENTS

We would like to thank Blake LeBaron for helpful discussions and suggestions during the preparation of this chapter. Financial support by the Netherlands Organization of Scientific Research under grants R46-319 and B45-163 is gratefully acknowledged. W.A. Brock would like to thank the NSF under grant #SBR-9422670, and the Vilas Trust for financial support.

ENDNOTES

1. There seem to be only a few attempts to fit or calibrate non-linear chaotic models to economic or financial data. The heterogeneous beliefs exchange rate models by DeGrauwe, DeWachter and Embrechts (1993) may be seen as a step in that direction. The work by Sterman (1989) shows that in experiments, in a simulated macroeconomic system, agents use suboptimal decision rules, which in about 40% of the cases lead to cycles and chaotic fluctuations.

2. Recall that our adaptive belief system has been formulated in deviations from the fundamental p_t^*. So far, we have assumed an IID stochastic process for dividends, with corresponding fundamental price $p_t^* = \bar{p} = \bar{y}/(R-1)$, where $\bar{y} = E_{ht}\{y_{t+1}\}$ is common expectations on dividends. Financial analysts often consider non-stationary stochastic earnings processes, e.g. a geometric random walk with a drift μ, i.e. $\ln(y_{t+1}) = \ln(y_t) + \mu + \varepsilon_{t+1}$, $\varepsilon_{t+1} \sim N(0, \sigma^2)$, which often fits earnings data fairly well. In that case, the fundamental solution is $p_t^* = A_1 y_t$, where $A_1 = \exp(\mu + \sigma^2/2)/(R - \exp(\mu + \sigma^2/2))$. Assuming this dividend process, it seems natural to compare deviations x_t in the model to linearly detrended logs of IBM prices.

3. For the time series in Figure 1.6, the initial state is $x_0 = x_{-1} = x_{-2} = -0.066$ and $n_j = 1/4,\ 1 \leqslant j \leqslant 4$.

4. See also Figure 1.3(e), where a chaotic series of 500 observations, converging to the same strange attractor, is shown.

5. To see this, writing in deviation form $x_t = p_t - p_t^*$, yields $R_{t+1} = v_{t+1} - Rp_t = p_{t+1}^* + x_{t+1} + y_{t+1} - Rx_t - Rp_t^* = v_{t+1}^* - Rp_t^* + x_{t+1} - Rx_t = E_t v_{t+1}^* - Rp_t^* + v_{t+1}^* - E_t v_{t+1}^* + x_{t+1} - Rx_t = (1 + A_1)\varepsilon_{t+1} + x_{t+1} - Rx_t = p_t^* r_{a,t+1} + \bar{f}_{t+1}/R - \bar{f}_t$.

6. We would like to thank Kim Sau Chung for carrying out the estimation exercise in Section 1.4.

COMMENTS

F. TAKENS AND H. NIJMEIJER

F. TAKENS

The authors intend to explain, by deterministic models, based on economical principles, the dynamic, if not chaotic, behaviour of economical and financial time series. This is related to the question whether phenomena such as the business cycle are due to random perturbations or whether they are caused by intrinsic instabilities of the economy, considered as a deterministic system.

To be more explicit, the purpose is to explain the following, so called, *stylized facts*, by deterministic models for adaptive belief systems:

(1) The autocorrelation function of individual security returns is approximately zero at all leads and lags.
(2) The autocorrelation function of most measures of volatility and volume (detrended) is positive and dies off as the lag increases.
(3) The cross-autocorrelation function between volume measures and volatility measures is contemporaneously positive with rapid falloff with leads and lags.

The question whether the stylized facts are explained by the (deterministic) models presented here is somewhat complicated from a methodological point of view. In this chapter this aspect is treated in a rather *ad hoc* way—the authors admit that this chapter is only a first step in tackling this difficult problem. Here I try to outline possible refinements of the methods to verify whether a given type of model, such as the present adaptive belief models, explains these stylized facts.

The stylized facts are expressed in terms of (cross) autocorrelations. We first consider a simpler case where we wish to explain 'facts' that are expressed only in terms of autocorrelations of a single time series. These autocorrelations determine and are determined by linear stochastic models, optimally fitted to observed data. So the first thing to do is to take experimental data (in the present chapter this is the time series of IBM data—it seems important to extend this collection considerably) and try to fit linear stochastic models. This consists of estimating the order (Akaike (1969)) and then estimating the relevant autocorrelations.

Then the test, whether our deterministic models explain the 'facts', consists of: (1) generating time series from this deterministic model, (2) fitting a linear stochastic model to these simulated data and (3) verifying whether the linear stochastic models (for the experimental data and for the simulated data) are not significantly different. Therefore, the proposal is to use stochastic models in order to put the 'facts' to be explained in a more quantitative form even if we finally want to model the data with a deterministic model.

In the chapter the stylized facts, which take in the place of the above 'facts' to be explained, are formulated in terms not only of autocorrelations but also of cross-autocorrelations with volatility. Therefore it seems natural to replace the linear stochastic models (AR) by ARCH or GARCH models when making the stylized facts quantitative. The above strategy should, however, still be applicable.

Then there is another aspect where I think the present approach should be adjusted. It is clear that when describing reality by mathematical models, all the elements which are not included in the model, but which influence the dynamics, should be considered as some form of 'noise'. If one uses simple models as in the chapter, one has to accept that there is a considerable amount of 'noise'. This should be taken into account when comparing time series of the model with experimental time series.

In the chapter there are simulations where noise is added, but this is problematic: adding noise, as it is done here, is a way to simulate measurement errors. Instead we should consider here dynamical noise, i.e. random perturbations of the *state* at each time step. From simple experiments with the logistic system one can see a significant difference between the effects of measurement noise and dynamical noise in systems with strong non-linearity. This was analyzed in Takens (1996), in which paper it was argued that the question whether the complexity of the behaviour of a given dynamical system is due to non-linearity (or chaos) or whether it is due to dynamical noise may very well be not meaningful.

This means that the two contrasting viewpoints, mentioned at the beginning of the introduction, might admit a synthesis in the sense that both strong non-linearities and some noise may play a role and that the question which of the two is the more important is irrelevant.

As a whole this method of trying to make models that are economically meaningful and which show behaviour comparable to the behaviour of the real economy is an interesting one and deserves further exploration.

The presentation of the models in this chapter could have been better. It may, of course, not be easy for a non-economist to follow the justification of a model for the economy, especially if the argument contains many references to related literature, but in this chapter I found some complications quite unnecessary. In particular, the way the economical agent optimizes his or her decision z_t at time t by finding a maximum as described in formula (2) is puzzling. It is not really explained what is constant and what is variable in this formula, but the resulting formula (3) seems only possible when assuming that the price p_t at time t is already known (or at least fixed). Then it turns out that this price at time t depends on the decision z_t. This means that there is an additional uncertainty in the wealth of the investor at time $t + 1$ which should have been incorporated into the variance $V_{ht}(W_{t+1})$ of the type h investor at time $t + 1$.

It may be that I missed certain points, but in any case I was not able to assess the justification of these models.

Finally, I wish to point out that the behaviour of financial time series from a non-linear point of view was considered earlier by Zeeman (1974) and I think that the ideas in that paper are still relevant as a complement to the considerations in the chapter.

H. NIJMEIJER

One of the outstanding challenges in theoretical economic analysis, is the derivation of 'acceptable' models for various economic processes. Indeed, unlike the case in physics an economic model is, and will be a subjective matter. A usual prerequisite is that the model is of a sufficiently simple (predictable) nature. Given the fact that the real data to be fitted by the model, are subject to noise, or at least unmodelled exogenous effects, the economist faces a difficult task.

The chapter forms an attempt to arrive at a dynamic model for what the authors call Adaptive Belief Systems. There are two opposite explanations possible for the existing fluctuations in economic and financial markets. Either the changes in fundamentals are generated by exogenous random effects, or the observed fluctuations in fundamentals are caused by nonlinearities in the describing dynamics. The first, neoclassical, viewpoint is connected to the concept of rational expectations; the second, Keynesian, viewpoint typically uses notions as market psychology and animal spirits. The debate between both doctrines is far from being settled but its outcome may have some important consequences in economic policy making. The Adaptive Belief Systems proposed by Brock and Hommes form an attempt to include traders from both viewpoints in an asset pricing model. Typically, in the model traders may dynamically adapt their viewpoint depending on the market price development. The derived dynamic models (depending on a different number of traders) with the inclusion of standard effects in the dynamic pricing model, turn out to be non-linear and, depending on certain parameter variations, may exhibit various bifurcations of the equilibrium solution(s). As is known from dynamical systems theory this may lead to an onset of chaos in the model. Clearly the preceding analysis is deterministic and has to be embedded in a stochastic context. This is in particular needed when one wishes to test whether the obtained non-linear model would agree with an explicitly given data set as the IBM stock prices and returns. To some extent the observed market data match with the Adaptive Belief pricing model. Of course, as the authors remark in their conclusion '. . . much more work is needed to arrive at definite conclusions'.

After the above summary of the chapter some comments seem relevant. First, and perhaps most important, the authors indirectly make contact with the difficult analysis of whether a given time series is generated through a linear (AR) process or by a process also containing non-linearities. This type of analysis has recently received a lot of attention in the physics literature and more specifically in an area which is called 'control of chaos'. For a collection of papers in this field we refer to Ott *et al.* (1994). Specific attention for the question of 'detecting' non-linearities (or even stronger, chaos) in a noisy time series is given in the paper Theiler *et al.* (1992) (see also Kostelich and Schreiber (1993)) where a so called 'surrogate data analysis' is proposed. When applied to a set of data coming from physical systems various discriminating statistics for, among others, testing nonlinearity, estimating the Lyapunov exponent and computing the correlation dimension (a measure for chaos in the time series) have successfully been applied. Indeed, also among economists quite similar questions have been investigated – most notably the first author of the reviewed chapter has been active in this direction, but in this case the problem is apparently more difficult since most economic time series are relatively short in comparison with physical data sets. For this reason definite conclusions are very difficult to obtain in an economic context, though the forementioned references seem to be useful.

A second point that may need further investigation is the nontrivial extension of the Adaptive Belief pricing model with a large number of traders with possibly different changing viewpoints. Of course, one would conjecture that the typical features the authors obtain for models with few different traders remains true, but this is certainly not directly clear. A related issue that deserves further attention is the notion of 'feedback' that is implicitly present in the asset price dynamics. The parameter-changes that may cause for certain bifurcations typically depend ('react') on the time-evolution of the traders. It is desirable to incorporate such state-dependency of the parameters in the model.

Despite the above comments, the authors have initiated an interesting way of modelling some complicated fluctuations in economics and finance. Further data analysis is required for demonstrating its relevance.

REPLIES

W.A. BROCK AND C.H. HOMMES

F. TAKENS

We would like to reply briefly, to the two general points and to one specific point raised by Floris Takens. Firstly, Takens outlines an interesting research strategy to test statistically whether some class of non-linear deterministic models, such as our adaptive belief systems, generates stylized facts observed in actual data: (1) generate time series by the (noisy) non-linear deterministic model, (2) fit a stochastic model, e.g. a linear or a GARCH-model, to this series, and (3) test whether the stochastic models fitted to the simulated data and the experimental data are not significantly different. It seems to be worthwhile to apply this strategy to the adaptive belief models. In the chapter, as a first step we only presented some preliminary empirical exercises and compared autocorrelation functions (ACFs) of simulated and actual data. We see the fact that there are some similarities between the simulated series and the data, as a useful first step to uncover non-linear economic laws that could play a role in explaining asset price fluctuations in financial markets. We believe that extensions of the adaptive belief systems would be necessary, in order for the model to survive the testing strategy suggested by Takens.

The second general point concerns dynamical noise. We agree with Takens that (large) dynamical noise should be present in a model describing real financial markets. Our calibration exercise of the adaptive belief system with small additive noise on monthly IBM-data, illustrates that the model is able to generate time series, similar to actual data. Takens raises the interesting point that (see Takens (1996) '. . . the question whether the complexity of the behaviour of a given dynamical system is due to non-linearity (or chaos) or whether it is due to dynamical noise may very will be not meaningful'. This may be a very difficult point to deal with in a useful manner. For example, Bickel and Bühlmann (1996) have shown that the closure of the set X of MA-processes, i.e.

$$X = \left\{ X_t = \sum a_j \varepsilon_{t-j}, \; -\infty < t < \infty \right\}$$

under a 'suitable' metric is unexpectedly large, indeed so large, that '... given even an infinite long data sequence, it is impossible (with any test statistic) to distinguish perfectly between linear and non-linear processes (including slightly noisy chaotic processes)'. (Bickel and Bühlmann (1996, p. 12128)). Hence, in applied work, parsimony of the representation may play a key role. For example, the fact that low-order moving average processes can be represented as high-order autoregressive processes does not detract from the desirability of the low-order moving average processes in practical estimation and forecasting work. Unfortunately it is beyond the scope of our work here to say anything more about Takens' interesting point.

In applications such as economics and finance, in the presence of a large amount of dynamical noise, there may still be some robust qualitative or even robust quantitative features that might be relevant. For example, the strange attractors in our adaptive belief systems are characterized by an irregular switching between phases of optimism with increasing prices, phases of pessimism with decreasing prices and phases of close to fundamental price fluctuations. In the presence of additive noise, this irregular pattern remains roughly the same. On the other hand, dynamical noise dramatically changes the timing of the switching between the different phases. But even in the presence of dynamical noise, the fluctuations can still be characterized as irregular switching between the same three phases. Dynamical noise shows that exactly the moment of switching, which is triggered by a rational switching of traders' beliefs, is difficult to predict.

In the chapter, we did not investigate systematically how dynamical noise affects the ACFs in the adaptive belief system. In another recent paper (see Hommes and Van Eekelen (1996)) a simple partial equilibrium market model with dynamical noise, that reduces to the quadratic map with dynamical noise, is investigated. By numerical simulations it is shown that for parameter values close to the period three window, even in the presence of dynamical noise, the ACF's have strongly significant lags 1 and 3. From an economic viewpoint, the detailed bifurcation structure of a non-linear model, with stable cycles for extremely small parameter intervals, is not so important, but the global features, such as significant autocorrelations, that are persistent against dynamical noise, are much more relevant.

Finally, Takens raises the issue '... but the resulting formula (3) seems only possible when assuming that the price p_t at time t is already known (or at least fixed) ...', in the third to last paragraphs of his comments. Equation (3) gives what economists call the 'Walrasian' demand function, i.e. each trader is viewed as a 'price taker' and draws up a schedule what it would demand at each price

p_t. The market is viewed as finding the price p_t that equates the sum of these demand schedules to the supply and that is the meaning of Equation (4). While this treatment may be standard in economics, Takens raises a deep point in questioning it. Indeed economists such as Grossman (see Grossman (1989)) questioned the validity of the standard Walrasian framework and have built an alternative framework. We can do no better than quote Grossman at length, 'The Walrasian demand function is derived by finding the x that maximizes expected utility subject to each unit of x having a cost of p. The demand function specifies a desired level of holdings of the security at each particular price p, irrespective of whether or not p is a market clearing price. It is the outcome of a thought experiment in which the consumer imagines that he faces a particular price p chosen at random and then decides how much of the security to purchase given that it will cost p. The crucial deviation from this framework, which I have focused upon, assumes that the consumer faces a price that is a real offer of another person, or the outcome of a market process. Hence the fact that a particular price is offered is itself information about what someone else thinks about the future payoff[1] (see chapters 7 and 8)', see Grossman (1989, pp. 1–2). Grossman's notion of equilibrium might do a better job of meeting Takens' concern 'This means that there is an extra uncertainty in the wealth of the investor at time $t + 1$, which should have been incorporated in the variance $V_{ht}(W_{t+1})$ of the type h investor at time $t + 1$'. De Fontnouvelle (1995) generalizes evolutive dynamics frameworks like ours to non-Walrasian concepts of demand functions like Grossman's.

H. NIJMEIJER

Here is a brief reply to the two main points raised by Henk Nijmeijer. Firstly, the surrogate data method propagated in physics is a technique to set up tests of linear null models by replicating autocorrelation functions (ACF). For surrogate data methods little is known about the statistical properties (e.g. consistency, power against different alternatives, etc), whereas we know some of these properties for bootstrap. While the method of surrogate data has some differences from the bootstrap method introduced by Efron (cf. Maddala and Rao (1996) for time series applications in finance), bootstrap is more general because it can be used to set up tests of much more general null models than linear ones. Bootstrap methods have been used extensively in economics in the last decade or so, as specification tests of null models. For an extensive discussion, see e.g. Brock and De Lima (1996) and Brock (1996) plus references given in those papers. In particular, Brock, Lakonishok and LeBaron (1992) have used bootstrap-based specification tests or 'goodness of fit' tests of the null hypothesis of several parametrizations of the Efficient Market Hypothesis (EMH), such as a random walk or a GARCH-model.

Ultimately we will want to test our adaptive belief model by nesting standard 'established' financial models (efficient markets based models) into our more general theory discussing deviations from the 'benchmark' efficient markets model. We will want to use trading profits and other economically motivated quantities to set up precise statistical tests of the 'extra free parameters' introduced by our theory. Since the surrogate data method is organized around the autocorrelation structure and since this is a linear structure, we do not see how to generalize the surrogate data method to handle these more general non-linear models. Bootstrap based methods seem to be better fit for this task.

The second point raised by the discussant concerns the extension of the model to a large number of different trader types. This is indeed an important topic for future work. In an ongoing research project (see Brock and Hommes (1997)), we introduce a so-called Large Type Limit (LTL) of the adaptive belief system, where the number of different types tends to infinity. This work is intended to provide some analytical background for the more computationally oriented 'Artificial Economic Life' literature.

As both Takens and Nijmeijer point out in their comments, in non-linear dynamics in economics and finance, a lot of work remains to be done.

REFERENCES

Akaike, H. (1969) Fitting autoregressive models for prediction. *Annals of the Institute of Statistical Mathematics, Tokyo* **21**, 243–7.

Altug, S. and Labadie, P. (1994) *Dynamic Choice and Asset Markets*. Academic Press, San Diego.

Anderson, S., de Palma, A. and Thisse, J. (1993) *Discrete Choice Theory of Product Differentiation*. MIT Press, Cambridge, MA.

Anderson, E., Hansen, L., McGrattan, E. and Sargent, T. (1995) Mechanics of forming and estimating dynamic linear economies. Department of Economics, The University of Chicago.

Arthur, W.B., Holland, J.H., LeBaron, B., Palmer, R. and Taylor, P. (1996) Asset pricing under endogenous expectations in an artificial stock market. In W. Arthur, D. Lane and S. Durlauf (eds) (1997) *The Economy as an Evolving Complex System II*. Addison-Wesley, Redwood City, CA.

Baak, S. (1996) Tests for bounded rationality: an application to the U.S. cattle industry. Working paper, Department of Economics, UW Madison.

Barnett, W.A. and Chen, P. (1988) The aggregation-theoretic monetary aggregates are chaotic and have strange attractors: an econometric application of mathematical chaos. In W.A. Barnett *et al.* (eds) *Dynamic Econometric Modelling*. Cambridge University Press, Cambridge, MA.

Benhabib, J. and Day, R.H. (1982) A characterization of erratic dynamics in the overlapping generations model. *Journal of Economic Dynamics and Control* **4**, 37–55.

Bickel, P.J. and Bühlmann, P. (1996) What is a linear process? *Proc. Natl. Acad. Sci. USA* **93**, 12128–31.

Boldrin, M. and Montrucchio, L. (1986) On the indeterminacy of capital accumulation paths. *Journal of Economic Theory* **40**, 26–39.

Boldrin, M. and Woodford, M. (1990) Equilibrium models displaying endogenous fluctuations and chaos. *Journal of Monetary Economics* **25**, 189–222.

Bollerslev, T. (1986) Generalized autoregressive conditional heteroskedasticity. *Journal of Econometrics* **31**, 307–27.

Bollerslev, T., Engle, R. and Nelson, D. (1994) ARCH models. *Handbook of Econometrics*, vol. IV. North-Holland, Amsterdam.

Box, G.E.P., Jenkins, G.M. and Reinsel, G.C. (1994) *Time Series Analysis. Forecasting and Control*, 3rd edition. Prentice Hall, Englewood Cliffs, NJ.

Brock, W.A. (1986) Distinguishing random and deterministic systems. Abridged version. *Journal of Economic Theory* **40**, 168–95.

Brock, W.A. (1993) Pathways to randomness in the economy: emergent non-linearity and chaos in economics and finance. *Estudios Económicos* **8**, 3–55.

Brock, W.A. (1995) Asset price behavior in complex environments. Forthcoming in W. Arthur, D. Lane and S. Durlauf (1997) *The Economy as an Evolving Complex System: II*. Addison-Wesley, Redwood City, CA.

Brock, W.A. and De Lima, P.J.F. (1995) Nonlinear time series, complexity theory and finance. SSRI working paper 9523, Department of Economics, University of Wisconsin

Brock, W.A. and Hommes C.H. (1995) Rational routes to randomness. SSRI working paper 9506. Department of Economics, University of Wisconsin, *Econometrica*, in press.

Brock, W.A. and Hommes, C.H. (1996) Heterogeneous beliefs and routes to chaos in a simple asset pricing model. Discussion paper TI96-147/8, Tinbergen Institute, University of Amsterdam.

Brock, W.A. and Hommes, C.H. (1997) Adaptive beliefs and the emergence of complex dynamics in asset pricing models. Working paper, Department of Economics, University of Wisconsin.

Brock, W.A., Hsieh, D.A. and LeBaron, B. (1991) *Nonlinear Dynamics, Chaos and Instability. Statistical Theory and Economic Evidence.* MIT Press, Cambridge, MA.

Brock, W.A., Lakonishok, J. and LeBaron, B. (1992) Simple technical trading rules and the stochastic properties of stock returns. *Journal of Finance* **47**, 1731–64.

Brock, W.A. and LeBaron, B. (1996) A structural model for stock return volatility and trading volume. *Review of Economics and Statistics* **78**, 94–110.

Brock, W.A. and Sayers, C.L. (1988) Is the business cycle characterized by deterministic chaos? *Journal of Monetary Economics* **22**, 71–90.

Chavas, J.-P. (1995) On the economic rationality of market participants: the case of expectations in the U.S. pork market. Working paper, UW Madison, Department of Economics.

Day, R.H. and Huang, W. (1990) Bulls, bears and market sheep. *Journal of Economic Behaviour and Organization* **14**, 299–329.

Dacorogna, M.M., Müller, U.A., Jost, C., Pictet, O.V., Olsen, R.B. and Ward, J.R. (1995) Heterogeneous real-time trading strategies in the foreign exchange market. *European Journal of Finance* **1**, 383–403.

De Bondt, W.F.M. and Thaler, R.H. (1985) Does the stock market overreact? *Journal of Finance* **40**, 793–808.

De Fontnouvelle, P. (1995) Informational strategies in financial markets: the implications for volatility and trading volume dynamics. Department of Economics, Iowa State University.

DeGrauwe, P., DeWachter, H. and Embrechts, M. (1993) *Exchange Rate Theory. Chaotic Models of Foreign Exchange Markets*, Blackwell, Oxford.

Gallant, R., Rossi, P. and Tauchen, G. (1993) Nonlinear dynamic structures. *Econometrica* **61**, 871–907.

Grandmont, J.-M (1985) On endogenous competitive business cycles. *Econometrica* **53**, 995–1045.

Grandmont, J.-M. (1994) Expectations formation and stability of large socioeconomic systems. CEPREMAP working paper 9424.

Grossman, S. (1989) *The Informational Role of Prices*. MIT Press, Cambridge, MA.

Guilliaume, D., Dacorogna, M., Dave, R., Muller, U., Olson, R. and Pictet, O. (1994) From the bird's eye to the microscope: a US survey of new stylized facts of the intra-daily foreign exchange markets. Olson & Associates, Zürich, Switzerland.

Hommes, C.H. (1991) *Chaotic Dynamics in Economic Models. Some Simple Case-studies.* Wolters-Noordhoff, Groningen.

Hommes, C.H. (1996) On the consistency of backward looking expectations. The case of the cobweb. Forthcoming in *Journal of Economic Behaviour and Organization*.

Hommes, C.H. and Van Eekelen, A. (1996) Partial equilibrium analysis in a noisy chaotic market, *Economics Letters* **53**, 275–82.

Kostelich, E.J. and Schreiber, T. (1993) Noise reduction in chaotic time-series data: a survey of common methods. *Physical Review E* **48**, 1752–63.

LeBaron, B. (1994) Chaos and nonlinear forecastibility in economics and finance. *Phil. Trans. R. Soc. Lond. A* **348**, 397–404.

LeBaron, B. (1995) Experiments in evolutionary finance. Forthcoming in W. Arthur, D. Lane, and S. Durlauf, (eds) (1997) *The Economy as an Evolving Complex System: II.* Addison-Wesley, Redwood City, CA.

Lux, T. (1995) Herd behaviour, bubbles and crashes. *The Economic Journal* **105**, 881–96.

Maddala, G. and Rao, C. (1996) *Handbook of Statistics Volume 14: Statistical Methods in Finance*. North-Holland, New York.

Medio, A. and Negroni, G. (1996) Chaotic dynamics in overlapping generations models with production. In W.A. Barnett, A.P. Kirman and M. Salmon (eds) *Nonlinear Dynamics and Economics*, Cambridge University Press, Cambridge, pp 3–44.

Nishimura, K. and Sorger, G. (1996) A survey on cycles and chaos in infinite horizon optimal growth models. Forthcoming in *Studies in Nonlinear Dynamics and Econometrics*.

Ott, E., Sauer, T. and Yorke, J.A. (eds) (1994) *Coping with Chaos*. John Wiley, New York.

Palis, J. and Takens, F. (1993) *Hyperbolicity and Sensitive Chaotic Dynamics at Homoclinic Bifurcations*. Cambridge University Press, New York.

Ramsey, J.B., Sayers, C.L. and Rothman, P. (1990) The statistical properties of dimension calculations using small data sets: some economic applications. *International Economic Review* **31**, 991–1020.

Rosen, S., Murphy, K. and Scheinkman, J. (1994) Cattle cycles. *Journal of Political Economy* **102**, 468–92.

Scheinkman, J.A. and LeBaron, B. (1989) Nonlinear dynamics and stock returns. *Journal of Business* **62**, 311–37.

Sorger, G. (1996) Imperfect foresight and chaos: an example of a self-fulfilling mistake. Forthcoming in *Journal of Economic Behaviour and Organization*.

Sterman, J.D. (1989) Deterministic chaos in an experimental economic systems. *Journal of Economic Behaviour and Organization* **12**, 1–28.

Stokey, N. and Lucas, R. (1989) *Recursive Methods in Economic Dynamics*. Harvard University Press, Cambridge, MA.

Takens, F. (1996) The effect of small noise on systems with chaotic dynamics. In S.J. van Strien and S.M. Verduyn Lunel (eds), *Stochastic and Spatial Structures of Dynamical Systems*. North-Holland, Amsterdam.

Thaler, R. (1994) *Quasi-rational Economics*. Russell Sage Foundation, New York.

Theiler, J., Eubank, S., Longtin, A., Galdrikian, B. and Farmer, J.D. (1992) Testing for nonlinearity in time series: the method of surrogate data. *Physica D* **58**, 77–94.

Vilder, R.G. de (1995) *Endogenous Business Cycles*. Tinbergen Institute Research Series 96, University of Amsterdam.

Zeeman, E.C. (1974) On the unstable behaviour of stock exchanges. *J. of Math. Economy* **1**, 39–49.

2

Non-linear Dynamics and Predictability in the Austrian Stock Market

E.J. DOCKNER, A. PRSKAWETZ AND
G. FEICHTINGER

2.1 INTRODUCTION

One of the challenges of modern capital market analysis is to develop theories that are capable of explaining the movements in asset prices and returns. According to Fama (1970) the returns' dynamic is driven by the efficient market hypothesis (EMH), i.e. all relevant public (and private) information is reflected in current prices. Any price movements are therefore caused only by the arrival of new and unexpected information. A simple way to formalize the EMH is to make use of the random walk model. Let x_t be the returns of a stock, then the random walk model for prices impies that

$$f(x_{t+1}|\varphi_t) = f(x_{t+1})$$

where $f(.)$ is the density function of x_t and φ_t the information available at time t. In economic terms the model implies that the latest available price of a financial asset is the best forecast for future prices. Hence, according to the random walk model (or the EMH) there is no way to *systematically beat the market* by applying quantitative forecasting methods.

While many empirical studies of the 1970s and 1980s seem to support the EMH, there is mounting evidence in more recent studies that stock markets fail to be (informationally) efficient. Financial economists have identified returns'

System Dynamics in Economic and Financial Models. Edited by C. Heij, J.M. Schumacher, B. Hanzon and C. Praagman © 1997 John Wiley & Sons Ltd

anomalies like the Monday effect or the small firm size effect which clearly contradict the EMH. The Monday effect refers to the phenomenon that returns are systematically smaller on Monday than on any other day of the week. The small firm size effect refers to the phenomenon that the returns of small firms are systematically different from those of larger ones. Moreover, latest research in non-linear dynamical systems has pointed out that simple systems can generate very complicated orbits that look like the outcome of a purely random system. As a consequence, one can conclude that linear techniques might not be appropriate to test for the EMH, i.e. search for structure in asset returns. To demonstrate this argument consider the following example.

In Figure 2.1 we plot a chart of a series generated by the following deterministic system

$$z_{t+1} = 4z_t(1 - z_t)$$

$$p_{t+1} = p_t - 0.5 + z_t$$

with the initial conditions set equal to $p_0 = 1000$, $z_0 = 0.3$. Figure 2.2 presents the charts of the daily prices of stocks traded at the Vienna stock exchange. Both charts share common characteristics such as unpredictable movements up and down. Things become even more interesting when the series plotted in Figure 2.1 is used to be tested for the EMH. Econometric estimation shows that a linear test of the form

$$x_{t+1} = \alpha + \beta x_t + \epsilon_t$$

with $x_t = \ln p_t - \ln p_{t-1}$ fails to reject the EMH although profitable short-run forecasts are possible since the series is generated by a deterministic system. This observation has led financial economists to apply statistical techniques from chaos theory for analysing stock market data.

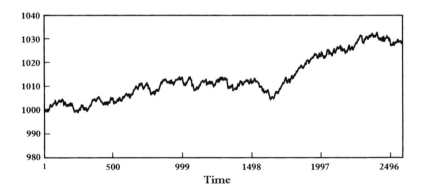

Figure 2.1 Chaotic time series

Based on these new techniques, recent empirical studies document non-linearities in stock market data. Lux (1994) surveys the empirical evidence and points out that although statistical tests with stock market data reject the hypothesis of i.i.d. data-generating processes, algorithms that have been developed to distinguish between simple deterministic (chaotic) and stochastic systems fail to identify a low-dimensional attractor for these data. In contrast, exchange rate data are compatible with low-dimensional chaos with the estimated correlation dimension lying between 2 and 3.

The empirical analyses of non-linearities in stock market data are mainly conducted with index series (cf. Scheinkman and LeBaron (1989), Brock (1988), Peters (1991) and Reiner, Ginter and Schnabl (1992)) based on graphical and statistical techniques related to the correlation integral and the BDS statistic. Analysing index data is comparable to studying well-diversified portfolios. Hence these series might suffer from the fact that non-linearities in the individual time series might have been 'washed out'.

In this chapter we take up two issues. First, we are looking for non-linearities and deterministic chaos in index as well as in individual stock returns. We make use of nearest-neighbour forecasting techniques to distinguish between chaos and noise. For this we apply two alternative nearest-neighbour forecasting techniques to the raw returns. Next, we filter the data by making use of a linear and a GARCH filter to capture existing dependencies in return series and then apply again the same forecasting techniques together with appropriate test statistics to detect remaining non-linearities. Second, our interest is to study whether or not the non-linear behaviour of index series (portfolios) is different from that of single stocks. Most of the research so far has neglected to study the consequences of diversification (i.e. reduction in risk due to mixed portfolios) with respect to non-linear behaviour of asset returns.

Our main result is that while the raw returns demonstrate predictable linear (autoregressive) structure that can be explained by thin trading effects (low liquidity) at the Vienna Stock Exchange, for the linearly filtered series a classical GARCH model is appropriate for capturing all the non-linear dynamics in the series. This result implies that for both the index series and the individual stocks the application of nearest-neighbour forecasting methods to the linearly filtered series does not provide any improvement in the predictability of stock returns relative to the random walk model.

As pointed out in the above example, the interest in applying chaos theory (or the theory of non-linear dynamical systems) to finance is rooted in the fact that simple non-linear deterministic dynamical systems like the tent or the logistic map can generate trajectories that look like random processes comparable to processes of asset returns. Chaotic systems are characterized, among other things, by the sensitive dependence on the initial state and hence a limited forecastability in the long run. This concept of limited forecastability together with complex dynamical behaviour is, however, of interest to researchers in economics and finance and has led to an enormous amount of empirical work searching for chaos in macroeconomic, exchange rate or financial time series. In the initial phases of this work statistical techniques as well as graphical tools were developed that supported the search for chaotic systems by means of the Grassberger–Procaccia correlation dimension (see Takens (1983)). The reason behind this is the fact that dynamical systems with a low dimension can be classified as deterministic while those with large dimensions are stochastic. First evidence in that respect showed, that while many asset returns series are characterized by correlation dimensions well above five, exchange rate series were compatible with low-dimensional chaos. Beyond the strong evidence that asset series do not necessarily show low-dimensional chaos it was found that many of the series showed evidence for interesting non-linear behaviour. This has led to studies that included in a second phase test statistics to check whether the time series follow an i.i.d. process after appropriate filtering or not. The most common statistic in that respect is the BDS test (see Brock, Hsieh and LeBaron (1991)).

The BDS test is designed to test for i.i.d. structures but not for chaos *per se*. It is useful, however, because it is well defined, and has power against many types of linear and non-linear structures. Hence the BDS test has a positive and a negative side. On the one hand, it is able to detect many structures in the data, and, on the other, a rejection of the null hypothesis is not very informative about the remaining structure. This fact has led to the development of additional techniques that allow for a better discrimination between deterministic and stochastic non-linearities. One such class of techniques are the nearest-neighbour forecasting methods originating from chaos theory. The idea behind these techniques is the following. For a low-dimensional non-linear deterministic process the phase space embedding in terms of the m-histories of the observed time series exhibits spatial correlation. This correlation can be exploited to improve forecasts by means of local approximation techniques. Such an approach is not fruitful in the case of random series, because they lack the spatial correlation. Therefore the performance of a forecasting algorithm based on nearest-neighbour techniques is a tool to distinguish random from chaotic behaviour. Here it is important to note that the BDS test as described in the next section is also based on the spatial correlation but makes use of it globally rather than locally.

In this chapter we employ two alternative forecasting techniques proposed by Finkenstädt (1995) and Fernández-Rodríguez and Martín-González (1996), hereafter abbreviated as F(1995) and FRMG(1996), respectively, and apply their corresponding test statistics to discriminate between deterministic and random behaviour of the time series. Hence, the issue here is not so much to improve the forecasting performance but to distinguish between chaos and noise.

The chapter is organized as follows. In the next section we briefly describe some concepts of statistical chaos theory that can be applied to test for non-linearities in the stock market. In Section 2.3 we present the data sets used and briefly comment on some summary statistics. Section 2.4 is devoted to the description of the nearest-neighbour forecasting techniques and the corresponding tests to identify non-linearities in the returns series. In Section 2.5 we present the empirical evidence for Austrian stock returns and Section 2.6 concludes the chapter.

2.2 STATISTICAL TECHNIQUES FOR ANALYSING NON-LINEARITIES IN STOCK MARKET DATA

Consider a time series of observations $\{x_t\}_{t=1,\cdots,N}$ that is generated by the following deterministic system:

$$x_t = h(z_t)$$

$$z_t = F(z_{t-1}) \qquad z_0 \text{ given}$$

z_t is the unobservable state variable of the system that is driven by the state dynamics $F(.)$ ($F: \mathbb{R}^n \to \mathbb{R}^n$) and $h(.)$ ($h: \mathbb{R}^n \to \mathbb{R}$) is a measurement function that translates the unobservable state variable into the observation x_t. In case that the functions F and h would be known, they could be used together with the initial condition to forecast future observations of x_t. In financial time series analysis, however, neither F nor h are known so that the dynamics as well as the dimension of the data-generating process need to be recovered from the univariate series $\{x_t\}_{t=1,\cdots,N}$, the asset returns that are observed. Since we are interested in the non-linear and possibly deterministic properties of the returns-generating system we need to employ a technique that allows us to do that. Takens (1983) supplies an answer to this problem. Define the m-histories as

$$x_t^m = (x_t, x_{t+1}, \cdots, x_{t+m-1})$$

then for $m \geqslant 2n + 1$ the dynamical properties of $\psi^m: \mathbb{R}^m \to \mathbb{R}^m$ defined by

$$\psi^m(x_t^m) = x_{t+1}^m$$

are the same as the dynamic properties of F. m is called the embedding dimension. Thus, for m large enough, the dynamical properties of the m-histories will be similar to that of the unknown state variable z_t. Since we are also interested in the true dimension n of the returns-generating system we need to apply a notion of dimension that allows us to calculate an estimate for n based on the series $\{x_t\}$. The concept that can be applied is that of the correlation dimension.

Consider the correlation integral defined as

$$C_m(\varepsilon) = \lim_{N \to \infty} \frac{2}{N(N-1)} \sum_{t<s} I_\varepsilon(x_t^m, x_s^m)$$

with $I_\varepsilon(x_t^m, x_s^m) = 1$ for $|x_t^m - x_s^m| < \varepsilon$ and $I_\varepsilon(x_t^m, x_s^m) = 0$ otherwise. According to Grassberger and Proccacia the correlation dimension is specified as

$$D = \lim_{\varepsilon \to 0} \frac{\ln C_m(\varepsilon)}{\ln \varepsilon}$$

If the series $\{x_t\}$ is the outcome of a sequence of random events that are i.i.d. then the correlation dimension of x_t^m is m. On the other hand, if the $\{x_t\}$ are generated by a low-dimensional system then estimates of the correlation dimension $\hat{D}$ should converge to a finite value as the embedding dimension is subsequently enlarged.

Based on the correlation integral Brock, Dechert and Scheinkman (BDS) (cf. Brock et al. (1991)) introduced a statistical test for testing the null hypothesis that a given series is i.i.d.. In particular, they show that for a given series $\{x_t\}$ the statistic

$$W_{m,N}(\varepsilon) = \sqrt{N} \frac{C_{m,N}(\varepsilon) - [C_{1,N}(\varepsilon)]^m}{\sigma_{m,N}(\varepsilon)}$$

has a standard normal asymptotic distribution under the independence hypothesis. $\sigma_{m,N}(\varepsilon)$ is the estimated standard deviation under the null hypothesis.

From the BDS statistic it becomes obvious that it tests for i.i.d. structures using the fact that for any independent series x_t the following holds:

$$P(d^m(x_t, x_s) < \epsilon) = P(d^1(x_t, x_s) < \epsilon)^m$$

where

$$d^m(x_t, x_s) \equiv \sup_{j=0,\ldots,m-1} |x_{t+j} - x_{s+j}|$$

and $P(.)$ is the probability of each event, and sup is the supremum norm or maximum.

The BDS test can be applied to test for existing structures in return series. In particular, we will apply several time series models to our data and judge on the basis of the BDS test applied to the corresponding residual whether or not they are capable of capturing all the dynamic structure present in the data. If after fitting a GARCH model to the returns series the standardized residuals pass the BDS test, we can conclude that all the existing structure in the data is properly taken into account with a time-varying conditional variance. If, in contrast, the null hypothesis of the BDS test is rejected, we get an indication that additional structure is present. This is particularly important after fitting the non-linear GARCH model. In that case we then apply nearest-neighbour forecasting techniques to distinguish between noise and deterministic non-linearities. The nearest-neighbour forecasting techniques that are employed in this study are presented in Section 2.4 of this chapter.

2.3 UNIVARIATE TIME SERIES MODELS FOR AUSTRIAN STOCK MARKET DATA

Our data set consists of six different time series of daily asset prices for stocks traded at the Vienna Stock Exchange. We make use of the ATX (Austrian Traded Index) and the WBI (Wiener Börsekammer Index), two stock indices over the sample period of January 1986 to June 1996. While the WBI includes all the stocks traded at the Stock Exchange, the ATX consists of only a small number of the most liquid stocks. Besides the two indices we use four individual stocks for which daily prices over different sample periods are available: CA (Creditanstalt-Stamm) and CA preferred (CA-Vorzug) over the sample period July 1991 to June 1996; OMV (Österreichische Mineralölverwaltung) over the sample period January 1990 to June 1996 and LEYKAM over the period January 1986 to June

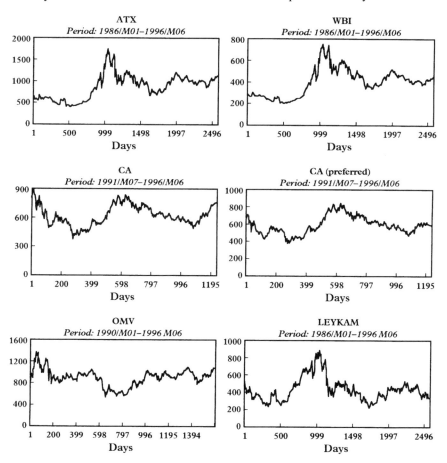

Figure 2.2   Selected Austrian stock market prices

1996. Individual charts for the indices as well as the stock series can be found in Figure 2.2. Simple inspection of the price series shows that they are not stationary so that we employ continuously compounded returns for our analysis.

Table 2.1 reports the sample length for all series as well as some simple descriptive statistics. The statistics demonstrate that the returns are characterized by well-known stylized facts found for returns of financial data: excess kurtosis (fat tails), volatility clustering (i.e. the fact that large changes in the returns tend to be followed by large changes and vice versa) as well as large statistically significant first-order autocorrelations. The correlation coefficients range from 0.12 to 0.37 and are higher for the index series than for the individual stocks. The statistically significant first-order autocorrelations are in line with international experience but are large, which can be explained by a thin trading argument that applies for the Austrian market. The AR structure in the data implies some predictability of asset returns and hence should be reflected when applying nearest-neighbour forecasting techniques. Since our interest is to identify non-linear structures in the returns we primarily make use of the linearly filtered series. In a next step we apply a GARCH(1,1) filter to all the series reported here. Since it turns out that all our data are characterized by a leverage effect (i.e. the observation that volatility tends to be higher in a down market rather than in an up market) we in fact estimate the Glosten, Jagannathan and Runkle (GJR) model (see Glosten *et al.* (1993)). This can be summarized as follows:

$$x_t = \epsilon_t h_t^{0.5} \quad \text{or} \quad x_t | \varphi_t \sim N(0, h_t)$$

where the conditional variance h_t satisfies the dynamic equation

$$h_t = \alpha_0 + \alpha_1 x_{t-1}^2 + \beta_1 h_{t-1} + \gamma_1 D_{t-1} x_{t-1}$$

where D_{t-1} is a dummy variable that takes values of 1 if $x_{t-1} < 0$ and 0 otherwise, ϵ_t are the standardized residuals and x_t are the returns.

In Table 2.1 we report in parentheses the descriptive statistics for the normalized GJR residuals. Here we find that the kurtosis declines, which is in accord-

Table 2.1 Descriptive test statistics for stock returns and residuals of fitted GJR models

	Number of observations	Standard deviation	Skewness	Kurtosis	ρ_1
ATX returns	2575 (2574)	1.24	0.09 (−0.56)	9.93 (5.88)	0.33 (0.04)
WBI returns	2568 (2567)	0.99	0.28 (−0.79)	20.70 (14.23)	0.37 (−0.01)
CA returns	1223 (1222)	1.72	−0.01 (−0.12)	4.40 (3.28)	0.12 (0.02)
CA (preferred)	1223 (1222)	1.60	0.02 (−0.07)	6.05 (1.99)	0.20 (0.01)
OMV returns	1591 (1590)	1.70	0.19 (−0.31)	6.10 (4.91)	0.27 (0.05)
LEYKAM returns	2565 (2564)	1.82	−0.07 (0.00)	4.58 (5.24)	0.29 (0.07)

Numbers in parentheses are the corresponding values for the residuals of the fitted GJR models, ρ_1 indicates the autocorrelation coefficient of order one.

Table 2.2 BDS statistic for stock returns and residuals of fitted GJR models

	σ	ε	Embedding dimension				
			2	4	6	8	10
ATX returns	1.24	$0.5^*\sigma$	23.14*	32.45*	49.20*	82.58*	158.50*
		$1^*\sigma$	22.80*	28.28*	34.39*	42.31*	53.56*
		$1.5^*\sigma$	20.84*	24.46*	27.75*	30.76*	34.09*
GJR residuals	1.00	$0.5^*\sigma$	14.16*	20.34*	32.66*	57.34*	119.04*
		$1^*\sigma$	2.40*	3.91*	5.47*	6.71*	7.52*
		$1.5^*\sigma$	5.98*	7.28*	7.90*	7.70*	7.31*
WBI returns	0.99	$0.5^*\sigma$	22.04*	27.81*	39.49*	62.24*	110.72*
		$1^*\sigma$	23.51*	27.16*	31.77*	37.39*	45.11*
		$1.5^*\sigma$	22.67*	25.25*	27.35*	28.98*	30.87*
GJR residuals	1.00	$0.5^*\sigma$	15.19*	18.90*	28.38*	46.42*	85.83*
		$1^*\sigma$	−3.66*	−2.74	−0.45	1.60	2.91*
		$1.5^*\sigma$	0.51	1.29	1.83	1.80	1.61
CA returns	1.72	$0.5^*\sigma$	7.02*	8.79*	11.82*	15.57*	25.83*
		$1^*\sigma$	8.11*	9.67*	10.86*	11.80*	13.61*
		$1.5^*\sigma$	8.21*	10.12*	11.16*	11.85*	12.92*
GJR residuals	1.00	$0.5^*\sigma$	4.45*	3.51*	4.01*	3.17*	0.82
		$1^*\sigma$	9.57*	7.39*	7.10*	6.62*	5.83*
		$1.5^*\sigma$	2.88*	1.36	1.42	1.26	0.82
CA (preferred) returns	1.60	$0.5^*\sigma$	7.56*	7.37*	9.91*	14.31*	17.30*
		$1^*\sigma$	6.81*	7.01*	7.95*	9.25*	10.19*
		$1.5^*\sigma$	6.72*	7.00*	7.60*	8.07*	8.28*
GJR residuals	1.00	$0.5^*\sigma$	0.55	3.86*	7.04*	10.77*	12.16*
		$1^*\sigma$	3.77*	3.99*	4.46*	4.32*	4.01*
		$1.5^*\sigma$	1.44	1.88	1.97	1.63	1.26
OMV returns	1.70	$0.5^*\sigma$	13.48*	18.15*	27.57*	45.77*	78.67*
		$1^*\sigma$	13.81*	17.01*	20.81*	25.42*	30.85*
		$1.5^*\sigma$	12.82*	15.04*	17.14*	18.92*	20.81*
GJR residuals	1.00	$0.5^*\sigma$	−3.48	−2.66	−1.63	0.49	2.22
		$1^*\sigma$	2.52*	2.36*	1.72	1.24	0.51
		$1.5^*\sigma$	0.77	0.75	0.44	0.15	0.36
LEYKAM returns	1.82	$0.5^*\sigma$	19.87*	32.39*	54.48*	102.29*	214.17*
		$1^*\sigma$	19.13*	24.43*	29.61*	37.34*	49.47*
		$1.5^*\sigma$	17.70*	20.70*	22.36*	24.40*	27.30*
GJR residuals	1.00	$0.5^*\sigma$	0.42	4.39*	7.65*	11.02*	12.74*
		$1^*\sigma$	4.98*	5.41*	4.75*	4.15*	3.81*
		$1.5^*\sigma$	2.82*	2.47*	1.41	1.01	0.98

Test statistics that are larger than the (one-sided) 1% critical value 2.33 are marked with *; the corresponding 5% critical value is 1.65; σ indicates the standard deviation.

ance with other empirical evidence and that the first-order autocorrelation has been removed. As a specification test for the appropriateness of the GJR specification we can employ the BDS test reported in Table 2.2 for different embedding dimensions and various ranges of ϵ.

Here we find that a GJR model substantially reduces the value of the BDS statistic for all series and that only in the case of the ATX GJR residuals does the potential for an additional non-linear structure exist. Since the sample size of the BDS test increases with increasing values of ϵ—which is in favour of any asymptotic test statistic like the BDS test—the fact that the BDS statistic becomes less significant with increasing values of ϵ for all other innovation series can be regarded as evidence for i.i.d. residuals.

Whether the structure in the ATX GJR residuals is due to deterministic or stochastic non-linearities will be examined by means of nearest-neighbour forecasting techniques in the following sections.

2.4 A NEAREST-NEIGHBOUR APPROACH TO FORECAST NON-LINEAR TIME SERIES

Though the behaviour of chaotic systems is unpredictable in the long run ('sensitive dependence on initial conditions'), the deterministic structure of chaotic systems makes short-term prediction possible. The improvement of short-term prediction of non-linear deterministic processes constitutes a potential measure to distinguish between low-dimensional deterministic (chaotic) and high-dimensional deterministic or stochastic systems. Whereas a genuine white-noise process will not be predictable at all, low-dimensional non-linear processes are short-term predictable.

In this chapter we concentrate on the nearest-neighbour approach of Farmer and Sidorowich (1987) to investigate the short-term predictability of Austrian stock market returns. The algorithm is based on the analysis of time series in an m-dimensional space and exploits spatial correlations to improve short-term forecasts of possible non-linear or even chaotic processes. The basic idea behind this algorithm is that parts of time series some time in the past might have a resemblance to parts in the future. To predict t time steps ahead, similar past patterns of behaviour are located in terms of near neighbours. The time evolution of these nearest neighbours t time steps ahead is exploited to yield the desired prediction. The algorithm uses only information local to the points to be predicted and makes no attempt to fit a function to the whole time series at once.

The nearest-neighbour approach to forecast non-linear time series is also related to the techniques of charting (technical analysis) applied in financial markets to produce short-term forecasts (see Elms (1994)). Chartists consider the chart of stock indices and try to infer the future behaviour of the stock prices based on observed up- and downturns in the past. Both methods seek to construct forecasts of future behaviour based on matching patterns observed in past behaviour.

To investigate the short-term predictability of the Austrian stock market returns, we apply two alternative algorithms as implemented by F(1995) and FRMG(1996). Both authors develop a simple non-parametric test of non-linear deterministic structure by exploiting the nearest-neighbour approach to forecast non-linear time series.

The first two steps are common to both algorithms (see F(1995)):

1. Transform the scalar series x_t, $t = 1, \ldots, N$ into a series of m-dimensional vectors X_t, $t = 1, \ldots, N - \tau(m - 1) = \overline{N}$ of m observations sampled from the original time series at intervals of τ units:

$$X_t = (x_t, x_{t+\tau}, \ldots, x_{t+\tau(m-1)})$$

with m referred to as the embedding dimension and τ as the delay parameter. The sequence of m-histories constitutes an m-dimensional object, which is—under certain conditions (see Broomhead and King (1986))—topologically conjugate to the attractor of the true dynamical system underlying the time series. In order to simplify, we shall only consider the case $\tau = 1$. Setting the delay equal to one implies that vectors in the m-dimensional embedding space have an alternative representation as segments of m sequential observations from the original time series.

2. Divide the series X_t into two parts, the *fitting set* $F = \{X_1, \ldots, X_{n_f}\}$ and the *testing set* $T = \{X_{n_f+1}, \ldots, X_{n_f+n_t}\}$ with $n_f + n_t = \overline{N}$.

The selection of nearest neighbours in both algorithms differs with respect to the set from which nearest neighbours are chosen.

3. (a) In FRMG(1996) the fitting set is updated, that is, for each m-history in the testing set $X_i \in T$, the distances to all m-histories preceding X_i are computed and the p nearest neighbours X_{i_k}, $k = 1, \ldots, p$ are determined.

   (b) In F(1995), for each m-history in the testing set $X_i \in T$, only the distances to the m-histories in the fitting set F are computed, and the p nearest neighbours $X_{i_k} \in F$, $k = 1, \ldots, p$ are determined.

   To compute the distances, we use the sum of absolute values.

Predictions are modelled as a convex linear combination (also called *Simplicial Predictor* by FRMG(1996)) of the last coordinate of the vectors following the p nearest neighbours. That is,

$$\hat{x}_{i+m} = \alpha_1^i x_{i_1+m} + \alpha_2^i x_{i_2+m} + \ldots + \alpha_p^i x_{i_p+m} \qquad i = n_f + 1, \ldots, N - m \quad (1)$$

with $X_{i_k} = (x_{i_k}, x_{i_k+1}, \ldots, x_{i_k+m-1})$, $k = 1, \ldots, p$ representing the p nearest neighbours to the point $X_i = (x_i, \ldots, x_{i+m-1})$, $i = n_f + 1, \ldots, N - m$. The proposed algorithms differ only in the specification of the weights α_k^i, $k = 1, \ldots, p$.

Having selected p nearest neighbours, the fourth step of the forecast algorithm involves the specification of the predictor.

4. (a) FRMG(1996) introduce the *Barycentric Predictor*

$$\hat{x}_{i+m}^{bar} = \frac{1}{p} x_{i_1+m} + \ldots + \frac{1}{p} x_{i_p+m}, \qquad i = n_f + 1, \ldots, N - m$$

where all weights are set equal to $1/p$. The authors show (see FRMG(1996), Proposition 2, p.18) that in a time series generated by a collection of i.i.d. random variables, the Barycentric Predictor is the local Simplicial Predictor that minimizes the mean quadratic prediction error.

(b) In F(1995) the distances to $p = (m + 1)$ nearest-neighbours are used to compute exponential weights, where neighbours with a larger distance are assigned lower weights:

$$w_k^i = \frac{e^{-\|X_i - X_{i_k}\|}}{\sum_{k=1}^{m+1} e^{-\|X_i - X_{i_k}\|}}$$

$$k = 1, \ldots, m + 1; \; i = n_f + 1, \ldots, N - m - (t - 1)$$

with $\|.\|$ as the absolute norm and X_i and X_{i_k} defined as in (1). Contrary to FRMG(1996), not only one-step-ahead but also t time-step-ahead predictions are defined. The nearest neighbours are followed t periods later and the predictions for $x_{i+m+(t-1)}$, $i = n_f + 1, \ldots, N - m - (t - 1)$ are obtained as

$$\hat{x}_{i+m+(t-1)} = \sum_{k=1}^{m+1} w_k^i x_{i_k+m+(t-1)} \qquad i = n_f + 1, \ldots, N - m - (t - 1)$$

with t representing the prediction time.

The final step is whether the algorithm really has improved the short-term forecasts for which we have to measure the relationship between the predicted values and the observed values in the testing set T. For each predictor introduced in the previous step a simple non-parametric statistical hypothesis test of non-linear determinism versus random behaviour is introduced in FRMG(1996) and F(1995) respectively.

5. (a) FRMG(1996) show that when the time series is purely random, the distribution of the barycentric prediction error for embedding dimension m and p nearest-neighbours

$$\epsilon_{i+m}^{\text{bar}}(m, p) = \hat{x}_{i+m}^{\text{bar}} - x_{i+m} \qquad i = n_f + 1, \ldots, N - m$$

is $N(0, \sigma(1/p + 1)^{1/2})$ distributed with σ as the standard deviation of the entire time series. Next, they compute the sample variance s^2 of the barycentric prediction error $\sigma_{\text{bar}}^2 = (1/p + 1)\sigma^2$ for a set of $r = [(n_t - 1)/m]$ ([ ] denotes the integer part of a number) independent forecast errors

$$s^2 = \frac{1}{r - 1} \sum_{j=1}^{r} \left(\epsilon_{n_f+1+jm}^{\text{bar}} - \overline{\epsilon^{\text{bar}}} \right)^2$$

where $\overline{\epsilon^{\text{bar}}}$ represents the mean of the r independent barycentric prediction errors. The fact that the transformation $(r - 1)s^2/\sigma_{\text{bar}}^2$ follows a χ_{r-1}^2-distribution if the time series is purely random can be used to build up a non-parametric test of deterministic non-linear structure. For a given significance level α, the time series under investigation is generated by a collection of i.i.d. random variables if

$$a(\alpha) \leqslant \frac{(r - 1)s^2}{\sigma_{\text{bar}}^2} \leqslant b(\alpha)$$

where $[a(\alpha), b(\alpha)]$ is the critical region for a given significance level α. The alternative hypothesis that there exists a causal or deterministic non-linear correlation between the observations in the testing set and its precedents in the fitting set implies low prediction errors and consequently

$$\frac{(r - 1)s^2}{\sigma_{\text{bar}}^2} \leqslant a(\alpha)$$

(b) In order to set up a non-parametric statistical test, F(1995) suggests computing the Spearman *rank correlation coefficient* r_s, which is the ordinary correlation coefficient taken from the rankings of the fitted and realized values in the testing set. For large data sets r_s is $N(0, 1/(n - 1))$ distributed, with n representing the number of data points, and the test statistic

$$t = r_s\sqrt{n - 1} \sim N(0, 1)$$

follows the standard normal distribution under the assumption that both samples are random. Therefore, the test of independence involves testing the null hypothesis H_0: $r_s = 0$ against the alternative hypothesis H_a: $r_s > 0$ and to use the one-sided critical values from the standard normal distribution. While the realized values in the testing set are random under the null hypothesis, the forecasting algorithm imposes dependence up to degree $m - 1$ between successive entries in the set of predictions. It has been shown by F(1995)—in terms of a simulation study as well as a theorem saying that the dependence itself becomes negligible when the sample size of the fitting set is large enough—that this specific dependence does not influence the distribution of the test statistic.

It should be pointed out that the predictions (in both algorithms) are conditioned on three parameters: the embedding dimension m, the number of nearest neighbours p and the splitting of the data set into a fitting and testing set. The choice of these parameters involves some judgement by the user. For example, if m is too small, information will be lost, if the embedding dimension is too high an appropriate neighbourhood might not be located as the additional coordinates might significantly increase the distance between points that were originally close to one another. Since the selection of these parameters is data driven, the common procedure is to search across permutations of these parameters with the resulting forecast performance as the selection criterion.

In the next section we apply the forecast algorithms to the Austrian stock market returns and the residuals of the corresponding GJR models.

2.5 NON-LINEAR FORECASTS FOR AUSTRIAN STOCK MARKET RETURNS

We use the forecast algorithms introduced in the previous section as a test of misspecification to be applied to the post-fitting stage, that is, to the residuals of the GJR models fitted to the linearly filtered stock market returns. For comparison we also apply the forecast algorithms to the stock market returns prior to any filtering process.

Figure 2.3 shows the test results of the algorithm as implemented by Finkenstädt applied to the Austrian stock market returns and the residuals of the corresponding GJR models for various embedding dimensions and choosing a fitting set in the order of approximately 9/10 of the data set. (All calculations have been performed using the GAUSS program kindly provided by B. Finkenstädt.) For all returns, the correlation coefficient is significant for one-step-ahead predictions at the 1% significance level, and stays—with the exception of CA (preferred) returns—below the critical 1% value for higher-order prediction time steps. The short-term predictability is most pronounced in the case of ATX, LEYKAM and CA (preferred) returns with the highest correlation coefficients for one-step-ahead predictions approximately for embedding dimension $m = 6$. WBI, CA and OMV returns display a much lower correlation coefficient for one-step-ahead predictions. The short-term predictability of stock market returns is not surprising, since these series are characterized by large statistically significant first-order autocorrelations (see Table 2.1). If applied to the residuals of the corresponding GJR models, the forecast algorithm indicates significant (at the

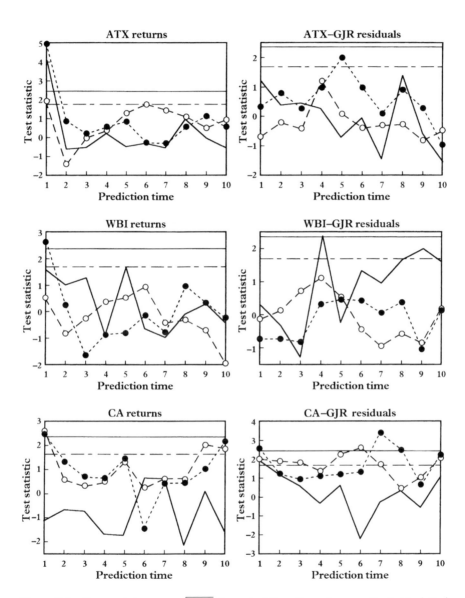

Figure 2.3 Test statistic $t = r_s\sqrt{n-1}$ for embedding dimension $m = 2, 6, 10$ plotted against prediction time for stock returns and residuals of fitted GJR models. The solid line (—) corresponds to $m = 2$, (– ● – ● –) to $m = 6$, (– ○ – ○ –) to $m = 10$; the horizontal solid line (—) shows the 1% critical level, and (– – –) the 5% critical level.

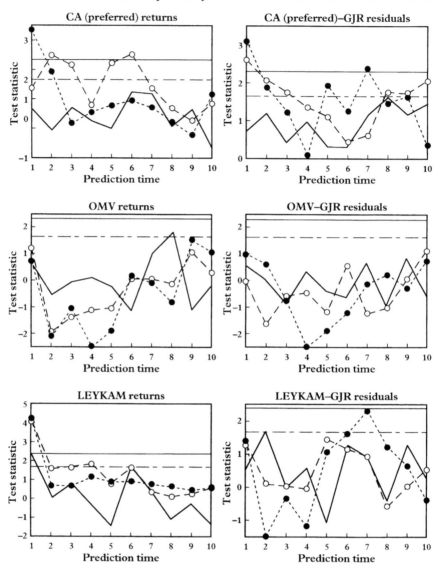

Figure 2.3 (*continued*)

1% as well as the 5% level) one-step-ahead predictions only in the case of CA and CA (preferred) returns.

Table 2.3 summarizes the result of the forecast algorithm as defined by FRMG(1996) for various embedding dimensions. The fitting set is initialized with 9/10 of the data set, while the number of neighbours is set equal to 2% of

Table 2.3 Test statistic $(r - 1)s^2/\sigma_{bar}^2$ for embedding dimension $m = 2, 4, 6, 8, 10$ for stock returns and residuals of fitted GJR models.

m	Test statistic	r	Critical region	Test statistic	r	Critical region
	ATX returns			ATX-GJR residuals		
2	32.53*	126	[95.49, 157.35]	108.62	126	[95.49, 157.35]
4	13.84*	63	[41.68, 85.16]	44.35	63	[41.68, 85.16]
6	9.86*	42	[24.78, 60.06]	29.94	42	[24.78, 60.06]
8	7.26*	31	[16.79, 46.98]	26.05	31	[16.79, 46.98]
10	7.23*	24	[11.69, 38.08]	17.72	24	[11.69, 38.08]
	WBI returns			WBI-GJR residuals		
2	57.87*	128	[97.25, 159.60]	99.37	128	[97.25, 159.60]
4	26.55*	64	[42.51, 86.33]	52.38	63	[41.68, 85.16]
6	10.56*	42	[24.78, 60.06]	29.77	42	[24.78, 60.06]
8	13.85*	31	[16.79, 46.98]	32.09	31	[16.79, 46.98]
10	11.86*	25	[12.40, 39.37]	15.14	25	[12.40, 39.37]
	CA returns			CA-GJR residuals		
2	39.33	60	[39.22, 81.62]	56.56	60	[39.22, 81.62]
4	18.45	30	[16.05, 45.72]	24.39	30	[16.05, 45.72]
6	7.72*	20	[8.91, 32.85]	15.02	19	[8.23, 31.53]
8	7.71	14	[5.01, 24.74]	9.14	14	[5.01, 24.74]
10	4.08	11	[3.25, 20.48]	6.43	11	[3.25, 20.48]
	CA (preferred) returns			CA (preferred)-GJR residuals		
2	37.32*	60	[39.22, 81.62]	48.20	60	[39.22, 81.62]
4	22.09	30	[16.05, 45.72]	20.68	30	[16.05, 45.72]
6	9.27	20	[8.91, 32.85]	9.53	19	[8.23, 31.53]
8	11.77	14	[5.01, 24.74]	9.01	14	[5.01, 24.74]
10	4.99	11	[3.25, 20.48]	5.34	11	[3.25, 20.48]
	OMV returns			OMV-GJR residuals		
2	39.98*	80	[55.86, 104.98]	55.05	79	[55.02, 103.82]
4	17.27*	39	[22.45, 56.39]	26.26	39	[22.45, 56.39]
6	16.10	26	[13.12, 40.65]	21.32	26	[13.12, 40.65]
8	9.01	19	[8.23, 31.53]	16.50	19	[8.23, 31.53]
10	4.75*	15	[5.63, 26.12]	12.13	15	[5.63, 26.12]
	LEYKAM returns			LEYKAM-GJR residuals		
2	65.64*	126	[95.49, 157.35]	185.60	126	[95.49, 157.35]
4	43.58	63	[41.68, 85.16]	44.97	62	[40.86, 83.98]
6	30.78	42	[24.78, 60.06]	58.43	41	[24.43, 59.34]
8	10.85*	31	[16.79, 46.98]	27.83	31	[16.79, 46.98]
10	21.06	24	[11.69, 38.08]	15.93	24	[11.69, 38.08]

Critical regions are computed for a 5% significance level. Test statistics that are outside the critical region are marked with *.

the data set as suggested in FRMG(1996). The results clearly indicate a deterministic non-linear structure for ATX and WBI returns, while the evidence is slightly less in the case of OMV and LEYKAM returns and even less in CA and CA (preferred) returns. Though the overall results are in accordance to the patterns in Figure 2.3, that is, all stock returns exhibit short-term predictability, the significance of the test results for each return differs between both algorithms. Compared with the BDS statistic (Table 2.2), the forecast algorithm in Table 2.3 gives the same results. That is, the ATX and WBI returns are most obviously not i.i.d., while the CA and CA (preferred) returns are at the least significantly different from i.i.d. variates. Applied to the residuals of the corresponding GJR model, the test statistic of the barycentric prediction error misses significance for all returns. Hence, in the case of the GJR residuals the results of both algorithms differ.

Summing up, both algorithms indicate that Austrian stock market returns exhibit short-term predictability, while the hypothesis that the residuals of the fitted GJR model are random i.i.d. variates is rejected only in the case of CA and CA (preferred) returns and only by applying the forecast algorithm as proposed by F(1995).

Left with these differing results, the question remains whether the GJR filter, applied to the linearly filtered stock market returns, captures all deterministic structures in the Austrian stock market returns. From the results of the forecast algorithms we can conclude that all deterministic structure has been captured by the specified GJR model or, in other words, there is no structure left which could improve short-term predictability compared to a pure white-noise series. The omitted structure as indicated by the BDS statistic might therefore be of a stochastic non-linear or stochastic linear type.

2.6 CONCLUSIONS

In this chapter we have applied nearest-neighbour forecasting methods to Austrian financial data to discriminate deterministic from random structures in asset returns. It was found that none of the residual series tested exhibits a non-linear deterministic structure that can be used to improve predictability. This result is in line with international research on asset returns.

The forecast algorithms presented in this chapter are of practical relevance. That is, if the forecast algorithm indicates further structure in the innovation process, this information can be used to improve forecasts. Conversely, even if the BDS statistic indicates further structure in the innovation process, we have no clue how to use this information to yield better forecasts.

An additional byproduct of our results is that we find no difference in the dynamical behaviour of individual stocks relative to indices. Both seem to be largely driven by GJR-type conditional variance dynamics.

COMMENTS

D.S.G. POLLOCK, J.C. ENGWERDA
AND H. NIJMEIJER

D.S.G. POLLOCK

The chapter by Dockner *et al.* is a product of the vigorous activity which is to be found nowadays in the field of the non-linear analysis of time series. The activists draw their methods from many subject areas, including that of chaotic processes where the so-called nearest-neighbour forecasting techniques have originated.

Such a spirit of eclecticism has much to recommend it, not least because it facilitates the re-examination of some techniques of prediction which have been thrust aside from the academic mainstream, even though they have long been popular among non-academic practitioners.

In their chapter the authors allude to the often-derided methods of the chartists who base their predictions of stockmarket values upon their ability to recognize peculiar patterns of financial movements which have been seen in the past. They go some way towards validating these methods.

Some academic theorists seem to believe that the activities of the chartists are akin to those of the fortune-tellers who discern the future from the patterns of tea leaves in empty cups. This is surely an unfair criticism of the chartists. The chapter by Dockner *et al.* is notable for the fact that it expounds a methodology for determining whether or not a stock market index is amenable to the techniques of the chartists. At the same time, it gives an indication of how such techniques can be systematized.

Classical Methods of Time-series Analysis

The continuing dominance of the classical methods of time-series analysis might be taken as a proof of their power and their generality. The present-day innovators, who depart from these methods fail, sometimes, to recognize this generality; and they may be mistaken in the matter of where the deficiencies of the methods lie.

The central notion which underlies the classical methods is that of stationarity. Stationary processes have no history in the usual sense. One segment of a stationary process, if it is of sufficient length, is much like any other segment; and the mathematical formulation of this condition is that every set of m consecutive elements taken from the series is generated by the same m-dimensional probability density function. This may seem to be a very stringent condition, However, it is often possible to transform a non-stationary series so that it conforms to the conditions of stationarity well enough to allow the classical methods to be applied successfully.

The power of the classical methods resides in the remarkable result that all stationary time series can be represented by linear models. This is the burden of the famous Cramér–Wold theorem, which indicates that stationary processes have moving-average representations. That is, all stationary time series can be depicted as the result of applying a linear filter to a white-noise sequence; and for all practical purposes this can be a one-sided causal filter. The theorem does not guarantee that the filter is finite, but is does impose enough restrictions to ensure that it can be approximated to an arbitrary degree of accuracy by the rational transfer function of an ARMA model.

Nearest-neighbour Forecasting Techniques

The point of departure of Dockner *et al.* is the assumption that not all segments of m elements have the same distribution. When different probability density functions apply in different eras, we are confronted by a heterogeneous stochastic system. Some segments of a heterogeneous time series will be more alike than others. The forecasting prescription of the nearest-neighbour techniques is to find the segments which most closely resemble the one which is to be extrapolated, and then to form the extrapolation on the basis of their common properties.

Two methods are suggested. The first is to apply conventional stationary procedures to the selected segments as if they have all originated in the same stationary process. The second method is to form barycentric convex combinations of the points which lie ahead of the selected segments and to use these combinations as the forecasts.

To use such techniques is to invite the question of how and why the segments of a time series might differ. A stock market index, for example, often resembles a seismic record. It is quiescent for long periods which are interspersed by short periods of frenzied or volatile activity. This sort of behaviour has been reproduced successfully by the so-called ARCH and GARCH models. Compared with ARMA models, they use a limited number of additional parameters to characterize the variation in the volatility of the time series. The remaining parameters of the model are global parameters which are applicable to all periods.

The nearest-neighbour techniques embody no global parameters. This is both their strength and their weakness. On the one hand, they avoid imposing untenable assumptions about the existence of an underlying statistical structure. On the other hand, they attribute so little structure to the phenomena in question that the statistical efficiency of the forecasts is liable to suffer greatly in circumstances where classical parametric forecasting models might be appropriate.

The nearest-neighbour forecasting techniques have arisen in the context of chaotic dynamic systems. With such systems, the trajectories of the variables can be described exactly in terms of generating mechanisms which embody a strictly limited number of parameters and whose output is heavily dependent upon a limited set of initial conditions. Such a mechanism seems to be the very opposite of a random process, and it would appear to have little in common with the sorts of processes which, in common imagination, are supposed to underlie the stock markets indices.

Chaotic Processes and Stochastic Processes

The use of so-called deterministic methods to analyse a social system poses an odd paradox; and Dockner *at al.* highlight the paradox by declaring repeatedly their intention of using nearest-neighbour forecasting techniques to distinguish chaotic deterministic non-linearities from random noise. It seems that the authors have in mind a dichotomy far more fundamental that the mere distinction between stationary stochastic systems and heterogeneous stochastic systems which we have employed above. To resolve the paradox, we need to discover precisely what is meant by randomness.

When they talk of stochastic or random processes, statisticians usually have in mind an abstract mathematical formulation which is underpinned by the well-known axioms of probability which were propounded originally by Kolmogorov (1950) in the 1930s. It seemed that, once they had adopted these axioms, statisticians were freed for ever from any further need to define the concepts of randomness and probability.

It is generally agreed that whatever fulfils Kolmogorov's axioms deserves to be called a probability measure. It is also agreed that a random variable is simply defined as a mapping from a sample space, upon which a probability measure has been imposed, onto the real line. However, it is inevitable that, into the interstices of this bald and rigorous system of axioms, will be inveigled any number of unexamined and unexplicit notions concerning the nature of randomness.

Matters of definition come to a head when the statisticians are challenged to generate a sequence of random numbers. Then two possibilities are open to them. Either the random numbers can be generated by a physical device which depends upon radioactive or thermionic emissions or they can be generated by use of a computer algorithm. The computer algorithms, which are nowadays used predominately in generating random numbers, are simply non-linear deterministic systems of a sort which can be described, without fear of contradiction, as chaotic systems. Physical devices are rarely used because they are inconvenient and because they cannot be relied upon to maintain stable relative frequencies over long periods.

If we accept that the output of a classical random number generator is the closest that we shall ever come to realizing the concept of pure randomness, then the endeavour of Docker *et al.* to distinguish between randomness and deterministic chaos assumes a very different aspect from the one which it presents at the outset. It becomes nothing more than an attempt to determine which of two closely related computer-based analogies is best applied in describing an empirical series.

Causality and Indeterminacy

A confusion over the distinction between chaos and randomness is bound to arise unless an adequate set of categories is adopted at the outset of the discussion. Let us therefore replace the dichotomy of randomness versus determinism by a fourfold classification which depends upon two dichotomies.

The first dichotomy is a distinction between causal and acausal processes. For the second dichotomy, we must distinguish between events which are determinate, in the sense of being precisely predictable from a finite number of initial conditions, and events which are indeterminate in the sense of not being precisely predictable.

Most scientific enquiry proceeds on the basis of a belief in universal causality. It is usually maintained that every event is caused by its antecedents. A notable exception, in recent times, has occurred in quantum mechanics where it was proposed in the 1930s that subatomic events are affected by a fundamental acausality (see Frank (1946), for example). However, there is nothing in quantum mechanics which compels this belief (see, for example, Bohm (1984)). Even though they may be indeterminate, there is no need to believe that subatomic events occur without cause.

Table 2.A Causality and determinacy

	Determinate	Indeterminate
Causal	Laplacian determinism	Ideal chaotic systems
Acausal		Classical quantum mechanics

The debate on the issue of causality versus acausality is essentially a metaphysical one. It makes little difference to the practice of science whether the indeterminacy of subatomic events or of social events is the result of acausality (or of 'pure randomness' if one wishes to use such a synonym) or whether it is, more understandably, the result of our inability to comprehend more than a few of an infinite number of peculiar factors and circumstances affecting these events.

Thus there are two observationally equivalent metaphysical outlooks. The first conceives of a world with a finite number of entities which is beset by fundamental acausality. The other conceives of a world which is wholly causal but with an infinite number of entities or with a number so large that it can be regarded as infinite.

What is pertinent to the present discussion is the notion that the randomness of an ideal chaotic process—as distinct from its realisation via a computer of finite accuracy—is a consequence of the non-denumerability of the values within its domain. Without knowing precisely the values of its initial conditions, there is no way that we can learn to predict such a process with accuracy; and therefore it is essentially indeterminate.

It is interesting to compare the randomness of a chaotic process with the randomness entailed by the spectral representation of a stationary stochastic process which depicts a time series as a combination of perfectly regular harmonic components. The randomness here arises precisely because the Fourier–Stieltjes integral comprises a non-denumerable infinity of components. When the integral is replaced by a finite sum, then a perfectly regular periodic function results; albeit that, if the sum comprises many components, we may have to wait for a long time before we can detect a cycle.

Our discussion is best summarized with the help of Table 2.A. Here the horizontal axis, which spans the dichotomy between determinate and indeterminate phenomena, is the scientific axis. The vertical axis, which spans the dichotomy between events with causes and events without, is the metaphysical axis. By maintaining such familiar distinctions as the one from physics between Laplacian determinism and classical quantum mechanics, one is liable to introduce an element of metaphysics into a discourse which can afford to be purely scientific.

J.C. ENGWERDA

The authors of this chapter address the question whether there is empirical evidence for the presence of deterministic chaos in the Austrian stock market. First, the data is filtered by a GARCH(1,1) filter, and then the occurrence of chaos is tested with the BDS statistic, a non-parametric test for the innovations of the filtered data being i.i.d. Only for one of the six time series analysed, the

ATX series, do the authors report evidence that the innovations of the filtered series might possess an additional non-linear structure. In the second part of the chapter it is investigated whether similar conclusions can be obtained if one uses local forecasting techniques. Two techniques, reported by Finkenstädt and Fernández-Rodríguez *et al.*, respectively, are implemented. Using the Finkenstädt technique for the filtered series, significant one-step-ahead predictions are found for two of the series, CA and CA (preferred). But using the Fernández-Rodríguez *et al.* technique none of the residuals of the filtered series seems to be short-term predictable.

These findings raise a number of questions. It seems that both local forecasting techniques are unable to provide us, under all circumstances, with answers that are in agreement with the findings of the BDS statistic. For the Finkenstädt procedure this holds in only three cases, for the technique of Fernández-Rodríguez *et al.* in five situations. Furthermore both techniques are somehow not able to determine the remaining non-linear structure of the filtered ATX series, exactly the job they were supposed to do. Of course, the forecasts made depend on the choice of the predictor. So, one way to proceed might be to look for more ingenuous predictors. In this respect the question can, for example, be posed as to why the type of non-linearity should be time-invariant. It might be interesting to consider only neighbours that date back not too long ago. On the other hand, this absence of agreement might also be due to a lack of data, or to a wrong choice of the parameters in both algorithms.

Another problem that arises in this context is the validity of the various premises made. In particular, the noise-free setting assumption seems to be a strong one. It is well known (see Brock and Dechert (1985)) that if this assumption is violated, then it is very difficult to discern whether a given time series still has some non-linear structure. In other words, even if the BDS statistic gives evidence for IID structure in a time series, in general, then we cannot conclude that there does not exist non-linear structure in the studied time series if we are not sure about the absence of noise. In view of this it may be the case that the BDS statistics obtained here for the CA and CA (preferred) time series do not contradict the statistics obtained using the local forecasting technique of Fernández-Rodríguez *et al.* This technique might even be a better testing technique for an i.i.d. structure than the BDS statistic, given this 'noisy' context. This is a rather fundamental point, because the question whether the innovation process obtained after filtering is either a white-noise or a non-linear process that is disturbed by a white-noise process with some small variance plays a fundamental role in answering a question such as whether the efficient market hypothesis holds.

Altogether, these comments make two points clear. First, that there is a need for a systematic analysis of test procedures for i.i.d. structures. Second, a better theoretical understanding is needed about the working of financial markets.

H. NIJMEIJER

As the authors note in the introduction to the chapter, one of the true challenges in economic analysis is the derivation of descriptive models for economic processes. In the chapter the authors take up this question for the dynamics in capital markets, and more specifically, for the Austrian stock market. In particular—and in this regard the work is intimately related to Chapter 1 in this volume written by W.A. Brock and C.H. Hommes—a study of non-linearity and deterministic chaos is made for time series coming from the Austrian stock market. Using two very recently developed tests that exploit the nearest-neighbour approach to forecast non-linear time series, the conclusion is obtained that none of the residual series of the Austrian stock market exhibits a non-linear deterministic structure that could improve the predictability of the series. As stated, the subject of the chapter is connected with that of Brock and Hommes and as such it is worth comparing both chapters. Also the comments on that chapter (including the references therein) seem relevant in the present case.

Another point that seems at present to be quite standard in (chaotic) time series analysis is to disregard any possible explicit time dependency in the system dynamics. On a conceptual level this excludes some important and, in many circumstances, relevant non-linearities in the system. In this regard it is interesting to note that P.C. Young and D.J. Pedregal in Chapter 6 in this volume precisely emphasize the use of linear time-varying systems for modelling economic data series. Perhaps in future research even the linearity postulate will not automatically be accepted. From a non-linear dynamics viewpoint this is quite natural. The imposed linear dynamics as described in equation (1) in Section 2.4 of the chapter may not be true for the given time series, but, for instance, the time series obtained by taking the logarithmic time series could obey such a linear relation.

It would be interesting to see whether, given the above comments, the conclusions of the chapter would hold for similar time series as the one studied in this chapter.

REPLIES

E.J. DOCKNER, A. PRSKAWETZ AND
G. FEICHTINGER

We are grateful for the suggestions and comments of all discussants.

D.S.G. POLLOCK

Professor Pollock's comment raises two very important issues, some of which go beyond the scope of our chapter. What we find of special interest is his detailed discussion on new developments in time-series analysis in comparison to classical methods. The fact that any random number generator performed on a computer constitutes a non-linear deterministic system makes clear that the concept of randomness used in the chapter has to be well specified. From that point of view we need to clarify that the aim of our chapter is to distinguish between low-dimensional deterministic (chaotic) and high-dimensional deterministic or stochastic systems (see the first paragraph of Section 2.4 in the chapter). That is, we implicitly assume that high-dimensional deterministic systems (as a random number generator) are identical to stochastic systems in the sense that our forecast algorithms will yield no further information compared to a random walk.

J.C. ENGWERDA

We would like to clarify that the aim of our chapter is not to assess whether the Austrian stock market is characterized by deterministic chaos. In fact, we only use the definition of deterministic chaos to introduce the concepts of non-parametric tests like the BDS test, the correlation dimension or the forecast algorithms—tests designed to have high power against non-linear deterministic and deterministic chaotic time series. But none of these tests can be regarded as a test for chaos, they are simply tests for i.i.d.. In the chapter we try to stress that while the BDS statistic is quite general (since it is not very informative about the remaining structure), the forecast algorithms might be regarded as complementary w.r.t. testing the null hypothesis of i.i.d. innovations. That is, if the forecast algorithm indicates further structure in the innovation process, this information can be used to improve the random walk forecasts. On the other hand, even if the BDS statistic indicates a further structure in the innovation process, we have no clue how to use this information to yield better forecasts. Since the focus of the chapter is to identify any structure which is of practical relevance (to that end: improving forecasts), we do not stress the differences between a white-noise and a non-linear process that is disturbed by a white-noise process, although we acknowledge the importance of the issue raised in the comment. With respect to the latter issue we wish to point out that Finkenstädt has demonstrated that her test based on nearest-neighbour forecasting techniques is robust with respect to adding noise to the data.

H. NIJMEIJER

Professor Nijmeijer draws attention to the fact that time-series analysis based on concepts from non-linear dynamical systems theory disregards any possible explicit time dependency in the system dynamics. This comment refers to a basic premise of time-series analysis based on chaos theory. The basic concept (e.g. the correlation integral) is to investigate the system dynamics in the space domain and not to rely on time concepts.

REFERENCES

Bohm, D. (1984) *Causality and Chance in Modern Physics,* Routledge and Kegan Paul, London.

Brock, W.A. (1988) Nonlinearity and complex dynamics in economics and finance. In P.W. Anderson *et al.* (eds), *The Economy as a Complex Evolving System,* Addison-Wesley, Reading, MA.

Brock, W.A. and Dechert, W.D. (1985) Theorems on distinguishing deterministic and random systems, Department of Economics, University of Wisconsin, Madison, Wisconsin and Department of Economics, University of Houston, Houston, Texas.

Brock, W.A., Hsieh, D.A. and LeBaron, B. (1991) *Nonlinear Dynamics, Chaos, and Instability: Statistical Theory and Economic Evidence.* The MIT Press, Cambridge, MA.

Broomhead, D.S. and King, G.P. (1986) Extracting qualitative dynamics from experimental data. *Physica* **20D**, 217–36.

Elms, D. (1994) Forecasting in financial markets. In J. Creedy and V.L. Martin (eds), *Chaos and Non-linear Models in Economics,* Edward Elgar, pp. 169–86.

Fama, E.F. (1970) Efficient capital markets: a review of theory and empirical work. *Journal of Finance* **25**, 383–417.

Farmer, J.D. and Sidorowich, J.J. (1987) Predicting chaotic time series. *Physical Review Letters* **59**, 845–87.

Fernández-Rodríguez, F. and Martín-González, J. (1996) Testing nonlinear predictability in noisy economic time series. Working paper, Universidad de Las Palmas, Departmento de Economía Aplicada.

Finkenstädt, B. (1995) *Nonlinear Dynamics in Economics: A Theoretical and Statistical Approach to Agricultural Markets.* Lecture Notes in Economics and Mathematical Systems, **426**, Springer, Berlin.

Frank, P. (1946) Foundations of Physics. In *International Encyclopaedia of Unified Science* **1**. University of Chicago Press, Chicago.

Glosten, L.R., Jagannathan, R. and Runkle, D. (1993) On the relation between the expected value and the volatility of the nominal excess return on stocks. *Journal of Finance* **48**, 1779–1801.

Kolmogorov, A. (1950) *Foundations of Probability,* Chelsea Publishing Co., New York.

Lux, T. (1994) Complex dynamics in speculative markets: a survey of the evidence and some implications for theoretical analysis. Working paper, University of Bamberg.

Peters, E.E. (1991) *Chaos and Order in the Capital Markets.* John Wiley, New York.

Reiner, R., Ginter, M. and Schnabl, H. (1992) Some remarks on forecasting of stock returns. In P. Gritzmann *et al.* (eds), *Operations Research '91.* Physica, New York.

Scheinkman, J.A. and LeBaron, B. (1989) Nonlinear dynamics and stock returns. *The Journal of Business* **62**, 311–37.

Takens, F. (1983) Distinguishing deterministic and random systems. In G. Borenblatt *et al.* (eds), *Nonlinear Dynamics and Turbulence.* Pitman Publishing, London.

3
Predictability and Economic Time Series

P. ORMEROD AND M. CAMPBELL

3.1 INTRODUCTION

It is fifty years since the path-breaking article by Klein (1947), which used a very small econometric model of the US economy to carry out short-term forecasts. Since then, and especially during the past two to three decades, an intensive research programme has been carried out by the economic modelling community, involving the application of increasingly sophisticated time-series econometrics and of apparently more sophisticated economic theory.

Most existing macroeconomic models, whatever their differences, are based upon the theoretical synthesis which became 'Keynesian' economics. Depending upon the various strengths of key linkages, these models are capable of generating a wide range of different policy simulation results, from those close to the position of pure monetarism to ones in which fiscal policy can have a permanent effect on the economy. The criticisms which follow apply equally well, however, to the minority of models which describe themselves in alternative terms, such as 'supply-side'.

During the past thirty years or so, many short-term forecasts for GDP growth in the developed economies have been published, by both public and private sector bodies and a large literature exists on their evaluation. Three points are clear from this evidence. First, no single institution or methodology has a better record than any other. A particular approach may from time to time perform better, but in the longer run there are no unambiguous rankings of accuracy (see, for example, the major survey by Wallis (1989)).

System Dynamics in Economic and Financial Models. Edited by C. Heij, J.M. Schumacher, B. Hanzon and C. Praagman © 1997 John Wiley & Sons Ltd

The second, and related, point is that there is no substitute for genuine *ex ante* forecasts for evaluating any particular approach. Econometricians devote a great deal of effort to building models of the past which give good forecasts on hold-out samples, and there are many examples in the literature of such work. But the error term on data outside the period over which the equation was estimated often exhibits a non-zero mean and a variance considerably greater than that expected on the basis of in-sample performance (see, for example, the chapters by leading US and UK modellers in Ormerod (1979) discussing the essential task of choosing error terms with non-zero mean on key equations when carrying out such a forecast). Chatfield (1995), a statistician rather than an econometrician, notes the existence of this phenomenon more widely than with just economic data.

Further, the accuracy of even one-year-ahead forecasts of GNP growth is, by any normal scientific criteria, very poor. Again, from time to time apparent improvements may appear to have taken place, so that McNees (1988), for example, in a survey of US forecasts claimed that 'annual forecasts for real GNP have improved over time'. But these putative improvements do not persist. The experience of the UK Treasury in the most recent ten-year period is entirely typical. The average one-year-ahead forecast error of GDP growth has been 1.5 percentage points, which is only very slightly lower than the actual annual average growth rate of the UK economy. The OECD (1993) note more generally for the G7 economies that over the 1987–92 period one-year-ahead forecasts of growth in national output and inflation could not beat the naive rule that next year's growth/inflation will be the same as this year's. These forecasts were carried out by the governments of the G7 countries, the IMF and the OECD itself, a set of organizations embracing a range of ideological and economic views. Of course, the raw output of the models is adjusted by the forecasters, but such literature as exists on this topic suggests that the unadjusted forecasts of the models tends to be even worse (see, for example, Clements (1995) for a list of such references).

In short, genuinely *ex ante* one-year-ahead forecasts of GDP/GNP growth in the Western economies, despite the very substantial research programme which has been dedicated to improving them, typically show errors whose first and second moments are similar to those of the actual data itself. This is not merely of academic interest, for a great deal of economic policy debate in the West is still conducted in terms of short-term prospects for the economy, and what the government could or should do to improve them. If short-term forecasting is not possible in any meaningful sense, short-term government intervention loses its validity. The key motivation of our chapter is to try to explain the phenomenon of the short-term forecasting record.

Further empirical evidence of the difficulty of constructing reasonable forecasts for, say, the growth of national output has emerged recently from the application of non-linear estimation techniques to macroeconomic data series.

Potter (1995) and Tiao and Tsay (1994) investigated quarterly changes in real US GNP (national output) from 1947 through 1990, using the first difference of the natural log of GNP. Tiao and Tsay used a threshold auto-regressive model in which the data series was partitioned into four regimes determined by the patterns of growth in the previous two quarters. Potter also takes the threshold auto-regressive approach, partitioning the data into just two regimes on slightly different criteria with respect to past growth than Tiao and Tsay.

Both the above papers showed that non-linear techniques were superior to linear auto-regressive representations of the data in terms of in-sample fit to post-war quarterly data on US GNP growth. However, the variance of the model error is barely less than the variance of the data, the former being 90% of the latter in the Tiao and Tsay model and 88% in Potter's best model. And this is the weakest possible test of forecasts, given that the fitted values of the model represent one-step-ahead in-sample predictions.

The idea that the business cycle is intrinsically unpredictable is not new. In the 1920s Fisher (1925) suggested that the business cycle was inherently unpredictable because, in modern terminology, the dimension of the problem is too high relative to the available number of observations. He argued that movements over time in the volume of output were 'a composite of numerous elementary fluctuations, both cyclical and non-cyclical', and quoted approvingly from his contemporary Moore who wrote that '[business] cycles differ widely in duration, in intensity, in the sequence of their phases and in the relative prominence of their various phenomena'. In such circumstances, even though some deterministic structure exists, given the limited amount of data available, it would be virtually impossible to distinguish data generated by such a system from data which was genuinely random. In the 1930s, Slutsky (1937) argued that economic data were in fact generated by a series of random shocks, and that transformations of random data based upon the principle of moving summation could generate data which looked very similar to genuine time-series macroeconomic data on output.

The main aim of this chapter is to examine the validity of the hypothesis that the business cycle is inherently unpredictable, in the sense that it is not possible to systematically generate forecasts of short-term growth of output which have errors whose variance is substantially less than the variance of the data.

In Section 3.2 we describe the technique of singular spectrum analysis, which is designed to characterize the general properties of a time series. In Section 3.3 we apply the technique to quarterly data of post-war growth in real national output in both the United States and the United Kingdom.

3.2 SINGULAR SPECTRUM ANALYSIS

The Santa Fe Institute time series competition presented researchers with a number of unidentified time series of data. From the outset, three distinct goals were specified, as Gershenfeld and Weigend (1993) point out in their introduction to a description of the competition; first, to forecast, or to 'accurately predict the short-term evolution of the system'; second, to model or to 'find a description that accurately captures features of the long-term behaviour of the system'. A clear distinction was made between these two aims, and indeed was demonstrated in the results of the competition. The third goal, described as 'system characterization', is to determine fundamental properties of the system, such as the degree of randomness. It is this last aim which is the focus of this chapter. It is a question which is prior to any attempt to represent the data by any particular model. Singular spectrum analysis (SSA) can be used to identify such general properties of a time series. A clear and accessible description is provided by Mullin (1993), and more formal accounts by Broomhead and King (1986) and Vautard and Ghil (1989).

The purpose of SSA is not, it must be stressed, to identify or build any particular model of the data. It provides information about the deterministic and stochastic parts of behaviour in a time series even when the series is short and noisy. Heuristically, the technique could be thought of as decomposing the data and identifying, should they exist, the principal periodic cycles in the data. In addition, it gives a measure of the signal-to-noise ratio of the data. The technique thus provides information on how far any particular model—whatever it might be—may be able to predict future movements in the data.

The task of obtaining a model, be it linear or non-linear, to represent the data would be an entirely separate and subsequent undertaking. Even if singular spectrum analysis of a data series identifies the existence of cycles or similar structure and suggests the existence of a signal of reasonable strength, the problems of capturing the behaviour of the data in an explicit model may still be formidable.

The information provided by SSA does not tell us, for example, whether an explicit model of a data series should be univariate or multivariate since, as we describe below, it identifies the degree of consistency or structure present in a *single* series. There is some potential for confusion between the sense in which econometricians use the word 'structure' and what we mean by it with respect to SSA. The issues surrounding SSA and the choice of a model can be illustrated by an example.

Suppose that the price of wheat was determined completely by the number of sunspots. The choice of sunspots as the illustrative explanatory variable is made because the sunspots series is clearly, in econometrician's terms, an exogenous variable. The price of wheat could, obviously, only exhibit such regularities of behaviour and signal-to-noise ratio as were found in the time series data on sunspots. If the sunspots series had a strong and consistent periodicity, it would be possible to build a univariate model of the wheat price that gave very accurate forecasts without knowing that the price depended on the number of sunspots. But if the sunspots were white noise, so, too would be the price of wheat, and a univariate model would not be able to produce forecasts that were of any use.

A clever econometrician might eventually discover, even if the sunspots were white noise, that the price of wheat depended upon them and build what econometricians call a 'structural' model. But, by definition in this example, the complete lack of structure in the data would mean that meaningful forecasts of the price of wheat could not be made. More generally, if the price was determined by a number of factors in addition to sunspots, then the properties of the singular spectrum analysis of the wheat price would be similar to those of the underlying factors. SSA would not tell us anything about *which* factors determined the price of wheat, but would tell us about their regularity and consistency and, hence, whether meaningful forecasts could be carried out *regardless* of whether a univariate or multivariate model were used.

SSA identifies characteristics of a series by finding the dominant patterns or structure in smaller sections or windows of the data. For example, for a series $X(t)$ where t runs from 1 to N, we choose a number m which is small by comparison with N and define vectors x_t in m-dimensional space by taking the m consecutive observations centred on t, i.e.

$$x_t = (X(t - (m - 1)/2), \ldots X(t - 1), X(t), X(t + 1), \ldots X(t + (m - 1)/2)$$

These vectors are called *m-histories* and m is chosen so that the length of time spanned by the observations in the embedded vector is long enough to include any structure in the data. We will also refer to the series of vectors x_t as the *embedded series* derived from $X(t)$ and call m the *embedding dimension*.

The embedded series x_t forms a cloud of points in Euclidean space. In general, any regularity or consistency in the series $X(t)$ will give the embedded series some discernible structure. For example, if the series is predominantly periodic, the embedded series will be largely confined to two dimensions rather than extending in all of the dimensions of Euclidean space. In this case the embedded series is essentially the same as a scatter plot of the series against the lagged value of the series. On the other hand, if the original series is genuinely random and entirely lacking in structure then the embedded series will be a relatively symmetric ball without any significant pattern.

The regularity or structure present in a data series is measured by taking the embedded series to be approximately an ellipsoid and calculating its principal axes or directions in Euclidean space and calculating the (root mean square) projection of the vectors x_t on to those principal directions. This amounts to finding the eigenvectors and eigenvalues of a matrix of covariance coefficients of the series $X(t)$. The eigenvalues of this matrix, which are typically arranged in decreasing order, are usually referred to as the singular spectrum of the series. This phrase is by no means ideal, for the technique of singular spectrum analysis relies on both the eigenvalues and eigenvectors of this matrix.

The eigenvectors and eigenvalues obtained in this way from the embedded series of m-histories indicate, respectively, the characteristic patterns in the data that exist over a period of time covered by m observations and the relative significance or strength of those patterns.

The ability of SSA to identify structure is not limited to series generated by linear or only mildly non-linear systems such as a periodic series. Provided the dimension of the embedding space is large enough to cover the time scale of the structure in the series, complex or even chaotic systems will also show some degree of regularity. As is to be expected, SSA finds less evidence of structure, the more complex or chaotic the system. However, this should not be seen as a shortcoming of the technique, for it is not clear that there is a distinction between a very complex system with a large number of contributing factors and a genuinely random process either in practice or in theory. (Thinking in terms of economics, the Fisher and Slutsky hypotheses represent, respectively, these two distinct concepts, but if either is true, the implications for predicting the business cycle are the same.)

Following this overview, we now give a more precise mathematical description of SSA. A more detailed account is given in Vautard and Ghil (1989). We assume that the series $X(t)$ where $t = 1, \ldots, N$ has sample mean 0 and sample variance σ^2. The estimate C_k of the kth covariance coefficient of the series $X(t)$ for positive and negative integer values of k is defined by

$$C_k = 1/N \sum_{t=1, N-|k|} X(t)X(t+k) \tag{1}$$

The coefficient C_0 equals the variance σ^2. Let m be the embedding dimension and denote by Γ the $m \times m$ matrix of covariance coefficients with (i, j) entry C_{i-j}, i.e.

$$\Gamma_{i,j} = C_{i-j}$$

and in accordance with the definition of the m-histories x_t, we take the indices i and j to run from $-(m-1)/2$ to $(m-1)/2$. We introduce a scaling factor and define the matrix A by

$$A = 1/m\Gamma \tag{2}$$

The development of singular spectrum analysis is based on this matrix.

It is well known that the covariance matrix Γ given by the estimate in equation (1) is non-negative definite. Therefore since it is also symmetric, the eigenvalues λ_k of the matrix A are non-negative and can be arranged in decreasing order,

$$\lambda_1 \geqslant \lambda_2 \geqslant \ldots \geqslant \lambda_m \geqslant 0$$

We call the eigenvalues of the matrix A the *singular spectrum* of the series X.

Since the sum of the eigenvalues equals the trace of the matrix A, we have

$$\sum \lambda_k = C_0 = \sigma^2$$

where σ^2 is the variance of the series X. By normalizing series to have variance 1, this scaling provides a basis for comparing the singular spectrums for different series.

Let ρ_k for $k = 1 \ldots m$ be the eigenvectors of A. Like the m-histories x_t, the eigenvectors are indexed from $-(m-1)/2$ to $(m-1)/2$. The eigenvectors are orthogonal and we assume that they have norm 1. Therefore they form an orthonormal basis for the m-dimensional embedding space. The symmetry of the covariance coefficients about 0, i.e. $C_k = C_{-k}$ for $k \neq 0$, can be shown to give the eigenvectors a similar property. The eigenvectors are either odd or even functions of their index, i.e. $\rho_k(i) = -\rho_k(-i)$ in the case of the odd eigenvectors or $\rho_k(i) = \rho_k(-i)$ for even eigenvectors. It follows that for odd eigenvectors $\rho_k(0) = 0$.

We can measure the components of the original series $X(t)$ corresponding to each of the eigenvectors of A. For each k define a derived series $X_k(t)$ by

$$X_k(t) = \sum_i X(t+i)\rho_k(i) \qquad (3)$$

where the sum over the index i runs from $-(m-1)/2$ to $(m-1)/2$. This could be written more simply as (x_t, ρ_k), the usual inner product of the vectors x_t and ρ_k. In other words, $X_k(t)$ is a projection of $X(t)$ on to the eigenvector ρ_k.

The variance of $X_k(t)$ indicates the size of the component ρ_k in the series $X(t)$, and can be calculated easily. The matrix with columns $X_k(t)$ can be written as ΞP where Ξ is the matrix or row vectors x_t and P is the matrix of column vectors ρ_k. The covariance matrix Γ is approximately equal to $1/N\Xi^{tr}\Xi$, the difference between this estimate and equation (1) is due to 'edge effects'. Therefore, since $A = 1/m\ \Gamma$, for the variance–covariance matrix of the derived series we have

$$1/N(\Xi P)^{tr}(\Xi P) = 1/NP^{tr}\Xi^{tr}\Xi P \approx mP^{tr}AP = m \operatorname{diag}(\lambda_k)$$

where $\operatorname{diag}(\lambda_k)$ is the diagonal matrix with the eigenvectors λ_k on the main diagonal. It follows that the derived series are uncorrelated and that $X_k(t)$ which measures the component of $X(t)$ corresponding to ρ_k has variance λ_k.

The original series can be reconstructed from the projections $X_k(t)$ by inverting equation (3). Each embedded vector x_t can be written as the sum $\sum_k X_k(t)\rho_k$ over k from 1 to m. The series $X(t)$ is just the 0th component of the vectors x_t, i.e.

$$X(t) = \sum_k X_k(t)\rho_k(0)$$

This also leads to a way of filtering the series. Taking the first r terms in this sum rather than all the terms from 1 to m, amounts to extracting those components of the series corresponding to the first r eigenvectors. This would be appropriate if the eigenvectors $r + 1$ to m had been identified as representing noise. Mullin (1993) and Medio (1992) give applications of this means of filtering.

Estimates of correlation coefficients play a central role in SSA. There is no satisfactory sampling theory for estimates of such coefficients, although approximations can be made (see, for example, Priestley (1981)). It is therefore even more difficult to try to estimate the statistical significance of the singular spectrum. In practice, it is a matter of judgement to infer from the estimated spectrum and the number of eigenvectors which exhibit regular patterns of behaviour, the degree of structure in the data. In Section 3.3 below we also describe what is effectively a bootstrapping procedure which provides further information.

By way of illustration of the SSA technique, we examine the series generated by the differential equation investigated by Medio (1992)

$$(D/n + 1)^n x = rx(1 - x) \tag{4}$$

where D is the differential operator d/dt and n and r are parameters. This is clearly related to the widely studied iterated quadratic map. We choose values $n = 10$ and $r = 5$, generating a series which Medio demonstrates to be mildly chaotic. Equation (4) was integrated numerically and the value recorded every 0.1 time units to give a series of 250 observations. The resulting data series M_1 is plotted in Figure 3.1, along with a second series M_2 obtained from the first by

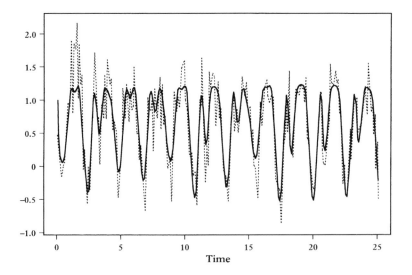

Figure 3.1   The series M_1 and M_2

adding noise generated from the normal distribution. The ratio of the variance of the noise to the variance of the original series is approximately 0.3.

The series M_1 is quasi-periodic with a period of about 2 time units. Therefore we should choose the embedding dimension m so that it covers this interval. Figure 3.2 shows the singular spectrum of M_1 for embedding dimensions of 30 and 50 which correspond to time intervals of 3 and 5 units of time respectively, since we record values of the series every 0.1 time units. The eigenvalues are plotted on a $\log_{10}$-scale. Two points should be noted. First, the values range over a full three orders of magnitude. Second, the singular spectrums fall away rapidly, suggesting a considerable degree of structure since the embedded series is largely restricted to the directions corresponding to the dominant eigenvalues. This is also the pattern in embedding dimension as low as 10.

Figure 3.3 compares the singular spectrum of M_2 with that of M_1 for embedding dimension $m = 30$. The first part of the spectra are virtually identical but the eigenvalues associated with M_2 soon reach a floor that is much larger than the smallest eigenvalues of M_1. This floor corresponds to the noisy component of M_2. The embedded series derived from M_2 is still dominated by the structure in the series M_1 but it also extends in every other direction as a result of the added noise. The qualitative nature of this result is not affected by the choice of m.

Although this is an artificial example, it illustrates that even in the presence of considerable noise, SSA can identify underlying structure. It is important to note that the results of the SSA do not in any way point us to the choice of any particular model as a way of representing the data. They simply show that a

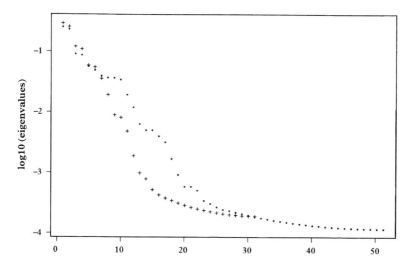

Figure 3.2   Singular spectrum for M_1 for embedding dimensions 30 and 50

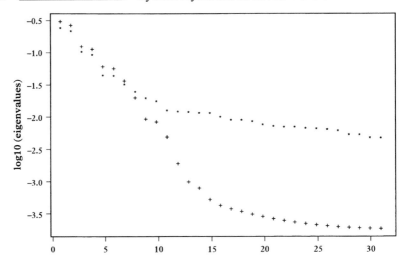

Figure 3.3 The singular spectra for M_1 (shown as $+$) and M_2 (shown as $\cdot$)

component of sufficient structure exists within the data to enable a potentially reasonable model to be built. Of course, without knowledge of equation (4) and being confronted with data for M_2, the practical search for such a model may be a formidable undertaking.

3.3 APPLICATIONS OF SSA TO US AND UK QUARTERLY GDP DATA

For both the USA and the UK, we examined the quarterly growth in real national output, on a seasonally adjusted basis over the post-war period. Growth was defined in the conventional way in applied economics, namely as the first difference of the log of real national output. For the USA, the sample period was from 1947Q2 through 1990Q4, the same as that used in the Potter and Tiao and Tsay articles quoted above. For the UK, the sample period was 1955Q2 through 1995Q3. The two series are plotted in Figures 3.4(a) and 3.4(b), respectively. (Gross National Product is the data series for the USA and Gross Domestic Product for the UK, in accordance with the usual conventions of applied economics. There is a small difference between these two definitions of national output which is more important for the USA than it is for European economies, and which need not concern us here.)

Visual inspection of the two data series does not immediately suggest any obvious periodicity. Mullin (1993) suggests that information on the choice of m, the embedding dimension of the data, can potentially be provided by the

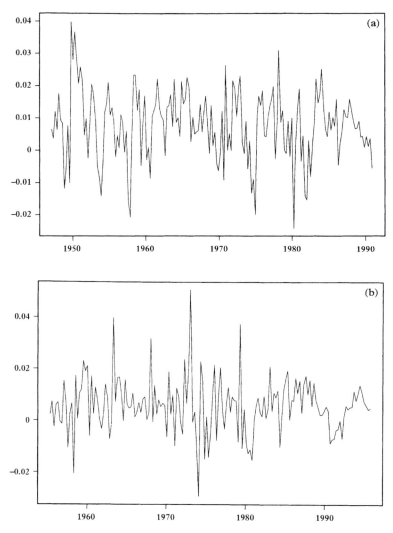

Figure 3.4   (a) US quarterly changes in log GNP; (b) UK quarterly changes in log GDP

autocorrelation function (ACF). But in these examples, as in a range of other series we have investigated, it is not very helpful. The use of formal criteria such as the AIC to choose the embedding dimension leads to values of m which are very low—three, for example, in the case of the US data. Lags 1 and 2 are significantly different from zero at the conventional 5% level with the US data, but they are the only ones. The values at lags 5 and 14 are larger than the others in absolute value, but are not significant. For the UK, no single value of the ACF is significantly different from zero, the largest absolute values being at lags 6, 8, and 12. As a much better guide, it has become the convention in economics to regard the business cycle as lasting anything between two or three to seven or eight years. Accordingly, by choosing $m = 41$, in other words, spanning a window of ten years of data, in the first instance, we make adequate allowance for any such potential structure.

Figure 3.5 plots the resulting singular spectra of US and UK data. The results are drastically different for both series from the examples given in Section 3.2. In neither case does the spectrum show evidence of much structure. The largest eigenvalue is relatively small and the eigenvalues do not fall away rapidly. The range of the eigenvalues is only one order of magnitude. There may be somewhat more structure to the US data since the larger eigenvalues are greater relative to the rest than those of the UK, but the difference is only small. Experimenting with different values of the embedding dimension, m, does not alter these results.

The eigenvectors associated with the six largest eigenvalues are plotted in Figures 3.6(a) and 3.6(b) for the USA and the UK, respectively. Here there is a marked difference between the two countries. As discussed in Section 3.2, the vectors represent principal directions in the cloud of points formed by the embedded series. They therefore indicate the pattern or regularity that exists in the data on the time scale covered by the choice of embedding dimension. For the US data, the first four eigenvectors have a strong pattern of regularity. By contrast, for the UK only the first two show any regularity at all, and the remainder are highly irregular.

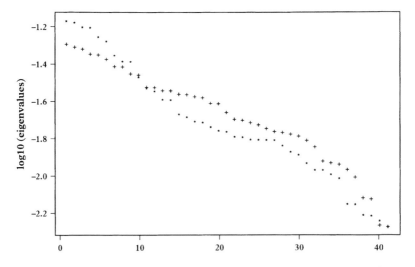

Figure 3.5 The singular spectrums for UK (+) and the USA (·) quarterly changes in national output

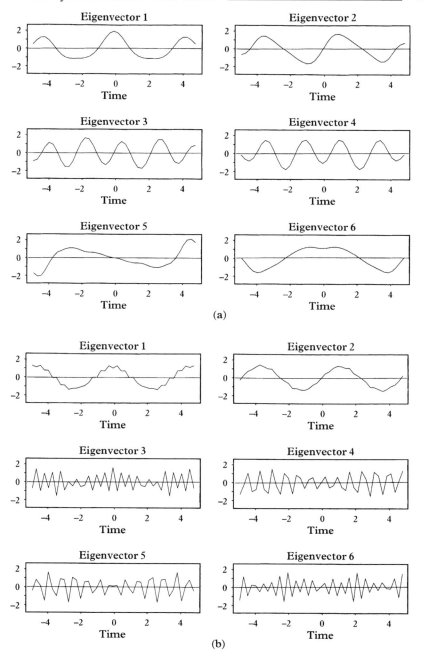

Figure 3.6 The eigenvectors associated with the largest eigenvalues for (a) US GNP and (b) UK GDP

The pattern of the eigenvalues does in fact look similar to that of a purely random series and, therefore, to try to assess the significance of these results, we carried out a bootstrapping exercise. From each of the original series, a random draw with replacement was carried out to generate a new data series of the same length. By construction, there is only a small probability that this series has any discernible structure. The singular spectrum of this artificial data was calculated, and the procedure repeated 500 times.

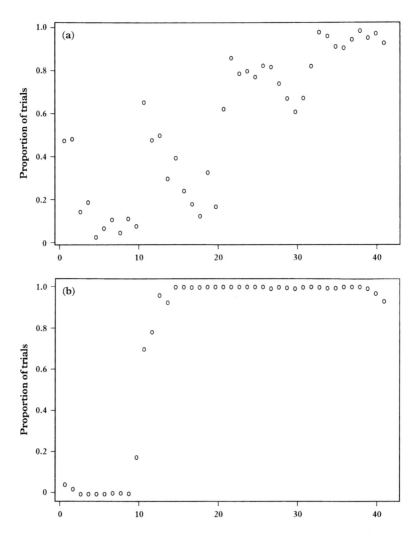

Figure 3.7 The proportion of trials for which each eigenvalue is larger than the corresponding value for (a) UK GDP and (b) US GNP

This exercise confirms the impression gained from inspection of the singular spectrums and eigenvectors for each of the data series.

The singular spectrum of the UK data seems to be indistinguishable from the spectrum of the artificially generated random series. For example, in terms of the largest eigenvalue of each spectrum, no less than 256 of the random series have one which is larger than that of the UK data itself. The proportion of trials for which the eigenvalue is larger than the corresponding value of the original series is plotted for each successive eigenvalue in Figure 3.7(a). The proportion shows some pattern of fluctuation but this is not at all significant. The variation is typical of what is observed when any one of the artificially generated series is compared with the remaining trials.

The results for the US data are quite different. In this case, the spectrum of the original series is distinct from those of the artificially generated random series. Figure 3.7(b) repeats the exercise of Figure 3.7(a) for the US data. For the first ten values, the proportion of trials in which the artificial data have eigenvalues larger than the actual data is very small, and there is then a very clear crossover point. It is important to remember, however, that the range of the singular spectrum of the US data is small, so that the larger values do not dominate the rest. The degree of structure is therefore not large.

Overall, taking into account the evidence from the eigenvalues, the eigenvectors and the results of the bootstrapping exercise, the clear interpretation of this analysis is that quarterly changes in real GDP in the UK possess no underlying structure. To all intents and purposes, it is indistinguishable from a random series. This offers strong support for the Fisher–Slutsky hypothesis that the business cycle is inherently unpredictable. Although the US data does show some small sign of structure or regularity, it is small and is by no means so clear as to contradict the hypothesis.

3.4 CONCLUSION

The programme of research in macroeconomic modelling and forecasting now spans a period of some fifty years. Particularly during the most recent decades, a great deal of work has been carried out. The content of the models follows closely the fashions of economic theory. Perhaps more importantly, the methodology of time series econometrics which is used to build empirical equations for forecasting has become very much more sophisticated.

But despite these apparent advances, the forecasting record of the models remains poor. Indeed, from a scientific standpoint it is hard to avoid the phrase 'very poor'. For forecasts of macroeconomic variables such as the growth in national output (GNP or GDP) and inflation, the track record of conventional forecasts is really no better than the simple rule that next year's value will be the same as this year's.

The use of statistical techniques for non-linear modelling is relatively new in macroeconomics. A small number of studies suggest that such techniques can improve upon linear models in terms of the power of the in-sample fit. But even in terms of just one-quarter-ahead forecasts for GDP growth, say, the variance of the forecast errors of such models is still around 90% of the variance of the actual data.

In this chapter we apply the technique of singular spectrum analysis to post-war quarterly series of GNP/GDP growth in the USA and the UK. The technique has been developed over the past decade or so, and is well established in the literature on the analysis of dynamic systems. It is designed to characterize the general properties of a time series such as the degree to which the series has some discernible structure or the extent of the noise present in the data. In other words, singular spectrum analysis can be used to identify consistent or regular features of data, for example periodicity or more general systematic behaviour, and also provides information about the nature of the random or noisy component of a series.

The results suggest very clearly that the inability to make satisfactory forecasts of GDP growth, in the sense that the variance of the forecast errors over time is less than the variance of the data, arises from fundamental characteristics of the data. This is particularly the case for the UK, where singular spectrum analysis suggests that the series is effectively indistinguishable from a purely random series. The data for the USA appear to possess a certain amount of structure, but the series is heavily dominated by noise.

The idea that movements in GDP over the course of the business cycle are inherently unpredictable is not new in economics, and some of the early quantitative thinking about the cycle, by for example Fisher (1925) and Slutsky (1937) in the 1920s and 1930s, advanced this as a hypothesis. The use of singular spectrum analysis confirms the validity of the hypothesis.

If this evidence existed purely in isolation we would suggest that the chapter offered strong but not conclusive support for the hypothesis that meaningful short-term forecasts of real output growth could not be carried out. However, it does not by any means exist in isolation. The actual *ex ante* forecasting record of the past thirty or more years supports it. The conclusion we draw is that the forecasting record is poor, not necessarily because of bad economic theory or bad statistical technique on the part of the forecasters, but because of a deep lack of structure in the data. In the current state of scientific knowledge, short-term economic forecasting is a fairly hopeless task.

A great deal of economic policy in the West since the Second World War has been and still is conducted on the basis of short-term forecasts of the economy. Governments try to anticipate the movements of the economy over the course of the business cycle and to take action to correct any adverse consequences which would arise if such predictions were correct. Again, criticisms of such a strategy are by no means new, with Milton Friedman, for example, in the 1950s arguing that government intervention was as likely to increase the overall variance of GDP growth over the course of the cycle as it was to reduce it. Keynes was in many ways a rather delphic economist, and it is certainly possible to interpret his *General Theory*, written in the 1930s, in the same way. Singular spectrum analysis confirms this view.

It must be emphasised, however, that the results of this chapter cannot be interpreted to mean that governments should never intervene in the economy. Keynes, after all, was writing at a time, not when it was predicted that there would be a major depression, but when the economies of the West were actually in one and he was addressing the question of what governments could do about it. The results of this chapter are not concerned with this latter point. Rather they show that the attempts of governments to anticipate and correct short-term fluctuations over the course of the business cycle are in general fruitless, given the inherent properties of the data series involved.

COMMENTS

F.C. PALM, C.H. HOMMES,
A.H.Q.M. MERKIES AND P.C. YOUNG

F.C. PALM

It is a pleasure to discuss the stimulating chapter by Ormerod and Campbell (hereafter denoted as OC), in which the authors investigate the predictability of time series using singular spectrum analysis (SSA) to determine fundamental properties of a time series. The main objective of the chapter is to present the SSA technique and to illustrate its ability to identify low-dimensional structure in economic series. The technique is applied to quarterly data of post-war growth in real national output in the USA and in the UK. The authors conclude that there may be some structure in US data but that the UK data possess no underlying structure and are indistinguishable from a random series. My comments on the chapter are mainly concerned with the conditions under which SSA can be applied and the relationship with alternative techniques for detecting structure in economic and other time series, and with a comparison of the empirical findings with results in the literature using different techniques for similar time series. Finally, some conclusions are made.

To see under which conditions SSA can be applied, it is worth briefly describing the technique as used in practice. For a given time series X_t of length N, obtain the sample autocovariance matrix up to lag $(m - 1)$ where m is called the embedding dimension. Next, obtain the eigenvalues of the sample auto-covariance matrix (divided by m) and arrange them in decreasing order. These eigenvalues are called the singular spectrum (SS) of the series X_t. Plotting the eigenvalues arranged in decreasing order against their index yields the graph of the SS. If this graph shows a truncation point beyond which the eigenvalues are (close to) zero, the system has a dimension equal to the value of the truncation point. The technique basically relies on the principal components associated with the sample autocovariance matrix up to order $(m - 1)$. If, for instance, there were two eigenvalues which were large compared to the rest, this would indicate that a two-dimensional model might well give a good account of the time series X_t.

In order to implement SSA, several conditions have to be fulfilled. First, the sample autocovariance matrix has to contain information on the basic structure of the series. If the series is second-order stationary and N is fairly large, the sample autocovariance matrix will be an accurate estimate of the second moments of X_t and SSA is expected to lead to reliable results on the structure of the underlying process for X_t. In fact, then the autocovariance matrix could be used to obtain the Wold representation of the series X_t, even if the process generating X_t is non-linear. If, however, X_t is non-stationary the sample auto-covariance matrix might be, at best, a local approximation of the underlying structure. At worst, the value of the sample autocovariances could be so sensitive to the specific sample period observed that little is revealed about the structure of the underlying process of X_t.

As a corollary of my comment, I would emphasize the need for checking the stationarity of the series under investigation and for transforming non-stationary series into stationary ones, e.g. by differencing the observations before applying SSA. There is by now a huge literature on how to detect and deal with unit roots and other forms of non-stationarity.

Second, one should realize that the underlying process for X_t might be highly structured whereas its Wold or MA representation is rather densely parameterized.

To illustrate this, consider an unobserved component model (see e.g. Harvey (1989)) of the form $X_t = T_t + S_t + \epsilon_t$, where the trend component is $T_t = T_{t-1} + \beta_{t-1} + u_t$ with $\beta_t = \beta_{t-1} + \eta_t$ and the seasonal component is $S_t = -\sum_{i=1}^{s-1} S_{t-i} + a_t$ and ϵ_t, u_t, η_t and a_t are independently distributed white noises with zero expectation and variances σ_ϵ^2, σ_u^2, σ_η^2 and σ_a^2, respectively. The model describes the time-series properties of many economic series quite well. First differencing and first seasonal differencing lead to a series which is stationary and can be represented as a moving average process of order $s + 1$.

The model is parsimoniously parameterized with four parameters only. The $(s + 1)$th order MA process leads when inverted to an infinite autoregression. SSA would probably not detect the non-linear restrictions on the autoregressive parameters implied by the restricted MA($s + 1$) process (if $s \geq 4$).

This point holds true more generally. Some highly structured non-linear processes have a densely parameterized autoregressive representation. In such a case the non-linear structure might not be detected by SSA. Testing and modelling the non-linear structure, e.g. along lines proposed in Granger and Teräsvirta (1993) among others, is required in this case.

Third, it is important to realize that structure will sometimes be detected only when the sampling frequency is increased. For instance, as a result of a low sampling frequency, a generalized autoregressive conditional hetero-scedastic (GARCH) structure in the conditional expectation of a GARCH-in-mean process might not be detected from the data (see e.g. Drost and Nijman

(1993)) when the data are sampled at a lower frequency than that at which they are generated.

Fourth, the embedding dimension m has to be determined. While I am sympathetic to the proposal by the authors of using prior information on the series, I believe that formal model-selection criteria (which penalize for dense parameterizations) such as Akaike's information criterion or Schwarz's Bayesian criterion could be used to determine the value of m. Formal selection criteria are preferred to using an informal judgemental analysis of the autocorrelation function of X_t.

Fifth, it would also be useful to have a formal method for selecting the truncation point in the SS. For instance, under stationarity and ergodicity large sample distribution for eigenvalues and eigenvectors of an estimated covariance matrix could be used to obtain formal testing procedures (see e.g. Anderson (1963); Girshick (1939)).

As far as the forecasting performance of the models advocated and used by OC is concerned, it would be worth comparing it with that of alternative approaches to forecasting macroeconomic time series.

The finding by Ormerod and Campbell that there is not much structure in quarterly observations for real output growth rates in the USA and the UK is not surprising. Aggregation across products and services, economic agents and time leads to flattening of the spectral density of a time series. For instance, for real GNP or GDP annual growth rates in, respectively, 9 and 18 OECD countries, Garcia-Ferrer *et al.* (1987) and Zellner and Hong (1989), among others, find that pure autoregressive models (of order 3) did not produce substantially improved forecasts when compared to naive no-change forecasts or random-walk based forecasts. Autoregressive-leading indicator models, however, outperformed several naive and purely autoregressive models.

For instance, this occurred when real stock returns and changes in the real money supply lagged one or two periods were added as leading indicators to a pure autoregression of order three. These indicator variables are close to being white noise and therefore could be part of the noise term in the pure autoregression that also appeared to be serially uncorrelated. By including leading indicators which are white noise, in fact, a measurable (white noise) component was extracted from the disturbance of the autoregressive model. In this way, Garcia *et al.* (1987) and Zellner and Hong (1989) effectively attempted to forecast white noise along lines suggested by Granger (1983) and achieved an improvement in forecast performance that could not have been realized if only a univariate SSA had been applied to the output growth rates.

In conclusion, the technique of SSA can be helpful in detecting underlying structures in economic data. As pointed out in my comments, it applies to series which exhibit enough regularity and structural stability to determine the matrix of autocovariances.

In my view, whenever SSA is used it should be complemented with the use of formal model-selection criteria to determine the embedding dimension of the model and formal test procedures to determine the truncation point in the SS. Whenever one suspects the presence of some non-linearity, it is appropriate to adopt testing procedures for non-linearity and/or model explicitly the non-linearities.

I join the authors in their belief that many aggregate economic time series do not exhibit much structure beyond the non-stationarity as long as univariate time series models are used. When leading indicators are introduced or when data are analysed in a multivariate set-up using, for example, pooling and shrinkage techniques, the precision of forecasts can be substantially improved as has been shown by Garcia-Ferrer *et al.* (1987) and Zellner and Hong (1989), among others.

C.H. HOMMES

The chapter addresses an old theme in economics: is there any forecastable structure in business cycle data such as GNP growth rates or inflation series? Irving Fisher (1925) suggested that '... the business cycle is inherently unpredictable, because, in modern terminology, the dimension of the problem is too high relative to the available number of observations'. In the 1930s Slutsky argued that fluctuations in economic data are generated by a series of exogenous random shocks, and are thus inherently unpredictable. Despite much research effort and the development of sophisticated econometric techniques and economic theory the authors argue that the unpredictability remains: '... not only is the forecasting record poor, but it shows no signs of improving over time despite the considerable resources devoted to research by conventional economic modellers'.

The aim of the chapter is to examine the validity of the 'classical' hypothesis that the business cycle is indeed inherently unpredictable. This is done by applying singular spectrum analysis (SSA) to analyse post-war quarterly data of first differences of logs of US and UK seasonally adjusted GNP. The authors arrive at the strong conclusion that 'The results suggest very clearly that the inability to make satisfactory forecasts of GDP growth, in the sense that the variance of the forecast errors over time is less than the variance of the data, arises from fundamental characteristics of the data. This is particularly the case for the UK, where SSA suggests that the series is effectively indistinguishable from a purely random series.'

It seems to me that this conclusion is too strong, given the evidence presented in the chapter. In particular, I would like to discuss the results in the light of the contrasting (endogenous) viewpoint that (a significant part of) business cycle fluctuations are caused by non-linear economic laws (see also Chapter 1 in this volume by Brock and Hommes). A low-dimensional non-linear deterministic model with a strange attractor, subject to small noise, is in some sense an alternative explanation of business fluctuations, somewhere between Fisher's and Slutsky's approach. It has only few (say, less than 10) degrees of freedom and therefore does not suffer from Fisher's problem of too many dimensions. It also has a certain degree of unpredictability, since chaotic series can be very erratic, even 'random looking' and are very sensitive to noise.

The question then arises whether, if the opposing endogenous viewpoint were correct, SSA would be able to distiguish this alternative. The authors suggest that SSA indeed would be able to detect chaos, but I find the evidence presented not convincing, since SSA may be very sensitive to (dynamic) noise. In fact, the problem is similar to earlier work on testing for chaos in economic and financial series. For example, in their pioneer work Brock and Sayers (1988) tested several macroeconomic time series for low-dimensional chaos. They found little evidence for chaos but they did find some for non-linearity in some of the series. However, they also emphasized that '. . . evidence for chaos is weak, but the tests may be too weak to detect it' (Brock and Sayers (1988, p. 71)). The problem is that the methods employed are very sensitive to noise.

The authors seem to be aware of these problems and they do apply SSA to a 'mildly chaotic series', but this chaotic series is in fact almost periodic (see Figure 3.1 in the chapter). Already by 'eye inspection' it is clear that there has to be structure in this series. In addition, SSA is applied to a noisy chaotic series obtained after adding a normal random variable to the mildly chaotic series, with a signal-to-noise ratio of 1/3. Indeed, SSA does find structure in this noisy chaotic series. The authors then claim that '. . . even in the presence of consider-able noise, SSA can identify underlying structure'. However, the noisy chaotic series clearly has some underlying, (quasi-periodic) structure; readers may judge for themselves by looking at Figure 3.1 in the chapter. In particular, it seems that the noisy chaotic series must have some strongly significant autocorrelations (see e.g. Hommes (1996) on sample autocorrelations of chaotic series in the non-linear cobweb model). The noisy chaotic series is thus very different from the GNP data, which have (close to) zero autocorrelations at all lags. The bottom line is that SSA may work for mildly chaotic time series with *additive* noise, but it is unclear how SSA performs on chaotic series with close to zero autocorrela-tions, subject to *dynamic* noise.[1] It is interesting to note that Medio (1992, p. 282), applying SSA to financial data, suggests finding 'rather strong evidence for chaoticity in the DM/$ daily exchange rate'.

As the authors correctly point out, there is no statistical theory concerning the significance of the singular spectrum. The bootstrapping exercise in the chapter, as applied to the macro series, is therefore interesting. SSA is used for 500 different runs of scrambled data sets of the same length. Each scrambled series is obtained by randomly drawing from the original series with replacement. This suggests that, if there is any structure at all, it is difficult to detect. In future work it would be interesting to apply similar bootstrapping techniques to time series generated by several other null models, such as low-order AR(k), ARCH or GARCH models when fitted to economic or financial data, or to chaotic models with and without different levels of (dynamic) noise, etc., (see e.g. Brock, Hshieh and LeBaron (1991) for a similar approach to bootstrapping for chaos tests based upon the correlation dimension).

SSA may be a useful tool in analysing business cycle data, but it seems that much more work on SSA would be needed to make such a strong case as suggested in the chapter. The debate concerning exogenous random shocks versus endogenous non-linear economic 'laws' as an explanation of business cycles has not been settled. The truth is probably somewhere in between the two alternatives and this makes the debate so hard to settle.

Endnote

1. The authors use *additive* noise in their analysis, where an i.i.d. random variable ϵ_t is added to each observation x_t. In the simplest case of *dynamic* noise added to a dynamical system, one has $x_{t+1} = F(x_t) + \epsilon_t$, so that the noise affects the dynamics. Small additive noise will not change the structure of the series very much, even if the series is chaotic. However, in a chaotic system small dynamic noise typically changes the time series dramatically, because of the sensitive dependence upon initial conditions.

A.H.Q.M. MERKIES

Summary

Ormerod and Campbell (OC) deal with the classical question whether empirical economic time series display enough regularity to detect business cycles. If they do, better economic forecasts are possible in principle. OC approach the question with a technique called singular spectrum analysis (SSA), discussed earlier, among others, by Broomhead and King (1986), Vautard and Ghil (1989) and by Mullin (1993). The SSA method is applied to a constructed series and to quarterly GDP data of the USA and the UK. OC do not find any regularity in both empirical series, which in their view confirms the opinion held by Fisher and Slutsky in the 1920s and 1930s that business cycles are unpredictable.

From the presentation by OC one gets a fairly clear view of their technique. For m odd the SSA method can alternatively be described as follows. OC construct from the time series $X(t)$ of length N a matrix Ξ, the tth row of which is $X(t-(m-1)/2)$, ..., $X(t-1)$, $X(t)$, $x(t+1)$, $X(t+(m-1)/2)$. Hence each of the m columns of Ξ contains the time series $X(t)$ shifted one position as compared to adjacent columns. As an example, take $m = 3$ and $N = 5$:

$$
\Xi = \begin{bmatrix}
 & & X(1) \\
 & X(1) & X(2) \\
X(1) & X(2) & X(3) \\
X(2) & X(3) & X(4) \\
X(3) & X(4) & X(5) \\
X(4) & X(5) & \\
X(5) & &
\end{bmatrix}
$$

Because the authors assume that $X(t)$ has zero sample mean $\Xi'\Xi$ equals the matrix of auto(co)variances of $X(t)$, except for the different constants N or $N-1$ in the denominators. For m even a similar matrix Ξ can be thought to underly the matrix of auto(co)variances. The SSA method of OC is nothing else than a principal component analysis of the m 'histories' contained in the matrix Ξ in the sense of the principal component study of Stone (1947), whose 'histories' consisted of m *different* macroeconomic time series instead of lagged series of one variable. Just as in Stone's analysis, which has been repeated a number of times, the crucial point is that only a very limited number of principal components may be needed to describe the m 'histories'. If only two components are sufficient to describe $X(t)$ its pattern is not basically different from a Brownian motion. Then there is not enough regularity in the series to hope for a forecasting method that beats the random walk.

Evaluation

As SSA is a principal component analysis, all the advantages and disadvantages of principal component analysis hold. One of the disadvantages is that principal components are not invariant to changes in units of measurement. This implies that the results will be different if one starts the analysis with autocorrelations instead of autocovariances. In general, the results are sensitive to transformations of the data.

OC assume zero sample mean of their time series, ignoring forecasting performance from deterministic parts in the series.

The conclusion that 'movements in GDP over the business cycle are inherently unpredictable' does not follow from the analysis of the chapter. Proving the non-existence of something requires far more than an analysis of this kind. The authors may only conclude that they have not found any regularity in the series with the particular form in which they used SSA. Other variations of SSA, such as starting from autocorrelations or a SSA after first taking logs of the data, might have shown different results. Then it may be that other methods are superior to SSA in detecting the existence of regularities. It is also quite credible that business cycles have to be defined differently than assumed in the chapter, e.g. in real GNP instead of nominal GNP or the co-movement of many economic variables (see e.g. Zarnowitz (1992)). The latter is e.g. the general stand taken by Blanchard and Fisher (1989).

There is a massive literature on the existence of business cycles since Tinbergen's seminal study in 1936 and Haberler's *Prosperity and Depression* (1937). OC make no reference to these authors. A proper survey is, for example, Belongia and Garfinkel (1992) or, with special attention to the role of money, Van Els (1995). The authors do not refer to Tinbergen (1936) or (1939), referring instead to Klein (1947) as 'path-breaking'.

To support the suggestion of the chapter that the forecasting performance of prevailing models with respect to business cycles is poor, OC refer to Wallis (1989). In view of the widespread use that is made of macroeconomic models this reference is not sufficient to convince the reader that macroeconomic forecasting is a dismal art. First, in generating economic forecasts insight is gained in ongoing economic developments, enabling policy makers to evaluate alternative policies conceived. This additional insight is not valued in *ex-post* analyses of forecasting errors. Second, evaluating forecasting performance is not a simple matter. Even if the analysis is restricted to business cycles predictions, there are different aspects to consider such as definitions (see above), time horizon, exogenous information available, expert knowledge used to adapt outcomes of models, etc. The present view on forecasting is at variance. 'Econometric forecasting is alive and well' remark Diebold and Watson (1996) in their introduction to the special issue on econometric forecasting of the *Journal of Applied Econometrics*. And although 'It is easy to find criticisms of economic forecasts' and 'a great deal of this criticism is probably deserved' a 'substantial rethinking of standard practices is worth attempting' according to Granger (1996). See also Hamilton and Lin (1996) in the same issue of *JAE* and the optimistic view expressed by Blanchard (1992).

It should be noted that there is a different kind of spectral analysis requiring Fourier transforms (see for a simple introduction e.g. Chatfield (1975)). Spectral analysis of this type has been applied within the realm of seasonality (see e.g. Nerlove (1964)).

P.C. YOUNG

Differencing data is often carried out without full regard to its noise amplification effects, and consequent signal/noise ratio reduction. This criticism could be applied to the GNP/GDP examples in this chapter and leads, I believe, to the overstrong statement in the last sentence of Section 3.3 of the chapter. 'Although the US data show some small sign of structure or regularity, it is small and is by no means clear as to contradict the hypothesis [that the series is not distinguishable from a random series].' There is, I believe, quite clear evidence of significant and economically meaningful structure in the US GNP data which becomes visible if the data are analysed by other means, rather than differencing.

In other words, I would claim that the noise amplification induced by differencing has obscured the underlying 'signal': namely the economic quasi-cycle. My evidence for this is shown in Figures 3.A and 3.B.

Figure 3.A is a plot of two normalized (standardized) variables: the detrended US GNP data, obtained by detrending to remove the low-frequency trend; and the private investment/GNP (PI) ratio (as introduced in our own chapter for this book (Chapter 6) and an associated paper (Young and Pedregal, 1996) which takes the analysis further). It is clear that these signals have very similar temporal character-istics ('stylized facts' to use the currently topical but rather unattractive jargon). Figure 3.B, which compares the AR(13) spectra of the two variables, shows that the spectral properties are also very similar with the following major peaks:

AR(13) spectrum Private investment ratio			AR(13) spectrum Detrended GNP		
Freq.	Period	Amp.	Freq.	Period	Amp.
0.043	23.27	43.39	0.047	21.33	67.23
0.094	10.67	9.97	0.102	9.85	12.30
0.188	5.33	1.66	0.180	5.57	2.78

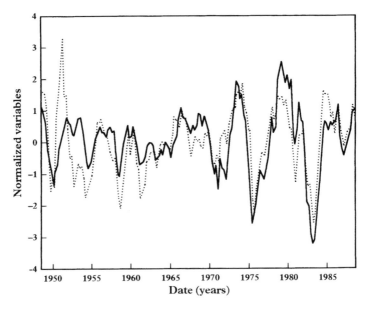

Figure 3.A Comparison of the normalized Private Investment/GNP ratio (dashed line) with the normalized detrended GNP (full line) for the USA between 1948 and 1988

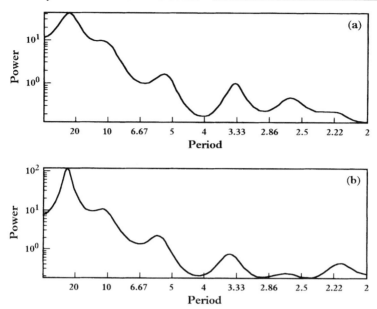

Figure 3.B Comparison of the AR(13) spectra for the normalized Private Investment/ GNP ratio (a) and the normalized detrended GNP (b)

The peaks in these spectra are typical of amplitude modulated quasi-cycle behaviour and it will be noted that peaks at around 10–11 and 5.3–5.5 quarters (as well as the lesser peaks not shown above) appear to be the harmonics of a fundamental cycle at around 21–23 quarters, which is consistent with an economic quasi-cycle of around 5 years.

Of course, detrending is often itself criticized since, if used carelessly, it can create quasi-cycle behaviour that is a consequence of the filtering process. In this case, however, the resulting detrended GNP series is being compared with the PI ratio, which is obtained *without filtering of any kind,* so the cyclical character- istics in this case cannot have been induced. Since the probability that such high correlation is occurring by chance seems very low indeed, I believe we must conclude that the quasi-cycle exposed in the above manner is a real, and important, aspect of the US economy. At the very least, it makes the authors' claim that the series is hardly distinguishable from a random series rather suspect. Since I get the impression that they see attractions in the existence of a economic quasi-cycle, perhaps they would like to 'soften' their conclusion in the light of the above discussion.

REPLIES

P. ORMEROD AND M. CAMPBELL

The various discussants have offered a range of interesting comments. Before responding directly, a general point from our chapter is worth re-emphasizing. During the past thirty years or so, many short-term forecasts for GDP/GNP growth in the developed economies have been published, by both public and private sector bodies and a large literature exists on their evaluation. The accuracy of even one-year-ahead forecasts of growth is, by any normal scientific criterion, very poor. They typically show errors whose first and second moments are similar to those of the actual data itself. Forecasts over a longer time horizon than one year are even worse. This provides support for the strength of the conclusion which we draw.

Not surprisingly in a book of this kind, many of the contributors expressed the view, both at the conference itself and in written comments, that non-linear models offer a way forward in terms of improving short-term forecasting accuracy. There are a number of points to make on this.

It is hard to prove a negative conclusion, but the experience of building explicit non-linear models has so far offered little improvement on the actual forecasting record. A number of recent papers, examples of which we cite in our chapter, offer strong evidence that, while such models are superior to a simple linear model, nevertheless they have very little predictive power on normal scientific criteria.

In any event, the only real test of any approach, no matter how carefully it is evaluated in advance, is in its genuinely *ex ante* forecasting record. Many claims are made in the applied economics literature for the ability of models to predict hold-out samples of past data. But the record of truly *ex ante* forecasts made about the future speaks for itself. To re-emphasize a point made above, the errors of such predictions have first and second moments which are similar to those of the actual data itself, a fact which the various apologists for the forecasting profession cannot explain away.

The discussants raise the question as to the ability of SSA to identify structure in highly non-linear data series. Given the relatively small number of observations available for most macroeconomic data series (no more than 200), one has to be cautious about the power of the tests for non-linearity and chaos which have been applied. But the pioneering article by Brock and Sayers (1988) found evidence of a certain amount of non-linearity but not chaos in macro-economic data. This conclusion is still believed to be valid by researchers in this area. Financial market data are a quite separate issue. Our concern is with monthly or, more usually, quarterly data on economic output. The distinction between both the quality and quantity of financial data and that of other economic data such as output, inflation and unemployment is one which is often not appreciated by non-economists. The non-linear models which have been built on economic data such as output are better than, but not overwhelmingly superior to, linear ones.

In short, macroeconomic data appear to be only mildly non-linear. It has been demonstrated that SSA can identify structure with noisy data of this kind (see, for example, Broomhead and King (1986)). In the light of this, the theoretical ability of SSA to identify structure in highly complex, strongly non-linear data is not relevant in this particular context.

As it happens, SSA can identify structure in, say, the chaotic data of the Lorenz equations. We generated a series of 200 observations from a numerical solution of the Lorenz differential equations with an autocorrelation function similar to that of the US GNP growth data examined in our chapter. Clear evidence of structure in this data exists. We also generated a number of similar series by adding dynamic noise to the numerical solution of the equations. For small amounts of such noise, structure could still be identified, but as the amount of noise increased, this was no longer true.

However, if it really is the case that macroeconomic data are generated by a highly non-linear or chaotic system with large amounts of dynamic noise, almost by definition even short-term forecasting of any degree of accuracy cannot be carried out, and the problems of explicit modelling of such data are truly formidable regardless of the approach which is adopted.

We believe that non-linear approaches do have an important role to play in economics, but not in short-term forecasting. As Young hints at in his comment, we are sympathetic to the unjustly neglected work of Richard Goodwin (Goodwin (1965), for example), who accounts for both short-term business cycles and long-term growth by a Lotka–Volterra system of non-linear differential equations in which cycles are generated within the system by the interplay of unemployment and the share of profits in national income. Such a theoretical approach gives a valuable insight into the longer-run dynamics of capitalist economies (see, for example, Ormerod (1997)), but this is not the same thing at all as short-term forecasting accuracy.

Related to this is the long-standing theoretical question in economics as to whether business cycles in capitalist economies are due to random shocks or are endogenous to the system, arising, for example, from a non-linear deterministic structure. We are sympathetic as economists to the latter (a minority view in the profession). But our chapter is not intended to adjudicate on this debate, nor is it intended to survey the voluminous literature.

The lack of low-dimensional structure which we identify could arise, at one extreme, because the cycles are actually generated entirely by random shocks. Equally, at the other extreme, it could arise if the data were generated by a non-linear system comprising a very large number of factors. But if this latter were the case, we could never hope to identify the structure given the relatively small number of observations which are available on macroeconomic data. In either case, in the current state of scientific knowledge it would not be possible to make meaningful short-term forecasts.

The comments by Young are very interesting, but perhaps pay insufficient attention to the economics of the data he addresses. For example, fluctuations in private investment are a major cause of cycles in the overall economy, so it is not surprising to find a similarity between the share of private investment in national output and deviations of output from trend. Much of the attention of econometricians has been devoted to the share of consumption in the economy rather than investment. Young's empirical work is firmly in the theoretical tradition of Keynes, whose major book on the business cycle (1936) was devoted to investment rather than consumption, though he, too, believed that the cycle was inherently unpredictable.

The second point to note here is that Young uses US data and, in terms of continuity of post-war experience, the American economy is unusual. It is perhaps not unreasonable to detrend data over the whole of the post-war period for the USA, but this is certainly not the case for most other Western economies. Their behaviour has been marked by sharp breaks in the underlying trend of growth—most noticeably in the period before and after the oil price shocks of 1973/74—and discussions about the current underlying trend often create sharp disagreements among economists. In terms of practical forecasting, the use of detrended data creates the additional problem of forecasting the trend, which is a non-trivial problem in itself. A recognition of the discontinuous nature of much macroeconomic data is now being made even by leading econometricians such as Hendry, who had previously placed great emphasis on empirical models satisfying various tests of stability. For example, Hendry (1995) writes 'Society and social systems alter over time, laws change, and technological innovations occur, so establishing any invariants of an economic system is not easy'.

Young also draws attention to the problems that are associated with differencing of data—in this case the difference of the log of real output is taken to give the rate of growth of output. The growth rate is the variable which is of interest to policy makers, and so in one sense it is not a differenced variable at all. Leaving this point aside, we agree with Young that there is some evidence of a 5-year cycle in the US economy. However, the strength of this underlying cycle is not really sufficient to be of any use in generating successful short-term forecasts for, as we say, 'Although the US data does show some small sign of structure or regularity, it is small'.

Palm also comments on the choice of dependent variable in our analysis, namely the rate of growth of real GNP/GDP and argues that SSA should only be applied to stationary series. This is more demanding than is really necessary. Like classical spectral analysis, SSA should be seen as an exploratory tool. Any consistent trend should be removed and similarly any clear periodicity, e.g. seasonality, should be removed but otherwise mildly periodic behaviour does not invalidate the use of SSA.

As is well known, both the US and UK data series are stationary according to standard unit root tests. In the same spirit of exploratory data analysis, rather than trying to devise some way of finding a 'best' embedding dimension as Palm suggests, we use a range of embedding dimensions to ensure the robustness of any conclusion about the degree of structure.

REFERENCES

Anderson, T.W. (1963) Asymptotic theory for principal components analysis. *Annals of Mathematical Statistics* **34**, 122–48.

Belongia, M.T. and Garfinkel, M.R. (1992) *The Business Cycle: Theories and Evidence.* Kluwer Academic Publishers, Boston, MA.

Blanchard, O.J. (1992) For a return to Pragmatism in M.T. Belongia and M.R. Garfinkel (eds), *The Business Cycle: Theories and Evidence.* Kluwer Academic Publishers, Boston, MA, pp. 121–32.

Blanchard, O.J. and Fisher, S. (1989) *Lectures on Macroeconomics.* MIT Press, Cambridge, MA.

Brock, W.A., Hsieh, D. and LeBaron, B. (1991) *Nonlinear Dynamics, Chaos and Instability: Statistical Theory and Economic Evidence.* MIT Press, Cambridge, MA.

Brock, W.A. and Sayers, C.L. (1988) Are economic time series characterized by deterministic chaos? *Journal of Monetary Economics* **22**, 71–90.

Broomhead, D.S. and King, G.P. (1986) Extracting qualitative dynamics from experimental data. *Physica* **20D**, 217–36.

Chatfield, C. (1975) *The Analysis of Time Series: Theory and Practice.* Chapman and Hall, London.

Chatfield, C. (1995) Model uncertainty, data mining and statistical inference. *J. R. Statist. Soc. A* **158**.

Clements, M. P. (1995) Rationality and the role of judgement in macroeconomic forecasting. *Economic Journal* **105**, 410–20.

Diebold, F.X. and Watson, M.W. (1996) Introduction: Econometric forecasting. *Journal of Applied Econometrics* **11**, 453–4.

Drost, F.C. and Nijman, T.E. (1993) Temporal aggregation of GARCH processes. *Econometrica* **61**, 909–27.

Fisher, I. (1925) Our unstable dollar and the so-called business cycle. *Journal of the American Statistical Association*, June.

Garcia-Ferrer, A., Highfield, R.A., Palm, F. and Zellner, A. (1987) Macroeconomic forecasting using pooled international data. *Journal of Business and Economic Statistics* **5**, 53–67.

Gershenfeld, N.A. and Weigend, A.S. (1993) The future of time series: learning and understanding. in N.A. Gershenfeld and A.S. Weigend (eds), *Time Series Prediction: Forecasting the Future and Understanding the Past.* Addison-Wesley, Reading, MA.

Girshick, M.A. (1939) On the sampling theory of roots of determinantal equations. *Annals of Mathematical Statistics* **10**, 203–24.

Goodwin, R.M. (1965) A growth cycle. In C.H. Feinstein (ed.), *Socialism, Capitalism and Economic Growth.* Cambridge University Press, Cambridge.

Granger, C.W.J. (1983) Forecasting white noise. In A. Zellner (ed.), *Applied Time Series Analysis of Economic Data.* Bureau of the Census, US Department of Commerce, Washington, DC, pp. 308–14.

Granger, C.W.J. (1996) Can we improve the perceived quality of economic forecasts? *Journal of Applied Econometrics* **11**, 455–74.

Granger, C.W.J. and Teräsvirta, T. (1993) *Modelling Nonlinear Economic Relationships.* Oxford University Press, Oxford.

Haberler, G. (1937) *Prosperity and Depression.* George Allen & Unwin, London.

Hamilton, J.D. and Lin, G. (1996) Stock market volatility and the business cycle. *Journal of Applied Econometrics* **11**, 573–94.

Harvey, A.C. (1989) *Forecasting, Structural Time Series Models and the Kalman Filter.* Cambridge University Press, Cambridge.

Hendry, D.F. (1995) Econometrics and business cycle empirics. *Economic Journal* **105**, 1622–36.

Hommes, C.H. (1996), On the consistency of backward looking expectations. The case of the cobweb. Forthcoming in *Journal of Economic Behaviour and Organization*.

Keynes, J.M. (1936) *The General Theory of Interest, Employment and Money.* Macmillan, London.

Klein, L.R. (1947) The use of econometric models as a guide to the policy process. *Econometrica* **15**, 111–52.

McNees, S.K. (1988) How accurate are macroeconomic forecasts? *New England Economic Review* July/August, 15–36.

Medio, A. (1992) *Chaotic Dynamics: Theory and Applications to Economics.* Cambridge University Press, Cambridge.

Mullin, T. (1993) A dynamical systems approach to time series analysis. In T. Mullin (ed.), *The Nature of Chaos.* Oxford Scientific Publications, Oxford.

Nerlove, M. (1964) Spectral analysis of seasonal adjustment procedures. *Econometrica* **32**, 241–86.

OECD (1993), *Economic Outlook*, June, Paris.

Ormerod, P. (ed.) (1979) *Economic Modelling*, Heinemann, London.

Ormerod, P. (1997) Unemployment: a distributional phenomenon. In M. Rhodes (ed.) *A New Social Contract.* Macmillan, London (forthcoming).

Potter, S.M. (1995) A nonlinear approach to US GNP. *Journal of Applied Econometrics* **10**, 109–26.

Priestley, M.B. (1981) *Spectral Analysis and Time Series.* Academic Press, London.

Slutsky, E. (1937) The summation of random causes as the source of cyclical processes. *Econometrica* **5**, 105–46.

Stone, R. (1947) On the interdependence of blocks of transactions. Supplement to the *Journal of the Royal Statistical Society* **IX**, 1–32.

Tiao, G.C. and Tsay, R.S. (1994) Some advances in non-linear and adaptive modelling in time-series analysis. *Journal of Forecasting* **13**, 109–32.

Tinbergen, J. (1936) Kan hier te lande, al dan niet na overheidsingrijpen, een verbetering van de binnenlandse conjunctuur intreden, ook zonder verbetering van onze exportpositie? In *Praeadviezen voor de Vereniging voor de Staathuishoudkunde en de Statistiek*, Martinus Nijhoff, The Hague, pp. 62–108.

Tinbergen, J. (1939), *Statistical Testing of Business-Cycle Theories: Business Cycles in the United States of America, 1919–1932.* League of Nations, Geneva.

Van Els, P.J.A. (1995) Real business cycle models and money: a survey of theories and stylized facts. *Weltwirtschaftliches Archiv, Review of World Economics*, Band 131, 1995-Heft 2.

Vautard, R. and Ghil, M. (1989) Singular spectrum analysis in nonlinear dynamics, with applications to paleoclimatic time series. *Physica* **35D**, 395–424.

Wallis, K.F. (1989) Macroeconomic forecasting: a survey. *Economic Journal* **99**, 28–61.

Young, P.C. and Pedregal, D.J. (1996) Macro-economic relativity: government spending, private investment and unemployment in the USA 1948:1988. Tech. Rep. No. 137. Centre for Research on Environmental Systems and Statistics (submitted for publication).

Zarnowitz, V. (1992) What is a business cycle? In M.T. Belongia and M.R. Garfinkel (eds), *The Business Cycle: Theories and Evidence.* Kluwer Academic Publishers, Boston, MA, pp. 3–72.

Zellner, A. and Hong, C. (1989) Forecasting international growth rates using Bayesian shrinkage and other procedures. *Journal of Econometrics* **40**, 183–202.

SECTION 2
Non-linearities in
Empirical Modelling

$$4$$

Smooth Transition Models

T. TERÄSVIRTA

4.1 INTRODUCTION

During the last twenty years interest in non-linear time series models has increased in many fields of science, including economics. Once linearity is abandoned, there is an immense amount of parameterizations available for those who want to fit parametric non-linear models to data. Furthermore, non-parametric models form an important area of non-linear time series analysis; see, for example, Tjøstheim (1994) and Teräsvirta, Tjøstheim and Granger (1994) for recent surveys. In this chapter I shall consider a rather small but important subset of parametric non-linear models called *smooth transition models* and discuss some recent developments. Although the idea of smooth transition has been well known for a long while, these models have only recently found application in the analysis of economic time series.

The term 'smooth transition' in its present meaning first appeared in a paper by Bacon and Watts (1971). They presented their smooth transition model as a generalization to models of two intersecting straight lines with an abrupt change from one linear regression to another at some unknown change point. They also applied the model to two sets of physical data. A year later, Goldfeld and Quandt (1972, pp. 263–4) generalized the so-called two-regime switching regression model using the same idea. The switching regression model is a piecewise regression model with a finite number of regimes in which the value of a switching variable determines the regime that generates the corresponding value of the dependent variable. Goldfeld and Quandt proposed their generalization just to facilitate the estimation of switching regression models. Maddala (1977, p. 396) suggested it as an actual model for economic time series, although he did

System Dynamics in Economic and Financial Models. Edited by C. Heij, J.M. Schumacher, B. Hanzon and C. Praagman © 1997 John Wiley & Sons Ltd

not present any application. In time series analysis, similar developments took place somewhat later. In that literature, a univariate switching autoregression model is called the threshold autoregressive model. For a survey of these models with applications, see Tong (1990). Chan and Tong (1986) proposed a generalization of threshold autoregressive models analogous to the one that Goldfeld and Quandt suggested for switching regression models; see also Luukkonen, Saikkonen and Teräsvirta (1988). These smooth transition autoregressive models differ from many econometric switching regression models in that the transition (switching) variable is a lag of the dependent variable. This property makes the dynamics of the model quite complex but, at the same time, interesting and, for example, capable of characterizing various forms of asymmetric behaviour.

Goldfeld and Quandt (1972, pp. 263–4) and Chan and Tong (1986) both proposed that the smooth transition between regimes be modelled by using the cumulative distribution function of a standard normal variable as the transition function. Bacon and Watts (1971) applied the hyperbolic tangent function. Luukkonen, Saikkonen and Teräsvirta (1988) proposed the logistic function which is a close approximation to the cumulative normal distribution function and has become a popular choice in this field. The logistic function is also used in artificial neural network models which may be interpreted as overparameterized smooth transition models of a special kind. Teräsvirta (1997) mentioned a few, mostly multivariate, applications of smooth transition models to economic data. For univariate applications see, for example, Granger and Teräsvirta (1993, Chapter 9), Teräsvirta (1994, 1995), Mills (1995), Öcal (1995), Skalin and Teräsvirta (1996) and Van Dijk, Franses and Lucas (1996).

The plan of this chapter is as follows. The smooth transition regression model with some extensions and variants of it is presented in Section 4.2. Section 4.3 considers testing linearity against the smooth transition model. Section 4.4 discusses inference in smooth transition regression models. Section 4.5 mentions applications of the smooth transition framework to some common testing problems in econometrics. Testing Granger non-causality is used as an example; econometricians normally test this hypothesis in the linear framework. An empirical example of testing non-causality is presented in Section 4.6. Section 4.7 presents conclusions.

4.2 SMOOTH TRANSITION REGRESSION MODEL

Consider the following non-linear regression model:

$$y_t = x_t'\varphi + (x_t'\theta)G(\gamma, c; s_t) + u_t \qquad (t = 1, \ldots, T) \qquad (1)$$

where $x_t = (1, x_{1t}, \ldots, x_{pt})' = (1, \tilde{x}_t')' = (1, y_{t-1}, \ldots, y_{t-k}; z_{1t}, \ldots, z_{mt})'$ with $p = k + m$ is the vector of explanatory variables, $\varphi = (\varphi_0, \varphi_1, \ldots, \varphi_p)'$, and $\theta = (\theta_0, \theta_1, \ldots, \theta_p)'$ are parameter vectors and $\{u_t\}$ is a sequence of independent, identically distributed random errors. Some of the parameters φ_i and θ_j may be zero *a priori* or an equivalent restriction $\varphi_i = -\theta_i$ may hold for some i. In equation (1), G is a bounded continuous transition function, it is customary to bound G between zero and unity, and s_t is the transition variable. It may be a single stochastic variable, for example, an element of $\tilde{x}_t$, a linear combination of stochastic variables or a deterministic variable such as a linear time trend. Model (1) with a bounded continuous transition function G is called the smooth transition regression (STR) model. If x_t does not contain any z_{it} and, furthermore, $s_t = y_{t-d}$, model (1) is a smooth transition autoregressive (STAR) model; see, for example, Granger and Teräsvirta (1993) and Teräsvirta (1994). It is seen from equation (1) that the univariate STAR model is a member of the class of state-dependent models; for this rather general class of non-linear models see Priestley (1988, Section 5.1). It contains many well-known non-linear time series models. By writing model (1) as

$$y_t = x_t'(\varphi + \theta G) + u_t \tag{2}$$

it is seen that the combined parameter vector $\varphi + \theta G$ is a function of the transition variable s_t. Furthermore, the model is locally linear in x_t in the sense that if s_t is fixed the model is linear in remaining variables. A small change in s_t may not change the dynamic properties of the model much, although this may not be true for all values of s_t. If G is bounded between zero and one, the value of the combined parameter $\varphi_j + \theta_j G$ may fluctuate between φ_j and $\varphi_j + \theta_j$. This feature often makes model (1) easy to interpret. Furthermore, the dynamics of the model make it possible, for example, to characterize an economy with its dynamic properties in expansion being different from those in contraction. Teräsvirta and Anderson (1992), see also Granger and Teräsvirta (1993, Chapter 9), contains examples of STAR models of this kind. Two transition functions are highlighted here because despite their simplicity they give the STAR models rather different dynamic properties. For instance, function (3) is useful if the economy behaves differently in expansion from how it does in contraction. The LSTR2 alternative (4) is suitable for cases in which the process has similar dynamics at both ends of the range of observed values and different behaviour at least somewhere in the middle.

The practical applicability of model (1) depends on how G is defined. A few definitions have been suggested in the literature; see, for example, Granger and Teräsvirta (1993, Chapter 7). If G has the form

$$G_1(\gamma, c; s_t) = (1 + \exp\{-\gamma(s_t - c)\})^{-1} \qquad \gamma > 0 \tag{3}$$

then the STR model (1) is called the logistic STR or LSTR1 model. The transition function (3) is a monotonically increasing function of s_t. The restriction $\gamma > 0$ is an identifying restriction imposed to select one of two observationally equivalent parameterizations; the other one has $\gamma < 0$. The slope parameter

γ indicates how rapid the transition from zero to unity (unity to zero should one choose $\gamma < 0$) is as a function of s_t and the location parameter c determines where the transition occurs. If $\gamma \to \infty$ in function (3), (1) becomes a two-regime switching regression model with the switching variable s_t. In this special case, $s_t = c$ is the switch-point between the regimes $y_t = x_t'\varphi + u_t$ and $y_t = x_t'(\varphi + \theta) + u_t$. If $x_t = (1, y_{t-1}, \ldots, y_{t-k})'$ in model (1) and $s_t = y_{t-d}$, the limiting model is a two-regime threshold autoregressive model; see Tong (1990).

Monotonic transition may not always be a satisfactory alternative in applications. A simple non-monotonic alternative is

$$G_2(\gamma, c_1, c_2; s_t) = (1 + \exp\{-\gamma(s_t - c_1)(s_t - c_2)\})^{-1} \qquad \gamma > 0, \; c_1 \leqslant c_2 \quad (4)$$

where the restrictions on γ, c_1, and c_2 are identifying restrictions. For each $\gamma \neq 0$, there is an observationally equivalent parameterization with $\gamma < 0$, and the restriction $\gamma > 0$ is imposed to choose between them. Transition function (4) is symmetric about $(c_1 + c_2)/2$, and $G_2(\gamma, c_1, c_2; s_t) \to 1$ for $s_t \to \pm\infty$. The minimum value of G_2 remains between 0 and $1/2$ and the latter value is attained for $c_1 = c_2$. On the other hand, when $\gamma \to \infty$, $G_2(\gamma, c_1, c_2; s_t) \to 0$, for $c_1 < s_t \leqslant c_2$, whereas for other values $G_2(\gamma, c_1, c_2; s_t) \to 1$. This is a special case of a three-regime switching regression model in which the two outside regimes are identical. The STR model (1) with transition function (4) is called the LSTR2 model.

Jansen and Teräsvirta (1996) suggested model (1) with (4) as a generalization of the exponential STR (ESTR) model previously discussed in the literature; see Granger and Teräsvirta (1993, Chapter 7). The transition function of an ESTR model is defined as

$$G_3(\gamma, c; s_t) = 1 - \exp\{-\gamma(s_t - c)^2\} \qquad \gamma > 0 \quad (5)$$

which is closely related to the case $c_1 = c_2$ in (4). The corresponding univariate ESTAR model is in turn a generalization of the exponential autoregressive (EAR) model of Haggan and Ozaki (1981). The transition function of model (5) is symmetric about c and $G_3(\gamma, c; s_t) \to 1$ for $s_t \to \pm\infty$. However, when $\gamma \to \infty$, the transition function $G_3(\gamma, c; s_t) \to 1$ except that for $s_t = c$ the limit is zero. Thus for large values of γ it is difficult in practice to distinguish an ESTR model from a linear model. By introducing another parameter as in (4) one obtains an STR model with more useful limiting properties as $\gamma \to \infty$. Variants of the LSTR2 model have been used in generalizing threshold cointegration; see Anderson (1996).

Defining $s_t = t$ yields an important special case of the STR model. Then model (2) becomes

$$y_t = x_t'(\varphi + \theta G(\gamma, c; t)) + u_t \quad (6)$$

Model (6) can be interpreted as a linear model whose parameters change over time as a function of time. It contains as a special case the presence of a single structural break which has been the most popular alternative to parameter constancy in econometrics since its introduction by Chow (1960). This special case is obtained by completing model (1) by (3) with $s_t = t$ and letting $\gamma \to \infty$ in model (3). Lin and Teräsvirta (1994) defined another non-monotonic transition function (see also Jansen and Teräsvirta, 1996):

$$G(\gamma, c_1, c_2, c_3; s_t) = \left(1 + \exp\left\{-\gamma(t - c_1)(t - c_2)(t - c_3)\right\}\right)^{-1} \quad (7)$$

where $\gamma > 0$, $c_1 \leqslant c_2 \leqslant c_3$. In fact, Lin and Teräsvirta (1994) defined the exponent of function (7) directly as a third-order polynominal without requiring the roots to be real. This does not make any difference as far as testing parameter constancy is concerned; see Jansen and Teräsvirta (1996). On the other hand, if an STR model with (7) is to be estimated, restricting the roots to be real alleviates the potential problem of very high correlation between the estimator of θ, on the one hand, and that of γ and possibly c_1, c_2, and c_3, on the other. At the same time, one does not give up too much generality in the sense that model (7) still allows substantial flexibility in the transition function.

The STR model with $s_t = t$ is useful in practice because it offers an opportunity to test parameter constancy in linear models against smoothly changing parameters. For example, if seasonal parameters in econometric models are not stable they often change slowly over time. If the null hypothesis of parameter constancy is rejected it is possible to estimate the alternative model. This may often give useful information about where and how the parameter constancy breaks down and help to respecify the model to avoid instability. Examples include Jansen and Teräsvirta (1996), Lütkepohl, Teräsvirta and Wolters (1995), Wolters, Teräsvirta and Lütkepohl (1996) and Teräsvirta (1997).

The above smooth transition models do not contain a moving average component, although such an extension would be possible, at least in theory. In fact, Wecker (1981) (see also Granger and Teräsvirta (1993, Section 4.4)) defined a univariate asymmetric moving-average model in which a positive and a negative shock of the same size to the system cause a different, asymmetric response. This two-regime model can be generalized by making the transition between the regimes smooth, but this possibility is not considered any further here.

4.3 TESTING LINEARITY AGAINST SMOOTH TRANSITION REGRESSION

In practical non-linear dynamic modelling, testing linearity is important. If a linear model adequately describes the univariate process or the multivariate relationship between the economic variables the model builder is interested in, there is no need to fit a non-linear model to data. If the non-linear alternative under consideration is an STR or a STAR model then there exists another reason for testing linearity before doing any non-linear modelling. As an example, consider the LSTR1 model. It is seen from equations (1) and (3) that equation (1) is only identified when it is genuinely non-linear. If $\theta = 0$ in equation (1) then the parameters in (3) are not identified. Conversely, if $\gamma = 0$ in function (3) then θ and c may obtain any value without affecting the likelihood. A consequence of this complication is that the standard asymptotic distribution theory for the likelihood ratio or other classical test statistics for testing $\gamma = 0$ or $\theta = 0$ is not available. Davies (1977, 1987) first discussed solutions to this problem. Presumably the first econometric paper in which the problem received attention was Watson and Engle (1985). Other recent contributions include Andrews and Ploberger (1994) and Hansen (1996). In some of those papers it is assumed that the number of nuisance parameters (the ones only identified under the alternative) equals one. In STR models there are generally at least two nuisance parameters whichever way one formulates the null hypothesis. Saikkonen and Luukkonen (1988) and Luukkonen, Saikkonen and Teräsvirta (1988) proposed a way of dealing with this problem which can be applied to testing linearity against STR.

Consider again the LSTR1 model as the alternative to linearity. The identification problem may be circumvented by approximating equation (3) by a low-order Taylor expansion about the null hypothesis of linearity which is expressed as $\gamma = 0$. A third-order expansion has the form

$$T_3 = \delta_0 + \delta_1 s_t + \delta_2 s_t^2 + \delta_3 s_t^3 + R_3(\gamma, c; s_t) \tag{8}$$

where R_3 is a remainder and δ_j, $j = 0, 1, 2, 3$, are constants. When equation (8) is substituted for G in equation (1) one obtains, assuming that s_t is an element of $\tilde{x}_t$,

$$y_t = x_t'\beta_0 + (\tilde{x}_t s_t)'\beta_1 + (\tilde{x}_t s_t^2)'\beta_2 + (\tilde{x}_t s_t^3)'\beta_3 + u_t^* \tag{9}$$

where $\tilde{x}_t$ is as before, $u_t^* = u_t + (x_t'\theta)R_3(\gamma, c; s_t)$ and $\beta_j = \gamma\tilde{\beta}_j$, $j = 1, 2, 3$, $\tilde{\beta}_j$ being functions of the parameters of equation (1) such that $\tilde{\beta}_j \neq 0$ for $\gamma = 0$. Because of the factorization $\beta_j \neq \gamma\tilde{\beta}_j$, the original null hypothesis is transformed into H_0: $\beta_j = 0$, $j = 1, 2, 3$, against H_1': 'at least one $\beta_j \neq 0$' in equation (9). This hypothesis can be tested by an LM-type test in a straightforward manner. Note that $u_t^* = u_t$ when the null hypothesis is true. The standard Lagrange multiplier (LM) or score type test statistic (see, for example, Granger and Teräsvirta (1993, Chapter 6)) has an asymptotic χ^2 distribution with $3p$ degrees of freedom when H_0 (and H_0') holds. Similar theory applies when the alternative is an LSTR2 or an ESTR model but the auxiliary regression (9) in fact has power against both LSTR1 and LSTR2, as Teräsvirta (1994) pointed out.

The asymptotic theory requires in the STAR case that the univariate auto-regressive (null) model is stationary and ergodic and that all the moments appearing in the relevant quadratic form with the asymptotic χ^2 distribution under H_0' exist. This implies finite moments up to the eighth order when $s_t = y_{t-d}$. A corresponding moment condition is required in the multivariate case when testing linearity against STR.

The following practical remark is in order. When x_t has a large number of elements, the auxiliary null hypothesis H_0' will sometimes be large relative to the sample size. In that case the asymptotic χ^2 distribution is likely to be a poor approximation to the actual small-sample distribution. It has been found (see Granger and Teräsvirta (1993, Chapter 7) for discussion) that an F approximation works much better in the sense that the empirical size of the test remains close to the nominal size while power is good. The test can be carried out in stages as follows:

1. Regress y_t on x_t and compute the residual sum of squares $SSR_0 = (1/T)\sum_{t=1}^{T}\hat{u}_t^2$.
2. Regress $\hat{u}_t$ (or y_t) on x_t, $\tilde{x}_t s_t$, $\tilde{x}_t s_t^2$ and $\tilde{x}_t s_t^3$ and compute the residual sum of squares $SSR_1 = (1/T)\sum_{t=1}^{T}\hat{v}_t^2$.
3. Compute

$$F = \frac{(SSR_0 - SSR_1)/3p}{SSR_1/(T - 4p - 1)} \tag{10}$$

Under H_0': $\beta_1 = \beta_2 = \beta_3 = 0$, F has approximately an F distribution with $3p$ and $T - 4p - 1$ degrees of freedom.

The above theory works when $\{s_t\}$ is stationary. It continues to work when $s_t = t$; see Lin and Teräsvirta (1994). In that case, t is not an element of x_t. The auxiliary regression when testing parameter constancy of a linear model against STR with transition function (7) (based on a first-order Taylor approximation), is

$$y_t = x_t'\beta_0 + (x_t t)'\beta_1 + (x_t t^2)'\beta_2 + (x_t t^3)'\beta_3 + u_t^* \tag{11}$$

The F-statistic corresponding to equation (10) thus has $3(p + 1)$ and $T - 4p - 4$ degrees of freedom.

The above LM-type test is based on the assumption that the transition variable is known. This may not always be the case. For example, in applying STAR models it is often unclear *a priori* which lag is the right transition variable. The assumption of a known transition variable may be relaxed, however, and the test generalized accordingly. In fact Luukkonen, Saikkonen and Teräsvirta (1988) derived their linearity test against STAR under the assumption that the delay d in y_{t-d} was not known, and the reader is referred to that paper for more information. An example of this situation can be found in Section 4.6.

4.4 INFERENCE IN SMOOTH TRANSITION REGRESSION MODELS

After estimating the parameters of an STR model the model may be subjected to misspecification tests. A general assumption for conducting statistical inference in STR models is that the estimators of the parameters are consistent and asymptotically normal. Wooldridge (1994) recently discussed conditions for that in a much more general framework. Estimation of an STR model is carried out, among other things, under the assumption of no error autocorrelation and that of parameter constancy. These two assumptions thus have to be tested, and procedures to that effect are discussed here. Furthermore, it is of interest to try to find out whether or not the estimated STR model captures all non-linear features present in the data. Eitrheim and Teräsvirta (1996) considered LM and LM-type tests for these situations in STAR models, and they can be generalized to the multivariate (STR) case. The test of no error autocorrelation against autocorrelation of a given order is an LM test which can be carried out using an auxiliary regression. If the model is linear, the test collapses into the Breusch–Pagan test (Breusch and Pagan (1979)) of no error autocorrelation. This is an LM test for testing the null hypothesis of no error autocorrelation in linear models. Note that the standard Ljung–Box portmanteau (Ljung and Box (1978)) test based on squared autocorrelations of the observed series is not valid here. This is because the observations are estimated residuals from an STR or STAR model, and no asymptotic distribution theory is available for that case. If it is applied in any case in a standard way it is bound to be very conservative.

I briefly introduce the two other tests in Eitrheim and Teräsvirta (1996). The test of no remaining non-linearity is based on the following idea. Define the *additive* STR model

$$y_t = x_t'\varphi + (x_t'\theta)G(\gamma, c_1; s_t) + (x_t'\psi)H(\gamma_2, c_2; r_t) + u_t \qquad (t = 1, \ldots, T) \tag{12}$$

This STR model has two additive nonlinear components, and the transition function H where r_t is assumed an element of x_t may be defined analogously to equations (3) and (4). This implies that the possibly neglected non-linearity is of STR type. When adequacy of the standard STR model is the issue it can be investigated by testing H_0: $\gamma_2 = 0$ in equation (12). The identification problem may be circumvented in the same way as in testing linearity. This results in a test which is based on an auxiliary regression in the same way as a linearity test against STR. In fact, if $G \equiv 0$ in equation (12) then the test collapses into the linearity test discussed in the preceding section.

The parameter constancy test is based on the same idea as the one for linear models. Write the non-constant STR model as

$$y_t = x_t'\varphi(t) + x_t'\theta(t)G(s_t; \gamma, c) + u_t \tag{13}$$

where $\varphi(t) = \varphi + \lambda_1 H(t; \gamma_1, c_1)$ and $\theta(t) = \theta + \lambda_2 H(t; \gamma_1, c_1)$. Transition function H can be defined analogously to equations (3), (4) or (7), and the null hypothesis of parameter constancy implies $H \equiv 0$. An LM-type test can be constructed following the same principles as in the linear case. If $G \equiv 0$ then the test is identical to the one for linear models discussed in Section 4.3.

4.5 APPLICATIONS OF TESTS

The tests discussed in Sections 4.3 and 4.4 are useful in building and evaluating STR and STAR models but they also have other uses. The parameter constancy tests may be used for checking the stability of linear models as, for example, in Lütkepohl, Teräsvirta and Wolters (1995) and Wolters, Teräsvirta and Lütkepohl (1996). The linearity tests may be applied to testing a form of invariance of linear econometric equations. The alternative is that structural changes in the generating mechanism of conditioning variables (the marginal model) of the equation affect the parameters of that equation. Such an alternative may be formulated in terms of smoothly changing parameters. The transition variable of the transition function is one representing structural changes in the marginal model. The STR framework allows joint testing of weak exogeneity and invariance, i.e. super-exogeneity; for definitions of exogeneity, see, for example, Hendry (1995, Chapter 5). Details of the tests can be found in Jansen and Teräsvirta (1996).

The STAR model and tests of no additive non-linearity can also be used for testing Granger non-causality in non-linear models; for a survey of the literature on Granger causality, see Geweke (1984). Skalin and Teräsvirta (1996) recently considered this possibility. Let $\{y_t\}$ and $\{z_t\}$ be two stationary and ergodic sequences and assume that $\{y_t\}$ is generated by a STAR model. The null hypothesis of z not Granger-causing y can be formulated in terms of the following STR model:

$$y_t = \varphi' w_t + \theta' w_t G(y_{t-d}; \gamma_1, c_1) + \psi_1' v_t + (\psi_{20} + \psi_2' v_t) H(z_{t-e}; \gamma_2, c_2) + u_t$$

$$\gamma_1, \gamma_2 > 0 \qquad\qquad (14)$$

where $\{u_t\}$ is a sequence of independent, identically distributed errors, $w_t = (1, y_{t-1}, \ldots, y_{t-p})'$, $v_t = (z_{t-1}, \ldots, z_{t-q})'$, $\varphi = (\varphi_0, \varphi_1, \ldots, \varphi_p)'$, $\theta = (\theta_0, \theta_1, \ldots, \theta_p)'$, and $\psi_j = (\psi_{j1}, \ldots, \psi_{jq})'$, $j = 1, 2$. Model (14) is a special case of (12). Transition functions G and H are defined as above so that the null hypothesis 'z does not Granger-cause y' is in this framework equivalent to H_0: $\psi_1 = 0$, $\gamma_2 = 0$ against H_1: $\psi_1 \neq 0$ or $\gamma_2 > 0$ or both. In the standard bivariate test based on linearity, $G \equiv 0$ and $H \equiv 0$ a priori, and the null hypothesis of non-causality is $\psi_1 = 0$. As the delay e is usually unknown, an STR-based test is constructed following the suggestions in Luukkonen, Saikkonen and Teräsvirta

(1988). Let $Z = \{z_{t-1}, \ldots, z_{t-q}\}$ be a set of possible transition variables. Selecting the 'economy version' of the test (auxiliary regression (14) in Luukkonen, Saikkonen and Teräsvirta (1988)) leads to testing H_0: $\tilde{\beta}_j = 0$, $j = 1, \ldots, q, \tilde{\beta}_{ij} = 0, i = 1, \ldots, q; j = i, \ldots, q; \delta_j = 0, j = 1, \ldots, q$, in

$$\hat{u}_t = \beta_0' g_t + \sum_{j=1}^{q} \tilde{\beta}_j z_{t-j} + \sum_{i=1}^{q}\sum_{j=i}^{q} \tilde{\beta}_{ij} z_{t-i} z_{t-j} + \sum_{j=1}^{q} \delta_j z_{t-j}^3 + \tilde{\eta}_t \tag{15}$$

where g_t is the $(n \times 1)$ gradient vector of the parameters of the STAR model (14) under H_0 and $\hat{u}_t$ is the tth residual of equation (14) estimated under H_0. For the asymptotic theory to work, one has to assume that all necessary moments implied by the moment matrix of the asymptotically χ^2-distributed (under H_0) test statistic exist. The degrees of freedom of the approximating F-statistic equal $q(q + 1)/2 + 2q$ in the numerator and $T - n - q(q + 1)/2 - 2q$ in the denominator. The alternative defined by equation (14) can be generalized if desired. For example, the set of possible transition variables may contain lags of y_t as well. I do not discuss such extensions here.

4.6 EXAMPLES

In this section I consider an application of smooth transition models to testing Granger non-causality. It forms a part of a larger study (Skalin and Teräsvirta (1996)) of long annual Swedish macroeconomic time series. The cyclical properties of these series were previously investigated by Englund, Persson and Svensson (1992) using frequency domain techniques. I shall concentrate on two time series only, the annual volume of industrial production and the employment (hours worked in manufacturing) in 1861–1988. The series are expressed in natural logarithms and differenced once to achieve stationarity. Their graphs appear in Figures 4.1 and 4.2. The differenced series are found to be non-linear and an ESTAR model is selected and fitted to both of them. The industrial production is characterized by the following ESTAR model:

$$y_t = 2.87 \; y_{t-1} + \underset{(0.62)}{1.30} \; y_{t-2} + \underset{(1.38)}{2.00} \; y_{t-3} + \underset{(0.40)}{0.41} \; y_{t-4} - \underset{(0.40)}{0.89} \; y_{t-5}$$

$$-\underset{(0.32)}{0.56} \; y_{t-6} + [\; \underset{(0.010)}{0.073} \; - \underset{(1.44)}{2.87} \; y_{t-1} - \underset{(0.62)}{1.30} \; y_{t-2} - \underset{(1.38)}{2.25} \; y_{t-3}$$

$$-\underset{(0.40)}{0.41} \; y_{t-4} + \underset{(0.40)}{0.89} \; y_{t-5} + \underset{(0.32)}{0.56} \; y_{t-6} - \underset{(0.093)}{0.30} \; y_{t-7}]$$

$$\times [1 - \exp\{-\underset{(0.63)}{1.82} \; (y_{t-3} + \underset{(0.013)}{0.089} \;)^2\}/\hat{\sigma}^2(y)] + \hat{u}_t \tag{16}$$

Where the numbers in parentheses below the coefficients: (1.44), (0.62), (1.38), (0.40), (0.40) appear under the first line of equation (16).

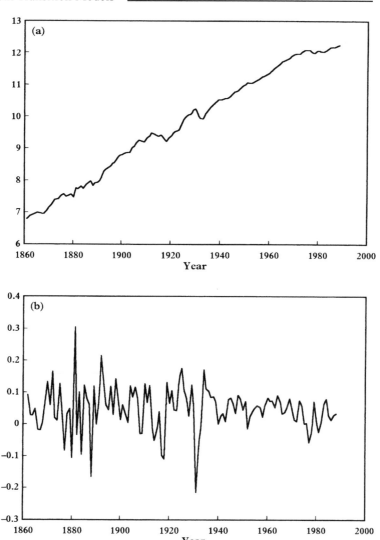

Figure 4.1 Logarithms of the annual volume of Swedish industrial production 1861–1988 (a) and first differences of the series (b)

$$s = 0.065 \qquad \text{skewness} = 0.22 \quad \text{excess kurtosis} = 3.1$$
$$\text{LJB} = 50 \ (10^{-11}) \quad \text{VR} = 0.85 \qquad R^2 = 0.23$$

where $\hat{\sigma}^2(y) = 0.0049$ is the sample variance of $\{y_t\}$, s is the residual standard error, LJB the Lomnicki–Jarque–Bera test of normality (Lomnicki (1961);

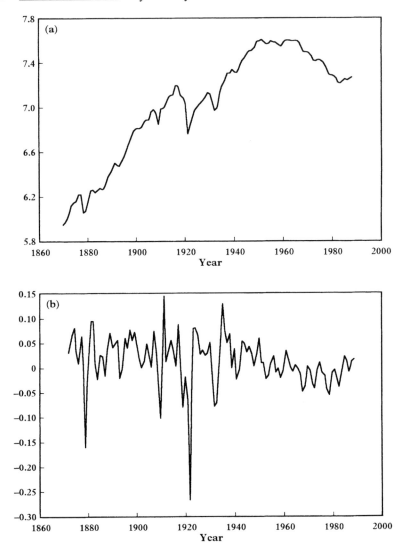

Figure 4.2 Logarithms of the annual employment, measured in hours worked in manufacturing, in Sweden 1861–1988 (a) and first differences of the series (b)

Jarque and Bera (1980)) of the error process (p-value in parentheses), VR is the ratio of the residual variance of the model to the residual variance of the corresponding linear AR model, and R^2 is the coefficient of determination. The coefficient of determination is rather low and the residuals not normal. This is due to the large turbulence in the series between the 1880s and the 1940s which is only partially captured by the STAR parameterization. Linear univariate models do even worse. The corresponding deterministic system has a unique stable stationary point at $y_\infty = 0.047$.

The estimated ESTAR model for the employment is

$$z_t = -\ 0.98\ -\ 3.53\ z_{t-1}\ -\ 9.65\ z_{t-2}\ +\ 6.16\ z_{t-3}\ +\ 3.52\ z_{t-4}$$
$$\quad\quad (0.73)\quad\ (2.25)\quad\quad (5.55)\quad\quad\ (5.26)\quad\quad\ (4.16)$$

$$+\ [\ 1.01\ +\ 3.53\ z_{t-1}\ +\ 9.65\ z_{t-2}\ -\ 6.16\ z_{t-3}\ -\ 3.52\ z_{t-4}]$$
$$\quad (0.73)\quad (2.25)\quad\quad (5.55)\quad\quad\ (5.26)\quad\quad\ (4.16)$$

$$\times\ [1 - \exp\{-\ 0.32\ (z_{t-1} +\ 0.17\quad)^2/\hat{\sigma}^2(z)\}] + \hat{u}_t$$
$$\quad\quad\quad\quad\ (0.17)\quad\quad (0.057) \tag{17}$$

$s = 0.038$ skewness $= -0.62$ excess kurtosis $= 2.4$

LJB $= 36\ (2 \times 10^{-8})$ VR $= 0.56$ $R^2 = 0.50$

where $\hat{\sigma}^2(z) = 0.0026$ is the sample variance of $\{z_t\}$. Also here, the system has a unique single stationary point at $y_\infty = 0.013$.

As to the interpretation of the equations, observe that in both models non-linearity is required mainly to characterize the local behaviour of the processes at low values. The estimates of c are small in both equations (16) and (17), -0.09 and -0.17, respectively. Several restrictions of type $\phi_j = -\theta_j$ have been imposed. This is an exclusion restriction making the combined parameter $\phi_j + \theta_j G_3$ equal zero for $G_3 = 1$ while the restriction $\phi_j = 0$ does the same for $G_3 = 0$. The non-linear component in equation (16) mainly explains responses of the system to some of the large negative shocks (note the estimate $c = -0.089$) between the 1880s and 1920s. For values of G_3 sufficiently close to zero, the lag polynomial of equation (16) contains a positive explosive root. It characterizes rapid positive movements in the growth rate after an initial negative shock. For large values of G_3, all roots are stationary. The lag polynomial then has a rather large, in absolute value, but negative root.

Equation (17) has the interesting property that for $G_3 = 1$, the corresponding linear equation (see equation (2)) is just a random walk with positive drift corresponding to an annual growth rate of 3%. Cyclical behaviour only occurs when the growth rate of employment steadily remains either positive but very low or negative. This is also observed from Figure 4.2. A fairly regular cycle emerges in the beginning of the late 1950s when employment is declining steadily.

Skalin and Teräsvirta (1996) contains a more thorough discussion of the properties and interpretation of the estimated STAR models whereas I proceed directly to the results of non-causality tests. They can be found in Tables 4.1 and 4.2. Table 4.1 contains the tests carried out in the STAR framework using equation (15). The outcome is somewhat sensitive to the lag length. The null hypothesis of production not causing employment is rejected more strongly the

Table 4.1 p-values of the Granger non-causality F-test based on the auxiliary regression (15): (a) industrial production (y) causes employment (z) under the alternative, (b) employment causes industrial production under the alternative

Direction of causality under H_1	Maximum lag q						
	4	5	6	7	8	9	10
$y \rightarrow z$	0.14	0.20	0.044	0.002	0.001	6×10^{-5}	6×10^{-5}
$z \rightarrow y$	0.010	0.026	0.036	0.089	0.048	0.094	0.0003

Table 4.2 p-values of the Granger non-causality F-test based on bivariate linear regression: (a) industrial production (y) causing employment (z) under the alternative, (b) employment causing industrial production under the alternative

Direction of causality under H_1	Maximum lag q						
	4	5	6	7	8	9	10
$y \rightarrow z$	0.050	0.084	0.14	0.33	0.40	0.23	0.043
$z \rightarrow y$	0.34	0.32	0.55	0.72	0.79	0.78	0.77

longer the maximum lag q in equation (15). Evidence against employment not causing production is less strong but also less sensitive to the choice of q. When the maximum lag equals 10 the rejection is overwhelming also in this direction. Thus, the tests indicate two-way causality between these variables.

These outcomes can be contrasted with what is obtained under the assumption of linearity using bivariate regressions; see Geweke (1984) for discussion. Those results can be found in Table 4.2. There is evidence about causality from production to employment at the 5% level at lags 5 and 10, although measured in p-values it is not particularly strong. On the other hand, the results indicate that employment does not Granger-cause production. This conclusion contradicts the one obtained using STR-based tests. Furthermore, statistical support for production causing employment is much stronger in the STR than in a completely linear framework.

Interpreting the outcomes of non-causality tests is, of course, not quite as straightforward as it seems above. The information set is bivariate, and adding more variables might change conclusions. However, STR models in this case fit the data better than the linear ones and thus provide a better starting-point for testing non-causality that the latter would do. The main lesson of this restricted example is that the model specification does affect the outcome of non-causality tests and that this possibility should be taken into consideration when undertaking bivariate tests of non-causality. The more extensive investigation by Skalin and Teräsvirta (1996) supports this conclusion. As is obvious from above, STR models offer a parametric extension to the standard linear framework for testing the non-causality hypothesis. For a recent non-parametric approach to this problem, see Bell, Kay and Malley (1996).

4.7 CONCLUSIONS

Smooth transition models are non-linear models with a flexible parameterization. They can be used for modelling various types of behaviour which cannot be adequately characterized with a linear model. In economic applications, the extra flexibility of smooth transition models is often needed to model series that contain rare or unusual events. Smooth transition models are locally linear in the sense discussed in Section 4.2, which facilitates their interpretation. Furthermore, the STR or STAR models form a well-defined class of models. Because of that, it has been possible to construct a feasible modelling strategy for this class; for discussion see, for example, Granger and Teräsvirta (1993, Chapter 7) and Teräsvirta (1994).

The STR model is useful not only for non-linear modelling *per se*. It also offers a useful framework for hypothesis (misspecification) testing in linear models. Tests of parameter constancy and super-exogeneity are examples of this. In this chapter I have chosen to emphasize the fact that one may also carry out bivariate Granger non-causality tests using STR models. The results support the claim that the outcomes of such tests are sensitive to the functional form of the underlying model.

All smooth transition models discussed in this chapter are single-equation models. Generalizing them to systems of equations is possible and many alternative ways of doing this exist, at least in theory. More work is needed in this area to find out how such extensions should best be parameterized and how useful they actually are in practice.

ACKNOWLEDGEMENTS

This research was supported in part by the Swedish Research Council of Letters and Social Sciences. I also wish to thank Joakim Skalin for help in preparing this chapter. Any errors and shortcomings are my own responsibility.

COMMENTS

M. BASSEVILLE, D. VAN DIJK,
P.H.B.F. FRANSES AND M. CAMPBELL

M. BASSEVILLE

The purpose of this chapter is to discuss smooth transition regression (STR) models. These models were introduced in the early 1970s as a generalization of switching regression models, which have been investigated also by Quandt (1958, 1960), Hinkley (1969, 1971); see Shaban (1980) for an annotated bibliography. When the transition (switching) variable is a lag of the dependent data, these models may exhibit complex dynamics (smooth transition autoregressive: STAR). When the transition variable is time, these models allow us to test parameter constancy in linear models. Inference in STR models is discussed, together with related tests of no error autocorrelation, of parameter constancy, and of no remaining non-linearities.

The author clearly advocates the usefulness of this class of parametric non-linear models, not only for non-linear modelling purposes but also for hypothesis testing in linear and non-linear models. For example, the parameter constancy test may be used for checking the stability of linear models, the linearity tests may be used for testing invariance in linear econometric relations, and the test of no additive non-linearity in STAR models can be used for testing Granger non-causality in non-linear models (even though the outcome of these tests does depend on model specification).

Because of the historical origin of the STR models and of my own experience of piecewise constant parametric models (called also change-point models), I would make the following comments:

- It may happen that piecewise constant models are relevant models even when the time series of interest exhibit more smooth transitions than actual abrupt changes. For example, it has been experimentally proven by André-Obrecht (1988) that piecewise constant autoregressive models of order two with white-noise input are of interest as a first step (segmentation) for the purpose of speech recognition, even though the relevant models for speech synthesis are known to be not only of autoregressive moving average type but also with additional impulsive input; see also Basseville and Nikiforov (1993). My question would thus be: are piecewise constant models still of interest in econometrics, and of lower or higher interest than STR models?

- Of course, this also raises the issue of the purpose of the (possibly non-linear) modelling. My own experience (on monitoring industrial processes) is that there is no unique model for a given set of time series, and that the choice of the model should basically be governed by the goal of the processing. For a given application, the best model for simulation has no reason to be the same as the best one for prediction, or for control, or for monitoring. My second question would thus concerns the underlying purpose of the modelling which is discussed in the chapter.

D. VAN DIJK AND P.H.B.F. FRANSES

The chapter by Timo Teräsvirta gives a comprehensive overview of the state of the art concerning various aspects of smooth transition regression (STR) models. Teräsvirta pays particular attention to tests for STR and diagnostic tests to examine the empirical adequacy of an estimated STR model. Teräsvirta (1994) and Granger and Teräsvirta (1993) incorporate these statistical tools into a sequential specification procedure for STR models, which consists of the familiar stages of testing, estimating and diagnostic checking.

Given the availability of this specification procedure, nothing seems to prevent a widespread application of this class of non-linear time series models. In our comment, we will elaborate on some practical issues, which any empirical researcher who seeks to apply STR models may wish to consider. To be more precise, we focus on the possible 'observational equivalence' of outliers and non-linearity in small samples and we provide some comments on evaluating forecasts from STR models.

Smooth transition models have been applied almost exclusively to study possible non-linearity of business cycles; see Teräsvirta and Anderson (1992), Teräsvirta, Tjøstheim and Granger (1994), and Öcal (1995), among others. At first sight, these studies seem to suggest that STR models are indeed useful in describing, for example, different properties of recessions and expansions. It has to be kept in mind, however, that many macroeconomic variables which reflect business cycle patterns are sampled only quarterly or monthly. Consequently, usually only series of moderate length are available, i.e. more than 100 observations is the exception rather than the rule. Possible non-linear properties in the data may then be most pronounced in only a small number of observations. For example, recessions often occur only once per decade and tend to last for not more than two or three quarters. From a practical point of view, one may then be tempted to regard these, say, 'non-linear data points' as aberrant observations, which can simply be removed by including dummy variables. If the primary goal of the econometric time series model is merely describing a time series, one may even justify this option by noting that estimating STR models often is not straightforward since several parameters in nonlinear functions are added. On the other hand, removing apparent outliers may destroy intrinsic nonlinearity, which could have been exploited to obtain better forecasts. Therefore, there seems to be a need for modelling strategies and tests which can distinguish nonlinearity from outliers and vice versa. A first step towards such a strategy is given in Van Dijk, Franses and Lucas (1996), where LM-type tests against smooth transition non-linearity are designed which are less sensitive to outlying observations. In short, these robust tests are obtained by estimating the linear model under the null hypothesis using a robust estimator.

As an example, consider Figure 4.A, which shows the seasonal differences of the quarterly index of US industrial production over the period 1962(iii)–1986(iv). Teräsvirta and Anderson (1992) model this series by a logistic smooth transition autoregressive (LSTAR) model, which seems to render an adequate description of the asymmetries observed between recessions and expansions. The circled observations indicate the recession periods as determined by the value of the transition function in their estimated model. When the LM-type tests as described in Teräsvirta's chapter are applied to this series, linearity is rejected

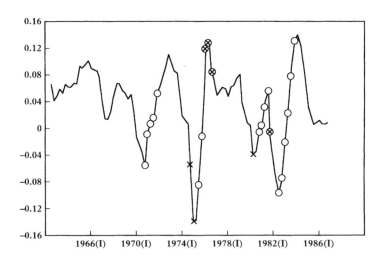

Figure 4.A US industrial production. Seasonal differences of quarterly index of US industrial production 1962(iii)–1986(iv). Circles indicate observations for which the estimated transition function is zero, crosses are observations that are identified as outliers in a robust estimation procedure

quite convincingly. The robust tests, on the other hand, do not reject the null hypothesis. The robust estimation procedure indicates that seven observations might be considered as outliers, marked by crosses in the figure, and that these observations roughly correspond with the recession periods around 1975 and 1981; see Van Dijk, Franses and Lucas (1996) for more details. Notice that these findings do not imply that STR models should not be used for these data. We merely find that any practitioner should make a decision whether or not to estimate complicated non-linear models of which characteristic features may only be reflected in a small number of observations.

Our second comment concerns the evaluation of forecasts from STR models, which, in a sense, is related to the issue of outliers. It is common practice to evaluate the adequacy of competing time series models by comparing their out-of-sample forecasting performance. If non-linearity is reflected by only a small fraction of observations, it may accidentally happen that the non-linear features do not become apparent in the period chosen (or available) for forecasting. Traditional measures of forecasting accuracy, such as the root mean squared forecasting error, treat all observations equally and, hence, may suggest that a linear model generates better forecasts, even though the non-linear model truly excels in forecasting data in specific regimes. Hence, an important topic for further research is the design of forecast evaluation criteria for non-linear time series models, which can incorporate this data-dependence.

M. CAMPBELL

The chapter by Teräsvirta is largely devoted to describing technical aspects of this class of non-linear models, statistical inference, testing for linearity, etc. Models are built for two Swedish data series, industrial production and employment and as a further application these techniques are used to test Granger non-causality.

The series for annual industrial production in Sweden runs from 1862 to 1988. Teräsvirta estimates a univariate smooth transition model for this series on the basis that the data are found to be non-linear. The non-linear model is an improvement on a linear autoregressive model of the same order, for example the residual variance of the non-linear model is 85% of the residual variance of the linear model. Nevertheless the standard error of the nonlinear model, which is 0.065, comes very close to the standard deviation of the data series itself, which is 0.070.

A similar non-linear model for employment is also reported which achieves a larger reduction in the residual variance but the estimated residual error of 0.038 is still a significant fraction of the standard deviation of the series 0.051.

In each case a single model is assumed to account for a very long period of time. It is far from clear either that this is a reasonable assumption to make, or that the use of non-linear techniques such as these add much to our under-standing of the data. In a recently published book the economic historian Angus Maddison (Maddison (1995)) argues 'economic growth has not been steady since 1820. There have been five distinct phases (1820–70, 1870–1913, 1913–50, 1950–73 and 1973–92). These were recognisable segments of the growth process ... The phases are identified, in the first instance, by inductive analysis and iterative inspection of measurable characteristics.'

Maddison takes into account evidence on the average growth rate of output, of productivity, and the overall environment, such as barriers to trade, freedom of capital movements, international migration, the world monetary order and exchange rate mechanisms. The separation of the history of capitalism into these periods is one which commands broad assent among economic historians.

Results that compare very favourably with those reported by Teräsvirta can be obtained by building a piecewise linear model that consists of very simple linear autoregressive models for each of the four periods 1862–1913, 1914–49, 1950–73 and 1974–88. (These periods have clearly been chosen, not with reference to any statistical analysis at all, but with reference to the phases identified by Maddison. For simplicity, the period 1862–69 is incorporated into the 1870–1913 phase.)

The Akaike information criterion is used to determine the order of a linear model for industrial production in each of the four periods.[1] According to this criterion the order of the models for the periods should be one, one, zero and zero respectively. The estimated models have standard errors of 0.0797, 0.0743, 0.0264 and 0.0384; and on pooling these estimates we arrive at a figure of 0.063 for the piecewise linear model. This estimate is slightly lower than the standard error of the model estimated by Teräsvirta. It should be noted that this reduction in standard error is obtained even though AR(0) models are used to represent the data since 1950. (The AIC does not give a very clear choice of order for all of the periods but virtually identical results are obtained for a variety of models of different orders.)

This approach is very simplistic mathematically, but even from a purely statistical point of view it is capable of explaining the data at least as well as the non-linear model, quite apart from the fact that it provides some insight into changes in behaviour of the economy over the last hundred years or so.

These results highlight an important general problem for modelling macro-economic data series. The chapter by Teräsvirta is an example of recent efforts in which mathematically sophisticated non-linear models are demonstrated to have greater explanatory power than linear alternatives. But even the most technically sophisticated models of many data series, such as those proposed by Teräsvirta, are very poor by any reasonable standard. The standard error of an equation is an estimate of the error of in-sample one-step-ahead forecasting. This is just about the least demanding measure of a model's explanatory power but it is often the case that this error is nearly as large as the standard deviation of the data. This is certainly true of all the models discussed above, non-linear and piecewise linear alike.

Endnote

1. These calculations were carried out using the statistical package S-PLUS.

REPLIES

T. TERÄSVIRTA

M. BASSEVILLE

First, I would like to thank the discussants for their comments which allow me to discuss several aspects of non-linear econometric modelling. Michèle Basseville is curious about the future of piecewise constant models in econometrics. They continue to enjoy considerable popularity. For example, the so-called Hidden Markov or Markov switching model of Lindgren (1978) is frequently applied to economic data. In this model, the process visits a finite number of linear models (states) according to a discrete unobserved variable which is usually modelled as a first-order Markov chain. In some other cases, there may exist economic theory that presupposes abrupt changes between states. Modelling markets with rationing with so-called disequilibrium models provides an example of this. On the other hand, if the postulated transition variable is an observable continuous variable then it may be useful to start from the assumption that the transition from the one extreme regime to the other is smooth and apply an LSTR1 model. The estimated transition function then tells whether or not a piecewise constant model would in fact be a reasonable choice. This should work well at least in cases where the piecewise constant model is expected to have two regimes.

It is certainly true that there often exist several reasonable models for a given set of time series. In econometrics, models are used not only for forecasting but also for policy analysis and for testing economic theories. Testing super-exogeneity in the STR framework is an example of a case in which the non-linear STR model is used for checking whether or not a possibly linear model can be used for policy analysis. Testing Granger non-causality between economic variables may, at least in some cases, amount to testing economic theory.

STAR and STR models are also suitable for forecasting. Forecasts for more than one period ahead may be obtained numerically as discussed in Granger and Teräsvirta (1993, Chapter 8). Alternatively, a separate (not necessarily an STR) model may be constructed for each forecast horizon. Non-linear structure in many of the STR models with economic variables is mainly required for modelling consequences of relatively rare events. If such an event does not occur in the forecasting period, the non-linear model may not produce any more accurate point forecasts than a simple linear model. The differences in forecasts may become apparent only if one compares not point forecasts but conditional forecast densities. While their means may be close to each other the densities themselves may be rather different from each other. The conditional forecast density of a forecast from a linear model with a symmetric error distribution is symmetric. The corresponding density for a conditional forecast from an STR model may be skewed and even bimodal. (For a nice way of representing sets of such densities see Hyndman (1995)). This is because the 'rare event' ignored by the linear model is allotted a positive probability in the non-linear forecast. Comparing forecasts may thus not just be a matter of selecting a prediction period and computing mean square errors of point forecasts from linear and non-linear models. The last point of Dick van Dijk and Philip Hans Franses is related to this problem. It is easy to agree with their argument that we have to develop evaluation criteria for forecasts from non-linear time series models and thus need further research in this area.

D. VAN DIJK AND P.H.B.F. FRANSES

The main point of Van Dijk and Franses concerns outliers and non-linearity. As discussed above, many economic time series are not inherently non-linear. Non-linear models often characterize relatively few 'rare events' in the series. Should the consequences of those be parameterized at all? Why not treat the deviating observations as possible outliers and analyse data free from their influence? Van Dijk and Franses illustrate their argument with an interesting example. Teräsvirta and Anderson (1992) fitted an LSTAR1 model to a quarterly US industrial production series. The authors found that non-linearity was needed to character-ize the recovery of the industrial production from a recession. This recovery was faster than what a linear autoregressive model would have predicted. Van Dijk and Franses apply linearity tests made robust against outliers and described in Van Dijk *et al.* (1996) to the same series. They do not reject linearity, and the outliers are depicted in their Figure 1. They are observations that belong either to recessions or to their immediate aftermath. This indicates that somehow the recessions and the ensuing recovery have dynamics different from the rest of the period. The figure thus does not contradict conclusions of Teräsvirta and Anderson.

The question then arises: what should one do in practice? If one only has the information in the data then the preferences of the modeller obviously determine the strategy. Suppose that avoiding any modelling of outliers is considered most important. Then one may choose the strategy Van Dijk *et al.* (1996) devised and robustify both linearity tests and estimation of STR models against outliers. If preference is given to parameterizing the dynamics of the process as well as possible one may begin with the ordinary testing and estimation procedures. At the evaluation stage of STAR or STR modelling it is possible to see how well the strategy worked. Suppose that the evaluation tests indicate that there is still considerable non-linearity left unexplained after fitting a STAR or an STR model to the data. In such a case a possible conclusion is that the series (a single one in the STAR case, more than one series in the STR case) contain too many irregularities (outliers) to be modelled with these models. Using robust procedures then emerges as a possible next choice.

The next question may be whether these preferences matter at all. In the above US industrial production example both strategies give rather similar insights. As already discussed above, the differences between them become obvious in forecasting. Linear models yield symmetric forecast densities whereas use of the LSTAR1 model leads to non-symmetric ones. The non-linear model may forecast better than the linear one in recessions (but then those were rare events). Suppose that the structure of the process following a STAR model remains unchanged over time. In that case the STAR model on average generates more accurate forecasts than the linear model. On the other hand, those rare events may in fact be unique and will not occur in the same form in the future. Then forecasts from a robust model probably have a higher precision than those generated by a STAR model. For example, those who view the Great Depression in the United States as a completely unique historical event may not want to model the long US GNP series with a STAR model as did Teräsvirta (1995). However, deciding whether or not the Great Depression indeed was such an event is not possible if one just has the information contained in the time series of the US GNP.

M. CAMPBELL

Michael Campbell finds that the estimated STAR models presented in the chapter are very poor by any reasonable standards. I should like to mention that the motivation of fitting STAR models to these two (and seven other) long Swedish macroeconomic time series is given in Skalin and Teräsvirta (1996) to which the reader of my chapter was referred. That paper also contains a detailed discussion of properties of the estimated models including parameter constancy tests and offers insight and interpretations. In the above, I have merely used the models as an empirical illustration of how to test the Granger non-causality hypothesis in the STR framework and, at the same time, considered the effect of the assumed functional form of the model on the outcomes. Nevertheless, Campbell makes a useful point: the results one obtains are conditional on prior assumptions one makes. Thus, if the world is assumed piecewise linear over time with known change-points the insight gained may be different from that obtained if one starts from the assumption that it is possibly non-linear with a constant structure over time. My hope is that the latter assumption is a fruitful one as well, although its many interesting consequences have not been the topic of my chapter.

REFERENCES

Anderson, H.M. (1996) Transaction costs and nonlinear adjustment towards equilibrium in the U.S. treasury bill market. Unpublished paper, Texas A & M University.

André-Obrecht, R. (1988) A new statistical approach for the automatic segmentation of continuous speech signals. *IEEE Trans. Acoustics, Speech, Signal Processing* **ASSP-36**, 29–40.

Andrews, D.W.K. and Ploberger, W. (1994) Optimal tests when a nuisance parameter is present only under the alternative. *Econometrica* **62**, 1383–1414.

Bacon, D.W. and Watts, D.G. (1971) Estimating the transition between two intersecting straight lines. *Biometrika* **58**, 525–34.

Basseville, M. and Nikiforov, I.V. (1993) *Detection of Abrupt Changes—Theory and Applications*. Prentice Hall Information and System Sciences Series, Englewood Cliffs, NJ.

Bell, D., Kay, J. and Malley, J. (1996) A nonparametric approach to nonlinear causality testing. *Economics Letters* **51**, 7–18.

Breusch, T.S. and Pagan, A.R. (1979) A simple test of heteroskedasticity and random coefficient variation. *Econometrica* **47**, 1287–94.

Chan, K.S. and Tong, H. (1986) On estimating thresholds in autoregressive models. *Journal of Time Series Analysis* **7**, 178–90.

Chow, G.C. (1960) Tests of equality between sets of coefficients in two linear regressions. *Econometrica* **28**, 591–605.

Davies, R.B. (1977) Hypothesis testing when a nuisance parameter is present only under the alternative. *Biometrika* **64**, 247–54.

Davies, R.B. (1987) Hypothesis testing when a nuisance parameter is present only under the alternative. *Biometrika* **74**, 33–44.

Eitrheim, Ø. and Teräsvirta, T. (1996) Testing the adequacy of smooth transition autoregressive models. *Journal of Econometrics* **74**, 59–75.

Englund, P., Persson, T. and Svensson, L. (1992) Swedish business cycles: 1861–1988. *Journal of Monetary Economics* **30**, 343–71.

Geweke, J. (1984) Inference and causality in economic time series models. In: Z. Griliches and M.D. Intriligator (eds), *Handbook of Econometrics*, Vol. 2, pp. 1101–44. North-Holland, Amsterdam.

Goldfeld, S.M. and Quandt, R.E. (1972) *Nonlinear Methods in Econometrics*. North-Holland, Amsterdam.

Granger, C.W.J. and Teräsvirta, T. (1993) *Modelling Nonlinear Economic Relationships*. Oxford University Press, Oxford.

Haggan, V. and Ozaki, T. (1981) Modelling nonlinear random vibrations using an amplitude-dependent autoregressive time series model. *Biometrika* **68**, 189–196.

Hansen, B.E. (1996) Inference when a nuisance parameter is not identified under the null hypothesis. *Econometrica* **64**, 413–30.

Hendry, D.F. (1995) *Dynamic Econometrics*. Oxford University Press, Oxford.

Hinkley, D.V. (1969) Inference about the intersection in two-phase regression. *Biometrika* **56**, 495–504.

Hinkley, D.V. (1971) Inference in two-phase regression. *Journal of the American Statistical Association* **66**, 736–43.

Hyndman, R. (1995) Highest-density forecast regions for non-linear and non-normal time series models. *Journal of Forecasting* **14**, 431–41.

Jansen, E.S. and Teräsvirta, T. (1996) Testing parameter constancy and super exogeneity in econometric equations. *Oxford Bulletin of Economics and Statistics* **58** 735–64.

Jarque, C.M. and Bera, A.K. (1980) Efficient tests of normality, homoskedasticity, and serial independence of regression residuals. *Economics Letters* **6**, 255–9.

Lin, C.-F. and Teräsvirta, T. (1994) Testing the constancy of regression parameters against continuous structural change. *Journal of Econometrics* **62**, 211–28.

Lindgren, G. (1978) Markov regime models for mixed distributions and switching regressions. *Scandinavian Journal of Statistics* **5**, 81–91.

Ljung, G.M. and Box, G.E.P. (1978) On a measure of lack of fit in time-series models. *Biometrika* **65**, 297–303.

Lomnicki, Z.A. (1961) Tests for departure from normality in the case of linear stochastic processes. *Metrika* **4**, 37–62.

Lütkepohl, H., Teräsvirta, T. and Wolters, J. (1995) Investigating stability and linearity of a German M1 money demand function. Stockholm School of Economics, Working Paper Series in Economics and Finance, No. 64.

Luukkonen, R., Saikkonen, P. and Teräsvirta, T. (1988) Testing linearity against smooth transition autoregressive models. *Biometrika* **75**, 491–9.

Maddala, D.S. (1977) *Econometrics*. McGraw-Hill, New York.

Maddison, A. (1995) *Monitoring the World Economy 1820–1992*. OECD, Paris.

Mills, T.C. (1995) Are there asymmetries or nonlinearities in the U.K. output? *Applied Economics* **27**, 1211–17.

Öcal, N. (1995) Nonlinear models for U.K. macroeconomic series. University of Manchester, School of Economic Studies, Discussion Paper No. 9526.

Priestley, M. (1988) *Non-linear and Non-stationary Time Series Analysis*. Academic Press, London and San Diego.

Quandt, R.E. (1958) The estimation of the parameters of a linear regression system obeying two separate regimes. *Journal of the American Statistical Association* **53**, 873–80.

Quandt, R.E. (1960) Tests of the hypothesis that a linear regression system obeys two separate regimes. *Journal of the American Statistical Association* **55**, 324–30.

Saikkonen, P. and Luukkonen, R. (1988) Lagrange multiplier tests for testing non-linearities in time series models. *Scandinavian Journal of Statistics* **15**, 55–68.

Shaban, S.A. (1980) Change point problem and two-phase regression: an annotated bibliography. *International Statistical Review* **48**, 83–93.

Skalin, J. and Teräsvirta, T. (1996) Another look at Swedish business cycles, 1861–1988. Stockholm School of Economics, Working Paper Series in Economics and Finance, No. 130.

Teräsvirta, T. (1994) Specification, estimation, and evaluation of smooth transition autoregressive models. *Journal of the American Statistical Association* **89**, 208–18.

Teräsvirta, T. (1995) Modelling nonlinearity in U.S. gross national product 1889–1987. *Empirical Economics* **20**, 577–97.

Teräsvirta, T. (1997) Modelling economic relationships with smooth transition regressions. Forthcoming in D. Giles and A. Ullah (eds), *Handbook of Applied Economic Statistics*. Marcel Dekker, New York.

Teräsvirta, T. and Anderson, H.M. (1992) Characterizing nonlinearities in business cycles using smooth transition autoregressive models. *Journal of Applied Econometrics* **7**, S119–S136.

Teräsvirta, T., Tjøstheim, D. and Granger, C.W.J. (1994) Aspects of modelling nonlinear time series. In R.F. Engle and D.L. McFadden (eds), *Handbook of Econometrics*, Vol. 4, pp. 2919–2957. Elsevier, Amsterdam.

Tjøstheim, D. (1994) Nonlinear time series analysis: A selective view. *Scandinavian Journal of Statistics* **21**, 97–130.

Tong, H. (1990) *Nonlinear Time Series. A dynamical system approach*. Oxford University Press, Oxford.

Van Dijk, D., Franses, P.H. and Lucas, A. (1996) Testing for smooth transition nonlinearity in the presence of outliers. Erasmus University Rotterdam, Econometric Institute Report 9622/A.

Watson, M.W. and Engle, R.F. (1985) Testing for regression coefficient stability with a stationary AR(1) alternative. *Review of Economics and Statistics* **67**, 341–6.

Wecker, W.E. (1981) Asymmetric time-series. *Journal of the American Statistical Association* **76**, 16–21.

Wolters, J., Teräsvirta, T. and Lütkepohl, H. (1996) Modelling the demand for M3 in the unified Germany. Stockholm School of Economics, Working Paper Series in Economics and Finance, No. 113.

Wooldridge, J.M. (1994) Estimation and inference for dependent processes. In R.F. Engle and D.L. McFadden (eds), *Handbook of Econometrics*, Vol. 4, pp. 2641–2739. Elsevier, Amsterdam.

5

Empirical Behaviour of Interest-rate Models

J.M. MORALEDA AND A.C.F. VORST

5.1 INTRODUCTION

Over the last two decades much financial research has been devoted to the development of valuation models for interest rate derivative securities, such as options, caps, collars and swaptions. Most models start with specifying a stochastic process for the dynamics of the prices of bonds, especially zero coupon or discount bonds. Since the cash flows from coupon-bearing bonds can be seen as linear combinations of the cash flows of discount bonds, the dynamics of the prices of coupon bonds readily follow. If we denote by $P(t, T)$ the price at date t of a discount bond that pays off one dollar at maturity date T, we set the T-maturity interest rate at time t, $R(t, T)$, equal to

$$R(t, T) = \frac{-\ln(P(t, T))}{T - t}.$$

The function $R(t, \cdot)$ is known as the yield curve at time t. Hence, modelling bond price dynamics is equivalent to modelling yield curve dynamics. The most general interest-rate derivative pricing model, the one developed by Heath, Jarrow and Morton (1992), models indeed for each T the dynamics of $R(\cdot, T)$ through a stochastic process. In fact, Heath, Jarrow and Morton (1992) describe the dynamics of forward rates instead of the dynamics of the different maturities interest rates, since this leads to equivalent results and is more convenient from a mathematical point of view. The forward rates are denoted by $f(t, T)$ and are related to the interest rates by

System Dynamics in Economic and Financial Models. Edited by C. Heij, J.M. Schumacher, B. Hanzon and C. Praagman © 1997 John Wiley & Sons Ltd

$$R(t, T) = \frac{1}{T - t} \int_t^T f(t, u)\, du.$$

Since changes in interest rates of different maturities are heavily correlated and in order to keep the model analytically tractable, the stochastic processes $f(t, T)$ for different maturities T are assumed to be functions of a fixed number of Brownian motions. Most popular are the models where all $f(t, T)$ depend on the development of just one Brownian motion. These are called one-factor models and can be completely described by the stochastic process of one single forward rate. In most cases, one uses the spot interest rate, $r(t) = f(t, t)$ as the descriptive variable. All other bond prices can be derived from the development over time of $r(t)$ in such a one-factor model. These are called term structure models. Having described a stochastic model for bond prices, one can derive theoretical prices of interest rate derivative securities using no-arbitrage arguments, as we will explain in the next section.

Most attention has been paid to the theoretical properties of these models, where very few papers have studied empirical issues. Most of this empirical work has focused on what the econometricians would call diagnostic checking or specification testing of the models. This means checking the assumptions of the model, computing statistics of the parameter estimates, studying their stability over time, etc. Typically, this strand of literature tests the models with bond price data. Brown and Dybvig (1986), Stambaugh (1988), Dybvig (1989), Chan et al. (1992) and Brown and Schaefer (1994) are examples of research where the main purpose is estimating different model parameters and subsequently testing with bond price data.

The main result from these studies is that relatively simple one-factor models such as Vasicek (1977) or Cox, Ingersoll and Rox (1985) fit bond price data remarkably well. A step further in the analysis of the empirical behaviour of the term-structure models is, though, to test how the models with these parameter values price options. This is of crucial interest, since these models are mainly developed for derivative pricing purposes. Surprisingly, this issue has been rarely addressed in the literature. Examples are Flesaker (1993), who analysed the continuous time version of the Ho and Lee (1986) model and Dietrich-Campbell and Schwartz (1986), who examined the two-factor Brennan and Schwartz (1982) model.

Some literature has approached the central question through estimating the model parameters with option data rather than with the underlying yield curve movements. In fact, the model parameters are estimated in the same way as the implied volatility for options on stocks is estimated from option and stock price data. Amin and Morton (1994) is probably the most relevant example that estimates implied parameters, also called implied volatilities, and compares different models. However, this approach has some theoretical inconsistencies. In particular, implied parameter techniques demand a different estimation on each trading day. The result is that the model parameters change daily, where term-structure models generally assume that the volatility parameters are constant or deterministic functions of time. The quoted authors have tried to reconcile this apparent inconsistency by different arguments, although a full understanding of the implied volatility estimation for models assuming only time-dependent parameters has not yet been obtained.

In this chapter we focus on the estimation of term-structure model parameters from historical yield curve movements. As in the previous literature, we analyse econometric issues such as the stability of the parameters. Our main interest, however, concerns the reliability of the estimated parameters to price options traded in the markets.

We use the general Heath, Jarrow and Morton (1992) framework for pricing options. However, for most interest rate derivative securities, such as American options which can be exercised prematurely, explicit calculation of prices in this kind of framework requires computationally intensive numerical methods. Recently, however, Li, Ritchken and Sankarasubramanian (1995) have developed a numerical algorithm that makes the evolution of the term structure Markovian for a broad class of models, as identified by Ritchken and Sankarasubramanian (1995). All models considered in this chapter can be included in this class. We estimate parameters for the Spanish market by minimizing the error between the forward rate changes produced by the models and those historically observed in the markets. The forward rates, however, are not directly observed in the markets. They rather have to be inferred from bond prices quoted in the debt markets as will be explained in Section 5.3. The parameters thus estimated are used to price derivative securities traded in the Spanish option markets. A comparison between the option prices given by the models and the prices quoted in the markets is provided.

This chapter compares three one-factor yield curve models. They have one, two and three parameters, respectively. The first is the continuous time version of the Ho and Lee (1986) model. Ho and Lee are credited for being the first to build a model that provides arbitrage-free prices which depend on an exogenously specified initial yield curve. Moreover, this process, contrary to traditional models, no longer involves an exogenous specification of the 'market price of risk'.

The Ho and Lee model, however, has the major disadvantage of only allowing parallel yield curves for any moment in the future. This is because the volatility structure of the interest rate dynamics is assumed to be a constant.

The second model under consideration is that of Hull and White (1990) or, equivalently, the exponentially decaying model by Heath, Jarrow and Morton (1992). This model adds a mean-reverting effect for the interest rates through a second parameter in the volatility specification. In fact, the volatility structure under this model is a strictly decreasing function of the time to maturity so that short-term interest rates are more volatile than long-term ones. As a result, this model captures the well-known effect that interest rates are pulled to some long-run average level over time.

Some recent empirical studies, however, have found that the mean reversion for the interest rates is not actually as straightforward as was generally believed. In fact, the volatility structure is not, frequently, a monotone decreasing function of the time to maturity as modelled by Hull and White (1990). Rather, it is initially upwards sloping, it reaches a maximum, and then, due to the mean reversion, it decreases with the time to maturity. This shape in the volatility for the interest rates is referred to in the financial literature as humped volatility structures.[1]

The third model we consider in this chapter is that of Moraleda and Vorst (1997). This model allows for humped volatility structures in the yield curve dynamics at the price of adding an extra parameter to the model.

The rest of this chapter is organized as follows. In Section 5.2 the general setting in which all the models are nested is presented. Section 5.3 describes the two different data sets that we will use. They record yield curve data and option price data, respectively. Section 5.4 outlines the methodology for the estimation of the models, while Section 5.5 presents the results achieved on both the volatility estimation and the fit to the option price data. Section 5.6 draws the main conclusions and summarizes the chapter.

5.2 THE MODELS

The yield curve dynamics can be equivalently modelled through three related variables: interest rates, forward rates and prices of discount bonds. The traditional approach focuses on the interest rate modelling. Vasicek (1977), for example, proposed the following characterization of the instantaneous spot interest rate dynamics:

$$\mathrm{d}r = (a - br)\,\mathrm{d}t + \sigma\,\mathrm{d}W(t) \tag{1}$$

where a, b and σ are non-negative constants, r is short-hand for $r(t)$, the spot interest rate, and $W(t)$ is a Brownian motion. Extensions of this stochastic differential equation yield well-known models in the financial literature. Thus, the extended Vasicek version of Hull and White (1990, 1993) follows from making the model parameters in equation (1) time dependent. In particular, by allowing a to be time dependent, Hull and White are able to incorporate the initial yield curve into their model. The Black and Karansinski (1991) model is obtained by assuming that $\ln(r)$ rather than r evolves according to the stochastic differential equation (1), and making the parameters a, b and σ time-dependent functions rather than constants. A number of *square root* models have also been proposed similar to equation (1). For example, the extended Cox–Ingersoll–Ross version of the Hull and White (1990) model has the second term of the right-hand side of equation (1) equal to $\sigma\sqrt{r}\,dW(t)$, so that this term also explicitly depends on r. Another possibility is to assume that $r = u^2$ and the underlying process u satisfies the stochastic differential equation (1) with a being a time-dependent function.

More recently, Heath, Jarrow and Morton (1992) have proposed to model the forward rates rather than the interest-rate dynamics. We derive all considered models under this framework as we outline below.

Consider a continuous-time economy where bonds are traded for all maturities and markets are frictionless. As explained in the Introduction, we denote by $P(t, T)$ the price at time t of a pure discount bond that pays \$1 at time T, and assume that $P(t, T) > 0$ for all $t \in [0, T]$. The instantaneous forward rate at time t for a maturity T, $f(t, T)$, is defined by

$$f(t, T) = -\frac{\partial \ln P(t, T)}{\partial T}$$

so that

$$P(t, T) = e^{-\int_t^T f(t,u)\,du} \tag{2}$$

For a fixed maturity T, Heath, Jarrow and Morton (1992) model the evolution of the instantaneous forward rates by the diffusion

$$df(t, T) = \alpha(t, T, f(t, T))\,dt + \sigma(t, T, f(t, T))\,dW(t) \tag{3}$$

with $f(0, T)$ given and deterministic, and where $\alpha(.)$ and $\sigma(.)$ are stochastic processes whose values are known at time t and $W(t)$ is a Brownian motion. Notice that both $\alpha(.)$ and $\sigma(.)$ can explicitly depend on the forward rates $f(t, T)$. The dependence of $\alpha(.)$ and $\sigma(.)$ on $f(t, T)$ will not be made explicit hereafter.

It should be noted that the same Brownian motion is used for all maturities. Hence, forward rates for different maturities are subject to the same single underlying stochastic process. This is why this is called a one-factor model. Portfolio managers can trade in all existing bonds and follow a dynamic portfolio strategy where they are buying and selling bonds over time. A dynamic arbitrage portfolio strategy is a strategy that initially requires no or a negative investment and at some fixed time the portfolio has a non-negative value with probability one and with a strictly positive probability the portfolio value is positive. Furthermore, there are no cash inflows or outflows from the portfolio meanwhile. In financial theory one assumes that dynamic arbitrage portfolio strategies do not exist, since all traders would be chasing the strategy, disturbing the prices to an equilibrium without further arbitrage opportunities.

Heath, Jarrow and Morton (1992) proved that at any moment in time arbitrage-free prices $g(t)$ of interest rates derivative securities with only a terminal payoff $g(T)$ at time T are given by

$$g(t) = E_t(e^{-\int_t^T r(u)\,du} g(T)) \tag{4}$$

where the expectation is taken with respect to the so-called risk adjusted process which is specified by equation (3) with the restriction that

$$\alpha(t,\,T) = \sigma(t,\,T) \int_t^T \sigma(t,\,u)\,du \tag{5}$$

Substituting equation (5) in (3) and integrating gives the instantaneous forward rate process under which theoretical arbitrage free prices should be calculated:

$$f(t,\,T) = f(0,\,T) + \int_0^t \sigma(u,\,T)\left(\int_u^T \sigma(u,\,y)\,dy\right)du + \int_0^t \sigma(u,\,T)\,d\tilde{W}(u) \tag{6}$$

where $\tilde{W}(u)$ denotes a Brownian motion under an equivalent martingale measure.

As follows from equation (6), the stochastic evolution of the forward rates under the risk-neutral process is fully characterized with the specification of an initial forward rate curve and the volatility function. The initial forward rate curve is observable in the market at any moment in time. The volatility function, in turn, plays a key role in the analysis. Its specification uniquely determines the drift term of the risk-adjusted process by the no arbitrage argument.

The spot rate at time t, $r(t)$, is given by

$$r(t) = f(t,\,t) = f(0,\,t) + \int_0^t \sigma(u,\,t)\left(\int_u^t \sigma(u,\,y)\,dy\right)du + \int_0^t \sigma(u,\,t)\,d\tilde{W}(u) \tag{7}$$

Once this general setting has been established, we can now discuss the particular models under consideration. Consider the framework given by equation (6) with

$$\sigma(t,\,T) = \sigma \frac{[1 + \gamma T]}{[1 + \gamma t]} e^{-(\lambda/2)(T-t)} \tag{8}$$

and where σ, γ and λ are non-negative constants. This choice for the volatility generalizes a number of term-structure models. In particular, we consider the following models (see Table 5.1):

Table 5.1 One-factor yield curve models

Model	Key	Volatility specification
1. Ho and Lee (1986)	HL	$\sigma(t,\,T) = \sigma$
2. Hull and White (1990)	HW	$\sigma(t,\,T) = \sigma\,e^{-(\lambda/2)(T-t)}$
3. Moraleda and Vorst (1997)	MV	$\sigma(t,\,T) = \sigma \dfrac{[1 + \gamma T]}{[1 + \gamma t]} e^{-(\lambda/2)(T-t)}$

1. *The constant volatility model (HL).* If we set $\lambda = \gamma = 0$, we get the continuous time version of the Ho and Lee (1986) model as derived by Heath, Jarrow and Morton (1992). This is a one-parameter model with the volatility function being constant. Hereafter, this is referred to as the HL model.

2. *The exponential volatility model (HW).* This second model is the extended Vasicek version of the Hull and White (1990) model or, equivalently, the exponentially decaying model by Heath, Jarrow and Morton (1992). It is obtained by setting $\gamma = 0$.[2] This generalizes the previous model by Ho and Lee (1986). What is more important, though, is that this approach models a very well-known effect for the interest rates dynamics known as mean-reversion. This means that interest rates are pulled over time to some long-run average level. Hence, it seems to imply that short-term rates are more volatile than long-term ones. This is denoted as the exponential volatility or HW model.

3. *The humped volatility model (MV).* We finally consider a three-parameters model introduced by Moraleda and Vorst (1997). These authors model yield curve dynamics with a volatility function as given by equation (8) with all parameters being strictly positive. This yields a humped volatility structure (for $2\gamma > \lambda$) that has been systematically found in recent empirical studies. Notice that this model still implies a mean-reverting process for the interest rates, as strongly supported by both economic theory and previous empirical evidence. What this model adds to the existing literature is a delay of the mean reverting effect. In fact, the volatility structure is upwards-sloping for the short-term rates. After reaching a maximum, the volatility decreases with time so that interest rates revert to their long-run average. After all, the empirical findings by Kahn (1991), Amin and Morton (1994), etc. point out that the mean-reverting effect is not as straightforward as was generally believed. This is precisely what Moraleda and Vorst (1997) modelled by adding an extra parameter to the previous model.[3] We refer to this as the humped volatility or MV model.

As explained in the Introduction, the final aim of this chapter is to test the models with real option data. If the options to be priced were European, which means that they cannot be exercised prematurely, their valuation would be fairly simple since equation (4) can be used. In fact, equation (4) can be explicitly further developed into an analytical formula in case the volatility is described by equation (8) (see Mercurio and Moraleda (1996)). Therefore, pricing European-style claims merely requires solving an analytic formula.[4]

For the case of American-style options, which can be exercised before the maturity date, this is not so easy. Since we use this kind of option data to test the models, we devote the next subsection to explain how to price these claims within a homogeneous framework for all models.

5.2.1 The Valuation of American-style Claims

In contrast to the European options, there are no analytic formulas for the valuation of American style claims. The expectation of the terminal payoff of the security considered should be calculated numerically, where T in equation (4) is the optimal exercise (stopping) time. This means discretizing the SDE (3). Discretizing in the option-pricing literature usually involves constructing a so-called binomial tree. The time interval until the maturity of the option is split in n intervals of equal length. From the initial value of r there are two possibilities of the interest rate at the end of the first interval. The probabilities for each of the two possible states sum to one. The changes in the interest rates and the probabilities are chosen such that the variance and expectation are equal to those given by equation (3) over the first continuous time interval. For each of the two possible rates at the end of the first interval, two new rates at the end of the second interval are possible. Hence after n intervals, there are 2^n possible rates at the end. The value of an American option is obtained by calculating backwards through the constructed binomial tree from the final payoffs. However, in each node the value of immediate exercise of the option is compared with the option value and if the first exceeds the last, the exercise value is put in that particular node. The American option value is the value at the initial point of the tree. However, for large n, the number of possibilities 2^n is too large to be computationally feasible. Hence, one usually constructs, if possible, recombining trees in such a way that in a tree an upward move of the interest rate value followed by a downward move results in the same node as a downward move followed by an upward one. In this way after n intervals only $(n + 1)$ nodes result and the required calculations are feasible. This is only possible if the process given by equation (3) is Markovian with the interest rate as the only state variable.

However, in the general case of Heath, Jarrow and Morton (1992), the process for the future short rate, r, depends on the full history of the short rate. Hence, it can be written as a Markov process only with an infinite number of states.

Recently, however, Ritchken and Sankarasubramanian (1995) have identified a class of volatility structures within the Heath, Jarrow and Morton (1992) paradigm that enable the evolution of the term structure to be made Markovian with respect to two state variables and thus reduce the number of different nodes at each instant considerably. As we show in this section, this class is fairly general.

The Ritchken and Sankarasubramanian (1995) class of models is given by equation (3), where we have the following specification for the volatility:

$$\sigma(t, T) = \sigma(t)h(t, T)$$

$$h(t, T) = e^{-\int_t^T \kappa(x)\, dx}$$

(9)

Here $\sigma(t)$, the volatility of the spot interest rate at date t, can depend on all information available at time t. In particular, $\sigma(t)$ can depend on the level of the spot interest rate itself, while $\kappa(x)$ is some deterministic function.

Ritchken and Sankarasubramanian (1995) show that bond prices at time t can be computed analytically according to

$$P(t,\ T) = \left(\frac{P(0,\ T)}{P(0,\ t)}\right) e^{-\beta(t,T)(r(t)-f(0,t))-\frac{1}{2}\beta^2(t,T)\phi(t)} \tag{10}$$

with

$$\beta(t,\ T) = \int_t^T h(t,\ u)\,\mathrm{d}u$$

and

$$\phi(t) = \int_0^t \sigma^2(u)h^2(u,\ t)\,\mathrm{d}u \tag{11}$$

As before, European options can be computed according to equation (4) where the expectation is now taken under the risk-neutral process:

$$\mathrm{d}r(t) = \mu(r,\ t)\,\mathrm{d}t + \sigma(t)\,\mathrm{d}\tilde{W}(t) \tag{12}$$

with

$$\mu(r,\ t) = \kappa(t)[f(0,\ t) - r(t)] + \phi(t) + \frac{\mathrm{d}}{\mathrm{d}t}f(0,\ t) \tag{13}$$

In contrast to the process described by equation (7), the process described by equation (12) can be discretized in a Markovian (or recombining) lattice in terms of two variables, namely $r(t)$ and $\phi(t)$. An efficient way to do this has been developed by Li, Ritchken and Sankarasubramanian (1995).

If $\sigma(t)$ in equation (9) is deterministic, as for all models considered here, then $\phi(t)$ in equation (11) also becomes deterministic and process (7) can be discretized in a recombining lattice in terms of a single variable, r. In particular, for all models in Table 5.1, the volatility of the instantaneous spot interest rate is a constant, $\sigma(t) = \sigma$. Hence, the stochastic integral driving the evolution of $r(t)$ in the right-hand side of equation (12) readily follows. This is indeed more convenient than the equivalent representation of the instantaneous spot rate dynamics described by equation (7) with the volatility functions in Table 5.1.

The models described in Table 5.1 fit in the framework of equation (9) by setting $\sigma(t) = \sigma$ and

$$h(t,\ T) = \frac{1+\gamma T}{1+\gamma t}\exp\left[-\frac{\lambda}{2}(T-t)\right]$$

where

$$\kappa(x) = \frac{\lambda}{2} - \frac{\gamma}{1 + \gamma x}.$$

A detailed exposition of this model and its analytical tractability can be found in Moraleda and Vorst (1997).

5.3 THE DATA

In order to describe the estimation procedures that are mostly used for our kind of models we first describe our data sets. This enables us to explain what kind of specific problems are involved in the estimation procedures. We have two different data sets. The first contains historical yield curves from the Spanish government bond market, that is, prices of coupon-bearing Treasury bonds. However, the term structure of interest rates is not directly observable for most maturities, since it consists of prices of zero coupon bonds. It has to be estimated, basically from bond prices. We devote some attention in this section to detail in which way the term structure has been estimated. The second data set records interest rate option prices. In particular, we took data on options on 10-year Treasury bond futures traded on MEFF (Spanish Exchange of Financial Futures).

5.3.1 The Term Structure Data

The term structure of interest rates provides a characterization at a specific date of interest rates as a function of time. There are three equivalent ways of specifying this characterization: the discount function, the spot rates for different maturities and the forward rates for different maturities. These functions can be readily computed only when zero coupon bond prices (sometimes referred to as strips) are quoted in the debt markets. However, this is not the case for most markets and certainly not for the Spanish government bond market. Estimation from coupon-bearing bonds has to be implemented to infer the term structure.

In the literature, spline techniques are used to estimate the discount function. McCulloch (1971, 1975) introduced the methodology of fitting the discount function by polynomial splines of different degrees. Steeley (1991) suggested using B-splines. Fong and Vasicek (1982) implemented exponential splines. Which of these techniques to use for estimating the term structure is not a trivial matter. While the estimation should be smooth, it should also approximate the actual bond prices as accurately as possible. It is likely that in the market, options on coupon-bearing bonds will be priced based on the market price of the underlying asset. If there is a large difference between the theoretical price from a term structure model of a coupon-bearing bond and its market price, it will be very probable that the theoretical value of the option is also incorrect. Not only will the mispricing in the option be approximately equal to the mispricing in the bond in absolute terms, but in relative terms it will certainly be larger since option prices are much lower than bond prices.

The estimation of the term structure used here was carried out by AFI according to McCulloch's polynomial (cubic) spline technique for estimating the discount function.[5] This produces estimates of the discount function as a continuous function of time and yields the forward rates to be a smooth function. This estimation was done from daily prices of Spanish government bonds quoted on the Madrid Stock Exchange. The sample we use lasts for 205 trading days covering the period from 8 July 1994 to 12 May 1995. On average, there are 17 daily bond prices. These bonds pay annual coupons. In order to have more short-term interest rates from 0 to 1 year, daily prices of REPOS on Treasury bills of the Spanish government were also used.

5.3.2 Bond Future Option data

We test the models in this chapter with options on Treasury bond futures traded on MEFF (Mercado de Futuros Financieros).[6] The sample lasts for 94 trading days. It covers the period from 9 January 1995 to 23 May 1995. All prices were taken during the time interval that lasts from 4.00 p.m. to the closing time of the market (5.15 p.m.). In the case of several trades of the same option, the one that was closest to 4.00 p.m. has been taken. This is because the yield curve data available in this chapter were taken also at 4.00 p.m. The sample contains 1085 options of which 538 are calls. The remaining 547 are puts.

The underlying asset of the option is a 10-year notional bond future also traded on MEFF. The underlying asset of the future is a notional bond theoretically issued at par at the day of the maturity of the future, with a maturity of 10 years, an annual coupon payment of 9% and a face value of 10 million Pts (roughly $82 000). There are, basically, four future contracts at any time traded on MEFF, with maturities in March, June, September and December. Specifically, the future contracts expire the third Wednesday of the maturity month. We collected closing prices of Treasury bond futures traded on MEFF. The closing price is computed by MEFF as the average of a number of trades (generally the last 12 trades before the market closes at 5.15 p.m.). In the period, two bond futures were mainly traded: March 95 and June 95.

The options on these bond futures are American-style. At each time, options of two different maturities are being traded. These are the first Wednesdays of the two closest months in which the bond futures mature, i.e., March, June, September and December. An additional option can be traded. It is written on the closest time-to-maturity future and it is referred to as the monthly option. The maturity of this option is also the first Wednesday of the closest month, but only when the month is not March, June, September or December. This means that the monthly option is called into existence only for those months in which no future matures. Eventually, we have then an option expiring on the first Wednesday of every month. The underlying asset is always the closest time-to-maturity future.

5.4 THE METHODOLOGY FOR THE ESTIMATION OF THE VOLATILITY FUNCTIONS

There are two ways of estimating the parameters of the models outlined in the previous sections. One possibility is to use time series of Government bond price data to estimate the parameters that specify the dynamics of the underlying interest rate process. The other choice is to estimate implied volatilities from option price data.

The procedure for estimating the implied volatility function is straightforward and very similar to that used for stock options. The problems that might arise are due to the more complicated expressions of interest rate movements and interest rate options compared to stock options.

We focus in this chapter on the estimation through time series of the volatility functions from a data set of changes in forward rates. The data was divided into 10 partly overlapping samples of 120 days each. For each trading date in these samples, t_i, the changes in forward rates for maturities T_j, with $T_j \in \{0.5, 1, 1.5, \ldots, 9.5\}$, were taken. As a result, each basic sample includes 120 observations of 19 variables. Our data, then, take the following form:

$$\Delta f(t_i, T_1) \ldots \Delta f(t_i, T_m) \qquad i = 1, 2, \ldots, n \qquad (14)$$

where $\Delta f(t_i, T) = f(t_i + 1, T) - f(t_i, T)$ for $i = 1, \ldots, n$ and $T = T_j$ with $T_j \in \{T_1 \ldots T_m\}$; and $\Delta t_i = t_{i+1} - t_i$. Note that keeping constant the set of forward rate maturities implies that as we move on the sample, t_i, the time-to-maturity of the forward rates, $\tau = T_j - t_i$, decreases.

To estimate the volatility functions of the models, we first need to discretize the process (6). Let us define $h > 0$ as the length of a, the discrete trading interval, where N intervals of size h compose a unit of time. In such a discrete time model, the instantaneous forward rate is defined by:

$$f(t, T) = -\frac{\ln(P(t, T + h)/P(t, T))}{h}$$

where $f(t, T)$ denotes the forward interest rate at time t for the investment period $[T, T + h]$ of length h.

Heath, Jarrow and Morton (1990a) have proved that the discrete-time setting of process (6) is given by

$$f(t, T) = f(0, T) + \sum_{j=1}^{\bar{t}} a_j \sigma(jh, T)C$$

$$+ \sum_{j=1}^{\bar{t}} \frac{1}{h} \ln \left\{ \frac{1 + p\left(\exp\left(-\sum_{i=j}^{\bar{T}} \sigma(jh, ih)Ch\right) - 1\right)}{1 + p\left(\exp\left(-\sum_{i=j}^{\bar{T}-1} \sigma(jh, ih)Ch\right) - 1\right)} \right\} \quad (15)$$

where $C = \sqrt{h/(q(1-q))}$ and q stands for objective probabilities,[7] with $0 \le q \le 1$; a_j is a Bernoulli random variable, taking the value 1 with probability q and the value 0 with probability $(1 - q)$, p is the risk-adjusted probability, with $0 \le p \le 1$; $\sigma(t, T)$ denotes the volatility function; $\bar{t} = t/h$ and $\bar{T} = T/h$.

According to equation (15) the forward rates will move upward if the Bernoulli random variable a takes the value 1, and downwards otherwise. The sizes of the movements are determined by the function σ. Therefore, the variable determining the direction of the movements of the forward rates is a_j in the model. This variable is sometimes referred to as the state variable.

For the constant volatility model (HL), the general model in equation (15) reduces to (Heath, Jarrow and Morton (1990a, page 430))

$$f(t, T) = f(0, T) + \sum_{j=1}^{\bar{t}} a_j \sigma C + \frac{1}{h} \ln \left(\frac{1 + p(e^{-\bar{T}\sigma C} - 1)}{1 + p(e^{-(\bar{T}-\bar{t})\sigma C} - 1)} \right) \quad (16)$$

with σ being a strictly positive constant.

In a number of studies,[8] principal component analysis has been used to determine a reduced number of variables to explain the stochastic evolution of the term structure of interest rates over time. Typically, the historical variability of the rates is for more than 95% explained with three orthogonal factors. The first factor essentially represents a parallel shift in the term structure, while the second and third factors describe the changes in the overall slope and curvature, respectively. These factors (factor loadings) constitute the volatility function of the Heath, Jarrow and Morton model (1990b). In particular, they assume proportional volatility functions given by

$$\sigma(t, T) = \sigma(T - t)f(t, T) \quad (17)$$

Assuming proportional volatility functions as equation (17) would have allowed us to take the factor loadings from the principal component analysis as the estimators of these functions. This is basically what Heath, Jarrow and Morton (1990b) do, leading to a straightforward estimation of the model. Moreover, such volatility functions match market data. But it results in an evolution of the term structure that is non-Markovian with the dramatic reduction in computational tractability that such models imply. Note indeed that function (17) cannot be embedded in the Ritchken and Sankarasubramanian (1995) class of volatilities given by equation (9).

Instead, simpler choices such as those in Table 5.1 lead to term structure dynamics that can be represented according to Markov processes with one state variable as shown in Section 5.2. Unfortunately, these specifications of the volatility cannot retain as much explanatory power as the former proportional ones. Furthermore, the volatility functions in Table 5.1 cannot be directly inferred from a principal component analysis. This is because these specifications of the volatility function no longer directly match the principal component extracted from the historical forward changes.[9]

An indirect estimation for the discrete-time processes has been proposed by Hess (1994). He proposes to take the factor scores as estimators of the state variables a_j in equation (15). As previously outlined, the state variables determine the direction of the movements of the yield curve. Thus if $a_j = 1$, the forward rates move upwards, while if $a_j = 0$, the movement of the term structure is downwards. The size of the movements of the yield curve, and how they affect each maturity of the forward rates, is determined by the specification of the volatility function. As a very first approximation, we can proceed as follows. Let the state variable a_j be equal to 1 if the jth factor score occurs to be positive at time t_j. Consequently, when the factor scores are negative we set a_j equal to 0. But this would just be a rough approximation. Implicitly, we would be assuming that the time interval between observations (Δ) and in the model (h) are the same and, hence, only one movement of the yield curve per trading day would be suitable in our estimation procedure.

To obtain a better fit, we can reduce h, the time step in our model. This would allow for several movements of the yield curve per trading day in the model, although only the daily effect is observed. Then the factor scores would no longer be estimated realizations of singular Bernoulli random variables. Instead, they would be sums of Δ/h realizations of the state variable. Thus, if we set $\Delta = nh$, then $a_j = \sum_{i=1}^{n} s_i$ where s is a Bernoulli random variable taking the values $\{0, 1\}$. The factor scores would be estimators of $a_j \in \{0, 1, 2, \ldots, n\}$, where a_j is the number of upward movements within the period and $n - a_j$ denotes the number of downward ones.

The problem we face is inferring the state variables in our model, sums of Bernoulli random variables, from the outcome of the factor analysis (specifically, from the factor scores). We proceed as follows. Let, for example, $n = 3$, so that $\Delta = 3h$, $a_j = \sum_{i=1}^{3} s_i$ and the factor scores being estimators of $a_j \in \{0, 1, 2, 3\}$, where a_j accounts for the upward movements and $3 - a_j$ denotes the downward ones. In order to maintain similar probability structures it is natural to proceed as follows. The intervals for which the factor scores are higher than 1 are understood as three upward movements in that particular trading day and we make

$a_j = 3$. If the factor scores (fs) are smaller than -1, the assumption of three downward movements is made and we set $a_j = 0$. Consistently, we make $a_j = 2$ if only two upward movements (and one downward) happened ($0 \leqslant fs_j < 1$), and finally we let $a_j = 1$ if $-1 \leqslant fs_j \leqslant 0$ which would mean that one upward (and two downward) movements took place at the time considered.[10]

With the state variables a_j so defined, it is now possible to estimate the parameters of the models in Table 5.1 with a non-linear optimization routine.[11] The function to be minimized is defined as the squared errors of the difference between the forward rate changes given by the models and the observed (historical) forward rate changes. To compute the forward rate changes given by the models we use the previously estimated state variables a_j.

5.5 RESULTS

For a fixed maturity T, the evolution of the forward rates was modelled by equation (3). Consider now the set of forward rate observations in our sample given by the maturity set $T_1, \ldots, T_m$ and arranged as shown in equation (14). Notice then that T_1 determines the largest data set to be considered: that where t_n equals T_1.

On the other hand, the largest data set possible would be desirable in order to obtain accurate estimates and to analyse the stability of the parameters through time. However, as explained by Hull (1995), the volatility function changes over time, and data that are too old may no longer be relevant. Furthermore, if, for example, T_1 is chosen to be two years, then the shortest maturity forward rates are disregarded for most of the observations. As a result, T_1 should be chosen to allow for sufficient number of historical observations, but reasonably small for the short-term yield curve not to be systematically disregarded. The choice in this chapter is $T_1 = 0.5$, i.e., half a year or 120 trading days. Hence, our largest possible choice for t_n is also half a year.[12]

The starting date in our option sample is 9 January 1995. At the preceding trading date, 6 January 1995, we take backwards 120 daily yield curve observations. For this data set we estimate the model parameters as explained in Section 5.4. We can then use the models in Table 5.1 to price the options in the market. However, over time, new information may arrive at the markets. It would not be too realistic to keep the estimated volatility constant for a long period. It is our choice in this chapter to re-estimate the model parameters every two weeks. In doing so, we take backwards again 120 trading days term structure observations and we re-estimate the model parameters. These new estimators are used for pricing options during the immediately following two weeks. After this the whole procedure is repeated. Overall, this routine is implemented ten times. The following subsection details the results of the estimation procedure.

5.5.1 Estimation of the Volatility Function

As explained in Section 5.4, we estimate the state variables of the models from a principal component analysis and from this, model parameters are estimated running an error minimization routine. The function to be minimized was defined as the squared errors of the difference between the forward rate changes given by the models and those observed in the markets. The remaining errors will be referred to as residual errors. Clearly, the lower the residual errors, the higher the explanatory power of the model. The precise coefficients to be estimated are the volatility function, $\sigma(t, T)$, and the probabilities p and q as given in equation (15). In all cases p and q have to be estimated, whereas the number of volatility parameters varies across the models.

Table 5.2 shows the parameter estimates for the three models considered for the ten sample periods. However, the estimated values for the objective probability, q, are not tabulated. Their values turned out to be 0.5 for all models and samples considered. This is in agreement with previous studies (see Hess (1994)). Moreover, it could have been to some extent expected, since the forward rate dynamics in equation (15) are hardly sensitive to the probability parameter p. Therefore, estimated values for p were not expected to differ much from those provided as initial condition in the estimation procedure.[13] The residual error (Res. err.) for each model and sample is also given in Table 5.2. It follows that the humped volatility model reduces the residual errors most, as could have been expected since this is a three-parameter model. We shall return to this point later in this section.

Table 5.2 also shows that γ is always positive for the MV model. Humped volatility shapes are just obtained in this model if $2\gamma > \lambda$. It is confirmed in Table 5.2 that this is the case for all samples considered apart from sample V, in which $2\gamma < \lambda$, so that the volatility is a decreasing function of time. Overall, therefore, nine out of the ten samples studied give empirical support to the humped volatility model. The shape of the hump is not uniform along the samples, though. In fact, the hump is rather sharp for samples I, II, III and IV while it is smoother and wider for samples VI to X. Figure 5.1 plots some of these shapes for illustrative purposes. Specifically, we draw the volatility function, $\sigma(t, T)$, for the MV model estimated from samples I, III, VIII and X (solid line). Notice that the volatility function for the HW model is also plotted (dotted line).

Comparison of the HW and MV volatility functions in Figure 5.1 leads to an interesting point. Indeed, λ in the HW model turns out to be negative in samples IV and VI to X making positive the overall sign of the exponential coefficient of this model.[14] Clearly, such an increasing volatility function is implausible for all maturities since it would lead to an explosion of interest rates. Therefore, negative values for λ in the exponential volatility model should be precluded. But this reduces the model to the constant volatility one for samples IV and VI to X.[15] Notice, moreover, that quite apart from the theoretical disadvantages of the

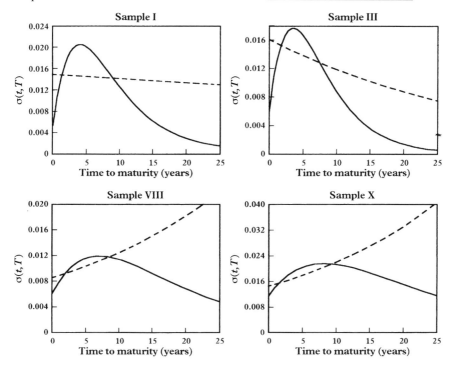

Figure 5.1 Volatility function for the HW (dotted line) and MV (solid line) model

constant volatility model, the differences in the residual errors become now apparent. This can be verified by comparing the residual errors (Res. err.) in Table 5.2 for the HW and MV model in samples I, II, III and V; and the HL and MV model in samples IV and VI to X where, as explained, the HW model reduces to the HL model.

It should be noticed, however, that the estimate for λ in the HW model results to be positive for samples I to III even though humped volatility structures are found for these samples with the MV model. As Figure 5.1 illustrates, this is because the downward part of the hump is dominant.[16] Although Figure 5.1 sufficiently clarifies this fact, it can be further verified by comparing the residual errors of both models in Table 5.2 for samples I to III.

In conclusion, not only are serious inconsistencies found when estimating the exponential volatility model but the fit to real yield curve data is largely improved by using the humped volatility model. Our yield curve data frequently reveals that the mean reverting effect is not as straightforward as generally believed.

We address next the analysis of the results for the probability parameters in Table 5.2. This table shows that both the risk-neutral and objective probabilities, p and q respectively, are very close to 0.5. In particular, q is systematically equal

Table 5.2 Models' parameter estimates

I

	σ	λ	γ	p	Res. err.
HL	0.0146	0.0108		0.5171	0.008 548
HW	0.0150	0.4587		0.5072	0.008 543
MV	0.0047		2.4401	0.5001	0.007 024

II

	σ	λ	γ	p	Res. err.
HL	0.0142	0.0306		0.4781	0.015 835
HW	0.0158	0.5244		0.4790	0.015 602
MV	0.0042		3.9045	0.4760	0.009 352

III

	σ	λ	γ	p	Res. err.
HL	0.0134	0.0613		0.4737	0.014 167
HW	0.0161	0.5162		0.4752	0.012 827
MV	0.0060		1.7886	0.4716	0.006 459

IV

	σ	λ	γ	p	Res. err.
HL	0.0146	−0.1501		0.5102	0.021 490
HW	0.0076	0.2208		0.4989	0.020 864
MV	0.0026		2.3531	0.4760	0.017 835

V^a

	σ	λ	γ	p	Res. err.
HL	0.0117	0.0070		0.4964	0.003 562
HW	0.0119	0.0844		0.4966	0.003 561
MV	0.0141		0.0052	0.4968	0.003 476

VI

	σ	λ	γ	p	Res. err.
HL	0.0157	−0.0042		0.4889	0.006 677
HW	0.0155	0.0827		0.4887	0.006 676
MV	0.0112		0.1517	0.4884	0.006 379

VII

	σ	λ	γ	p	Res. err.
HL	0.0148	−0.0932		0.4846	0.008 671
HW	0.0116	0.0066		0.4799	0.007 908
MV	0.0085		0.1460	0.4834	0.006 902

VIII

	σ	λ	γ	p	Res. err.
HL	0.0110	−0.0751		0.4667	0.009 941
HW	0.0086	0.2232		0.4549	0.008 622
MV	0.0061		0.4651	0.4884	0.007 783

IX

	σ	λ	γ	p	Res. err.
HL	0.0110	−0.1452		0.4758	0.010 543
HW	0.0085	0.2464		0.4722	0.007 789
MV	0.0039		1.3158	0.4759	0.007 480

X

	σ	λ	γ	p	Res. err.
HL	0.0183	−0.0844		0.5156	0.008 639
HW	0.0143	0.1851		0.5148	0.007 793
MV	0.0112		0.3680	0.4884	0.007 489

I–X stand for the 10 samples whose period are reported below. Each of these samples account for 120 daily observations of the yield curve. Sample I: 8 July 1994 to 6 January 1995; Sample II: 22 July 1994 to 20 January 1995; Sample III: 8 August 1994 to 3 February 1995; Sample IV: 23 August 1994 to 17 February 1995; Sample V: 6 September 1994 to 3 March 1995; Sample VI: 21 September 1994 to 17 March 1995; Sample VII: 4 October 1994 to 31 March 1995; Sample VIII: 17 October 1994 to 12 April 1995; Sample IX: 31 October 1994 to 28 April 1995; Sample X: 14 November 1994 to 12 May 1995.

[a] All parameters reported for sample V are estimated from the sample period 21 September 1994 to 3 March 1995. This is a subsample accounting for 100 days rather than 120. The estimation for the sample 6 September 1994 to 3 March 1995 turns out to be highly biased while the one reported seems steadier.

to 0.5 whereas p always lies in the interval [0.45, 0.52]. Moreover, the forward rates are hardly sensitive to changes in the objective probability coefficient, q. In turn, the yield curve dynamics are very sensitive to changes in the risk-neutral probability p. This proximity to 0.5 of both parameters is in agreement with a theoretical result by Heath, Jarrow and Morton (1990a). They proved that the discrete-time process (15) converges in probability to its continuous-time counterpart process (6) if and only if $p = q = 0.5$ in process (15). Thus, the limiting forward rate process is insensitive to the parameters p and q. Accordingly, these authors argue that an estimation procedure that involves inverting the contingent claims values (implied volatility estimation from option data) should be done with the limiting processes. This is because the option market is a continuous-time economy and, hence, the option value should be insensitive to the probabilities (see Heath, Jarrow and Morton (1990a), page 438). Whether this also applies to our model is discussed next.

In particular, we wish to study the estimates of the volatility function achieved by the discrete-time process where no restrictions are imposed on p and q, and the limiting process where p and q are forced to take their limiting value 0.5. We study four subsamples of each of the ten samples reported in Table 5.2. More precisely, the last date of each sample we take backwards 120 (entire sample whose results are shown in Table 5.2), 100, 80 and 60 observations. These subsamples are referred to as A, B, C and D, respectively. For ease of exposition we restrict our attention to the constant volatility model (HL).

Columns dt in Table 5.3 report the volatility parameters for the HL model estimated from the discrete-time process (16) where p and q were allowed to take any value in the interval [0, 1]. Columns ct in Table 5.3 show the estimation of the volatility function using the limiting process for the HL model. As previously explained, the limiting process is obtained by setting $p = q = 0.5$ in equation (16). Comparing columns dt and ct in Table 5.3, it is obvious that the dt estimators are more stable than those produced by the limiting process. Moreover, in many cases the ct volatility parameters are highly misestimated, yielding in some cases null values for the volatility in the HL model. That is, process (16) is very sensitive to the risk-neutral probability p, and although its value is very close to 0.5 (see Table 5.2), forcing it to take this exact value leads, in many cases, to a misspecification of the volatility coefficients. As a consequence, the probability parameters should be left free.

5.5.2 Yield Curve and Future Prices

Pricing options with the models in Table 5.1 only requires as inputs the initial yield curve on the valuation date and the volatility function parameters.[17] The volatility function is estimated as shown in Section 5.4. The initial yield curve has to be estimated from bond prices as explained in Section 5.3. It was explained in

Table 5.3 Estimates of σ for the constant volatility (HL) model

	I		II		III		IV		V	
	dt	ct	dt	ct	dt	ct	dt	ct	dt	ct
A	0.0146	0.0106	0.0142	0.0290	0.0134	0.0251	0.0146	0.0081	0.0171	0.0110
B	0.0124	0.0190	0.0113	0.0148	0.0158	0.0059	0.0137	0.0047	0.0117	0.0125
C	0.0134	0.0121	0.0147	0.0100	0.0127	0.0085	0.0139	0.0152	0.0109	0.0040
D	0.0129	0.0089	0.0135	0.0037	0.0119	0.0136	0.0144	0.0163	0.0163	0.0211

	VI		VII		VIII		IX		X	
	dt	ct	dt	ct	dt	ct	dt	ct	dt	ct
A	0.0157	0.0082	0.0148	0.0170	0.0110	0.0285	0.0110	0.0231	0.0183	0.0101
B	0.0140	0	0.0111	0	0.0102	0	0.0152	0.0352	0.0172	0.0105
C	0.0111	0	0.0144	0.0053	0.0166	0.0297	0.0165	0.0143	0.0192	0.0042
D	0.0157	0	0.0159	0.0181	0.0219	0.0149	0.0188	0.0184	0.0172	0.0095

I–X stand for the sample periods reported in the note to Table 5.2. Each of these samples accounts for 120 daily observations. A, B, C, D are subsamples of each of the previous samples. A accounts for the total sample, i.e. 120 observations, or, alternatively six-month yield curve data. B, C and D correspond to subsamples of 100, 80, and 60 observation respectively. Finally, dt denotes the discrete-time processes as given by equation (15) while ct denotes the limiting process, i.e., the probabilities p and q in equation (15) are fixed equal to 0.5.

Section 5.3 that the estimation of the term structure of interest rates is not trivial. Moreover, such estimation faces a tradeoff between smoothness and accuracy. To give some insights into the accuracy of the estimation of the term structure, we compute the errors we make in pricing bond futures. The 10-year Treasury bond futures are traded in MEFF, so that market prices are available. Their model price can be calculated from the yield curve. Moreover, these are the underlying instruments of the options we consider later in this chapter. Table 5.4 reports some descriptive statistics of the pricing errors defined as model price minus market price. Notice that the models systematically underprice the futures in the market. The errors, though, are not large. On average, we make an error of -0.35 and -0.60 percentage points over the nominal value of the bond futures of March 95 and June 95, respectively. This means a relative absolute error of, on average, 0.0044 and 0.0080.[18] It is important to realize that these errors may partially be caused by a lack of synchronicity of the data. Recall that the yield curve data were estimated with bond prices taken at 4.00 p.m. while the bond future data consists of closing prices. The closing price is computed by MEFF as the average of a number of trades (generally the last 12 trades before the market closes at 5.15 p.m.). Due to the liquidity of these instruments, most of the references for calculating the closing price are taken in the interval from 5.00 to 5.15 p.m. Therefore, there is roughly a gap of one hour between the different data sets. Given the underpricing of futures, it is likely that all option pricing models produce biased theoretical values. However, all models price bond futures exactly in the same way. They will all be affected by the same bias and, hence, the comparison between the models is still possible.

5.5.3 Option Pricing

Descriptive statistics for pricing errors of options produced by the different models are shown in Table 5.5. The pricing error is defined as model price minus

Table 5.4 Summary of bond future pricing errors

Bond future	Av. err.[a]	St. dev.[b]	Av. rel. abs. err.[c]
March-95	-0.35	0.23	0.0044
June-95	-0.60	0.43	0.0080

The sample period is 6 January 1995 to 26 May 1995. The total number of trading dates in the sample is 94. During 36 trading dates options with the March-95 bond future as the underlying asset were being traded. The June-95 bond future was the underlying asset of traded options on 91 trading dates. The price of the bond future is the same for all models considered. It depends on the initial yield curve. [a]Av. err. = Average error where the pricing error is defined as model price minus market price. [b]St. dev. err. = Standard Deviation of the errors defined as (a). [c]Av. rel. abs. err. = average of (Pricing error/Market price).

Table 5.5 Descriptive statistics for pricing errors

		All options			
Model	Av. error[a]	Var. err[b]	Av. abs. err[c]	Av. rel. abs. err.[d]	Sum sqr.err.[d]
HL	−0.09	0.09	0.21	0.39	103.42
HW	−0.11	0.09	0.22	0.40	106.19
MV	−0.11	0.10	0.24	0.45	118.93
		Call options			
Model	Av. error[a]	Var. err[b]	Av. abs. err[c]	Av. rel. abs. err.[d]	Sum sqr.err.[d]
HL	−0.17	0.07	0.22	0.40	57.31
HW	−0.20	0.07	0.25	0.45	62.20
MV	−0.20	0.08	0.26	0.47	67.24
		Put options			
Model	Av. error[a]	Var. err[b]	Av. abs. err[c]	Av. rel. abs. err.[d]	Sum sqr.err.[d]
HL	0.00	0.09	0.20	0.37	46.11
HW	−0.02	0.08	0.20	0.36	43.99
MV	−0.02	0.10	0.23	0.42	51.69

[a] Av. err. = Average error where the pricing error is defined as model price minus market price. [b] Var. err. = Variance of the errors defined as (a). [c] Av. abs. err. = average pricing absolute error. [d] Av. rel. abs. err. = average of (Pricing error/Market price). [e] Sum sqr. err. = Sum of the squared pricing error. All prices of both market and models were computed as a percentage of the face value of the underlying asset.

market price. All option prices are computed as percentage of the face value of the underlying asset. Notice that the option prices given by the models will be affected by the mispricing in the futures reported in Table 5.4. In particular, the mispricing in the option will be approximately equal to the mispricing in the bond future in absolute terms, but in relative terms it will certainly be larger since option prices are much lower than bond prices.

Table 5.5 shows that the constant volatility (HL) model provides the best fit to the data. In fact, it is the model that makes the lowest error on average and the total squared errors are also smaller. However, the mispricing for all models is very similar. They all drastically underprice the call options, while, on average, provide a better fit to the puts.

The main conclusion, however, that can be drawn from Table 5.5 is that the models poorly match the data. In fact, the average mispricing of the models ranges from 39% at best to 45% in the worst case. In both cases, this is the mispricing percentage over the options quoted in the market.

There are three reasons for these disappointing results. First, we use historical volatility, where options in the markets are priced based on expectation of the volatility of the underlying asset over the remaining time to maturity of the option. If, for example, the market expects certain announcements about the interest rate policy of the Central Bank or some other government agency, this might cause more uncertainty. Hence, traders might increase the volatility that they put in their models above the historically observed level. Second, although the derived theoretical prices are arbitrage-free prices this, of course, only holds if the dynamics of bond prices are indeed correctly described by the models. Since we cannot fully explain observed bond price dynamics with our models the theoretical prices do not have to be arbitrage-free prices. It is well known that market participants often use a model developed by Black (1976) for pricing bond options. If one applies this methodology to a large portfolio of options and bonds, Black's model certainly leads to inconsistencies. However Miltersen, Sandmann and Sondermann (1995) have recently proved that for individual bond options one can specify a dynamic process for the price of the underlying bond such that Black's model gives exactly the no-arbitrage price. The inconsistencies are due to the fact that if these processes really describe the price behaviour of a portfolio of bonds then there are arbitrage opportunities within the bond portfolio. Finally, the no-arbitrage argument is based upon the assumptions of continuous trading and frictionless markets. Hence, small arbitrage opportunities cannot be exploited due to market frictions. Market makers might increase the prices of options if there is a net demand for certain kind of options to just below the level at which arbitrage opportunities can be exploited in markets with frictions. We think that the first reason might be the most relevant for this study.

5.6 CONCLUSIONS

We have studied in this chapter the empirical behaviour of three one-factor interest rate models as developed by Ho and Lee (1986), Hull and White (1990) and Moraleda and Vorst (1997). The same general setting has been used for all models. In particular, they all have been embedded in the Ritchken and Sankarasubramanian (1995) framework. This is a general model within the Heath, Jarrow and Morton (1992) paradigm, that allows for pricing American options through recombining binomial trees. Moreover, the same estimation procedure has been run in all cases. Specifically, we have used an indirect estimation procedure from a principal component analysis. The model parameters have been estimated from daily yield curve data. The parameter estimates have been used to price bond future options traded in MEFF.

Humped volatility shapes as modelled by Moraleda and Vorst (1997) have been found in 90% of the samples studied. Moreover, serious inconsistencies are found when estimating the exponential volatility model. In particular, the exponential coefficient of this model, λ, has a negative estimated value in 60% of the samples. Since this makes interest rates explode, λ should be precluded to become negative.

The humped volatility model (MV) turns out to be the model that best explains the yield curve movements. In fact, it is the model that most reduces the residual errors but it also has one more parameter. This higher explanatory power is even more evident when restricting the exponential coefficient, λ, of the HW model to be non-negative. However, this ability no longer applies when pricing options. In fact, the simpler constant volatility model (HL) minimizes the option-pricing errors. Nevertheless, the errors are rather large for all models. There have been given three reasons that might cause this frustrating result. First, historical volatility might not be a correct indication of expected future volatility in the market. Second, the arbitrage-free prices are based on the assumption that the underlying bond prices are correctly described by our models. Finally, market imperfections do not allow the exploitation of all arbitrage opportunities.

ENDNOTES

1. See, for example, Kahn (1991), Heath *et al.* (1992) and Amin and Morton (1994) who have found, for different periods and currencies, humped volatility structures in the yield curve dynamics.
2. While the exponentially decaying model by Heath, Jarrow and Morton (1992) matches the initial term structure by construction, Hull and White (1990) allowed the drift parameter of Vasicek's model to be time dependent so that they exogenously fit the initial yield curve. As a result, both models are equivalent (see Moraleda and Vorst (1997) for a formal proof). Nevertheless, Hull and White (1990) were the first to incorporate the initial yield curve as observed in the markets to a model with Vasicek's volatility. For this historical reason we choose their name to refer to this model. However, as with the HL model, the derivation of the model that we use throughout this chapter is due to Heath, Jarrow and Morton (1992).
3. The Moraleda and Vorst (1997) model as given by equation (8) is somehow related to a previous model by Mercurio and Moraleda (1996) where humped volatilities are already modelled. The latter authors considered a volatility structure given by $\sigma(t, T) = \sigma[1 + \gamma(T - t)] \exp[-(\lambda/2)(T - t)]$, which is humped (for $2\gamma > \lambda$) and stationary. But such a choice leads to a model that cannot be used for pricing American-style claims with a recombining lattice. On the other hand, the Moraleda and Vorst (1997) model can price American options with recombining lattices, although it is no longer stationary.
4. Notice that most of the interest-rate derivatives can be written as portfolios of derivatives on discount bonds.
5. AFI stands for Analistas Financieros Internacionales (International Financial Analysts). We thank Amadeo Reynes and Inmaculada Gomez from AFI that kindly provided us with the estimation of the discount function, that, as explained in this section, fully characterizes the term structure of interest rates. Thus, we are given the estimated coefficients for the discount function for each day in the sample (for the different intervals into which the time horizon is divided). For doing this estimation, AFI used five knots in all the dates considered, i.e. the time horizon was divided in four parts. The size of these parts changes daily according to the usual criteria.
6. Spanish Exchange of Financial Futures. We thank Miguel Angel Rodriguez from MEFF who kindly provided us with the option and future data.

7. The objective probabilities are those of the general process (3), while the risk-adjusted probabilities are those of the the process under the no-arbitrage restriction (5).

8. Dybvig (1989), Heath, Jarrow and Morton (1990b), Steeley (1991) and Strickland (1993) are relevant examples.

9. Heath, Jarrow and Morton (1990b) choose a volatility function as (17). They use a data set of proportional changes in forward rates in order to run a principal component analysis. To directly match the outcome of such analysis, they select the observations in a convenient way (disregarding some forward rate maturities). In particular, they just look at forward rates whose time-to-maturity is given by $\tau_i = (T_{j+i} - t_j)$ with i denoting the different maturities considered and j standing for the different dates in the sample. By doing so, the outcome of the component analysis exactly matches their volatility function, which was precisely a function of the time-to-maturity.

10. This choice for the intervals of the factor scores seemed natural to us in relating the coefficients a_j and the factor scores from the factor analysis. Notice that the probabilities associated with a standard normal distribution for the intervals $\{(-\infty, -1], (-1, 0], (0, 1], (1, \infty)\}$ are $\{0.15, 0.35, 0.35, 0.15\}$. In the case of the considered state variables, the probability distribution for $a_j = \{0, 1, 2, 3\}$ is $\{1/8, 3/8, 3/8, 1/8\}$. However, different choices may be possible as long as they maintain a relationship as shown for the coefficients and the factor scores.

11. We used a Newton–Raphson routine that was run in Gauss.

12. Hull (1995), facing the historical estimation of stock volatility, advises a data set ranging from 90 to 180 daily observations.

13. The initial value for p in the estimation routine was chosen to equal 0.5 for all samples and models considered. As explained below, this is its limiting value.

14. Similar results for λ in the exponential volatility model were found by Amin and Morton (1994).

15. The volatility coefficients as shown in Table 5.2 have been used for pricing bond future options whose results are studied in the next section. This is similar to what Amin and Morton (1994) do but, as explained, if the model is to be used practically, negative values for λ should be precluded.

16. Note that the volatility functions in Figure 5.1 are plotted for 25 years to maturity. However, we use only yield curve data up to 10 years for estimating model parameters.

17. This is, of course, apart from the specific features of the options to be priced.

18. Both market and model prices of the bond futures are given in percentage over its nominal value. Thus, the average and standard deviation of the pricing errors are also given in the same unit. In turn, the average relative absolute error reported in the last

COMMENT

M.H.A. DAVIS

This chapter presents an econometric analysis of term structure models for interest-rate derivative pricing, in the context of the Spanish Treasury yield curve. I wish to comment mainly on the uses and abuses of these models rather than on the details of the parameter estimation procedure in which the authors are definitely more expert than I am.

The authors start off by reviewing some of the standard term structure models. As they point out, the starting point can be regarded as the collection $p(t, T)$ of prices at time t of zero-coupon bonds maturing at time T. The corresponding *yield* is $R = -\log p(t, T)/(T - t)$, so that $p(t, T) = \exp(-R(T - t))$, and the *forward rate* is $f(t, T) = -\partial \log p(t, T)/\partial T$; this is the rate available at time t over a short time interval $[T, T + dT]$. The *short rate* is $r(t) = f(t, t)$. Most term structure models either model the short rate as a diffusion process or are 'whole-yield' models modelling $f(t, \cdot)$ (this is the 'HJM' approach). A key result of HJM is that under the risk-neutral measure, needed for derivative pricing, the drift of the forward rate process is determined by the volatility, so the model is completely specified once the volatility function $\sigma(t, T)$ is given. One of the innovations here is a new parameterization $\sigma(t, T) = \sigma \, e^{-\lambda(T-t)/2}(1 + \gamma T)/(1 + \gamma t)$ introduced by the authors in another recent paper which allows for 'humped' volatility structures.

The market the authors are considering is the Spanish Treasury market. The yield curve is estimated, using cubic splines, from a rather limited number (around 17) government bonds together with some short-term interest rates. The options considered are options on Treasury bond futures. The authors do not explain in the chapter why they considered this particular market rather than a larger and more liquid one. Parameters are estimated for various specific models by a discretization of the basic HJM model, by minimizing mean square differences between forward rate changes predicted by the models and observed in the market. In general, the results support the use of the authors' own 'humped-volatility' model as providing a more realistic representation of the data. The fitted models are quite successful in predicting the prices of bond futures, but fail completely in estimating option prices. I do not think this is at all surprising.

From the trader's point of view, models are required for two closely related purposes: pricing and hedging. For the former, the models are invariably used in the following way: they are 'calibrated' to current market prices of liquid instruments (say, European swaptions) and then used to price some OTC product (say, a Bermuda swaption). I do not think there is any 'theoretical inconsistency' in this approach, as claimed by Moraleda and Vorst in their Introduction: the models are simply being used as interpolation formulas and should be thought of in that way, not as attempts at representing some 'true' price distribution. It is too much to expect that a model with parameters estimated from historical data will succeed in matching market option prices to an accuracy adequate for trading. Where reality intervenes is in connection with the second use of the model, namely hedging. The models are used (after calibration, of course) to determine hedge parameters which are then used to rebalance the book. The real test of a model is whether this procedure succeeds in capturing the value of the option as evaluated by the model. Recent work by myself and Han Lee (1996) and by El Karoui, Jeanblanc-Picqué and Shreve (1995) has shown that successful hedging is possible even if the model is quite inaccurate, as long as the volatility is not underestimated. My feeling is that models should be evaluated from this point of view rather than in terms of some abstract 'goodness of fit'.

REPLY

J.M. MORALEDA AND A.C.F. VORST

The discussant raises two main issues. First, he would like to know why we consider the Spanish bond and option market rather than a larger and more liquid one. Second, and probably more relevant, the discussant does not see any theoretical inconsistency in the 'implied volatility' technique. He explains the trader's point of view in which models are required for pricing and hedging. The discussant's opinion is that hedging is the real test for interest rate models.

The Spanish futures and options market (MEFF) is, as the discussant points out, certainly smaller and less liquid than, say, LIFFE or CBOT. However, MEFF is the fourth market in Europe closing the gap with respect to the French MATIF, ranked third after LIFFE and the German DTB. We agree with the discussant that a larger market such as LIFFE or CBOT may be more reliable for testing any model in terms of deepness and efficiency of the market. However, while some research and tests have been done using futures and option data from LIFFE and specially CBOT, little attention has been paid to other European countries' markets. Our study is, to our knowledge, the first investigating term-structure models from MEFF data. The interest shown by MEFF in our research and their efforts in providing us any required data also motivated our study of this particular market.

Concerning the question whether it is 'theoretically consistent' to use the models as interpolation tools for pricing OTC-products, we must say that we partly disagree with the discussant. As he explains, the standard procedure followed by banks and institutions is to calibrate the models (either equity, currency or interest rate models) to current market prices of actively traded derivatives and then use the estimated parameters for pricing more complicated and less liquid instruments. As also explained by the discussant, the models are therefore used as interpolation formulas. But the fact that they are used in this way does not mean that this is theoretically correct. In fact, if every single moment that one wants to price some particular derivative the model is calibrated to current market prices, one is actually changing the model parameters, say, every day (in practice this is even done several times per day). However, most of these models, and certainly those under consideration in this chapter, assume that model parameters are constant over time. It is therefore inconsistent to assume that the parameters are constant over time and then change them every single day (or every time we need to price some option). An extended discussion of these issues can be found in Amin and Ng (1995).

A different matter is that if the models are used as they are meant to, i.e. with constant parameters (say, estimated historically), they completely fail to match the option prices being traded in the markets. For this reason practitioners do not trust the models and use them simply as interpolation formulas. As long as these interpolation formulas give correct prices this might be fine, but it does not make the methodology theoretically consistent.

The discussant claims that the real test of term structure models is in both pricing and hedging. We agree with the discussant that hedging is a key concept and selecting a model should seriously regard this issue. Also the references given by the discussant are very relevant concerning this issue.

REFERENCES

Amin, K.I. and Morton, A.J. (1994) Implied volatility functions in arbitrage-free term structure models. *Journal of Financial Economics* **35**, 141–80.

Amin, K.I. and Ng, V.K. (1995) Heath, Jarrow and Morton implied volatility functions and conditional heteroskedasticity models: information in Eurodollar futures options. Working paper, Lehman Brothers, New York.

Black, F. (1976) The pricing of commodity contracts. *Journal of Financial Economics* **3**, 167–79.

Black, F. and Karasinski, P. (1991) Bond and option pricing when short rates are lognormal. *Financial Analysts Journal* **47**, 52–9.

Brennan, M. and Schwartz, E. (1982) An equilibrium model of bond pricing and a test of market efficiency. *Journal of Financial and Quantitative Analysis* **17**, 301–29.

Brown, R.H. and Dybvig, P.H. (1986) The empirical implications of the Cox–Ingersoll–Ross theory of the term structure of interest rates. *Journal of Finance* **41**, 617–30.

Brown, R.H. and Schaefer, S.M. (1994) The term structure of real interest rates and the Cox, Ingersoll and Ross model. *Journal of Financial Economics* **35**, 3–42.

Chan K.C., Karolyi, G.A., Longstaff, F.A. and Sanders, A.B. (1992) An empirical comparison of alternative models of the short-term interest rate. *Journal of Finance* **47**, 1209–27.

Cox J.C., Ingersoll, J.E. and Ross, S.A. (1985) A theory of the term structure of interest rates. *Econometrica* **53**, 385–408.

Davis, M. and Lee, H. (1996) Coping with model error in hedging interest rate derivative products. Presented at Global Derivatives '96, ICBI Conferences, Paris, April.

Dietrich-Campbell, B. and E. Schwartz (1986) Valuing debt options, empirical evidence. *Journal of Financial Economics* **16**, 321–43.

Dybvig, P.H. (1989) Bond and option pricing based on the current term structure. Working paper, Washington University, St Louis, Missouri.

El Karoui, N., Jeanblanc-Picqué, M. and Shreve, S.E. (1995) Robustness of the Black and Scholes formula. Preprint, Université Paris VI, September.

Flesaker, B. (1993) Testing the Heath–Jarrow–Morton/Ho–Lee model of interest rate contingent claims pricing. *Journal of Financial and Quantitative Analysis* **28**, 483–95.

Fong, H.G. and Vasicek, O.A. (1982) Term structure modeling using exponential splines. *Journal of Finance* **37**, 339–48.

Heath D., Jarrow, R. and Morton, A. (1990a) Bond pricing and the term structure of interest rates: a discrete time approximation. *Journal of Financial and Quantitative Analysis* **25**, 419–40.

Heath D., Jarrow, R. and Morton, A. (1990b) Contingent claims valuation with a random evolution of interest rates. *Review of Futures Markets* **9**, 55–76.

Heath D., Jarrow, R. and Morton, A. (1992) Bond pricing and the term structure of interest rates: a new methodology for contingent claims valuation. *Econometrica* **60**, 77–105.

Heath D., Jarrow, R., Morton, A.J. and Spindel, M. (1992) Easier done than said. *RISK* **5**, 77–80.

Hess, S.D. (1994) Estimation of discrete time multiple factor models of the term structure of interest rates. University of Konstanz, Faculty of Economics and Statistics, Technical report.

Ho, T.S.Y. and Lee, S.-B. (1986) Term structure movements and pricing interest rate contingent claims. *Journal of Finance* **41**, 1011–29.

Hull, J. (1995) *Options, Futures and Other Derivative Securities*, 3rd edition, Prentice-Hall, Englewood Cliffs, NJ.

Hull, J. and White, A. (1990) Pricing interest rate derivative securities. *Review of Financial Studies* **3**, 573–92.

Hull, J. and White, A. (1993) One-factor interest rate models and the valuation of interest-rate derivative securities. *Journal of Financial and Quantitative Analysis* **28**, 235–54.

Kahn, R. (1991) Fixed income risk modeling. In F.J. Fabrozzi (ed.), *The Handbook of Fixed Income Securities*, 3rd edition, pp. 1307–19. Business one Irwin, Homewood, IL.

Li A., Ritchken, P. and Sankarasubramanian, L. (1995) Lattice models for pricing American interest rate claims. *Journal of Finance* **1**, 719–37.

McCulloch, J.H. (1971) :'Measuring the term structure of interest rates. *Journal of Business* **46**, 19–31.

McCulloch, J.H. (1975) An estimate of the liquidity premium. *Journal of Political Economy* **83**, 95–119.

Mercurio, F. and Moraleda, J.M. (1996) An analytically tractable interest rate model with humped volatility. Discussion paper TI 96-116-2, Tinbergen Institute, Erasmus University Rotterdam, The Netherlands.

Miltersen K.R., Sandmann, K. and Sondermann, D. (1997) Closed form solutions for term structure derivatives with log-normal interest rates. *Journal of Finance* **52**, 409–30.

Moraleda, J.M. and Vorst, A.C.F. (1997) Pricing American interest rate claims with humped volatility models. Forthcoming in *Journal of Banking and Finance*.

Ritchken, P. and Sankarasubramanian, L. (1995) Volatility structures of forward rates and the dynamics of the term structure. *Mathematical Finance* **5**, 55–72.

Stambaugh, S.M. (1988) The information in forward rates: implications for models of the term structure. *Journal of Financial Economics* **21**, 41–70.

Steeley, J. (1991) Estimating the gilt-edged term structure: basic splines and confidence intervals. *Journal of Business Finance and Accounting* **18**, 513–29.

Strickland, C. (1993) An analysis of the Heath, Jarrow and Morton approach to pricing interest rate contingent claims. Working paper, FORC, University of Warwick.

Vasicek, O.A. (1977) An equilibrium characterization of the term structure. *Journal of Financial Economics* **5**, 177–88.

6
Data-based Mechanistic Modelling

P. C. YOUNG AND D. J. PEDREGAL

6.1 INTRODUCTION

Over many years, the first author has promoted a data-based approach to the modelling of environmental and other dynamic systems (see e.g. Young (1983, 1993); Young and Runkle (1989); Young and Beven (1994)). This favours simpler mathematical descriptions of complex dynamic processes, arguing that large, highly parameterized models can rarely be justified statistically because of the inherent limitations in the available time-series data. Coupled with the inability to perform planned experiments, such data deficiencies seriously restrict the *identifiability* of the parameters in such models (Young (1984)). This problem is exacerbated by the occurrence of *modal dominance* in dynamic systems; that is, the fact that the normal response of high-order dynamic systems is governed mainly by those few eigenvalues which define the identifiable dominant modes of the system. Such modal dominance is not often acknowledged in environmental modelling but it is often dramatic in its effect: for example, we have recently found that a linear, constant parameter, fourth-order transfer function model of the kind discussed in this chapter can explain over 99% of the dynamic behaviour associated with the perturbed dynamics of a very high order global carbon cycle simulation model (Young, Parkinson and Lees (1996)).

It seems obvious that, if sufficiently informative time-series data are available, the dominant modal structure should be identified directly from these data using objective methods of statistical inference. Unfortunately, while the simple 'black

System Dynamics in Economic and Financial Models. Edited by C. Heij, J.M. Schumacher, B. Hanzon and C. Praagman © 1997 John Wiley & Sons Ltd

box' time-series models obtained in this manner provide a reasonable basis for time-series forecasting and control applications, they almost always lack the kind of clear, mechanistic interpretation which is essential if the model is to be fully credible as a scientific theory of behaviour. *Data-based mechanistic* (DBM) modelling (see e.g. Young and Runkle (1989); Young (1993); Young and Beven (1994)) is a time-series approach to environmetric (or other systems) analysis which attempts to extend conventional, data-based, time-series methodology in a manner which enhances the model builder's ability to interpret the identified model in physical, biological, ecological or, in the present context, socio-economic terms.[1]

In the DBM approach, the model *structure* is first obtained by a process of objective statistical inference applied to the time-series data and based on a given general class of Unobserved Component (UC) models characterized by *linear* transfer function (TF) components whose parameters are allowed to vary over time and are estimated using a special form of recursive fixed interval smoothing (FIS: see e.g. Young (1984, 1988, 1989); Ng and Young (1990)). Since these time variable parameter (TVP) estimates will reflect any non-stationary and non-linear aspects of the observed system behaviour, they can be utilized to identify the nature of such non-linearity, often in the form of state dependent parameter (SDP) relationships, prior to final estimation of the model (e.g. Young (1993)). However, in the DBM approach, the model equations obtained in this manner are then only accepted as a credible theory of behaviour if, in addition to explaining the data well, they also provide a description which has direct relevance to the physical reality of the system under study.

Of course, while this novel approach should normally ensure that the model equations have such an acceptable physical (here macroeconomic) interpretation, it does not guarantee that this interpretation will necessarily conform to the current paradigm. Indeed, one of the most exciting, albeit controversial, aspects of DBM models is that they can tend to question such paradigms. For example, DBM methods have been applied successfully to the characterization of imperfect mixing in fluid flow processes and, in the case of pollutant transport in rivers, have led to the development of the *aggregated dead zone* (ADZ) model (e.g. Wallis, Young and Beven (1989)). Despite its initially unusual physical interpretation, the practical success of this ADZ model and its formulation in terms of physically meaningful parameters within an ordinary differential equation (ODE) setting, raises controversial questions about the utility, in this fluvial context, of the ubiquitous *advection dispersion model* (ADE) which preceded it as the most credible theory of pollutant transport in stream channels.[2]

In the present chapter, we outline this DBM approach to modelling and apply it to the problem of investigating a quite simple non-linear relationship between quarterly measures of the seasonally adjusted unemployment rate, GNP and total capital investment in the USA over the period 1948 to 1988, as shown in Figure 6.1.

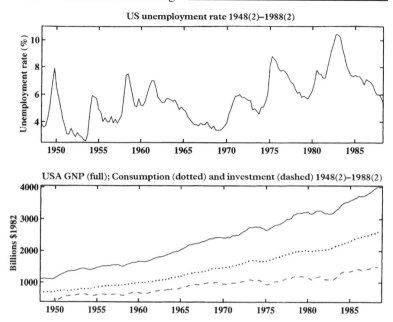

Figure 6.1 DBM modelling of US unemployment data: selected macroeconomic data for the USA 1948(2)–1988(2)

6.2 DATA-BASED MECHANISTIC MODELLING

It is assumed here that, in general, the macroeconomic system will be non-linear and/or non-stationary. Consequently, in discrete-time, sampled data terms,[3] the behaviour of a typical measured variable y_t, at the tth sampling instant, can be described by a general stochastic, dynamic equation of the form

$$y_t = \mathfrak{I}\{\chi_t, \mu_t\} \tag{1}$$

where $\mathfrak{I}\{\cdot\}$ is a reasonably behaved, non-linear function of the variables in an extended or *non-minimum state space* (NMSS) defined by the following NMSS state vector,

$$\chi_t = [y_{t-1} \cdots y_{t-n}\ \mathbf{u}_t^T \cdots \mathbf{u}_{t-m}^T\ \mathbf{U}_t^T \cdots \mathbf{U}_{t-q}^T]^T$$

where the superscript T denotes the vector/matrix transpose. We see that χ_t is composed of the past values of y_t, as well as present and past values of a deterministic exogenous (input) variable vector $\mathbf{u}_t$ with elements u_{it}, $i = 1$, $2, \ldots, r$; and the present and past values of a vector $\mathbf{U}_t$ of other exogenous variables, U_{jt}, $j = 1, 2, \ldots, s$. Finally, μ_t is an unobserved, zero mean, stochastic process with fairly general properties, which is the source of all stochasticity in the system and is assumed to be independent of the input variables u_{it} and U_{jt}.

This model assumes that y_t is causally related to the *primary* input variables u_{it}; while the vector $\mathbf{U}_t$ represents any other associated variables which *may* affect the system non-linearly but whose relevance in this regard may not be clear prior to time-series analysis. For instance, in the macroeconomic example considered later, y_t is the quarterly unemployment rate in the USA over the period 1948–88; u_{it}, $i = 1, 2, \ldots, r$ are functions of major macroeconomic variables that could reasonably be assumed to affect the unemployment rate (in the example, quarterly measures of GNP, G_t, and total capital investment, I_t, over the same period). The stochastic input μ_t then represents the effects of modelling error, measurement noise and any other input (or unobserved) variables not taken into account. Within this macroeconomic context, U_{it}, $j = 1, 2, \ldots, s$ could, for example, represent other economic variables or policy instruments that may possibly influence the unemployment rate levels, but whose relevance in this regard is not clear at the start of the analysis. The inclusion of such additional variables can prove useful in other application areas but they are not considered further in the present example.

For simplicity of presentation and because it relates directly to the later practical example, consider the case of two primary exogenous variables, so that $r = 2$. Following arguments similar to those presented in Young (1993), the non-linear model (1) can then often be represented exactly, or approximated via a process of statistical linearization, by the following additive UC model,

$$y_t = T_t + S_t + \frac{B_{1t}(L)}{A_t(L)} u_{1t} + \frac{B_{2t}(L)}{A_t(L)} u_{2t} + \xi_t \tag{2a}$$

where T_t is a low-frequency trend component which allows for non-stationarity in the mean of the series (which could be due to long-term non-linear effects); S_t represents any undamped seasonal (periodic) component; and ξ_t is a general (coloured) noise component that accounts for all the stochasticity in y_t not explained by T_t and S_t. In general, the exogenous inputs enter model (2a) via TVP or SDP transfer functions that are defined by ratios of the following polynomials in the lag or backward shift operator L (i.e. $L^i y_t = y_{t-i}$):[4]

$$A_t = 1 + a_{1t}L + \cdots + a_{nt}L^n$$

$$B_{1t} = b_{10t} + b_{11t}L + \cdots + b_{1mt}L^m$$

$$B_{2t} = b_{20t} + b_{21t}L + \cdots + b_{2qt}L^q$$

Here, the subscript t associated with the parameters indicates that they may vary over time, either because of temporal changes in the TF characteristics or because of state dependency arising from non-linearity. Finally, any pure time delays δ_i, $i = 1, 2$, affecting the TF relationship between each u_{it} and y_t can be accommodated by setting the δ_i leading coefficients of the $B_{it}(L)$ polynomial equal to zero, in each case.

In essence, equation (2a) can be considered as a UC model with TVP/SDP transfer function components introduced to allow for non-linear features in the data. This has some clear similarity with the structural model of Harvey (1989), but the structural model is not normally assumed to contain this type of TVP/SDP transfer function component applied to the exogenous variables. Indeed, such TF terms do not normally take on much significance in structural model analysis, which usually considers exogenous effects through additional regression terms or lagged dependent variables. In more traditional econometric terminology, equation (2a) might also be termed a TVP/SDP version of the 'distributed lag' class of models.

In the context of the later example, the long-term trend in the unemployment rate data (see Figure 6.1) can be explained well by one of the TF relationships and, as mentioned above, all the data are seasonally adjusted. As a result, it is only necessary to consider here the following simplified version of equation (2a):

$$y_t = \frac{B_{1t}(L)}{A_t(L)} u_{1t} + \frac{B_{2t}(L)}{A_t(L)} u_{2t} + \xi_t \tag{2b}$$

or

$$y_t = x_{1t} + x_{2t} + \xi_t \tag{2c}$$

where the two deterministic variables, x_{it}, $i = 1, 2$, which can be considered as the 'noise-free' outputs of the model, are defined by

$$x_{it} = \frac{B_{it}(L)}{A_t(L)} u_{it} \qquad i = 1, 2 \tag{2d}$$

and ξ_t is a stochastic term which, ideally, would be white noise but, more likely in practice, will be a general ARIMA process. However, both for simplicity and because we feel it yields a fairly generally applicable and useful model form, *it will be assumed that all the major dynamic features in the series* y_t *can be explained by the (possibly non-linear) effects of the exogenous inputs* u_{it}. In consequence, the residual ξ_t should then be capable of representation by a simple, constant parameter, pth-order Autoregressive (AR) process of the form

$$\xi_t = \frac{1}{C(L)} e_t = \frac{1}{1 + c_1 L + \ldots + c_p L^p} e_t \tag{2e}$$

where e_t is a zero mean, serially independent sequence of normally distributed random variables with variance σ^2 (discrete-time white noise); i.e. $e_t \sim NID(0, \sigma^2)$. This allows ξ_t to be a fairly general 'coloured noise' process with rational spectral density.

To summarize, the model to be considered in subsequent sections of the chapter is the following simplification of the general model (2a),

$$y_t = \frac{B_{1t}(L)}{A_t(L)} u_{1t} + \frac{B_{2t}(L)}{A_t(L)} u_{2t} + \frac{1}{C(L)} e_t \tag{3}$$

This is a two-input TF model, where the polynomials that define the TF characteristics are assumed to be possible functions of the time index t, in order to allow for non-linearity and/or time variability in the dynamic relationships. In the present context, these time-variable parameters will reflect the nature of any non-linear or non-stationary aspects of the system behaviour; and their statistical estimates, based on the data $\{y_t, u_{it}, i = 1, 2; t = 1, 2, \ldots, N\}$, should provide a potential source of information on the nature of the non-linearity and/or non-stationarity in the system. Most conveniently, however, the major source of non-linearity in the later example is associated with the input variable to only one of the TF relationships. As a result, the following simplified version of equation (3) is used in the example:

$$y_t = \frac{B_1(L)}{A(L)} b_t u_{1t} + \frac{B_2(L)}{A(L)} u_{2t} + \frac{1}{C(L)} e_t \tag{3a}$$

where b_t is a single time-variable parameter that allows for non-linearity in the first input;[5] and the TF polynomials are all defined by constant parameters, i.e. they are *linear* TFs.

6.2.1 Initial Parameter Estimation

The approximation of the non-linear system by a TVP model such as equation (3) is the key assumption in the first stage of DBM modelling. The multi-order and multivariable generalizations of this equation provide a fairly wide class of time-series model for stationary or non-stationary, linear or non-linear, stochastic systems; and the estimation of the (possibly) time-variable parameters of such a general model from the observed time series $\{y_t, u_{it}, i = 1, 2, \ldots, r\}$ provides a useful mechanism for the identification of a *time-invariant parameter* non-linear model of the system, which is the main objective of DBM analysis. As in previous publications (e.g. Young (1988, 1993); Young and Runkle (1989); Ng and Young (1990); Young and Beven (1994)), we propose here that such TVP estimation is based on a powerful *Kalman filter – fixed interval smoothing* (FIS) method of recursive estimation.

The details of FIS estimation are given in these prior publications and so it will suffice here to note that the FIS algorithm is applied to the following alternative vector form of model (3):

$$y_t = \mathbf{z}_t^T \mathbf{a}_t + \eta_t \qquad t = 1, 2, \ldots, N \tag{4}$$

where

$$\mathbf{z}_t^T = [-y_{t-1} \; -y_{t-2} \cdots -y_{t-n} \; u_{1,t} \cdots u_{1,t-m} \; u_{2,t} \cdots u_{2,t-q}]$$

$$\mathbf{a}_t = [a_{1t} \; a_{2t} \cdots a_{nt} \; b_{10t} \cdots b_{1mt} \; b_{20t} \cdots b_{2qt}]^T$$

and $\eta_t = A_t(L)\xi_t$. The FIS algorithm provides an estimate $\hat{\mathbf{a}}_{t|N}$ of the model parameter vector $\mathbf{a}_t$ at every sampling instant t, conditional on the time-series data $\{y_t, u_{1t}, u_{2t}\}$ over the whole observation interval $t = 1, 2, \ldots, N$. In addition, if the noise η_t is assumed to be discrete white noise with variance σ_η^2, it also yields an estimate, at each sampling instant, of the covariance matrix $\mathbf{P}_{t|N}^* = E\{\tilde{\mathbf{a}}_{t|N} \cdot \tilde{\mathbf{a}}_{t|N}^T\}$, where $\tilde{\mathbf{a}}_{t|N} = \hat{\mathbf{a}}_{t|N} - \mathbf{a}_t$ is the estimation error.

If η_t is not white noise, as seems likely in practice, then the FIS algorithm will tend to transfer any colour in the residuals to the estimates $\hat{\mathbf{a}}_{t|N}$ in order to produce a white innovations process in the recursive algorithm (see e.g. Young (1984)). It should be stressed, however, that the FIS algorithm is being used here as a non-parametric estimation device to identify any non-linearities in the data and *not* for final non-linear model estimation. Consequently, unless the residuals are large (indicating a poor explanation of the data) the TVP estimates in $\hat{\mathbf{a}}_{t|N}$ will still be accurate enough to indicate the main features of any non-linearity. Also, as we shall see, the estimated covariance matrix $\mathbf{P}_{t|N}^*$ provides a useful measure of the relative accuracy of the TVP estimates, which can often prove useful in evaluating the detailed nature of the estimated parameter variations and inferring possible state dependency/non-linearity.

The FIS estimate $\hat{\mathbf{a}}_{t|N}$ is generated on the basis of some assumed theoretical model for the temporal variations in the parameter vector $\mathbf{a}_t$. The simplest assumption, and one which has been found to work well in practice over many years, is that it propagates as a vector random walk, i.e.

$$\mathbf{a}_t = \mathbf{a}_{t-1} + \mathbf{v}_t \tag{5}$$

in which $\mathbf{v}_t$ is a zero mean, white-noise vector, with a (normally assumed) diagonal covariance matrix $\mathbf{Q}$, which is considered to be statistically independent of the residual noise term η_t in equation (4). Other non-stationary stochastic models of this Gauss–Markov form, such as the integrated (IRW) and smoothed random walks, provide alternative models for parametric change (see e.g. Young (1984)) but the simpler RW model proves sufficient in the present context.

In estimation terms, the most important parameters that follow from assumption (5) are the diagonal elements of the matrix, $\mathbf{Q}_{\mathrm{nvr}} = \mathbf{Q}/\sigma_\eta^2$. These noise variance ratio (NVR or 'hyper') parameters define the rate of temporal variation in the parameters relative to the variance σ_η^2 of the residual white noise in the 'observation' equation (4). In order to obtain $\hat{\mathbf{a}}_{t|N}$ using the FIS algorithm, the NVR parameters must be defined in some manner. In the later example, this is achieved by maximum likelihood optimization in the time domain.

One important caveat is necessary when pursuing this approach to TVP estimation: it is important that model (4) should not be over-parameterized, otherwise any temporal variation in the estimated parameters may be due to such over-parameterization rather than to the presence of real non-linear/non-stationary behaviour (see e.g. Young (1984)). Of course, knowledge of the system and straightforward observation of the system behaviour will often provide prior information on such matters. However, as a general heuristic rule, it is advisable to choose initially the *simplest possible* model that is capable of describing the observed behaviour and then, if necessary, increase the order of the model should this be suggested by subsequent analysis.

6.2.2 A Simple State-dependent Parameter Model

If, at this initial TVP estimation phase of the analysis, the estimated parameters appear sensibly constant over time, then it can be inferred that the system is predominantly linear and further analysis is not required. Otherwise, the analysis proceeds, with the aim of investigating the nature of the estimated parameter variation and attempting to identify whether these variations can be related to any of the variables in the NMSS vector χ_t; in other words, the FIS analysis is intended to *identify* any state dependency in the parameter variations which is associated with non-linear behaviour in the system.[6] At this stage it should be possible to develop some general non-linear representation of the estimated parameter variations $\hat{\mathbf{a}}_{t|N}$ in terms of the other measured variables in χ_t. Here, it is assumed that the number of other measured variables is such that all physically meaningful non-linear relationships can be explored on an individual basis in a reasonably straightforward fashion. As we shall see, this proves to be possible in the later example, which has particularly simple non-linear characteristics; and it has also been possible in environmental examples (e.g. Young (1993); Young and Beven (1994)).

The linearization approach used to derive the TVP model (4) suggests that any temporal variations in the linearized model parameters may well be identifiable as functions of the state χ_t. In the 1970s the first author suggested and utilized one of the simplest general assumptions which acknowledges such state dependency; namely that $\mathbf{a}_t$ is linearly related to (possibly non-linear) functions of χ_t by a parameter vector α_t, i.e.

$$\mathbf{a}_t = \mathbf{M}\{\chi_t\}\alpha_t \qquad (6)$$

In this chapter $\mathbf{M}_t = \mathbf{M}\{\chi_t\}$ is restricted to be a diagonal transformation matrix, functionally dependent upon χ_t; and α_t can be considered as the transformed parameter vector which should, ideally, have time-invariant elements if the introduction of the state dependency in this manner has proven completely successful in explaining the non-linearity.

6.2.3 Identification and Estimation of the State-dependent Model

In order that the state-dependent model (SDM) can prove useful in statistical terms, it is necessary to utilize the estimate $\hat{\mathbf{a}}_{t|N}$ of the TVP vector, together with its associated covariance matrix $\mathbf{P}^*_{t|N}$, to identify the nature of the potentially non-linear diagonal elements in the transformation matrix $\mathbf{M}_t$; and then to estimate the parameters which characterize these non-linear elements. There are two approaches to this problem (see Young and Beven (1994)): the one favoured here, which is used in the later practical example, applies when $\boldsymbol{\alpha}_t$ is time invariant, so that we can assume from equation (6) that $\hat{\mathbf{a}}_{t|N}$ can be approximated by the following regression equation:

$$\hat{\mathbf{a}}_{t|N} = \mathbf{M}_t \boldsymbol{\alpha} + \varepsilon_t \tag{7}$$

where ε_t is a zero-mean, white-noise vector with covariance matrix $\mathbf{P}^*_{t|N}$ which is introduced to allow for the uncertainty on the estimate $\hat{\mathbf{a}}_{t|N}$. This assumption suggests that a weighted least squares (WLS) estimate of $\mathbf{M}_t$ can be obtained by minimizing the following cost function: [7]

$$J = \sum_{k=1}^{k=N} [\hat{\mathbf{a}}_{t|N} - \mathbf{M}_t \boldsymbol{\alpha}]^{\mathrm{T}} \mathbf{W}_t [\hat{\mathbf{a}}_{t|N} - \mathbf{M}_t \boldsymbol{\alpha}] \tag{8}$$

where $\mathbf{W}_t = \mathbf{P}^{*~-1}_{t|N}$.

Note that the exact nature of the $\mathbf{M}_t$ diagonal elements is specified in relation to the NMSS state variables by reference to the FIS estimates $\{\hat{\mathbf{a}}_{t|N}, \mathbf{P}^*_{t|N}\}$, and *the physical nature of the system under consideration*. This emphasis is essential to the DBM approach: while the choice of non-linear transformation should not be *dictated* by the prior perception of the modeller about the nature of the non-linear system, it should be capable of a rational explanation in relation to the physical (macroeconomic in the present context) nature of the system. For instance, in the later example, only one significant non-linearity is identified, so that $\mathbf{M}_t$ becomes a simple scalar which appears strongly related to the inverse of GNP. As we shall see, this inverse relationship has important economic significance and so the resulting non-linearity is, therefore, acceptable on a DBM basis.

6.2.4 Final Estimation of the Non-linear Model

The primary aim of the FIS analysis in the previous section is to evaluate whether the system is linear or non-linear and, in the latter case, to identify a sensible functional form for each of the elements in the state-dependent transformation matrix $\mathbf{M}_t = \mathbf{M}\{\chi_t\}$; in other words, the analysis is aimed at *non-linear model structure identification*. Once we have identified a plausible form for the non-linear model in this manner, however, it is then necessary to estimate the non-linear model parameters against the time-series data by some form of numerical optimization (e.g. deterministic minimization of the model residual variance; maximum likelihood estimation; prediction error minimization, etc.), the exact nature of which will tend to depend on the identified form of the model. In the most desirable situation, this should then produce a final model with parameter estimates that are both consistent and efficient in statistical terms.

As an example, consider the TVP model (3). The identification stage in the analysis will, in general, suggest optimization of the following TF model:[8]

$$y_t = \frac{B_{1t}(\boldsymbol{\chi}_t, L)}{A_t(\boldsymbol{\chi}_t, L)} u_{1t} + \frac{B_{2t}(\boldsymbol{\chi}_t, L)}{A_t(\boldsymbol{\chi}_t, L)} u_{2t} + \frac{1}{C(L)} e_t \tag{9a}$$

where, nominally, all the parameters can be state dependent. In practice, however, we would expect only a subset of the parameters to be so dependent, with the others remaining time-invariant. Moreover, in the later example, equation (9a) takes on the even simpler form where the non-linearity resides only in relation to the first exogenous input (cf. equation (3a)):

$$y_t = \frac{B_1(L)}{A(L)} b(\boldsymbol{\chi}_t) u_{1t} + \frac{B_2(L)}{A(L)} u_{2t} + \frac{1}{C(L)} e_t \tag{9b}$$

so that there is only a single state-dependent parameter $b(\boldsymbol{\chi}_t)$ associated with the first input and all other parameters are time-invariant. In this example, therefore, the final estimation stage requires the consistent and, if possible, efficient estimation of the parameters in model (9b). Both for comparative purposes and to ensure that the finally estimated model is not sensitive to the method of estimation, this is achieved by the use of three different estimation procedures: the optimal refined instrumental variables (RIV) method; the prediction error minimization (PEM) algorithm available in the Matlab[TM] software package; and standard exact maximum likelihood (ML) estimation.

6.2.5 A Summary of the Complete DBM Procedure

In the case of a two input–single output system such as (9a), the analysis discussed in the previous subsections can be summarized as follows (the multiple input generalization is obvious):

1. Examine the available time-series data $\{y_t, u_{1t}, u_{2t}\}$ and use these to estimate the parameters in the best identified *constant parameter* TF model using a reliable method of TF model identification and estimation (we recommend a special form of *instrumental variable* (IV) estimation: see e.g. Section 6.2.6 below; Young (1984); Young and Beven (1994)). Apply

standard statistical tests to the model residuals, including tests for non-linearity (e.g. Billings and Voon (1986); White (1980); Engle (1982)): if the results indicate linearity then the linear model can be accepted and the analysis is complete. Alternatively, proceed to step 2.

2. Based on the analysis in step 1 and any knowledge about the physical nature of the system, select: (a) the variables that could characterize the NMSS vector; and (b) the simplest TF model that appears capable of characterizing the behaviour of the output variable y_t in relation to the observed inputs u_{1t} and u_{2t} (this will often be a first- or second-order dynamic model at most; and it may even be based initially on static relationships).

3. Use FIS estimation to obtain initial TVP estimates of the parameters in the model and define those parameters which show significant variation over the observation interval. If any time-variable parameters are identified, obtain the FIS estimate of the model parameter vector $\hat{\mathbf{a}}_{t|N}$ with the time-variable elements specified by step 2 but with all other parameters constrained to be constant; and note the relative accuracy of these estimates over time by reference to the appropriate elements of the estimated covariance matrix $\mathbf{P}^*_{t|N}$.

4. Examine the nature of the FIS estimated time variation in the parameters in relation to all the variables in the defined NMSS vector, using devices such as scatter plots, correlation analysis, etc.; in all cases taking into account the relative accuracy of the FIS estimates, as defined by $\mathbf{P}^*_{t|N}$ obtained in step 3.

5. On the basis of the results in step 4, define the nature of the diagonal elements in the transformation matrix $\mathbf{M}(k) = \mathbf{M}\{\chi(k)\}$; and then use WLS estimation (equation (8)) to estimate the parameters which characterize these SDM relationships.

6. The DBM philosophy requires that, if at all possible, any strong SDM relationships exposed in step 5 should be capable of physical (in the present context, macroeconomic) interpretation. This can often help to avoid the identification of potentially spurious non-linearities (i.e. nonsense correlations).

7. Use the estimates of the parameters in step 6 as starting values in a final model estimation stage, where the (hopefully constant) parameters in the identified non-linear model are estimated, based on the identified non-linear model form and all the relevant data in the NMSS vector. Again, at this stage, optimal IV estimation is recommended as a general approach to the problem (see Section 6.2.6) but any other appropriate methods could be used, as in the later example.

8. Analyse the residuals from the estimated model to ensure that there is no evidence of any residual non-linearity not identified in steps 1–6. This should include standard statistical diagnostic tests and non-linearity tests; see step 1.

6.2.6 A Systems Approach to Modelling Input–Output Behaviour: Optimal Instrumental Variable Identification and Estimation

Note that in the above approach to data-based non-linear modelling, optimal IV identification and estimation is recommended (see e.g. Young (1984); Young and Beven (1994)) as a general method of modelling the causal relationships between the input and output variables. This preference is linked strongly with the '*systems approach*' to modelling the *input–output behaviour* of stochastic, dynamic systems and contrasts somewhat with the more traditional methods advocated in the statistical and econometrics literature, where the emphasis tends to be placed more on the modelling of the stochastic effects. In systems modelling, it is the presumed causal mechanism between input and output variables that dominates attention because it is here that the description of the physical aspects of the system behaviour will normally reside and where the input–output mapping, which is so important to scientific understanding and to engineering applications such as control systems design, is contained. Within this systems context, the stochastic effects are often considered as a nuisance whose effect has to be avoided or negated, rather than something of *primary* importance.

This is not to say, of course, that the systems analyst is not cognisant of the significance of stochastic effects and the dangers of ignoring their presence in time-series analysis. Indeed, one of the major advances in time-series analysis in the twentieth century, the optimal state estimator or Kalman filter (Kalman (1960)), which we exploit in this chapter as part of the FIS estimation, is inherently stochastic. But, to many systems analysts, stochastic inputs are considered to arise for many and diverse reasons, such as: other inputs which affect the output but are not measurable; the result of measurement noise *which cannot be considered as having rational spectral density* and so is difficult to model explicitly in statistical terms; from the presence of higher-frequency but low-amplitude modes of dynamic behaviour that are not sufficiently excited by the input signal to be identifiable from the input–output data; and because of low-amplitude, additive, non-linear effects which yield characteristics that are, once again, not easily characterized by the more common stochastic models. As a result, the assumption that all these effects can be approximated adequately by a simple, normally distributed, stochastic process with rational spectral density is often difficult to justify.

The IV approach to identification and estimation is very appealing in circumstances such as these because it does not require any strong assumptions about the stochastic nature of any additive noise processes (which are simply required to be statistically independent of the chosen instrumental variables); nor concurrent estimation of a model for such noise, as in most other procedures, such as maximum likelihood (ML: e.g. Box and Jenkins (1970)), or prediction error minimisation (PEM: e.g. Ljung and Söderström (1983)). On the other hand, the IV method not only has respectable statistical credentials (e.g. Kendall and Stuart

(1961)) but its statistical efficiency can be enhanced quite simply *if* the noise process can be assumed to have rational spectral density (i.e. it is assumed to be the output of a transfer function, defined as the ratio of rational polynomials in the backward shift operator, whose input is a discrete-time white-noise process). For example, the IV methodology proposed by Young (e.g. 1970, 1984), where the instrumental variables are generated by the adaptively pre-filtered outputs of an iteratively updated 'auxiliary model' of the system, can be extended to an optimal RIV form (e.g. Young (1984, 1985); Young and Jakeman (1979, 1980); Jakeman and Young (1979)) which is asymptotically equivalent to maximum likelihood estimation and yields asymptotically efficient estimates of the TF model parameters *if the noise can be assumed to follow an ARMA process.*

This latter RIV methodology is used in the later macroeconomic example, where the estimation results are compared with those obtained using the alternative PEM and ML methods. In this particular practical example, there is little to choose between the methods which provide very similar results, thus verifying the efficacy of the final model estimation phase in the analysis. However, in other practical examples, such as those in which the input variables are of an impulsive kind, as in tracer experiments or rainfall-flow data, we have found that our RIV methods seem to offer some significant advantages.

6.3 EXPLORING THE RELATIONSHIP BETWEEN UNEMPLOYMENT, INVESTMENT AND GNP IN THE USA 1948(2) TO 1988(2)

The top graph in Figure 6.1 is a plot of the quarterly unemployment rate figures, y_t, in the USA over the period 1948(2) to 1988(2), a total sample size of $N = 161$. Below this are graphs of the quarterly GNP, G_t; total capital investment, I_t, and consumption, C_t, over the same period of time.[9] All these variables are non-stationary in the mean and, at first sight, there is little apparent relationship between them, except that all have experienced a predominant, upward, long-term trend since the end of the Second World War. Even in the case of the unemployment rate, where the shorter-term changes are much larger and more erratic, there has been a clearly discernible rise in mean level, particularly over the second half of the data. The objective of the analysis is to obtain a model for the variations in the unemployment rate in terms of the other variables, starting from the results of a previous analysis of these data (Young (1994)).

6.3.1 Initial Exploratory Analysis

The first author (Young (1994)) investigated a UC relationship between $\log(y_t)$ and $\log(G_t)$ which showed that the perturbations in $\log(y_t)$ about its long-term trend could be explained very well by a first-order linear TF relationship, using the perturbations of $\log(G_t)$ about its long-term trend as the assumed exogenous input. Although this use of log-transformed variables is the standard convention in the analysis of USA macroeconomic time series, it makes sense here to start with the raw, non-transformed data. This is justified for two main reasons: first, since the prime objective of our analysis is to infer, as objectively as possible, the nature of any non-linearities in the data, it seems sensible not to pre-judge the issue by imposing the specific log transform prior to non-linear model identification; second, the subsequent analysis does not suggest in any way that the log transform is appropriate. Indeed, if it is imposed, the resulting model does not explain the data as well as the model obtained without this constraint.

Bearing these arguments in mind, it makes sense to repeat the previous analysis using the non-transformed data y_t and G_t. This yields the following UC model:

$$y_t = T_t - \frac{0.0092}{1 - 0.464L} \nabla G_t + \xi_t$$

$$\xi_t = \frac{1}{1 - 0.913L + 0.180L^2 + 0.149L^3} e_t \qquad e_t \sim NID(0, \sigma^2)$$

(10)

where $\sigma^2 = 0.097$. The normally defined coefficient of determination for this model, based on the one-step-ahead prediction errors, is $R^2 = 0.967$; while that based on the model output response errors (see below) is $R_T^2 = 0.920$. Here, T_t is the long-term trend in y_t; while ∇G_t are the deviations of G_t around its long-term trend T_t^g, i.e., $\nabla G_t = G_t - T_t^g$. For this analysis, both T_t and T_t^g are modelled as integrated random walk (IRW) processes, i.e.

$$T_t = \frac{1}{(1 - L)^2} \eta_t \qquad \eta_t \sim NID(0, \sigma_\eta^2)$$

$$T_t^g = \frac{1}{(1 - L)^2} \eta_t^g \qquad \eta_t^g \sim NID(0, \sigma_{\eta^g}^2)$$

where the noise variance ratios (NVRs) associated with the white-noise inputs η_t and η_t^g are defined as follows, based on the analysis of the spectra for y_t and G_t (see Young (1994)):

$$NVR_\eta = \frac{\sigma_\eta^2}{\sigma^2} = 0.0006 \qquad NVR_{\eta^g} = \frac{\sigma_{\eta^g}^2}{\sigma^2} = 1.93$$

From these results, it is clear that the short-term *perturbations* of y_t and G_t about their long-term trends can be explained very well by a first-order TF with steady-state gain of -0.017 and time constant of 1.3 quarters.

Although model (10) exposes clearly a strong coherence between the short-term fluctuations of y_t and G_t about their trends, it does not provide an explicit relationship between these long-term trends, which are simply estimated individually on the basis of the spectral properties of each series. The previous analysis investigated a possible link between the second differences of the estimated trends, but a later theoretical result (Pedregal (1995); Young and Pedregal (1996a)) suggests that this arises because of a special, and quite surprising, property of FIS estimated trends.[10] Clearly, a superior approach in this situation would be to model the series in multivariable cointegration terms, as discussed elsewhere in this text. However, it would be more advantageous still, and certainly more consistent with the DBM philosophy, to explain the upward trend in unemployment rate in a manner that is explicitly related to the other macroeconomic variables and so is more meaningful in macroeconomic terms.

One hypothesis in this latter regard is that the long-term changes in the unemployment rate that are accounted for by T_t in model (10) are related, in some manner, to the long-term changes in capital investment I_t or consumption C_t. Considering I_t, this implies a model of the form (3) which, in this case, takes the specific form,[11]

$$y_t = c + \frac{b_{1t}}{1 + a_{1t}L} I_t + \frac{b_{2t}}{1 + a_{1t}L} \nabla G_t + \xi_t \tag{11}$$

where c is a constant which is introduced to allow for the difference in levels between the variables now that the trend term T_t has been omitted.

6.3.2 DBM Analysis: Non-linear Model Identification

Step 1 in the DBM approach outlined in Section 6.2 involves estimating the constant parameter version of model (11) and then using statistical tests on the residuals to see if there is evidence of non-linearity. In this case, the correlation-based tests of Billings and Voon (1986) suggest that some non-linearity is present but the ARCH-LM (Engle (1982); White (1980)) heteroscedasticity tests provide contradictory results. However, the relatively poor fit compared with that obtained using the UC model (10), as well as the quite distorted shape of the residuals, implies that some form of non-linearity may well be present. At least it suggests that this possibility should be investigated further.

Steps 2 and 3 of the DBM analysis are concerned with estimating any time variability in the model parameters. Bearing in mind the nature of model (10), initial TVP estimation suggests that, most of the time, variability in the parameters (and therefore the non-linearity) resides in the input (numerator) parameter b_{1t} of equation (11), with all the other parameters showing little evidence of any meaningful non-stationarity. Since there is only one time-variable parameter to estimate in this situation, it is only necessary to optimize the single

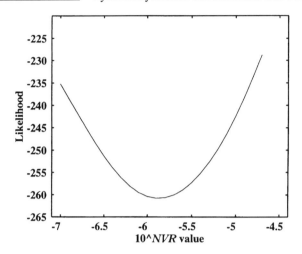

Figure 6.2 Initial TVP modelling: optimization of the *NVR* value for FIS time-variable parameter estimation

NVR parameter associated with the RW model of this parameter, with the *NVR* for the others all set to zero. Figure 6.2 shows the results of maximum likelihood optimization of this single *NVR* parameter in the time domain: the graph of the likelihood against the *NVR* (shown as the power of 10) suggests an $NVR = 1.26 \times 10^{-6}$. Figure 6.3 is a plot of the resulting FIS estimate $\hat{b}_{1t|N}$ of b_{1t}, with its estimated standard error band shown dashed: in this case, the

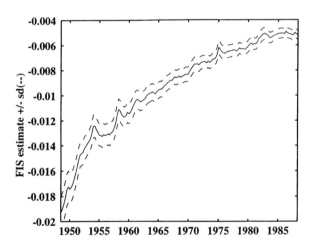

Figure 6.3 Initial TVP modelling: FIS estimate $b_{1t|N}$ of b_{1t} parameter variation with standard error band shown dashed

confidence band is fairly uniform, so that subsequent WLS estimation of a state-dependent relationship is not affected too much by the weighting effect. This is not always the case, however: in a recent rainfall-flow modelling example (Young and Beven (1994)) the weighting varies a great deal, depending upon the nature of the rainfall input, and the success of the subsequent SDM estimation is strongly dependent upon this weighting effect.

Steps 4 and 5 of the DBM analysis involve the investigation of the FIS estimate $\hat{b}_{1t|N}$ in Figure 6.3 to see if there are any feasible relationships with other available macro-economic variables. In this case, scatter plots of $\hat{b}_{1t|N}$ against both G_t and C_t expose a quite strong inverse relationship, as shown in Figure 6.4 for G_t, where $\hat{b}_{1t|N}$ is plotted against G_t^{-1}. Also shown on the plot is the resulting WLS estimated regression line: note that, inasmuch as the weighting has any effect on the estimation, it emphasizes the importance of the $\hat{b}_{1t|N}$ estimates associated with the lower values of G_t^{-1} (the higher values of G_t) in the top-left of the plot. These results suggest, quite clearly, that the b_{1t} parameter is inversely proportional to GNP; or equivalently, that a linear dynamic relationship appears to exist between the long-term changes in the unemployment rate y_t and I_t/G_t.

Step 6 of the DBM analysis requires us to ascertain whether any non-linear relationships inferred during steps 4 and 5 are capable of macroeconomic interpretation. In this case, the new variable $RI_t = I_t/G_t$ has clear macroeconomic significance: it can be interpreted as a direct measure of *relative capital investment*; that is, the total capital investment, as defined in this chapter, as a

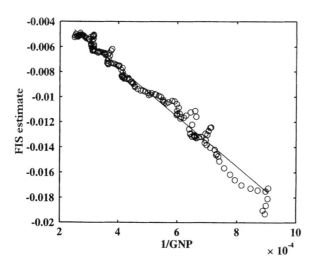

Figure 6.4 The SDP modelling stage: WLS estimation of the state-dependent relationship between the FIS estimate $b_{1t|N}$ and $1/G_t$

proportion of the GNP. RI_t is plotted in the upper graph of Figure 6.5(a), together with the ratios of private investment to GNP (RPI_t) and government spending to GNP (RGI_t); while its inverse relationship with the unemployment rate is illustrated in Figure 6.5(b), which shows how, when inverted and scaled accord-

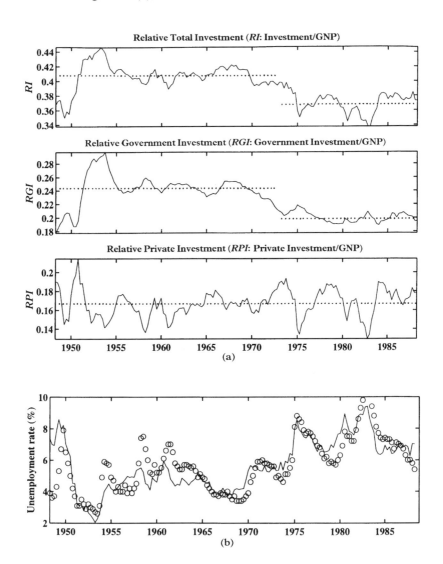

Figure 6.5 The SDP modelling stage. (a) The identified Relative Investment variable RI_t (top) and its constituent parts: Relative Government Investment RGI_t (middle); and Relative Private Investment RPI_t (bottom). (b) Scaled, inverted Relative Investment and the unemployment rate series (circles)

ingly, RI_t exhibits a very strong, visible (and mostly lead) correlation with the unemployment rate over much of the historical period (the correlation coefficient between y_t and RI_t is -0.81).

Figure 6.5(a) is interesting because it reveals that the decline in our objectively inferred variable RI_t is mostly due to the decline of public (government) rather than private investment, since the latter exhibits a roughly constant mean level over the whole period.[12] The relationship revealed in Figure 6.5(b) does not, of course, prove that there is any causative mechanism between the rather worrying decline of RI_t (especially public investment) over the past half century, particularly since 1970,[13] and the growth in the unemployment rate, but it does provide food for thought in this regard. Later analysis which takes these ideas further is reported in Young and Pedregal (1996b). As far as our current analysis is concerned, however, Figure 6.5(b) suggests strongly that, if I_t in model (11) is replaced by RI_t, then it is likely that both the long- and short-term changes in the unemployment rate can be explained well by a constant parameter TF model, without the need for any trend term.

It is interesting to note that, following this analysis, we discovered that RI_t is similar, but not the same as, one of the 'great ratios' mentioned by King et al. (1991);[14] the other being *relative consumption* $RC_t = C_t/G_t$, which could also have been used in this analysis (see later, Section 6.4). However, it is important to stress the differences between the present analysis and that of King et al., which is devoted mainly to demonstrating the possibility of cointegration relationships between macroeconomic variables. In order to achieve this goal, however, it proves necessary to define the 'great ratios' only for the macroeconomic variables relating to the *private* economy (i.e. the ratio of private investment to 'private GNP', defined by King et al. as GNP minus government expenditure). With these definitions, it is then possible to demonstrate that the 'great ratios' are stationary, implying that the variables utilized in their definition are cointegrated. In our analysis, on the other hand, RI_t is clearly not stationary; indeed, the main importance of this ratio to our analysis lies in its ability to reflect, and possibly to explain, the long-term non-stationary behaviour of the unemployment rate series. More precisely, the cointegration properties of the 'great ratios' defined for the 'private' variables is what enables us to relate non-stationary variables by a stable TF, making both sets of results compatible.

6.3.3 DBM Analysis: Final Model Estimation

Having identified a plausible model structure relating the unemployment rate y_t to RI_t and ∇G_t, it remains to carry out the final step in the DBM analysis and use a statistically efficient estimation procedure to identify and estimate the final, constant parameter TF model. Here, as mentioned previously, this has been achieved using three separate estimation procedures: namely, RIV, PEM and ML estimation. All three methods identify, quite unambiguously, a model of the form:

$$y_t = c + \frac{b}{1 + a_1 L} RI_t + \frac{b_2}{1 + a_1 L} \nabla G_t + \frac{1}{1 + c_1 L + c_2 L^2} e_t \qquad e_t \sim NID(0, \sigma^2)$$

$$\nabla G_t = G_t - T_t^g \qquad T_t^g = \frac{1}{1 - L^2} \eta_t^g \qquad \eta_t^g \sim NID(0, 0.0308) \qquad (12)$$

where, on comparison with equation (10), we see that the long-term trend T_t has been effectively replaced by the sum of the constant c and the TF relating the relative investment variable RI_t to y_t; while the AR(3) noise process has been modified slightly to AR(2). Note that, in estimating this model, the NVR value defining the IRW model for the trend T_t^g was estimated simultaneously with the other TF model parameters using iterative RIV optimization and the same ∇G_t was then used for both PEM and ML estimation.

The comparative parameter estimates, standard errors and diagnostic test results obtained from the three estimation methods are listed in Tables 6.1–6.3. Here, R^2 denotes the usual coefficient of determination defined in terms of the one-step-ahead prediction errors; while R_T^2 is the coefficient of determination defined in terms of the TF model response errors $\tilde{y}_t = y_t - \hat{y}_t$, where $\hat{y}_t$ is defined as follows:

$$\hat{y}_t = \hat{c} + \frac{\hat{b}_1}{1 + \hat{a}_1 L} RI_t + \frac{\hat{b}_2}{1 + \hat{a}_1 L} \nabla G_t \qquad (13)$$

and the 'hats' denote the estimated values of the parameters. R_T^2 is usually a more discerning measure of model fit than R^2 and is often the favoured measure in systems modelling. It will be noted that all three estimation

Table 6.1 RIV estimation results

Parameter	Estimate	SE	T-statistic
c	10.470	1.21	8.65
a_1	−0.585	0.045	−12.94
b_1	−20.647	2.626	−7.86
b_2	−0.0043	0.0007	−6.05
c_1	−1.018	0.077	−13.2
c_2	0.234	0.078	3.02

$\sigma^2 = 0.1048 \qquad R_T^2 = 0.884 \qquad R^2 = 0.964$
Jarque–Bera: $\qquad$ 0.279 $\qquad$ Prob $= 0.87$
Q(4): $\qquad$ 2.165 $\qquad$ Prob $= 0.14$
Q(8): $\qquad$ 5.340 $\qquad$ Prob $= 0.07$
Steady-state gains: $G_1 = -49.7426$; $G_2 = -0.0104$; time constant, $T_c = 1.865$ quarters

Table 6.2   PEM estimation results

Parameter	Estimate	SE	T-statistic
c	10.566	1.43	7.39
a_1	−0.593	0.052	−11.51
b_1	−20.976	3.064	−6.85
b_2	−0.0042	0.0007	−5.71
c_1	−1.086	0.078	−13.88
c_2	0.293	0.078	3.76

$\sigma^2 = 0.1019$ $R_T^2 = 0.884$ $R^2 = 0.965$

Jarque−Bera: 0.251   Prob = 0.88

Q(4):   2.756   Prob = 0.10

Q(8):   5.321   Prob = 0.07

Steady-state gains: $G_1 = -51.47$; $G_2 = -0.0102$; time constant, $T_c = 1.911$ quarters

Table 6.3   ML estimation results

Parameter	Estimate	SE	T-statistic
c	11.588	1.48	7.82
a_1	−0.527	0.054	−9.82
b_1	−22.648	3.253	−6.96
b_2	−0.0055	0.0007	−7.37
c_1	−1.022	0.077	−13.33
c_2	0.226	0.077	2.94

$\sigma^2 = 0.1048$ $R_T^2 = 0.881$ $R^2 = 0.964$

Jarque−Bera: 0.297   Prob = 0.86

Q(4):   1.471   Prob = 0.22

Q(8):   5.936   Prob = 0.05

Steady-state gains: $G_1 = -47.83$; $G_2 = -0.0116$; time constant, $T_c = 1.559$ quarters

methods yield quite similar models with good explanations of the data: the R_T^2 values vary from 0.8838 for RIV and PEM to 0.8808 for ML; while R^2 ranges from 0.9655 for PEM through 0.9644 for RIV to 0.9639 for ML. Also shown in results are: the Jarque−Bera, Q(4) and Q(8) diagnostic statistics (see Jarque and Bera (1980); Ljung and Box (1978)), which verify the statistical adequacy of the models in each case; the TF steady-state gains, G_1 and G_2; and the common time constant T_c associated with the $1 + \hat{a}_1 L$ denominator polynomial.

Figures 6.6–6.8 confirm graphically the satisfactory nature of the residuals in the RIV case: Figure 6.6 is a plot of the response error $\tilde{y}_t$ and its associated autocorrelation function; Figure 6.7 presents similar graphs for the model prediction errors e_t; and Figure 6.8 exhibits plots of the cross-correlation functions between e_t and the two inputs, RI_t and ∇G_t. It is clear that the colour in the response error $\tilde{y}_t$ is successfully purged by the AR(2) noise model and the

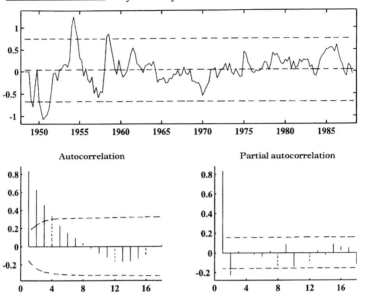

Figure 6.6 RIV response error diagnostics of final RIV estimation: model response error $\tilde{y}_t$ (top) together with its simple and partial autocorrelation functions (bottom)

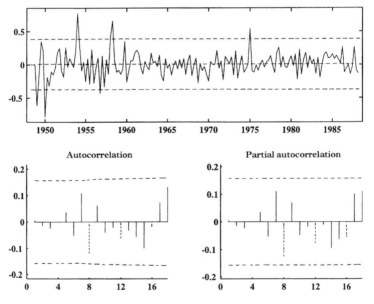

Figure 6.7 RIV prediction error diagnostics of final RIV estimation: model residuals (one step ahead prediction errors e_t) (top), together with their simple and partial autocorrelation functions (bottom)

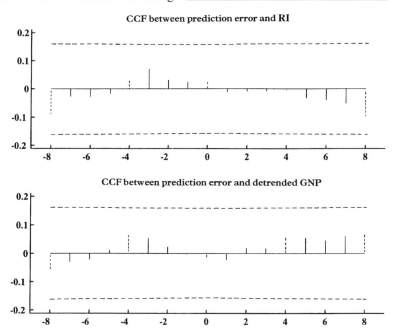

Figure 6.8 Final RIV estimation: cross-correlation functions between the model residuals e_t and the two input variables

resulting prediction errors e_t are serially uncorrelated. Also, the e_t are not significantly correlated with the exogenous inputs, as required. Finally, all the non-linearity tests discussed previously in Section 6.3.2 now indicate that there is no significant residual non-linearity.

The top graph in Figure 6.9 is a plot of $\hat{y}_t$ for the RIV model compared with the unemployment rate series: here, $\hat{y}_t$ can be interpreted as an estimate of the 'noise-free' output from the model, that is, the output due to the exogenous inputs alone. This variable is considered to be of primary importance in most systems and control modelling studies because it shows how well the TF model is relating the exogenous inputs (which are often manipulatable control inputs) to the output. The graph below this compares the one-step-ahead predictions from the RIV model with the unemployment rate series: not surprisingly, the fit to the data in this case is very close given the high $R^2 = 0.9644$. It is clear from these graphs and the error plots in Figures 6.6 and 6.7 that the modelling errors are larger before 1960 than after this date. This may be caused by additional factors that have not been taken into account in the present analysis: for instance, price controls, the Korean War and the Treasury–Fed accord. This suggests that further improvement in the model may be possible if such additional factors are considered over this period.

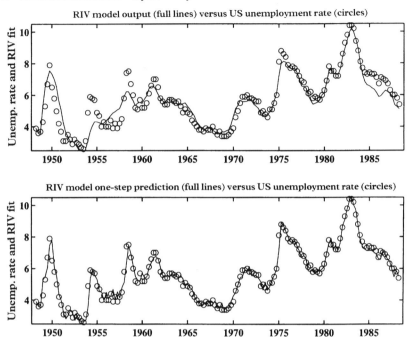

Figure 6.9 Final RIV estimation: model output response $\hat{y}_t$ (top) and one-step-ahead predictions (bottom) compared with the unemployment rate series (circles)

Finally, and most importantly, Figure 6.10 shows the contributions that the exogenous inputs make to explaining the variations in the unemployment rate: at the top, for reference, is a repeat plot of $\hat{y}_t$ compared with the unemployment rate series; while below this are the estimated 'noise-free' outputs of the two TFs and the constant term c, that additively produce $\hat{y}_t$. As might be expected, the effect of the detrended GNP input ∇G_t, in the bottom plot, is to explain mainly the shorter-term fluctuations in the unemployment rate; while the main effect of relative investment input RI_t plus the constant c, in the middle plot, is to model the long-term upward variations. In this sense, it can be seen that the primary objective of introducing this latter variable, namely to replace the long-term trend component T_t associated with model (10), has been achieved: this is illustrated in the middle plot, where the T_t from model (10) is shown as a dashed line.

Since almost identical results to those shown in Figures 6.6–6.10 are obtained from the PEM and ML estimated models, these are not presented here. However, for completeness, there is one other result worth mentioning: this is the estimation of an alternative model with different denominators in the two transfer functions, which clearly has potential attractions in this example. However, this

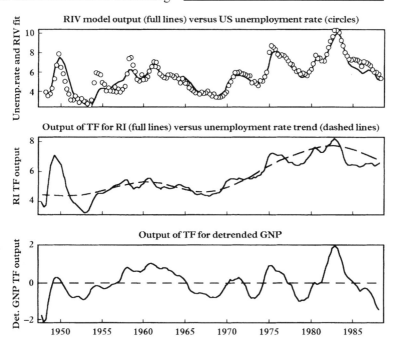

Figure 6.10 Final RIV estimation: contributions of the outputs from the TFs for each input variable (lower plots) to the total model output $\hat{y}_t$ (top). The dashed line in the middle plot is the long term trend estimated in a previous study (Young (1994))

produces only a marginal improvement in fit, as shown by the R_T^2 and R^2 values of 0.894 and 0.966, respectively. On the other hand, the standard errors on the parameters are all increased substantially, while the model characteristics remain quite similar: for example, neither the denominator $(0.572 \pm 0.11; -0.555 \pm 0.15)$ nor numerator $(-21.754 \pm 5.22; -0.0046 \pm 0013)$ TF coefficients differ significantly from the values of -0.5925 ± 0.05, -20.9756 ± 3.0638 and -0.0042 ± 0.0007 obtained in the common denominator model case. On the basis of parsimony, therefore, it seems reasonable to reject this model in favour of the common denominator TF models given above.

6.4 DISCUSSION

The primary purpose of the modelling study in the previous section is to illustrate the application of DBM modelling within a macroeconomic context and it is not intended, in any sense, as a serious, in-depth study of the US economy over the past forty years. Nevertheless, the analysis yields some results that are interesting in their own right and provide considerable food for thought. In particular, model (12) shows that there has been a quite strong and sustained relationship between the relative decline in capital investment in the USA over this period and the concurrent, long-term growth in the unemployment rate; a relationship which appears particularly well defined after 1970. Of course, in explaining the data rather well, the model does not *prove* that there is any causal link between these two important economic indicators: indeed, it is extremely difficult, if not impossible, to prove that causative mechanisms exist between economic variables because the variables are simply observed (measured) passively during the normal operation of the system, and planned experiments, which could remove the ambiguity, are not possible. On the other hand, it is also clear from the analysis that the possibility of such causality, which has such important economic implications, is very well supported by our analysis and is deserving of further detailed evaluation, which we have now initiated (see Young and Pedregal (1996b)).

Perhaps the most important contribution of the modelling exercise is that it focuses attention on the behaviour of various derived economic indicators, in the form of our, objectively inferred, versions of the 'great ratios'. Figure 6.5(a), for example, suggests that the decline in the most important of these indicators, relative investment RI_t, is due mainly to the decline of public (government) rather than private investment: in particular, standard statistical tests (augmented Dickey–Fuller and Chow structural change) show unambiguously that the mean level did not remain constant along the entire period. Specifically, the mean of the former (shown dotted) has declined significantly from a roughly constant level of $24.48 \pm 0.69\%$ of GNP (i.e. 0.2448 ± 0.0069) in the period 1955–69 to $20.07 \pm 0.72\%$ of GNP in the period 1973–88; meanwhile private investment, while very volatile in the short term, has remained at a roughly constant level ($16.68 \pm 1.45\%$ of GNP) over the whole period.

Finally, Figure 6.11 compares RI_t with other 'great ratios' that are suggested by our analysis and behave in a similar manner. The top graph shows the inverted RI_t (as suggested by the model), while the lower two graphs present the concurrent changes in relative consumption ($RC_t = C_t/G_t$) and the consumption–investment ratio (C_t/I_t). The pattern of variation in these ratios (particularly the latter) is very similar indeed to RI_t, so that either of them could replace RI_t in model (12). Although the model parameters would then be different, the message of the model would remain largely the same. In the case of C_t/I_t, for instance, it would show that the increase in the long-term trend of the unemployment rate is highly correlated with the changes in this ratio, which exhibits a statistically significant rise from 1.461 ± 0.045 over the period 1955–69 to 1.723 ± 0.088 in the period 1973–88. However, this rise occurs at the same time as the decline in RI_t and the concurrent rise in RC_t: in other words, a possible movement of national resources from the investment to consumption.

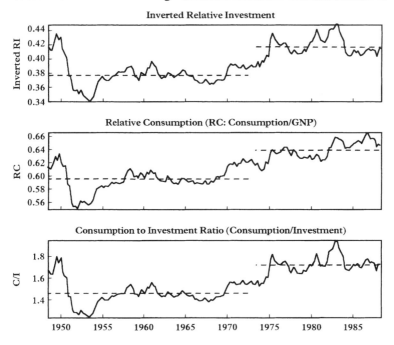

Figure 6.11 Some 'great ratios': Relative Investment (inverted, at top), Relative Consumption (middle) and Consumption to Investment Ratio (bottom)

6.5 CONCLUSIONS

This chapter has two main objectives: first, to introduce the data-based mechanistic (DBM) approach to modelling non-linear, stochastic dynamic systems; and second, to show how this reasonably objective and relatively prejudice-free methodology can be applied to the analysis of a well known set of macroeconomic time series. Previously, the DBM approach has been utilized successfully for the modelling of environmental, biological and engineering systems, but its general formulation in time series terms makes it potentially applicable to any stochastic dynamic system where sufficient observational time series data are available, either from planned experiments or, as in the macroeconomic example considered here, from the monitoring or collection of data during the normal operation of the system.

In addition, since closely related methods of analysis have already been used successfully for the forecasting and seasonal adjustment[15] of economic and business time series (e.g. Young (1988); Young, Ng and Armitage (1989); Ng and Young (1990)), it would appear that this general approach to modelling has potential for further application in all areas of economic data analysis and modelling, not only those involving time-series data.[16] Indeed, the fact that we have been able to use these techniques to extract rather interesting facts from the well-known, and much-analysed, set of macroeconomic time series data for the USA, facts that do not appear to have been highlighted before in this particular form, is testimony to its effectiveness in this regard. Moreover, the use of the same DBM model analysis for the elucidation of dominant modal behaviour in large environmental models (Young, Parkinson and Lees (1996)) suggests that a similar approach might also be advantageous in connection with large macroeconomic simulation and forecasting models.

Finally, we believe the economic facts that we have highlighted here are of some potential importance in macroeconomic terms. While the modelling exercise has clearly not proven that there is a causative link between the relative reduction in capital investment, particularly government spending, over the last quarter century and the long-term rising trend in the unemployment rate over this same period, it is clear from the analysis that the possibility of such causality, which has such important economic implications, is very well supported by our analysis and is deserving of further study. For this reason, we believe that the initial analysis reported here should lead to further and more detailed examination of this most important question.

In this latter regard, a subsequent paper (Young and Pedregal (1996b)), whose main purpose is to study the determinants of unemployment in the USA, takes the illustrative modelling exercise reported in the present chapter one step further and develops a purely relativistic model of US unemployment, in which the unemployment rate y_t (i.e. unemployment as a proportion of the available labour force) is related to relative government investment RGI_t, and relative private investment RPI_t, as discussed in this chapter and plotted in Figure 6.5(a). We believe that this improved model is quite significant in economic terms: it raises important questions about the management of the US economy over the past quarter century and suggests that an economic theory of relativity, involving the explanation of dynamic relationships between purely relative measures of the major macroeconomic variables, may help economists to better understand the vagaries of economic behaviour.

ACKNOWLEDGEMENTS

The authors are most grateful to the UK Engineering and Physical Sciences Research Council (EPSRC) for supporting part of the research reported in this chapter under grant no. ESA7088.

ENDNOTES

1. Of course, sufficient time-series data are not always available and the scientist must then make recourse to a mechanistic simulation model of some sort. However, the DBM methodology can still prove useful in this alternative context since it can provide a means of establishing reduced order DBM model to approximate closely the higher-order *simulation model* dynamics (see e.g. Young, Parkinson and Lees (1996)). Clearly, such an approach could also provide a method for evaluating and approximating large macro-economic models, although we have not yet investigated this.

2. Here we are referring to the simplest version of the ADE and our comments do not imply that other, more sophisticated, versions of the model may not perform better. However, to compete with the ADZ, they would have to be similarly parsimonious in their parameterization. This would be difficult given the parametric efficiency of the ADZ model, with lengthy reaches modelled by a first-order ODE with only two parameters.

3. Note that all of the analysis described in the chapter can be modified simply for application to stochastic, dynamic systems described by continuous-time differential equations or transfer functions in the discrete-time differential (or delta) operator (see e.g. Young and Jakeman (1980); Young (1993); Young (1996a)).

4. In the systems literature this is denoted by either z^{-1} or q; while some statistical texts use B (e.g. Box and Jenkins (1970)).

5. In the systems literature, this would be termed a *bilinear* TF relationship.

6. State dependency is not essential to the analysis. In engineering applications, for example, 'hard non-linearities' (e.g. dead zone, limiting, hysteresis) may be identified directly as elements in the system (Young (1996b)).

7. In the Gaussian case, where ε_t is assumed to have a zero-mean, normal distribution, this can be considered as quasi-maximum likelihood estimation.

8. One implication of this model is that the non-linear relationship is affine in form and, clearly, final estimation is simpler if this is the case. The affine form is reasonably general, however, since non-affine systems can often be converted to affine form (e.g. Co (1996)).

9. All data were obtained from Citibase. Using the Citibase mnemonics for the series, the precise definitions of the variables are *LHUR* (Unemployment rate), *GNP82* (GNP), *GC82* (Consumption), *GGE82* (Government Investment), *GPI82* (Private Investment). Total investment were obtained by the addition of *GGE82* and *GPI82*. We would like to thank Richard Todd and R. Shawn Hewitt from the Federal Reserve Bank of Minneapolis for kindly supplying the data.

10. These references show that, when the IRW model is used for FIS trend estimation and detrending, the fourth difference of the estimated trend is *exactly* equal to the detrended series, lagged by two samples and rescaled by a factor that is *exactly* equal to the *NVR* parameter used in the FIS estimation. Young and Pedregal (1996a) also show that, since FIS estimation is *exactly* equivalent to deterministic regularization, Wiener–Kolmogorov–Whittle smoothing and cubic smoothing spline estimation, this result also applies to these methods.

11. The possible use of C_t will be discussed later.

12. This decline in public investment has been discussed elsewhere in the economic literature (see e.g. Gramlich (1994)).

13. See also the discussion in Young (1994, p. 204) about the significance of 1970 in relation to the long-term behaviour of GNP.

14. Although these authors follow the normal convention and use log-transformed variables.
15. Related FIS techniques to those described here, which are part of the microCAP-TAIN computer program, have been used by the UK Department of Employment for seasonal adjustment of the Labour Force Survey data.
16. E.g. the approach to non-linear model identification used in DBM analysis can be compared with some methods of non-parametric regression analysis (e.g. Hastie and Tibshirani (1990)) which are applicable to other forms of economic data.

COMMENTS

T. KLOEK AND J.C. ENGWERDA

T. KLOEK

In my opinion the models and methods proposed in this fascinating paper deserve the careful attention of all time-series econometricians (TSE). The authors should be congratulated on the way they succeed in describing a complicated set of procedures.

The first author has worked in this area for more than thirty years. Most of his work has appeared in the engineering literature. The application in the present chapter is based on macroeconomic time series. The final model in this paper resembles a Box and Jenkins type transfer function (TF) model. Differences with the Box–Jenkins approach include the way non-stationarity is handled (not by differencing), the specification search (starting from models with time-varying parameters, TVP) and some of the estimation methods (the emphasis on recursive instrumental variables, RIV). Most of the ingredients of the chapter will be familiar in some form to TSE; it is the way they are mixed which is original.

TVP modelling can be viewed as a member of the family of flexible modelling approaches, together with kernel smoothing, splines and other approaches. So far TVP have played a larger role in engineering than in econometrics. Early attempts in econometrics around 1970 appear not to have been very successful; see Cooley and Prescott (1976) and Pagan (1980) for theoretical approaches and further references. A more successful approach was presented by Doan, Litterman and Sims (1984). Their exercise contains a vector autoregression (VAR) with ten variables (and hence ten equations) and six lags, so that the total number of regression parameters equals 610 (including ten intercepts). Their approach (which they call Bayesian) experiments with several values for eight hyperparameters to construct their priors. Because they construct point estimates to maximize their posterior density rather than integrate, the differences with maximum likelihood are rather small. The versions of their model that produce the best forecasts over a longer horizon show very little parameter variation. This is in accordance with the final model of the present chapter. A recent contribution to this literature by Phillips (1996) deserves attention.

A different type of flexible time-series modelling has appeared in financial econometrics. It concentrates on conditional variance estimation. It started with Engle (1982) and there is now an abundant literature, recently reviewed by Bollerslev, Engle and Nelson (1994). Its success is mixed. My impression is that there is a tendency to make these models more flexible than is desirable.

The Young–Pedregal (YP) model concentrates on means rather than variances. Therefore, I compare it with the Doan *et al.* approach. The YP specification is more parsimonious but also more non-linear. It is unclear if it is feasible to apply their approach to the ten-variable data set of Doan *et al.* The TVP in YP is in two parts. As a first step trends are removed using a local linear trend filter and a Kalman filter algorithm. This is of the same type as the approach in Harvey (1989). Only the methods to identify the noise variance ratio (*NVR*) differ. My conjecture is that both approaches are unnecessarily complicated.

The second step is in the specification of the transfer function. The authors postulate a relation between long-term changes in unemployment and capital investment (I). The problem of common trends (or cointegration) is informally addressed but it is clear that further research on this issue is in order. It is unfortunate that they give so little explicit attention to the estimation of the TVP version of the TF model (3) in the chapter, but immediately make the step to (3a) where only one variable parameter is left. This may save space, but it makes it impossible for the reader to get an impression of the practical possibilities and problems of estimating a flexible model like (3). Figure 6.4 in the chapter, where the authors show the linear dependence between their TVP estimate $\hat{b}_{1t|N}$ and $1/G_t$, may be interesting, but it is important to be convinced that this type of trick also works when there are six or ten TVP around.

Further, one of the attractive features of TVP modelling is that the issue of unit roots becomes less important. A root of a time series may be temporarily equal to unity and temporarily smaller. In any case the deviations between a variable and its trend will be reasonably stationary. In the very long run it is incredible that time series are stationary or relations linear or parameters constant. This argument was put forward by Day (1993).

Finally, it may be interesting to learn from the growing literature on cross-section based flexible modelling. In particular, the problem of selecting the bandwidth in kernel smoothing must be closely related to the problem of estimating *NVR* in TVP time-series modelling. See Wand and Jones (1995) for a good survey of this literature.

The best way to evaluate the approach proposed is to apply it to one's own data. This leads to the question how to apply DBM modelling. The description of the procedures of the authors is incomplete. Of course, some of the references may be consulted, but several of these appeared in journals that are not readily available in economics libraries. There is a book (Young (1984)), but given the numerous new developments this badly needs a revised edition. I have already mentioned the overconcise description of the TVP estimates of the TF. The authors are also very brief about the specification of the orders of the polynomials in model (12) in the chapter. This equation contains common factors. This is easily seen by rewriting model (12) as

$$(1 + a_1 L)(1 + c_1 L + c_2 L^2) y_t = c^* + (1 + c_1 L + c_2 L^2) b_1 RI_t$$

$$+ (1 + c_1 L + c_2 L^2) b_2 \nabla G_t + (1 + a_1 L) e_t$$

The common factor hypothesis states that the polynomials of y_t, RI_t and ∇G_t have the factor $(1 + c_1 L + c_2 L^2)$ in common. This restriction can be tested against the alternative that these polynomials are distinct. Hendry (1995, p. 269) and others warn against this type of specification unless one starts with more general specifications and tests to see whether the implicit restrictions can be accepted; see also Mizon (1995). On the other hand, it should be noted that the present specification which makes use of TVP and moving average (MA) error components is more general than the autoregressive distributed lag (AD) specification advocated by Hendry and his colleagues.

The economic ideas of the authors must have been inspired by Keynes. Contemporary authors use different explanatory variables such as interest rates, real wage costs and oil crisis dummies when discussing unemployment or employment. See, for instance, Bierens and Broersma (1993) and Palm and Pfann (1993) and the literature quoted there. But whether the example makes economic sense is of secondary importance. It is desirable that economists can apply this approach themselves. In other words, there is a need for user-friendly software. If that is not made available the approach has no future. In this context it is important to know what is the maximum dimensionality of the problems to be handled. I have already mentioned the Doan *et al.* (1984) approach which several readers would consider as a benchmark. Of course, the present approach is more ambitious.

Despite the terse description of some details, I find this chapter highly interesting. One could only hope that this approach will form a stimulus for new research in econometrics. The following issues deserve further attention:

1. Extension of the present approach to the case where the data series contain one or more common trends.
2. Finding a simpler procedure for determining noise variance ratios.
3. Incorporating checks to prevent overfitting as a standard part of the procedure.
4. Comparison of the DBM modelling with other flexible approaches. I have already mentioned the Doan *et al.* (1984) Bayesian VAR approach, and the approach in Bierens and Broersma (1993). Another suggestion by Bierens is ARMA memory index modelling. See Bierens (1994) for more detailed

references. So far the Harvey (1989) approach is mainly univariate. It seems that a multivariate version of the STAMP package is currently being developed or just completed.
5. Reconstructing the approach in the light of the interesting suggestions made by Davies (1995), which emphasize robustness (weak topologies) and adequacy regions.

If only 10% of all the research time now devoted to unit root/cointegration research could be redirected to this area we would enter a fascinating period.

J.C. ENGWERDA

In this chapter the authors propose a methodology for the modelling of complex dynamic processes, which they call data-based mechanistic (DBM) modelling. The basics of the procedure are outlined in Section 6.2.5. The basic philosophy behind the approach is that the available time-series data should determine both the structure of the model and its final parameters. This view is motivated by the facts that, first, many processes cannot be modelled using large, highly parameterized models due to limitations in the available time-series data and, second, the normal response of these processes is, usually, governed by only a few dominant modes. This philosophy agrees with the behavioural framework used by Willems (1986) and Van Overschee and De Moor (1994) and coworkers. In that approach the basic assumption is made that the available time series are generated by a linear model, from which in a mechanistic way a (dynamic) input–output model is designed that can replicate the data and that can be used in trying to understand the dynamics of the underlying process. Note that this last part of the modelling is, particularly in economics, an important one. Indeed, although the approach may produce a mathematically completely sound input–output relationship, it must also provide a description which has direct relevance to the physical reality of the process. This point is also stressed in the DBM approach.

In the DBM approach the linearity assumption is dropped and replaced by a general non-linear relationship of the type (2a) and the assumption that the measured variable is causally related to a number of *a priori* chosen variables. In particular, this last assumption is in conflict with the behavioural approach, and an interesting question is to what extent this assumption can be dropped in the DBM approach, for this would definitely make the DBM approach even more DBM. On the other hand, one should keep in mind that for identifiability reasons it is a great advantage to use as much *a priori* information on causality structure in the model as possible, which stresses the tension between the DBM approach and the presumed knowledge of the process.

Given these *a priori* assumptions on the model, the authors describe in a very clear way all the details of the data-based process of obtaining the structure of the model and then estimating its (possibly time-varying) parameters. It is very impressive to see how various econometric techniques are used to arrive at a final model, and the authors illustrate the various stages (and problems) in the approach by means of an illuminating example. The example clearly demonstrates the (dis)advantage of the DBM approach. It produces a model that is at variance with the mainstream macroeconomic literature, and as such may initiate a discussion on existing macroeconomic paradigms.

However, I also have some comments. First, it would have been valuable to see how well the final model forecasts unemployment figures. Second, the question remains whether we captured the most important explanatory variables for explaining unemployment figures (what about the number of potential workers?). Third, the question arises to me whether the fact that a ratio of two macroeconomic figures is obtained as an explanatory variable might not be due to the fact that there are some subjective elements in the measurement of macroeconomic data (redefinitions of variables, indexing etc.). A ratio of variables, which somehow cancels these effects, may therefore be a better explanatory variable.

⎯⎯⎯⎯ REPLIES ⎯⎯⎯⎯

P.C. YOUNG AND D.J. PEDREGAL

T. KLOEK

1. Dr Kloek's short review of TVP methods in econometrics is a fair one and he correctly stresses the differences between these various methods and our DBM approach. There is, however, a little misunderstanding about the procedures used in DBM analysis, which probably arises from our inadequate description of the methodology rather than any fault on Dr Kloek's part. In particular, while the estimation and removal of trends can form part of the analysis, as it does in the empirical example, it is not essential to the DBM approach: if a physical (here macroeconomic) explanation of the trend behaviour is possible, then we believe it should always be included in the model in preference to a stochastic trend. The unemployment example described in the present chapter, for instance, is intended merely to illustrate the application of the DBM approach and it is not meant to be a definitive statement on the modelling of unemployment behaviour in the US economy. Indeed, an alternative and more economically meaningful model can be obtained from similar analysis, which we have now referred to in the chapter for clarification, after receiving an initial draft of Dr Kloek's comments.

    As we now point out, in this subsequent analysis (see Young and Pedregal (1996b)), the explanatory variables are modified so that there is no need at all for any trend estimation and removal. More specifically, government spending and private investment, both measured relative to GNP, are utilized as explanatory variables, with the long-term movements in the former accounting for the long-term non-stationarity in the unemployment figures; and the extreme volatility of the latter, about a reasonably constant mean value, explaining the shorter term and rather large fluctuations. Not only does this lead to a model which has interesting and controversial Keynesian connotations (see 6 below), but it also explains the data a little better than its cruder progenitor described in the present chapter.

2. As Dr Kloek points out, while the DBM approach has similarities to the structural modelling (SM) methodology of Harvey and others (since it shares with them the exploitation of recursive KF and FIS smoothing algorithms), it also has some marked differences which are worth noting. First, there are conceptual differences: the DBM approach starts with the assumption that the relationships may be non-linear and utilizes FIS estimation to identify the presence and nature of any non-linearity; also it assumes that TF components relating the explanatory (exogenous) variables to the dependent variable will probably be required in the UC model and it utilizes optimal RIV methods to identify and estimate these TF relationships (see also 5 below).

    At a more detailed technical level, there are two other differences worth emphasizing. First, trends are normally assumed to be described by an integrated random walk (IRW) model, rather than the local linear trend (LLT) model, since the former often yields a smoother, more trend-like long-term component (although we now note that the IRW trend model, considered as 'a LLT model with the variance of the white noise in the level equation constrained to zero', is receiving more attention in structural modelling circles than before: see our comments on the chapter by Harvey and Koopmans in this volume). Second, we estimate the *NVR*s (or signal-to-noise ratios) as hyperparameters, normally using a special kind of optimization in the frequency domain;[1] whereas, in SM, the noise variances are normally estimated directly using time or frequency domain ML methods.

3. Dr Kloek feels that both DBM and SM approaches are 'unnecessarily complicated'. Certainly, simpler and more 'hands-on' manual approaches to DBM analysis are possible (and available, for instance, in the *micro*CAP-TAIN software package, where the user can choose manual selection of *NVR* values based on spectral or Bayesian considerations; or, alternatively, select automatic optimization). Such manual approaches may well be desirable in some circumstances but, in general, we feel that the automatic optimization of parameters in parsimonious UC models is rather more objective, yet still relatively simple. Dr Kloek is also perceptive when he draw parallels between NVR optimization and bandwidth selection in kernel regression and smoothing. We have recently shown how FIS estimation and such smoothing methods are closely related, with the former utilizing *implicit* (and stochastically optimal) kernel smoothing, while the latter *explicitly* involves such methods in a rather more *ad hoc* manner (Young and Pedregal (1996a), (1996c)).

4. It is true that, in its present form, the DBM approach to non-linear model identification could not be applied easily and successfully to larger-dimension multivariable TF models. However, research on such extensions is proceeding with funding from the UK Engineering and Physical Sciences Research Council (whose assistance we gratefully acknowledge). In addi-

tion, the whole philosophy behind DBM analysis stresses the need for parametrically efficient models and the avoidance of overparameterization (see e.g. Young, Parkinson and Lees (1996)). Consequently, we do not envisage it being used for the *simultaneous* estimation of 'six to ten' TVPs. Indeed, for such estimation to be successful, it would probably be necessary to look for transformations in the data which would create orthogonal variables and so tend to hinder the important physical interpretation stage, which is the aspect which most differentiates DBM analysis from the more usual 'black box' methods of time-series analysis.

5. We agree that our description of the DBM methodology is rather brief but it was impossible to include more within the page limitations. We apologize for this but hope that interested readers will be stimulated to read the other papers referred to in the chapter, which amplify on various aspects of the methodology. On the specific point raised by Dr Kloek, however, it should be emphasized that the orders of the TF polynomials are specified during an identification stage in the analysis, which exploits the fact that the *instrumental product matrix* (IPM), which is an essential feature of RIV estimation, becomes near singular when the model is overparameterized. Consequently, a statistic based on the inverse of the IPM (see Young, Jakeman and McMurtrie (1979)) is able to detect the possibility of overparameterization, so ensuring a well identified model and avoiding the presence of pole-zero cancellations in the TF model.

Such an identification step, with its ability to avoid the presence of common factors, is of obvious importance in relation to the other point raised by Dr Kloek; namely the apparent difficulty of the common factors which emerge when the model equation (12) in our chapter is manipulated into its alternative ARMAX form. Clearly, as Dr Kloek suggests, such common factors are a problem *if one attempts to identify the model directly in this particular regression-like ARMAX form*. But the common factors in this ARMAX model are not relevant at all if, as in our approach (and, indeed, that of Box and Jenkins), the identification analysis is directed *entirely* at a TF model form, such as (12). This is an important matter which we have discussed thoroughly in two previous papers on this subject (Jakeman and Young (1981, 1983)). These demonstrate certain statistical advantages associated with the TF model formulation and, in particular, draw attention to the identification problems that can occur when ARMAX model identification is applied to time series data generated by TF models. For example, if the data are generated by a multi-input TF model of the form,

$$y_t = \sum_{i=1}^{m} \frac{B_i(L)}{A(L)} u_{it} + \frac{D(L)}{C(L)} e_t \qquad (1)$$

then, in order to avoid the common factor problem pointed out by Dr Kloek, ARMAX identification would need to be applied to the ARMAX model

$$A(L)y_t = \sum_{i=1}^{m} B_i(L)u_{it} + F(L)e_t \qquad (2)$$

where $F(L) = D(L)A(L)/C(L)$ is nominally infinite dimensional and, for estimation purposes, will always need to be approximated by a finite dimensional MA process. Depending upon the nature of the polynomials in its definition, this MA approximation may involve a large number of parameters and so lead to an ARMAX model which is not very parsimonious in comparison to the true TF model that generated the data. In the case of the TF model (12) (which we would emphasize is very well identified, as demonstrated by the diagnostic statistics and acf/ccf correlation analysis shown in our chapter) this is not too important, however, since simple manipulation of the model into the ARMAX form (2) shows that the nominally infinite MA polynomial $F(L)$ is given by

$$F(L) = 1 + 0.433L + 0.2068L^2 + 0.1092L^3 + 0.0628L^4 + \dots \qquad (3)$$

which is well approximated by the first three or four terms shown here. Thus, *in this case*, the TF model has only marginal advantage in terms of parsimony (TF: five parameters; ARMAX: six to seven parameters) and either can be considered to describe the data reasonably well.[2] But this will not always be the case: we believe it is safer, in general terms, to consider linear time-series modelling in TF rather than ARMAX terms; a decision which is, of course, the basis of the very well-tested and successful Box and Jenkins approach to time-series analysis. There are also other statistical advantages of the TF model and these are discussed in the above references.

6.   We agree to some extent that 'the economic ideas of the authors must have been inspired by Keynes'. As we point out, one of the most exciting, albeit controversial, aspects of DBM models is that they can tend to question existing paradigms or, in the case of Keynes, resuscitate much older paradigms that have gone out of favour for some (often unscientific) reasons. What is so comforting in the case of our unemployment example, and which is made even clearer in the subsequent analysis referred to in 1 above, is that the Keynesian interpretation has not been imposed upon the analysis by prior conjecture but has emerged fairly objectively from the DBM analysis. It could be argued, of course, that the original selection of the explanatory variables was inspired in some way by Keynesian thinking but, even if this was (subconsciously) the case, the model structure, particularly the use of relativistic variables, did not emerge from any explicit Keynesian considerations. Also, we would emphasize that we are not inferring, in any sense, that

the US government have been consciously acting in a Keynesian-inspired manner (just the opposite, it would appear). Rather, we are simply pointing out that there is some evidence in the data that *naturally occurring* Keynesian-type mechanisms may have been at work in the US economy and led to the long-term rise in the background level of unemployment since 1970.

J.C. ENGWERDA

1. While Dr Engwerda rightly draws attention to some similarities between our DBM approach and the data-based behavioural methodology of Willems *et al.*, we feel that there are considerable differences in both the philosophy and methodology associated with the two approaches which makes their comparison rather difficult. Also, his remarks on the assumption of causality make us realize that the empirical example is a little misleading, since it does not explicitly seek to statistically justify the assumption that the major direction of potential causation is from the explanatory variables to unemployment. In fact, testing this assumption is the normal approach used in DBM analysis and it usually involves Granger-type causality analysis (see e.g. Lütkepohl (1991)) applied to a vector autoregressive (VAR) model of the complete data vector, in this case $X_t = [y_t \; RI_t \; \nabla G_t]^T$. This VAR model contrasts with the uni-directional TF model (12) since it allows for dynamic interaction between all the variables, so permitting significant feedback effects to be identified between all three variables, if there is evidence of their presence.

This multivariable causality analysis is presented more fully in the subsequent modelling study referred to in comment 1 of our response to T. Kloek, which describes our development of an improved unemployment model. There, following standard practice (see e.g. Priestley (1989)), the Akaike Information Criterion identifies a third-order, VAR(3) process for $X_t = [y_t \; RGI_t \; RPI_t]^T$, where now RGI_t and RPI_t are the two relative investment variables (government and private, respectively), i.e.

$$X_t = c + A_1 X_{t-1} + A_2 X_{t-2} + A_3 X_{t-3} + \varepsilon_t \qquad \varepsilon_t \sim NID(0, \Sigma_\varepsilon)$$

in which c is a vector of constants, A_i, $i = 1, 2, 3$, are 3×3 dimensional matrices of parameters and Σ_ε is the covariance matrix associated with the white noise-input vector ε_t. The causality tests in this case reject the possibility of significant feedback effects between the unemployment variable y_t and the explanatory variables (RGI_t, RPI_t) and so justify our use of the uni-directional TF model.

2. We agree that forecasting results would have provided additional insight into the value and validity of the model. Once again, however, we have to plead

space limitations and refer the reader once again to the subsequent modelling study, where forecasting results for the improved model mentioned above, are presented. As shown in Figure 6.A, these show that the model provides a very reasonable forecast of the unemployment variations up to 1995, based on forecasts of the two explanatory variables RGI_t and RPI_t over the period 1988(2) to 1998(2) (rather difficult exercises in their own right). To obtain these forecasts, dynamic harmonic regression (DHR) models were identified and estimated for the two explanatory variables up to 1988(2) and these were appended to the model for Kalman filter-based forecasting.[3] Note that the new unemployment data up to 1995 (shown as crosses on Figure 6.A) were not used in this forecasting analysis and the forecasts represent true 40-step-ahead (10-year) predictions, based only on data up to 1988(2). It is clear that the forecasts (actually carried out prior to acquisition of the new data) have proven quite reasonable and are consistent with what one might expect, given the nature of model (3) in the chapter and the forecast explanatory variables. The main discrepancy is that the forecast level of unemployment is about 1% higher than that realized over the forecast period. However, this is well within the forecast accuracy and, presumably, arises mainly because of errors in the predicted changes in the explanatory variables. Thus far, however, we have been unable to obtain later figures for these variables.

Finally, we would like to thank Dr Kloek and Dr Engwerda for the various additional references and useful suggestions they have provided, all of which help to clarify and enhance our chapter. Such thoughtful comments and discerning questions are always welcome in the evaluation of new ideas.

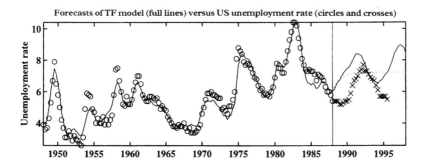

Forecasts of TF model (full lines) versus US unemployment rate (circles and crosses)

Figure 6.A Unemployment rate in the USA (circles and crosses) compared with forecasts of the TF model when (1) the explanatory variables are forecast using DHR models (full line) and (2) the inputs are assumed to remain constant at their mean levels between 1974 and 1988 (dotted line)

Endnotes

1. Normally in DBM modelling, the *NVR* parameters for trend and periodic components are optimized by fitting the UC model to the AIC identified AR spectrum of the data; while time-domain ML estimation (similar to that used in structural modelling) is utilized for TVP estimation in regression or TF models.
2. We have carried out a quick ARMAX analysis of the data and this confirms that at least a third-order MA is required to explain the data as well as the TF model (12).
3. DHR is a modelling technique by which a time series is assumed to be the addition of a number of periodic functions at different frequencies modulated by time variable parameters (see e.g. Ng and Young (1990) and Young (1988)).

REFERENCES

Bierens, H.J. (1994) Topics in advanced econometrics. Cambridge University Press, Cambridge.

Bierens, H.J. and Broersma, L. (1993) The relation between unemployment and interest rate: some international evidence. *Econometric Reviews* **12**, 217–56.

Billings, S.A. and Voon, W.S.F. (1986) Correlation based model validity tests for non-linear models. *International Journal of Control* **44**, 235–44.

Bollerslev, T., Engle, R.F. and Nelson, D.B. (1994) ARCH models. Chapter 49 in R.F. Engle and D.L. McFadden (eds), *Handbook of Econometrics, Volume IV.* Elsevier Science, Amsterdam.

Box, G.E.P and Jenkins G.M. (1970) *Time Series Analysis, Forecasting and Control.* Holden Day, San Francisco.

Co, T.B. (1996) Parameter estimation of nonlinear systems using modulating functions methods. In M.I. Friswell and J.E. Mottershead (eds), *Identification in Engineering Systems.* Swansea, University of Wales, pp. 87–96.

Cooley, T.F. and Prescott, E.C. (1976) Estimation in the presence of stochastic parameter variation. *Econometrica* **44**, 167–84.

Davies, P.L. (1995) Data features. *Statistica Neerlandica* **49**, 185–245.

Day, R.H. (1993) Complex economic dynamics: obvious in history, generic in theory, elusive in data. Chapter 1 in M.H. Pesaran and S.M. Potter (eds), *Nonlinear Dynamics, Chaos and Econometrics.* Wiley, Chichester.

Doan, T., Litterman R. and Sims C. (1984) Forecasting and conditional projection using realistic prior distributions. *Econometric Reviews* **3**, 1–100.

Engle, R.F. (1982), Autoregressive conditional heteroskedasticity, with estimates of the variance of UK inflation. *Econometrica* **50**, 987–1007.

Gramlich, E.M. (1994) Infrastructure investment—a review-essay. *Journal of Economic Literature* **32**, 1176–96.

Harvey, A.C. (1989) *Forecasting, Structural Time Series Models and the Kalman Filter.* Cambridge University Press, Cambridge.

Hastie, T.J. and Tibshirani R.J. (1990) *Generalized Additive Models.* Chapman & Hall, London.

Hendry, D.F. (1995) *Dynamic Econometrics.* Oxford University Press, Oxford.

Jakeman, A.J. and Young, P.C. (1979) Refined instrumental variable methods of recursive time-series analysis: Part II, multivariable systems. *International Journal of Control* **29**, 621–44.

Jakeman, A.J. and Young, P.C. (1981) On the decoupling of system and noise model parameter estimation in time-series analysis. *International Journal of Control* **34**, 423–31.

Jakeman, A.J. and Young P.C. (1983) Advanced methods of recursive time-series analysis. *International Journal of Control* **37**, 1291–1310.

Jarque, C.M. and Bera A.K. (1980) Efficient tests for normality, homoskedasticity and serial independence of regression residuals. *Economic Letters* **6**, 255–9.

Kalman, R.E. (1960) A new approach to linear filtering and prediction problems. *ASME Trans., Jnl. Basic Eng.* **83-D**, 95–108.

Kendall, M.G. and Stuart, A. (1961) *The Advanced Theory of Statistics Vol.2.* Griffin, London.

King, T.G., Plosser, C.I., Stock, J.H. and Watson, M.W. (1991) Stochastic trends and economic fluctuations. *American Economic Review* **81**, 819–40.

Ljung, G.M. and Box, G.E.P (1978) On a measure of lack of fit in time series models. *Biometrika* **66**, 67–72.

Ljung, L. and Söderström T. (1983) *Theory and Practice of Recursive Estimation.* MIT Press, Cambridge, MA.

Lütkepohl, H. (1991) *Introduction to Multiple Time Series Analysis.* Springer-Verlag, Berlin.

Mizon, G.E. (1995) A simple message for autocorrelation correctors: Don't. *Journal of Econometrics* **69**, 267–88.

Ng, C.N. and Young, P.C. (1990) Recursive estimation and forecasting of nonstationary time-series. *Journal of Forecasting* **9**, 173–204.

Pagan, A. (1980) Some identification and estimation results for regression models with stochastically varying coefficients. *Journal of Econometrics* **13**, 341–63.

Palm, F.C. and Pfann, G.A. (1993) Asymmetric adjustment costs in nonlinear labour demand models for the manufacturing sectors in the Netherlands and the UK. *Review of Economic Studies* **60**, 397–412.

Pedregal, D.J. (1995) *Comparación Teórica, Estructural y Predictiva de Modelos de Componentes no Observables y Extensiones del Modelo de Young.* PhD thesis, Universidad Autónoma de Madrid.

Phillips, P.C.B. (1996) Econometric model determination. *Econometrica* **64**, 763–812.

Priestley, M.B. (1989) *Spectral Analysis and Time Series.* Academic Press, London.

Van Overschee, P. and De Moor, B. (1994) N4SID: Subspace algorithms for the identification of combined deterministic–stochastic systems. *Automatica* **30**, 75–93.

Wallis, S.G., Young, P.C. and Beven, K.J. (1989) Experimental investigation of the Aggregated Dead Zone (ADZ) model for longitudinal solute transport in stream channels. *Proc. Inst. of Civil Engrs, Part 2* **87**, 1–22.

Wand, M.P. and Jones, M.C. (1995) *Kernel smoothing.* Chapman and Hall, London.

White, H. (1980) A heteroskedasticity-consistent covariance estimator and a direct test for heteroskedasticity. *Econometrica* **48**, 817–38.

Willems, J.C. (1986) From time series to linear system (Parts I, II, III). *Automatica* **22**, 561–80, 675–94, and **23**, 87–115.

Young, P.C. (1970) An instrumental variable method for real-time identification of a noisy process. *Automatica* **6**, 271–87.

Young, P.C. (1983) The validity and credibility of models for badly defined systems. In M.B. Beck and G. van Straten (eds), *Uncertainty and Forecasting of Water Quality.* Springer-Verlag, Berlin.

Young, P.C. (1984) *Recursive Estimation and Time-Series Analysis.* Springer-Verlag, Berlin.

Young, P.C. (1985) The instrumental variable method: a practical approach to identification and system parameter estimation. In H.A.Barker and P.C.Young (eds), *Identification and System Parameter Estimation 1985, Vols. 1 and 2.* Pergamon Press, Oxford, pp. 1–16.

Young, P.C. (1988) Recursive extrapolation, interpolation and smoothing of non-stationary time-series. In H.F. Chen (ed.), *Identification and System Parameter Estimation* Pergamon Press, Oxford, pp. 33–44.

Young, P.C. (1989) Recursive estimation, forecasting and adaptive control. In C.T. Leondes (ed.), *Control and Dynamic Systems, Vol. 30.* Academic Press, San Diego, pp. 119–65.

Young, P.C. (1993) Time variable and state dependent modelling of nonstationary and nonlinear time series. Chapter 26 in T. Subba Rao (ed.), *Developments in Time Series Analysis.* Chapman and Hall, London, pp. 374–413.

Young, P.C. (1994) Time variable parameter and trend estimation in nonstationary economic time series. *Journal of Forecasting* **13**, 179–210.

Young, P.C. (1996a) Identification, estimation and control of continuous-time and delta operator systems. In M.I. Friswell and J.E. Mottershead (eds), *Identification in Engineering Systems*. University of Wales, Swansea, pp. 1–17.

Young, P.C. (1996b) A general approach to identification, estimation and control for a class of nonlinear dynamic systems. In M.I. Friswell and J.E. Mottershead (eds), *Identification in Engineering Systems*. University of Wales, Swansea, pp. 436–45.

Young, P.C. and Beven, K.J. (1994) Data-based mechanistic modelling and the rainfall-flow nonlinearity. *Environmetrics* **5**, 335–63.

Young, P.C. and Jakeman, A.J. (1979) Refined instrumental variable methods of recursive time-series analysis: Part I, single input single output systems. *International Journal of Control* **29**, 1–30.

Young, P.C. and Jakeman, A.J. (1980) Refined instrumental variable methods of recursive time-series analysis: Part III, extensions. *International Journal of Control* **31**, 741–64.

Young, P.C., Jakeman, A.J. and McMurtrie, R. (1979) An instrumental variable method for model order identification *Automatica* **16**, 281–94.

Young, P.C., Ng, C.N. and Armitage, P. (1989) A systems approach to economic forecasting and seasonal adjustment. *International Journal on Computers and Mathematics with Applications* **18**, 481–501.

Young, P.C., Parkinson, S. and Lees, M.J. (1996) Simplicity out of complexity: Occam's Razor revisited. *Journal of Applied Statistics* **23**, 165–210.

Young, P.C. and Pedregal, D.J. (1996a) Recursive and en-bloc approaches to signal extraction. Submitted paper.

Young, P.C. and Pedregal, D.J. (1996b) Macro-economic relativity: government spending, private investment and unemployment in the USA. Tech. Rep. No. 148, Centre for Research on Environmental Systems and Statistics (submitted for publication).

Young, P.C. and Pedregal, D.J. (1996c) Recursive fixed interval smoothing and the evaluation of LIDAR measurements: a comment on the paper by Holst, Hössjer, Björklund, Ragnarsson and Edner. *Environmetrics* **7**, 417–27.

Young, P.C. and Runkle, D. (1989) Recursive estimation and modelling of nonstationary and nonlinear time-series. In *Adaptive Systems in Control and Signal Processing, Vol. 1*. Institute of Measurement and Control for IFAC, London, pp. 49–64.

SECTION 3
Trends and Non-stationarity

7
Cointegration Analysis

H.J. BIERENS

7.1 INTRODUCTION

7.1.1 What is Cointegration?

The basic idea behind cointegration is that if all the components of a vector time series process z_t have a unit root, or in other words, if z_t is a multivariate $I(1)$ process, there may exist linear combinations $\xi^T z_t$ without a unit root. These linear combinations may then be interpreted as long-term relations between the components of z_t, or in economic terms as static equilibrium relations.

For bivariate economic $I(1)$ processes, cointegration often manifests itself by more or less parallel shapes of the plots of the two series involved. Figure 7.1 displays a typical example of such a pair of cointegrated economic time series, namely the log of nominal income (upper curve) and the log of nominal consumption (lower curve) in Sweden[1] from 1861 to 1988.

According to Friedman's (1957) permanent income theory, the long-run marginal propensity to consume from permanent income should be close to one. With the logs of consumption and income being unit root with drift processes, the modern interpretation of the permanent income hypothesis therefore is that the difference of the logs of consumption and income is stationary: $\xi = (1, -1)^T$. However, income in Friedman's theory is net income rather than gross income, so that the long-run marginal propensity to consume from gross income might be less than one. In any case, Friedman's theory predicts that the logs of consumption and income are cointegrated. The time series displayed in Figure 7.1 will be used in an empirical application in Section 7.6.

System Dynamics in Economic and Financial Models. Edited by C. Heij, J.M. Schumacher, B. Hanzon and C. Praagman © 1997 John Wiley & Sons Ltd

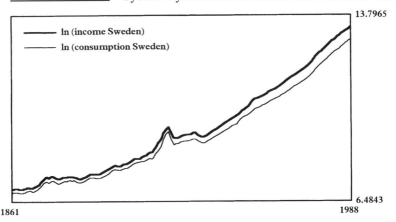

Figure 7.1 Logs of nominal income and consumption in Sweden from 1861 to 1988

7.1.2 The Literature on Cointegration

The concept of cointegration was first introduced by Granger (1981) and elaborated further by Engle and Granger (1987), Engle and Yoo (1987, 1991), Phillips and Ouliaris (1990), Stock and Watson (1988), Phillips (1991) and Johansen (1988, 1991, 1994), among others.

Working in the context of a bivariate system with, at most, one cointegrating vector, Engle and Granger (1987) propose to estimate the cointegrating vector $\xi = (1, \xi_2)^T$ by regressing the first component $z_{1,t}$ of z_t on the second component $z_{2,t}$, using OLS (which is called the cointegrating regression), and then testing whether the OLS residuals of this regression have a unit root, using the Augmented Dickey–Fuller (ADF) test. See Fuller (1976), Dickey and Fuller (1979, 1981) and Said and Dickey (1984) for the latter. However, since the ADF test is conducted on estimated residuals, the tables of the critical values of this test in Fuller (1976) no longer apply. The correct critical values involved can be found in Engle and Yoo (1987). Phillips and Ouliaris' (1990) tests are also based on these residuals, but instead of using the ADF test for testing the presence of a unit root they use further elaborations of the Phillips (1987) and Phillips–Perron (1988) unit root tests. Both types of tests have absence of cointegration as the null hypothesis. Park (1990) proposes a test for unit root and cointegration using the variable addition approach, by regressing the OLS residuals of the cointegrating regression on powers of time and testing whether the coefficients involved are jointly zero. The same idea has been used by Bierens and Guo (1993) to test (trend) stationarity against the unit root hypothesis. However, also Park's approach requires consistent estimation of the long-run variance of the errors of the true cointegrating regression by a Newey–West (1987) type estimator, which sacrifices a substantial amount of asymptotic power of the test. Cf. Bierens and Guo (1993) for the latter. Also the tests of Hansen (1992) and Park (1990) are based on a single cointegrating regression, and both tests employ variants of the instrumental variables estimation method of Phillips and Hansen (1990). Finally, Boswijk (1994, 1995) links the single-equation and system approaches by using structural single-equations as a basis for cointegration analysis.

The above approaches test the null or alternative hypothesis of absence of cointegration, but if the tests indicate the presence of cointegration in systems with three variables or more we still do not know how many linear independent cointegrating vectors there are. In such cases one may use the approach of Stock and Watson (1988), which is a multivariate extension of the Engle–Granger and Phillips–Ouliaris tests. The basic idea is to linearly transform the q-variate cointegrated process z_t with, say r linear independent cointegrating vectors such that the first r components of the transformed z_t are stationary and the last $q - r$ components, stacked in a vector w_t, say, are integrated. The transformation matrix involved can be consistently estimated using principal components of z_t. Then test whether w_t is a $q - r$ variate unit root process, using a multivariate version of the ADF test or the Phillips (1987) test. The critical values of this test differ according to whether the initial value z_0 is non-zero or not and whether the unit root process z_t has drift or not.

In a series of influential papers, Johansen (1988, 1991) and Johansen and Juselius (1990) propose an ingenious and practical full maximum likelihood estimation and testing approach, based on the following error correction model (hereafter ECM) for the q-variate unit root process z_t:

$$\Delta z_t = \Pi_0 d_t + \sum_{j=1}^{p-1} \Pi_j \Delta z_{t-j} + \gamma \beta^{\mathrm{T}} z_{t-p} + e_t \qquad (1)$$

Here $\Delta z_t = z_t - z_{t-1}$, d_t is a vector of deterministic variables, such as a constant and seasonal dummy variables, the Π_j, $j > 0$, are $q \times q$ and β and γ are $q \times r$ parameter matrices, where β and γ are of full column rank, with r the number of linear independent cointegrating vectors (the columns of β), the e_t are i.i.d. $N_q(0, \Sigma)$ errors, and $\det (I - \sum_{j=1}^{p-1} \Pi_j L^j)$ has all its roots outside the unit circle. Note that if $r = q$, so that then the matrix $\gamma \beta^{\mathrm{T}}$ is of full rank, and if $d_t = 1$, then model (1) generates a stationary AR(p) process z_t.

ECM (1) is based on the Engle–Granger (1987) error correction representation theorem for cointegrated systems, and the asymptotic inference involved is related to the work of Sims, Stock and Watson (1990). By step-wise concentrating all the parameter matrices in the likelihood function out, except the matrix β, Johansen shows that the maximum likelihood estimator of β can be derived as the solution of a generalized eigenvalue problem. Likelihood ratio tests of hypotheses about the number of cointegrating vectors can then be based on these eigenvalues. Moreover, Johansen (1988) also proposes likelihood ratio tests for linear restrictions on the cointegrating vectors.

Initially, Johansen (1988) considered the case where d_t is absent. Later, Johansen (1991) extended his approach to the case where d_t contains an intercept and seasonal dummy variables, and in Johansen (1994) also a time trend in d_t (but no seasonal dummy variables) is allowed. These three cases lead to different null distributions of the likelihood ratio tests of the number of cointegrating vectors. Moreover, also possible restrictions on the vector of intercepts or the vector of trend coefficients may lead to different null distributions. Thus application of Johansen's tests actually requires some *a priori* knowledge of the true parameters of ECM (1).

Phillips' (1991) efficient error correction modelling approach differs from that of Johansen (1988) in that Phillips specifies the ECM directly on the basis of the cointegrating relations $z_{1,t} = Bz_{2,t} + u_t$, with u_t a stationary zero mean Gaussian process, leading to an ECM of the form

$$\Delta z_t = \begin{pmatrix} I_r & -B \\ O & O \end{pmatrix} z_{t-1} + v_t \qquad (2)$$

where r is the number of cointegrating relations and v_t is a stationary Gaussian process with long-run variance matrix $\Omega = \lim_{n\to\infty} \text{var}\,[(1/\sqrt{n})\Sigma_{t=1}^{n} v_t]$. Phillips shows that under the i.i.d. assumption on v_t the maximum likelihood estimator of B is efficient, and that this efficiency carries over to the case with dependent errors v_t if B is estimated by maximum likelihood on the basis of model (2) with i.i.d. $N(0, \Omega)$ errors v_t, provided Ω is replaced by a consistent estimator. In contrast to Johansen's maximum likelihood method, however, Phillips' efficient maximum likelihood approach has not yet been widely applied in empirical research, probably due to the fact that the limiting distribution of the maximum likelihood estimator of the matrix B depends on the long-run variance matrix Ω.

The Stock and Watson (1988), Phillips (1991) and Johansen (1988, 1991, 1994) approaches require consistent estimation of nuisance and/or structural parameters. In a recent article (Bierens (1997)) I have proposed consistent cointegration tests that do not need specification of the data-generating process, apart from some mild regularity conditions, or estimation of (nuisance) parameters. Thus these tests are completely non-parametric. They are conducted analogously to Johansen's tests, including the test for parametric restrictions on the cointegrating vectors, namely on the basis of the ordered solutions of a generalized eigenvalue problem. Moreover, as in Johansen's approach, one can consistently estimate a basis of the space of cointegrating vectors, using the eigenvectors of the generalized eigenvalue problem involved. However, the two matrices are constructed independently of the data-generating process on the basis of weighted means of z_t and Δz_t, respectively, where the weights involved are Chebychev time polynomials (cf. Hamming (1973)) of even order.

7.1.3 Contents of this Chapter

In this chapter I will review some new developments in cointegration analysis, in particular Johansen's (1988, 1991, 1994) maximum likelihood approach on the basis of ECM (1), and my non-parametric cointegration approach. First, in Section 7.2, I will explain cointegration in more detail, and in Section 7.3 I will discuss (in an informal way) the Granger representation theorem that gives rise to the ECM specification (1). In Sections 7.4 and 7.5 I will review Johansen's and my non-parametric approach, respectively. The main reason for focusing on Johansen's approach is that it is presently the most popular one in empirical macroeconomic cointegration research, due to its own merits as well as the fact that Johansen's approach is now available in most time-series oriented econometric software packages. Finally, in Section 7.6 I will apply both the Johansen approach and my non-parametric approach to the Swedish data on the logs of consumption and income displayed in Figure 7.1.

7.2 INTRODUCTION TO COINTEGRATION

Consider the q-variate unit root process $z_t = z_{t-1} + u_t$, where u_t is a zero mean stationary process, and let z_t be observable for $t = 0, 1, 2, \ldots, n$. Due to the Wold decomposition theorem, we can write (under some mild regularity conditions), $u_t = C(L)v_t$, where v_t is a q-variate stationary white-noise process with unit variance, i.e.

$$E[v_t] = 0, \qquad E[v_t v_t^{\mathrm{T}}] = I_q \qquad E[v_t v_{t-j}^{\mathrm{T}}] = O \text{ for } j \neq 0 \qquad (3)$$

and $C(L)$ is a $q \times q$ matrix of lag polynomials: $C(L) = \sum_{k=0}^{\infty} C_k L^k$, where L is the lag operator. Since by construction the lag polynomial $C(L) - C(1)$ is zero at $L = 1$, we can write

$$C(L)v_t = C(1)v_t + (C(L) - C(1))v_t = C(1)v_t + (1 - L)D(L)v_t \qquad (4)$$

where

$$D(L) = \sum_{k=0}^{\infty} D_k L^k = (C(L) - C(1))/(1 - L) \qquad (5)$$

Denoting $w_t = D(L)v_t$ we now have $u_t = C(1)v_t + w_t - w_{t-1}$, hence

$$z_t = z_0 - w_0 + w_t + C(1)\sum_{j=1}^{t} v_j \qquad (6)$$

If v_t is a Gaussian process then by the white-noise assumption (3) the v_ts are i.i.d. $N_q(0, I_q)$. Since Johansen's approach is based on Gaussian maximum likelihood theory, this normality condition will be imposed. Moreover, we need regularity conditions that ensure that u_t and w_t are stationary processes. Therefore, I assume:

Assumption 1: The process u_t can be written as $u_t = C(L)v_t$, where v_t is i.i.d. $N_q(0, I_q)$, $C(L) = C_1(L)^{-1}C_2(L)$, with $C_1(L)$ and $C_2(L)$ finite-order lag polynomials, and $\det(C_1(L))$ has all its roots outside the complex unit circle.

Note that the condition on $C(L)$ implies that ΣC_k, $\Sigma C_k C_k^T$, ΣD_k and $\Sigma D_k D_k^T$ converge, so that together with the normality condition, it follows that u_t and w_t are stationary Gaussian processes. Cf. Engle and Yoo (1991). Moreover, Assumption 1 excludes the usual condition that also $\det(C_2(L))$ has roots all outside the unit circle. This is necessary because for cointegration we need to allow the matrix $C(1)$ to be singular.

As far as the non-parametric cointegration approach is concerned, Assumption 1 is more restrictive than necessary, but it will keep the argument below transparent, and focused on the main issues. See Phillips and Solo (1992) for weaker conditions in the case of linear processes. Also, in the non-parametric cointegration case we could assume instead of Assumption 1 that u_t is stationary and ergodic, so that we can write $u_t = \varepsilon_t + w_t - w_{t-1}$, where ε_t is a martingale difference process with variance matrix comparable with $C(1)C(1)^T$. Cf. Hall and Heyde (1980, p.136).

Now if $\mathrm{rank}(C(1)) = q - r < q$ then the process z_t is cointegrated: there exist r linear independent cointegrating vectors β_j, $j = 1, \ldots, r$, say, such that $\beta_j^T C(1) = 0^T$, hence it follows from equation (6) that $\beta_j^T z_t = \beta_j^T(z_0 - w_0) + \beta_j^T w_t$, $j = 1, \ldots, r$. Thus the $\beta_j^T z_t$s are now asymptotically stationary processes, in the sense that the stochastic intercept $\beta_j^T(z_0 - w_0)$ becomes independent of w_t if t approaches infinity, so that we then may condition on $z_0 - w_0$ and treat it as a constant.

Factorization (4) can be applied to the matrix $D(L)$ as well, so that, as in (4), $C(L)v_t = C(1)v_t + D(1)(1 - L)v_t + (1 - L)^2 G(L)v_t$, where $G(L) = (D(L) - D(1))/(1 - L)$. However, if there exists a cointegrating vector β such that $\beta^T D(1) = 0^T$ then, with $\varepsilon_t = G(L)v_t$ a stationary process, we would have $\beta^T u_t = \Delta^2 \beta^T \varepsilon_t$, hence $\sum_{j=1}^{t} \beta^T z_t = \beta^T(z_0 - \varepsilon_0 + \varepsilon_{-1})t + \beta^T \varepsilon_t$ is trend stationary. As we will see in the next section, this would violate one of the conditions for the existence of an autoregressive error correction representation of a cointegrated system. Also, we need to exclude this case for the non-parametric cointegration approach. Therefore I assume:

Assumption 2: Let R_r be the matrix of eigenvectors of $C(1)C(1)^T$ corresponding to the r zero eigenvalues. Then the matrix $R_r^T D(1)D(1)^T R_r$ is non-singular.

7.3 THE ERROR CORRECTION FORM OF A COINTEGRATED SYSTEM

Following the approach of Engle and Yoo (1991) I will now show that under some regularity conditions a cointegrated process can be modelled as an ECM of the type (1). This result is due to Granger (cf. Engle and Granger (1987)). For convenience the discussion will be confined to the bivariate case ($q = 2$) with one cointegrating vector.

Let β be the cointegrating vector. Without loss of generality we may normalize $\beta = (1, \beta_2)^T$. Consider the matrices

$$\Phi = \begin{pmatrix} 1 & \beta_2 \\ 0 & 1 \end{pmatrix} = \begin{pmatrix} \beta^T \\ \phi_2^T \end{pmatrix} \qquad V^{-1}(L) = \begin{pmatrix} \beta^T D(L) \\ \phi_2^T C(L) \end{pmatrix}$$

$$M(L) = \begin{pmatrix} 1-L & 0 \\ 0 & 1 \end{pmatrix} \qquad M^*(L) = \begin{pmatrix} 1 & 0 \\ 0 & 1-L \end{pmatrix}$$

Then

$$\Phi \Delta z_t = \begin{pmatrix} (1-L)\beta^T D(L) \\ \phi_2^T C(L) \end{pmatrix} v_t = M(L)V^{-1}(L)v_t$$

and $M^*(L)M(L) = (1-L)I_2$. Next, assume that $V^{-1}(L)$ is invertible with inverse $V(L)$. This assumption is related to Assumption 2: if Assumption 2 does not hold then $V^{-1}(1)$ is singular so that $V^{-1}(L)$ is not invertible. Furthermore, denote $A(L) = V(L)M^*(L)\Phi$. Then $(1-L)A(L)z_t = (1-L)v_t$, which yields the AR form of the model:

$$A(L)z_t = \mu_0 + v_t \tag{7}$$

where $\mu_0 = A(L)z_0 - v_0$. Now observe that

$$A(1) = V(1)M^*(1)\Phi = V(1)\begin{pmatrix} 1 & 0 \\ 0 & 0 \end{pmatrix}\begin{pmatrix} 1 & \beta_2 \\ 0 & 1 \end{pmatrix} = V(1)\begin{pmatrix} 1 & \beta_2 \\ 0 & 0 \end{pmatrix} = \gamma_1 \beta^T \tag{8}$$

where γ_1 is the first column of $V(1)$. Moreover, similar to equation (4) we can write

$$A(L) = A(1)L + (1-L)B(L) \tag{9}$$

Combining equations (7), (8) and (9) we get the ECM $B(L)\Delta z_t = \mu_0 - \gamma_1 \beta^T z_{t-1} + v_t$. Finally, assume that $B(0)$ is invertible and that $B(L)$ is a $(p-1)$-order lag polynomial, so that we may write $\Pi(L) = B(0)^{-1}B(L) = I - \Pi_1 L - \ldots - \Pi_{p-1}L^{p-1}$. Denoting $\pi_0 = B(0)^{-1}\mu_0$, $\gamma = -B(0)^{-1}\gamma_1$, and $e_t = B(0)^{-1}v_t$, we get the ECM $\Delta z_t = \pi_0 + \sum_{j=1}^{p-1}\Pi_j\Delta z_{t-j} + \gamma\beta^T z_{t-1} + e_t$.

Note that the lag of the level variable z_{t-1} does not matter. Without loss of generality we may replace $\Pi(L)$ by the lag polynomial $\Pi_*(L) = \Pi(L) - \Sigma_{j=1}^{p-1} \gamma \beta^T L^j$, which yields an ECM of the form (1) with $d_t = 1$.

7.4 JOHANSEN'S MAXIMUM LIKELIHOOD APPROACH

7.4.1 Introduction

Johansen's cointegration testing approach is based on maximum likelihood estimation and likelihood ratio testing of ECM (1), by step-wise concentrating the parameters out (i.e. maximizing the likelihood function over a subset of parameters, treating the other parameters as known), given the number r of cointegrating vectors, where the matrix β is the last to be concentrated out. Denoting the concentrated likelihood, given r and β, by $\hat{L}(r, \beta)$, and the maximum likelihood estimator of β given r by $\hat{\beta}_r$, where β and its maximum likelihood estimate are interpreted as zero vectors if $r = 0$, Johansen proposes two tests for the number of cointegrated vectors, namely the likelihood ratio test $-2 \ln (\hat{L}(r, \hat{\beta}_r)/ \hat{L}(r + 1, \hat{\beta}_{r+1}))$ of the null hypothesis that there are r cointegrated vectors (for $r = 0, 1, \ldots, q - 1$) against the alternative that there are $r + 1$ cointegrating vectors, and the likelihood ratio test $-2 \ln (\hat{L}(r, \hat{\beta}_r)/ \hat{L}(q, \hat{\beta}_q))$ of the same null hypothesis against the alternative that there are q cointegrated vectors. The latter alternative corresponds to the case where β is square and of full rank, which in turn corresponds to the case that z_t is stationary rather than a multivariate unit root process. Since the usual regularity conditions for maximum likelihood estimation do not apply in this case, the likelihood ratio tests involved have non-standard limiting null distributions. Moreover, given the number r of cointegrating vectors, Johansen also proposes a likelihood ratio test of parametric restrictions on β of the form $\beta = H\phi$, where H is a given $q \times s$ matrix of rank $s \leqslant r$ and ϕ is an unrestricted $s \times r$ matrix. For example, in the case $r = 1$, $q = 2$, one might wish to test whether β^T is proportional to $(1, -1) = H^T$. The likelihood ratio test statistic $-2 \ln [\sup_\phi \hat{L}(r, H\phi)/\hat{L}(r, \hat{\beta}_r)]$ involved has a limiting χ^2 null distribution with $r(q - s)$ degrees of freedom.

7.4.2 The Lambda-max and Trace Tests

I will now illustrate how Johansen's cointegration tests are conducted for the case where the data-generating process is a Gaussian ECM of the form (1) with $d_t = 1$ and $p = 2$, where z_t is observable for $t = -1, 0, \ldots, n$:

$$\Delta z_t = \pi_0 + \Pi_1 \Delta z_{t-1} + \gamma \beta^T z_{t-2} + e_t \qquad e_t \sim \text{i.i.d. } N_q(0, \Sigma) \qquad (10)$$

Given β, γ and Σ, the maximum likelihood estimates of π_0 and Π_1 can be obtained simply by regressing $\Delta z_t - \gamma \beta^T z_{t-2}$ on an intercept 1 and Δz_{t-1}, using

OLS. The residuals of this regression are $\hat{R}_{1,t} - \gamma\beta^T\hat{R}_{2,t}$, where $\hat{R}_{1,t}$ is the residual of the regression of Δz_t on 1 and Δz_{t-1}, and $\hat{R}_{2,t}$ is the residual of the regression of z_{t-2} on 1 and Δz_{t-1}. Now the log-likelihood function with π_0 and Π_1 concentrated out is of the form

$$-0.5n\ln(\det\Sigma) - 0.5\sum_{t=1}^{n}(\hat{R}_{1,t} - \gamma\beta^T\hat{R}_{2,t})^T\Sigma^{-1}(\hat{R}_{1,t} - \gamma\beta^T\hat{R}_{2,t}) + \text{rest}$$

where 'rest' stands for the terms that do not depend on parameters. Similarly, we can concentrate γ out, given β and Σ, by regressing $\hat{R}_{1,t}$ on $\beta^T\hat{R}_{2,t}$, which yields the estimate $\hat{\gamma}(\beta) = \hat{S}_{1,2}\beta[\beta^T\hat{S}_{2,2}\beta]^{-1}$, where $\hat{S}_{i,j} = (1/n)\sum_{t=1}^{n}\hat{R}_{i,t}\hat{R}_{j,t}^T$, $i, j = 1, 2$. Next, concentrate Σ out, given β, by substituting the well-known maximum likelihood estimator of the variance matrix of a normal distribution with zero mean vector:

$$\hat{\Sigma}(\beta) = (1/n)\sum_{t=1}^{n}(\hat{R}_{1,t} - \hat{\gamma}(\beta)\beta^T\hat{R}_{2,t})(\hat{R}_{1,t} - \hat{\gamma}(\beta)\beta^T\hat{R}_{2,t})^T$$

$$= \hat{S}_{1,1} - \hat{S}_{1,2}\beta(\beta^T\hat{S}_{2,2}\beta)^{-1}\beta^T\hat{S}_{2,1}$$

Thus, the concentrated log-likelihood now becomes $\ln(\hat{L}(r, \beta)) = -0.5n\ln(\det\hat{\Sigma}(\beta)) + \text{rest}$, hence the maximum likelihood estimator of β is found by solving the minimization problem

$$\min\det(\hat{S}_{1,1} - \hat{S}_{1,2}\beta(\beta^T\hat{S}_{2,2}\beta)^{-1}\beta^T\hat{S}_{2,1}) \tag{11}$$

where the minimum is taken over all $q \times r$ matrices β. It is a standard linear algebra exercise to verify that the minimization problem (11) is equivalent to

$$\min\det(\beta^T\hat{S}_{2,2}\beta - \beta^T\hat{S}_{2,1}\hat{S}_{1,1}^{-1}\hat{S}_{1,2}\beta)\det(\hat{S}_{1,1})/\det(\beta^T\hat{S}_{2,2}\beta) \tag{12}$$

Note that the solution involved is not unique, as we may freely multiply β by a conformable non-singular matrix. It is now quite easy to recognize the minimization problem (12) as a generalized eigenvalue problem: let $\hat{\lambda}_1 \geqslant \hat{\lambda}_2 \geqslant \ldots \geqslant \hat{\lambda}_q$ be the ordered solutions of the generalized eigenvalue problem $\det(\lambda\hat{S}_{2,2} - \hat{S}_{2,1}\hat{S}_{1,1}^{-1}\hat{S}_{1,2}) = 0$, let $\hat{B} = (\hat{b}_1, \ldots, \hat{b}_q)$ be the matrix of corresponding eigenvectors, normalized such that $\hat{B}^T\hat{S}_{2,2}\hat{B} = I_q$, and choose $\beta = \hat{B}\xi$, where ξ is a $q \times r$ matrix normalized such that $\xi^T\xi = I_r$. Then the minimization problem (12) becomes

$$\min_{\xi^T\xi=I_r}\det(I_r - \xi^T\hat{\Lambda}\xi)\det(\hat{S}_{1,1}) \tag{13}$$

where $\hat{\Lambda} = \text{diag}(\hat{\lambda}_1, \hat{\lambda}_2, \ldots, \hat{\lambda}_q)$. Clearly, the solution of equation (13) is $\xi^T = (I_r, O)$, hence the maximum likelihood estimator $\hat{\beta}_r$ of β, given the number r of cointegrating vectors, is equal to the matrix of the first r columns of $\hat{B}$: $\hat{\beta}_r = (\hat{b}_1, \ldots, \hat{b}_r)$. Moreover, $\det[\hat{\Sigma}(\hat{\beta}_r)] = \det(I_r - \hat{\Lambda}_r)\det(\hat{S}_{1,1})$, where $\hat{\Lambda}_r = \mathrm{diag}(\hat{\lambda}, \ldots, \hat{\lambda}_r)$, so that the maximum log-likelihood given r becomes:

$$\ln(\hat{L}(r, \hat{\beta}_r)) = -0.5n\sum_{i=1}^{r}\ln(1 - \hat{\lambda}_i) - 0.5n\ln[\det(\hat{S}_{1,1})] + \text{rest} \qquad (14)$$

Thus, the likelihood ratio test $-2\ln(\hat{L}(r, \hat{\beta}_r)/\hat{L}(r + 1, \hat{\beta}_{r+1}))$ of the null hypothesis that there are r cointegrated vectors against the alternative that there are $r + 1$ cointegrating vectors becomes $-n\ln(1 - \hat{\lambda}_{r+1}) \approx n\hat{\lambda}_{r+1}$, and the likelihood ratio test $-2\ln(\hat{L}(r, \hat{\beta}_r)/\hat{L}(q, \hat{\beta}_q))$ of the same null hypothesis against the alternative that there are q cointegrated vectors becomes $-n\Sigma_{i=1+r}^{q}\ln(1 - \hat{\lambda}_i) \approx n\Sigma_{i=r+1}^{q}\hat{\lambda}_i$. Johansen (1988, 1991) proves that under the null of r cointegrating vectors, $(\hat{\lambda}_1, \ldots, \hat{\lambda}_r)^{\mathrm{T}}$ converges in probability to a vector of constants between zero and one, and $n(\hat{\lambda}_{r+1}, \ldots, \hat{\lambda}_q)^{\mathrm{T}}$ converges in distribution to the vector of ordered eigenvalues $\lambda_1 \geq \ldots \geq \lambda_{q-r}$ of a stochastic a.s. positive definite $(q - r) \times (q - r)$ matrix which components are functionals of a $q - r$-variate standard Brownian motion. Therefore, the likelihood ratio test $-2\ln(\hat{L}(r, \hat{\beta}_r)/\hat{L}(r + 1, \hat{\beta}_{r+1})) \approx n\hat{\lambda}_{r+1}$ is called the *lambda-max* test, and the likelihood ratio test $-2\ln(\hat{L}(r, \hat{\beta}_r)/\hat{L}(q, \hat{\beta}_q)) \approx n\Sigma_{i=r+1}^{q}\hat{\lambda}_i$ is the *trace* test.

7.4.3 Testing Parametric Restrictions on the Cointegrating Vectors

As in equation (14) it can be shown that under the null hypothesis $\beta = H\phi$, where H is a given $q \times s$ matrix of rank $s \leq r$ with r given, and ϕ an unrestricted $s \times r$ matrix, the log-likelihood is $-0.5n\sum_{i=1}^{s}\ln[1 - \tilde{\lambda}_i] - 0.5n\ln[\det(H^{\mathrm{T}}\hat{S}_{1,1}H)] + \text{rest}$, where $\tilde{\lambda}_1 \geq \ldots \geq \tilde{\lambda}_s$ are the solutions of the generalized eigenvalue problem $\det(\lambda H^{\mathrm{T}}\hat{S}_{2,2}H - H^{\mathrm{T}}\hat{S}_{2,1}\hat{S}_{1,1}^{-1}\hat{S}_{1,2}H) = 0$ and the rest term is the same as in equation (14). Thus, the likelihood ratio test statistic involved is:

$$-2\ln(LR) = n\sum_{i=1}^{s}\ln(1 - \tilde{\lambda}_i) - n\sum_{i=1}^{r}\ln(1 - \hat{\lambda}_i)$$

$$+ n\ln[\det(H^{\mathrm{T}}\hat{S}_{1,1}H)] - n\ln[\det(\hat{S}_{1,1})].$$

Johansen (1988, 1991) proved that this likelihood ratio test has a χ^2 null distribution with $r(q - s)$ degrees of freedom.

7.4.4 Cointegrating Restrictions on the Intercept Parameters

The null distributions of the lambda-max and trace tests in the above case depends on whether the vector π_0 of intercept parameters in model (10) can be written as

$$\pi_0 = \gamma\mu \qquad \text{with } \mu \in \mathbb{R}^r \tag{15}$$

or not. If so, ECM (10) becomes $\Delta z_t = \Pi_1 \Delta z_{t-1} + \gamma[\mu + \beta^{\mathrm{T}} z_{t-2}] + e_t$, so that then $\beta^{\mathrm{T}} z_t$ is stationary about a constant μ rather than zero-mean stationary.

If we believe that the cointegrating restriction (15) on the intercept parameters holds, we can impose it as follows. First, concentrate Π_1 out, by regressing $\Delta z_t - \gamma(\mu + \beta^{\mathrm{T}} z_{t-2})$ on Δz_{t-1}. The residuals of this regression are $\hat{R}_{1,t} - \gamma(\mu, \beta^{\mathrm{T}})\hat{R}_{2,t}$, where $\hat{R}_{1,t}$ is now the residual of the regression of Δz_t on Δz_{t-1} alone, and $\hat{R}_{2,t}$ is now the residual of the regression of $(1, z_{t-2})^{\mathrm{T}}$ on Δz_{t-1}. Then proceed as before, with β replaced by $\beta_* = (\mu, \beta^{\mathrm{T}})^{\mathrm{T}}$. Note that in this case the size of the matrix $\hat{S}_{2,2}$ is now $(q+1) \times (q+1)$, and the sizes of the matrices $\hat{S}_{1,2}$ and $\hat{S}_{2,1}$ are now $q \times (q+1)$ and $(q+1) \times q$, respectively. The limiting null distributions of the lambda-max and trace tests, however, are different from the ones before. Thus, there are three cases with different null distributions:

1. The cointegrating restriction (15) on the intercept parameters does not hold and is not imposed.
2. The cointegrating restriction (15) on the intercept parameters holds but is not imposed.
3. The cointegrating restriction (15) on the intercept parameters holds and is imposed.

The problem with testing parametric restrictions on the cointegrating vectors in the latter case is that we cannot confine our attention to restrictions of the form $\beta = H\phi$ only, but that we have to include μ as well. Thus, we can only test restrictions of the form $\beta_* = (\mu, \beta^{\mathrm{T}})^{\mathrm{T}} = H\phi$, where H is now a given $(q+1) \times s$ matrix with rank $s \leqslant r$, and ϕ is a conformable matrix of free parameters. However, the parameter vector μ is in general of no (economic) interest, so that one has to re-estimate the model without imposing restriction (15) in order to test restrictions on β only.

7.4.5 Further Extensions

Along the same lines as above one may include seasonal dummy variables in the ECM, provided they are taken in deviation from their sample means so that they become orthogonal to the intercept, without affecting the null distributions of the lambda-max and trace tests. Moreover, recently Johansen (1994) considered also the case where a time trend is included in the ECM, i.e. $\Delta z_t = \pi_{0,0} + \pi_{0,1} t + \sum_{j=1}^{p-1} \Pi_j \Delta z_{t-j} + \gamma\beta^{\mathrm{T}} z_{t-p} + e_t$, where possibly cointegrating restrictions of the form $\pi_{0,1} = \gamma\delta$ are imposed on the trend parameters. In the latter case $\beta^{\mathrm{T}} z_t$ is trend stationary. Again, the null distributions of the lambda-max and trace tests differ from the cases with an intercept only, and between the cases where cointegrating restrictions on the trend parameters are imposed or not.

7.5 NON-PARAMETRIC COINTEGRATION ANALYSIS

7.5.1 Non-parametric Tests of the Number of Cointegrating Vectors

The basic idea behind my non-parametric cointegration approach is that the difference in asymptotic behaviour of certain weighted means of z_t and Δz_t under cointegration can be exploited to construct cointegration tests. In particular, these weighted means can be used to construct two random matrices such that cointegration tests can be based on their generalized eigenvalues, as in Johansen's approach. I will only outline the main ideas; for the details and the proofs I refer to Bierens (1997) and the separate appendix to that paper.

Denote the partial sums associated to z_t and Δz_t by $S_n^z(x) = 0$ if $x \in [0, n^{-1}]$, $S_n^z(x) = \sum_{t=1}^{[xn]} z_t$ if $x \in (n^{-1}, 1]$, and $S_n^{\Delta z}(x) = 0$ if $x \in [0, n^{-1}]$, $S_n^{\Delta z}(x) = \sum_{t=1}^{[xn]} \Delta z_t$ if $x \in (n^{-1}, 1]$, respectively. Then it is not difficult to prove that under Assumption 1

$$\begin{pmatrix} S_n^z(x)/(n\sqrt{n}) \\ S_n^{\Delta z}(x)/(\sqrt{n}) \end{pmatrix} \Rightarrow \begin{pmatrix} C(1)\int_0^x W(y)\,dy \\ C(1)W(x) \end{pmatrix} \tag{16}$$

where $W(.)$ is a q-variate standard Wiener process, and '$\Rightarrow$' means weak convergence (cf. Billingsley (1968)). The latter symbol will also be used to indicate convergence in distribution and convergence in probability, as these concepts are special cases of weak convergence.

Next, consider the following class of weighted means of z_t and Δz_t:

$$M_n^z(F) = \frac{1}{n}\sum_{t=1}^n F(t/n)z_t \qquad M_n^{\Delta z}(F) = \frac{1}{n}\sum_{t=1}^n F(t/n)\Delta z_t \tag{17}$$

where F is a continuously differentiable function on the unit interval $[0,1]$ with derivative f. Then it is straightforward to verify from equation (16) and Lemma 9.6.3 in Bierens (1994, p. 200) that

$$\begin{pmatrix} M_n^z(F)/\sqrt{n} \\ M_n^{\Delta z}(F)\sqrt{n} \end{pmatrix} = F(1)\begin{pmatrix} S_n^z(1)/(n\sqrt{n}) \\ S_n^{\Delta z}(1)/\sqrt{n} \end{pmatrix} - \int f(x)\begin{pmatrix} S_n^z(x)/(n\sqrt{n}) \\ S_n^{\Delta z}(x)/\sqrt{n} \end{pmatrix} dx$$

$$\Rightarrow \begin{pmatrix} C(1)\int F(x)W(x)\,dx \\ C(1)(F(1)W(1) - \int f(x)W(x)\,dx) \end{pmatrix} \sim N_{2q}(0, (C(1)C(1)^{\mathrm{T}}) \otimes \Sigma_F) \tag{18}$$

where

$$\Sigma_F = \begin{pmatrix} \iint F(x)F(y)\min(x,\,y)\,dx\,dy & \tfrac{1}{2}\left(\int F(x)\,dx\right)^2 \\[2mm] \tfrac{1}{2}\left(\int F(x)\,dx\right)^2 & \int F(x)^2\,dx \end{pmatrix}$$

(The integrals in equation (18), Σ_F and below are taken over the unit interval, unless otherwise indicated.) Note that if we choose F such that

$$\int F(x)\,dx = 0 \tag{19}$$

then Σ_F becomes a diagonal matrix, so that the two components on the right-hand side of equation (18) are then independent normally distributed:

Lemma 1: Under Assumption 1 and condition (19),

$$\begin{pmatrix} M_n^z(F)/\sqrt{n} \\[1mm] M_n^{\Delta z}(F)\sqrt{n} \end{pmatrix} \Rightarrow \begin{pmatrix} C(1)X_F\sqrt{\iint F(x)F(y)\min(x,\,y)\,dx\,dy} \\[1mm] C(1)Y_F\sqrt{\int F(x)^2\,dx} \end{pmatrix} \tag{20}$$

where X_F and Y_F are independent q-variate standard normally distributed random vectors depending on F in the following way:

$$X_F = \frac{\int F(x)W(x)\,dx}{\sqrt{\iint F(x)F(y)\min(x,\,y)\,dx\,dy}} \qquad Y_F = \frac{F(1)W(1) - \int f(x)W(x)\,dx}{\sqrt{\int F(x)^2\,dx}} \tag{21}$$

Note that in the case of cointegration the matrix $C(1)C(1)^{\mathrm{T}}$ is singular, so that the limiting normal distribution at the right-hand side of equation (20) is singular, hence for any cointegrating vector ξ we have $\xi^{\mathrm{T}} M_n^z(F)/\sqrt{n} \Rightarrow 0$ and $\xi^{\mathrm{T}} M_n^{\Delta z}(F)\sqrt{n} \Rightarrow 0$. This suggests that for cointegrating vectors ξ the rates of convergence of $\xi^{\mathrm{T}} M_n^z(F)$ and $\xi^{\mathrm{T}} M_n^{\Delta z}(F)$ will be different from the case in Lemma 1.

Lemma 2: Let Assumption 1 and condition (19) hold. If z_t is cointegrated then for each matrix $\Xi = (\xi_1, \ldots, \xi_r)$ of cointegrating vectors ξ_i,

$$\begin{pmatrix} \Xi^{\mathrm{T}} M_n^z(F)\sqrt{n} \\[1mm] \Xi^{\mathrm{T}} M_n^{\Delta z}(F)n \end{pmatrix} \Rightarrow \begin{pmatrix} \Xi^{\mathrm{T}} D(1)Y_F\sqrt{\int F(x)^2\,dx} \\[1mm] F(1)\Xi^{\mathrm{T}} D_* Z \end{pmatrix}$$

where Y_F and Z are independent q-variate standard normally distributed, with Y_F defined by (21) and $D_* = [\Sigma_{j=0}^{\infty} D_j D_j^{\mathrm{T}}]^{1/2}$ (c.f. (5)).

Comparing Lemmas 1 and 2 we see that the asymptotic behaviour, in particular the absolute and relative rates of convergence, of the statistics (17) differ substantially according to whether z_t is cointegrated or not. These differences can now be exploited in constructing non-parametric cointegration tests as follows.

Choose a sequence F_k, $k = 1, 2, \ldots, m$, with $m \geqslant q$, of continuously differentiable real functions on $[0,1]$ with derivatives f_k satisfying condition (19), i.e. $\int F_k(x)\,dx = 0$ for $k = 1, \ldots, m$, so that the random vectors

$$X_k = \frac{\int F_k(x)W(x)\,dx}{\sqrt{\int\int F_k(x)F_k(y)\min(x,\,y)\,dx\,dy}} \qquad Y_k = \frac{F_k(1)W(1) - \int f_k(x)W(x)\,dx}{\sqrt{\int F_k(x)^2\,dx}}$$

(cf. equation (21)) are mutually independent, together with conditions ensuring that these random vectors are also independent for $k = 1, 2, \ldots$. Such functions F_k do exist. For example, let

$$F_k(x) = \cos(2k\pi x) \qquad k = 1, 2, 3, \ldots \qquad (22)$$

In fact, this choice of F_k is 'optimal' in the sense that it maximizes a lower bound of the power function of the non-parametric cointegration test.

Next, construct the random matrices $\hat{A}_m = \sum_{k=1}^{m} a_{n,k} a_{n,k}^T$ and $\hat{B}_m = \sum_{k=1}^{m} b_{n,k} b_{n,k}^T$, where

$$a_{n,k} = \frac{M_n^z(F_k(\cdot))}{\sqrt{\int\int F_k(x)F_k(y)\min(x,\,y)\,dx\,dy}} \qquad b_{n,k} = \frac{\sqrt{n}\,M_n^{\Delta z}(F_k(\cdot))}{\sqrt{\int F_k(x)^2\,dx}}$$

Moreover, denote

$$\gamma_k = \frac{\sqrt{\int F_k(x)^2\,dx}}{\sqrt{\int\int F_k(x)F_k(y)\min(x,\,y)\,dx\,dy}} \qquad \delta_k = \frac{F_k(1)}{\sqrt{\int F_k(x)^2\,dx}}$$

Then it follows easily from Lemmas 1 and 2:

Lemma 3: Let rank $C(1) = q - r$, let R_{q-r} be the matrix of orthonormal eigenvectors of $C(1)C(1)^T$ corresponding to the $q - r$ positive eigenvalues, let R_r be the matrix of orthonormal eigenvectors corresponding to the r zero eigenvalues, and denote $R = (R_{q-r}, R_r)$. Then under Assumption 1:

$$\begin{pmatrix} I_{q-r} & O \\ O & nI_r \end{pmatrix} R^T \hat{A}_m R \begin{pmatrix} I_{q-r} & O \\ O & nI_r \end{pmatrix} = \begin{pmatrix} R_{q-r}^T \hat{A}_m R_{q-r} & nR_{q-r}^T \hat{A}_m R_r \\ nR_r^T \hat{A}_m R_{q-r} & n^2 R_r^T \hat{A}_m R_r \end{pmatrix}$$

$$\Rightarrow \begin{pmatrix} R_{q-r}^T C(1) \sum_{k=1}^{m} X_k X_k^T C(1)^T R_{q-r} & R_{q-r}^T C(1) \sum_{k=1}^{m} \gamma_k X_k Y_k^T D(1)^T R_r \\ R_r^T D(1) \sum_{k=1}^{m} \gamma_k Y_k X_k^T C(1)^T R_{q-r} & R_r^T D(1) \sum_{k=1}^{m} \gamma_k^2 Y_k Y_k^T D(1)^T R_r \end{pmatrix} \qquad (23)$$

and

$$\begin{pmatrix} I_{q-r} & O \\ O & \sqrt{n}I_r \end{pmatrix} R^{\mathrm{T}} \hat{B}_m R \begin{pmatrix} I_{q-r} & O \\ O & \sqrt{n}I_r \end{pmatrix} = \begin{pmatrix} R_{q-r}^{\mathrm{T}} \hat{B}_m R_{q-r} & \sqrt{n} R_{q-r}^{\mathrm{T}} \hat{B}_m R_r \\ \sqrt{n} R_r^{\mathrm{T}} \hat{B}_m R_{q-r} & n R_r^{\mathrm{T}} \hat{B}_m R_r \end{pmatrix}$$

$$\Rightarrow \begin{pmatrix} R_{q-r}^{\mathrm{T}} C(1) \sum_{k=1}^{m} Y_k Y_k^{\mathrm{T}} C(1)^{\mathrm{T}} R_{q-r} & R_{q-r}^{\mathrm{T}} C(1) \sum_{k=1}^{m} \delta_k Y_k Z^{\mathrm{T}} D_*^{\mathrm{T}} R_r \\ R_r^{\mathrm{T}} D_* \sum_{k=1}^{m} \delta_k Z Y_k^{\mathrm{T}} C(1)^{\mathrm{T}} R_{q-r} & R_r^{\mathrm{T}} D_* \sum_{k=1}^{m} \delta_k^2 Z Z^{\mathrm{T}} D_*^{\mathrm{T}} R_r \end{pmatrix}$$

where the X_is, the Y_js and Z are independent q-variate standard normally distributed.

Now at first one might think of employing these results for constructing cointegration tests by using the solutions of the generalized eigenvalue problem $\det(\hat{A}_m - \lambda \hat{B}_m) = 0$, as in Johansen's approach. However, the problem is that under cointegration both matrices converge in distribution to singular matrices. In deriving the limiting distribution of the generalized eigenvalues, Johansen used a result of Andersen, Brons and Jensen (1983), saying that the ordered solutions of the generalized eigenvalue problem $\det(P_n - \lambda Q_n) = 0$, where P_n and Q_n are stochastic matrices converging jointly in distribution to P_* and Q_*, say, converge in distribution to the ordered solutions of the generalized eigenvalue problem $\det(P_* - \lambda Q_*) = 0$, provided Q_* is a.s. non-singular. Due to the latter condition, this result cannot be used to derive the limiting distribution of the ordered solutions of the generalized eigenvalue problem $\det(\hat{A}_m - \lambda \hat{B}_m) = 0$. However, the following method will cure the problem.

Observe that part (23) of Lemma 3 implies

$$\frac{R^{\mathrm{T}} \hat{A}_m^{-1} R}{n^2} \Rightarrow \begin{pmatrix} O & O \\ O & V_{r,m}^{-1} \end{pmatrix}$$

where

$$V_{r,m} = R_r^{\mathrm{T}} D(1) \sum_{k=1}^{m} \gamma_k^2 Y_k Y_k^{\mathrm{T}} D(1)^{\mathrm{T}} R_r - \left(R_r^{\mathrm{T}} D(1) \sum_{k=1}^{m} \gamma_k Y_k X_k^{\mathrm{T}} C(1)^{\mathrm{T}} R_{q-r} \right)$$

$$\times \left(R_{q-r}^{\mathrm{T}} C(1) \sum_{k=1}^{m} X_k X_k^{\mathrm{T}} C(1)^{\mathrm{T}} R_{q-r} \right)^{-1} \left(R_{q-r}^{\mathrm{T}} C(1) \sum_{k=1}^{m} \gamma_k X_k Y_k^{\mathrm{T}} D(1)^{\mathrm{T}} R_r \right)$$

Note that by Assumption 2, this matrix is a.s. non-singular. Hence $R^{\mathrm{T}}(\hat{B}_m + n^{-2}\hat{A}_m^{-1})R$ converges in distribution to a non-singular block-diagonal matrix. Now using the result of Andersen, Brons and Jensen (1983) it follows straightforwardly:

Theorem 1: Let $\hat{\lambda}_{1,m} \geqslant \ldots \geqslant \hat{\lambda}_{q,m}$ be the ordered solutions of the generalized eigenvalue problem

$$\det(\hat{A}_m - \lambda(\hat{B}_m + n^{-2}\hat{A}_m^{-1})) = 0 \tag{24}$$

and let $\lambda_{1,m} \geqslant \ldots \geqslant \lambda_{q-r,m}$ be the ordered solution of the generalized eigen-value problem $\det(\sum_{k=1}^m X_k^* X_k^{*\mathrm{T}} - \lambda \sum_{k=1}^m Y_k^* Y_k^{*\mathrm{T}}) = 0$, where the X_i^*s and Y_j^*s are i.i.d. $N_{q-r}(0, I_{q-r})$. If z_t is cointegrated with r linear independent cointegrating vectors then under Assumptions 1 and 2, $(\hat{\lambda}_{1,m}, \ldots, \hat{\lambda}_{q,m}) \Rightarrow (\lambda_{1,m}, \ldots, \lambda_{q-r,m}, 0, \ldots, 0)$.

This result suggests using $\hat{\lambda}_{q-r,m}$ as a test statistic for testing the null hypothesis that there are r cointegrating vectors against the alternative that there are $r+1$ cointegrating vectors. The test involved is a left-sided one: the null is rejected if $\hat{\lambda}_{q-r,m}$ is smaller than a critical value. See Bierens (1997, Table 2) for the critical values involved.

The power of the test involved depends on the choice of m as well as on the choice of the functions F_k. As mentioned earlier, the choice (22) is 'optimal' in that it maximizes a lower bound of the power function of the test. However, the asymptotically equivalent functions $F_k(x) = \cos(2k\pi(x - 0.5/n))$ will do an even better job because then the test becomes invariant for drift in the multi-variate unit root process z_t, i.e. the case where $z_t = z_{t-1} + c + u_t$, where c is a vector of drift parameters and u_t is a zero mean stationary process satisfying Assumption 1. The matrices $\hat{A}_m$ and $\hat{B}_m$ then become

$$\hat{A}_m = \frac{8\pi^2}{n} \sum_{k=1}^m k^2 \left(\frac{1}{n}\sum_{t=1}^n \cos(2k\pi(t-0.5)/n)z_t\right)\left(\frac{1}{n}\sum_{t=1}^n \cos(2k\pi(t-0.5)/n)z_t\right)^{\mathrm{T}}$$

$$\hat{B}_m = 2n \sum_{k=1}^m \left(\frac{1}{n}\sum_{t=1}^n \cos(2k\pi(t-0.5)/n)\Delta z_t\right)\left(\frac{1}{n}\sum_{t=1}^n \cos(2k\pi(t-0.5)/n)\Delta z_t\right)^{\mathrm{T}}$$

The same lower bound of the power function of the test mentioned earlier depends on m, hence maximizing this lower bound with respect to m would yield a sensible choice for m. The resulting values for m for significance levels $s \times 5\%$, $s = 1, 2$, and $0 \leqslant r \leqslant 4$, $1 \leqslant q \leqslant 5$, can be expressed by

$$m = q + I(q \geqslant s+1)I(r=0) \tag{25}$$

where $I(.)$ is the indicator function.

7.5.2 Testing Linear Restrictions on the Cointegrating Vectors

Once the number r of cointegrating vectors is established, and $0 < r < q$, one may wish to verify whether there exist cointegrating vectors ξ satisfying the linear restriction $H_0: \xi = H\phi$, $\phi \in \mathbb{R}^s$, where H is a given $q \times s$ matrix with full column rank $s \leqslant r$ and ϕ is arbitrary. Thus, the null hypothesis is that the space spanned by the columns of the matrix H is contained in the space of cointegrating vectors. For example, in the case $q = 3$ we may wish to test whether there exists a cointegrating vector $\xi = (\xi_1, \xi_2, \xi_3)^T$ such that $\xi_1 + \xi_2 = 0$ and $\xi_3 = 0$, so that $H = (1, -1, 0)^T$.

At first one might think of mimicking Johansen's tests for these restrictions, on the basis of the matrices $\hat{A}_m$ and $\hat{B}_m + n^{-2}\hat{A}_m^{-1}$. However, this leads to a case-dependent null distribution. Therefore I propose two tests, the trace and the lambda-max, on the basis of the matrix $\hat{A}_m$ only. The recipe for the lambda-max test is as follows. Choose $m = 2q$. The lambda-max test is based on the maximum solution, say $\tilde{\lambda}_{\max}(H)$, of the generalized eigenvalue problem

$$\det[H^T\hat{A}_m H - \lambda H^T(\hat{A}_m + n^{-2}\hat{A}_m^{-1})^{-1}H] = 0 \qquad (26)$$

The test statistic involved is $n^2\tilde{\lambda}_{\max}(H)$, and we reject the null hypothesis if $n^2\tilde{\lambda}_{\max}(H)$ is larger than a critical value. See Bierens (1997, Table 4). The trace test statistic is n^2 times the sum of the solutions of equation (26), and the critical values involved are given in Bierens (1997, Table 3).

The choice of $m = 2q$ is somewhat heuristic: a lower bound of the power function is monotonically increasing in m, but too large an m may distort the size of the test. Since this lower bound of the power function is almost flat for $m > 2q$, I recommend the 'rule of thumb' $m = 2q$.

7.5.3 Consistent Estimation of a Basis of the Space of Cointegrating Vectors

Given that there are r linear independent (but unknown) cointegrating vectors $\xi_1, \ldots, \xi_r$, one can consistently estimate a basis of the space of cointegrated vectors as follows. Choose again $m = 2q$, and let $\hat{H}$ be the matrix of eigenvectors corresponding to the r smallest eigenvalues of the generalized eigenvalue problem

$$\det[\hat{A}_m - \lambda(\hat{A}_m + n^{-2}\hat{A}_m^{-1})^{-1}] = 0 \qquad (27)$$

where $\hat{H}$ is standardized such that

$$\hat{H}^T(\hat{A}_m + n^{-2}\hat{A}_m^{-1})^{-1}\hat{H} = I_r \qquad (28)$$

Then $\hat{H} = (\xi_1, \ldots, \xi_r)\hat{\Gamma}_r + O_p(1/n)$, where $\hat{\Gamma}_r$ is $r \times r$ with rank $(\hat{\Gamma}_r) = r$. Since the cointegrating vectors $\xi_1, \ldots, \xi_r$ can be chosen orthonormal, we can interpret this result also in terms of projections: The distances between the columns of $\hat{H}$ and their corresponding projections on the space of cointegrating vectors vanish at order $O_p(1/n)$.

7.5.4 Seasonal Drift

The above results apply to multivariate unit root processes with constant drift, but not to processes with seasonal drift. In the latter case one should replace z_t in the matrices $\hat{A}_m$ and $\hat{B}_m$ by seasonal moving averages $\bar{z}_t = (1/s)\Sigma_{\tau=0}^{s-1}z_{t-\tau}$, where s is the number of seasons. With this modification, the non-parametric approach is applicable to time series with seasonal drift.

7.5.5 Concluding Remarks

My non-parametric cointegration approach has some clear advantages over Johansen's maximum likelihood approach, in particular that it does not require one to specify a lag length p and the deterministic variables d_t of ECM (1), and that the critical values are case independent. This will become more clear in the empirical example in Section 7.6. However, there is also a disadvantage, namely that the non-parametric tests are not invariant for scale: replacing z_t by $z_t^* = Qz_t$ where Q is a non-singular matrix, the generalized eigenvalue problem (24) becomes $\det[\hat{A}_m - \lambda(\hat{B}_m + n^{-2}(Q^{\mathrm{T}}Q)^{-1}\hat{A}_m^{-1}(Q^{\mathrm{T}}Q)^{-1})] = 0$, and similarly the matrix $\hat{A}_m^{-1}$ in equations (26), (27) and (28) changes accordingly to $(Q^{\mathrm{T}}Q)^{-1}\hat{A}_m^{-1}(Q^{\mathrm{T}}Q)^{-1}$. Of course, asymptotically this does not matter, but in small samples it clearly will. On the other hand, due to the fact that for $k = 1, 2, 3 \ldots,$

$$\sum_{t=1}^{n} \cos\left(2\pi k(t - 0.5)/n\right) = 0 \qquad \sum_{t=1}^{n} t\cos\left(2\pi k(t - 0.5)/n\right) = 0 \qquad (29)$$

the tests are invariant for location shifts in Δz_t. Therefore, if all the variables in z_t are in logs the units of measurement of the original variables do not matter, due to equation (29), but one should be cautious in conducting the non-parametric tests to vector time-series processes z_t if not all components are in logs.

7.6 AN EMPIRICAL EXAMPLE

I will now apply my non-parametric and Johansen's likelihood ratio cointegration tests to the annual data on the logs of consumption and income in Sweden from 1861 to 1988. However, before conducting cointegration analysis, one should test first whether the time series involved are unit root processes or not. From Figure 7.1 it is obvious that the appropriate hypotheses to be tested are the unit root *with drift* hypothesis against *trend* stationarity. Therefore, I have conducted the Augmented Dickey–Fuller (ADF) t-test of the null hypothesis $\alpha = 0$ in the auxiliary regression $\Delta y_t = \alpha y_{t-1} + \sum_{j=1}^{p}\beta_j\Delta y_{t-j} + \gamma_0 + \gamma_1 t + \varepsilon_t$, with p depending on the sample size n (see Said and Dickey (1984)), and the Phillips–Perron (1988) test Z_α of the unit root with drift hypothesis against the trend stationarity hypothesis. The truncation lag p of the Newey–West (1987) estimator of the long-run variance of Δy_t employed by the Phillips–Perron test as well as the ADF lag length p have been chosen: $p = [5n^{1/4}] = 16$ for $n = 128$. The result is that for both time series the unit root with drift hypothesis cannot be rejected at the 10% significance level. Also, I have conducted the Bierens–Guo (1993) tests of the trend stationarity hypothesis against the unit root with drift hypothesis, and for both time series the null hypothesis of linear trend stationarity is rejected at the 5% significance level.

The results of the non-parametric cointegration tests, conducted at the 10% significance level, are as follows:

H_0	H_1	Test statistic	10% critical region	Conclusion
$r = 0$	$r = 1$	0.000 05	(0, 0.005)	Reject H_0
$r = 1$	$r = 2$	24.332 66	(0, 0.111)	Accept H_0

Thus the conclusion is that there is one cointegrating vector: $r = 1$. The estimate $\hat{\beta}$ of the parameter β in the cointegrating vector $(1, -\beta)^T$ is: $\hat{\beta} = 0.9444$, and the null hypothesis $\beta = 1$ is not rejected at the 10% significance level. The latter hypothesis corresponds to the hypothesis that the long-run marginal propensity to consume from income equals 1.

Next, I have conducted Johansen's tests on the basis of ECM (1) for $p = 1, \ldots, 6$, for the following five cases with respect to the deterministic part $\Pi_0 d_t$:

1. $\Pi_0 d_t = \pi_0$, where π_0 is not proportional to γ.
2. $\Pi_0 d_t = \pi_0$, where π_0 is proportional to γ but this restriction is not imposed.
3. $\Pi_0 d_t = \pi_0$, where π_0 is proportional to γ and this restriction is imposed.
4. $\Pi_0 d_t = \pi_0 + \pi_1 t$, where π_1 is proportional to γ but this restriction is not imposed.
5. $\Pi_0 d_t = \pi_0 + \pi_1 t$, where π_1 is proportional to γ and this restriction is imposed.

In cases 3 and 5 with test result $r = 1$ I have also tested whether the imposed cointegrating restriction holds. Moreover, for cases with test result $r = 1$ I have tested the hypothesis that the cointegrating vector $(1, -\beta)^T$ is equal to $(1, -1)^T$: $\beta = 1$. All tests are conducted at the 10% significance level and the results are presented in Tables 7.1–7.3.

Table 7.1 Johansen's test results for the number r of cointegrating vectors

Case 1		Case 2		Case 3		Case 4		Case 5	
p	r	p	r	p	r	p	r	p	r
1	1	1	1	1	2	1	1	1	1
2	2	2	1	2	2	2	1	2	1
3	2	3	1	3	2	3	1	3	1
4	0 or 2	4	0 or 1	4	2	4	0	4	0
5	0	5	0	5	1	5	0	5	0
6	0 or 2	6	0	6	1	6	0	6	0

Table 7.2 $\hat{\beta}$ and test of $H_0: \beta = 1$ for $r = 1$

	Case 1			Case 2				Case 3				Case 4				Case 5	
p	$\hat{\beta}$	H_0	p	$\hat{\beta}$	H_0	p	$\hat{\beta}$	H_0	p	$\hat{\beta}$	H_0	p	$\hat{\beta}$	H_0
1	0.9115	Reject	1	0.9448	Reject	5	0.9420	Accept	1	0.9245	Reject	1	0.9245	Reject
			2	0.9367	Reject	6	0.9442	Accept	2	0.9115	Reject	2	0.9115	Reject
			3	0.9397	Reject				3	0.9165	Reject	3	0.9165	Reject

Table 7.3   Test of H_0: $\pi_i = \gamma\mu$ for $r = 1$

Case 3		Case 5	
p	H_0	p	H_0
5	Reject	1	Reject
6	Reject	2	Accept
		3	Reject

The results in Table 7.1 where r takes two possible values are due to the fact that the lambda-max and trace tests gave different test results. The test result $r = 2$ would imply that both series are stationary, but the unit root and trend stationarity tests conducted on the single series indicate that they are unit root processes. For case 3 with $p = 5$ and 6 the imposed cointegrating restriction on π_0 is rejected, so that the result $r = 1$ in cases 2 and 3 should be ignored. In case 5 with $p = 1$ and 3 the cointegrating restriction on the trend parameter vector π_1 is rejected, which would imply the presence of a linear time trend in the drift. Since this is implausible, because then the growth rates of consumption and income have a linear trend and therefore grow to infinity themselves, there are only two cases with $r = 1$ left that make sense, namely case 1 with $p = 1$ and case 5 with $p = 2$. For both cases the cointegrating vector is the same, $\hat{\beta} = 0.9115$, and the hypothesis $\beta = 1$ is rejected. The latter result is probably more accurate than the corresponding result of the non-parametric test, because the non-parametric test of restrictions on the cointegrating vector seems less powerful than the corresponding Johansen test. See Bierens (1997).

The results in Tables 7.1–7.3 demonstrate that the Johansen approach is quite sensitive to the specification of the deterministic part $\Pi_0 d_t$ and the lag length p of ECM (1). Without *a priori* knowledge of the data-generating process or of the non-parametric test results it is very difficult to draw firm conclusions from Tables 7.1–7.3 as to whether there is cointegration or not. However, with the non-parametric test results at hand one can narrow down the Johansen test results to a set of results that are plausible, and this is exactly the right way to use the non-parametric tests. My non-parametric tests do not (and should not) compete with Johansen's tests. Both types of tests should be conducted in tandem as I did here, in order to get the maximum information from the data.

ACKNOWLEDGEMENTS

The helpful comments of Helmut Lütkepohl on a previous draft of this chapter are gratefully acknowledged.

ENDNOTE

1. I would like to thank Philip Hans Franses for providing me with this data set. The original sources of these time series are Krantz and Nilson (1975) and Melander, Vredin and Warne (1992).

COMMENTS

R. TSCHERNIG, M. DEISTLER AND M. WAGNER

R. TSCHERNIG

It is no exaggeration to say that the development of cointegration analysis has been one of the most important contributions to econometrics during the last one and a half decades. It has provided the basis for a statistically sound investigation of the long-run dynamics of multivariate (economic) time series if each single time series process is characterized by unit root non-stationarity. This has been of particular importance to economics, since economists are especially interested in the existence and the structure of long-run relationships among these time series. In general they can be interpreted as long-run equilibria. In other words, economists are interested in the existence, number and parameterization of cointegrating vectors. In his survey Bierens concentrates mainly on techniques of cointegration analysis that allow us to answer all three questions simultaneously. They are all based on multivariate time-series techniques. In contrast, single-equation techniques only allow us to answer the question of existence. Therefore they are only briefly sketched and commented on. Bierens presents two multivariate approaches in greater detail: the parametric Johansen maximum likelihood approach and his own recently developed non-parametric approach.

In his survey Bierens is very much concerned with the relevance of a *priori* assumptions on the underlying data-generating process for the various econometric techniques. In fact, he argues that in this respect the Bierens approach is clearly superior to the others due to its non-parametric nature. In this comment I would like to discuss this statement. First, I wish to summarize the line of argument in the chapter. For the error correction form of a cointegrated vector autoregressive time series process (equation (1) in the chapter)

$$\Delta z_t = \Pi_0 d_t + \sum_{j=1}^{p-1} \Pi_j \Delta z_{t-j} + \gamma \beta^{\mathrm{T}} z_{t-p} + e_t$$

Johansen was able to derive the concentrated likelihood function and the asymptotic distribution of the maximum likelihood estimator. Since the likelihood function is derived from the error distribution its specification requires knowledge of the order p of the process, the number of cointegrating relations r and the nature of the deterministic variables d_t. Thus, applying the likelihood ratio testing principle to testing r requires *a priori* knowledge of p and d_t. Furthermore, the choice of d_t influences the asymptotic null distributions depending on whether d_t is absent or contains an intercept or seasonal dummies or exhibits a time trend. As a consequence, Johansen's procedure depends on the econometric procedures to select the order p and the deterministic variables d_t.

In contrast, Bierens' non-parametric procedure does not require such preparatory methods. It therefore seems to suggest itself as an important alternative to existing techniques of cointegration analysis. However, the application of the Bierens method also requires a decision on an order parameter. It is the order m of the non-parametric random matrices $\hat{A}_m$ and $\hat{B}_m$. Equation (25) in the chapter provides an automatic rule for selecting values for m depending on q and r. They are derived in Bierens (1997) by maximizing the power of the test using the Chebychev inequality. Since, however, the Chebychev inequality does not exploit any deeper stochastic structure of the underlying problem, this rule is very conservative and should be viewed more as a rule of thumb. Since the exact relationship may depend on the short-run structure of the process and thus possibly on its order p, it follows that the choice of m may be the non-parametric counterpart of selecting p in parametric methods.

Nevertheless this has different implications. While the parametric Johansen method requires an appropriate choice of p for obtaining the correct null distribution, this is not the case for the Bierens method. For the latter, the choice of m influences only the power of the test.

The key issue is then whether the rule of thumb (25) in the chapter for selecting m implies a power function that really makes the Bierens procedure an interesting alternative to the Johansen procedure in real applications. To answer this question extensive Monte Carlo simulations are needed of which there is no report in the chapter. Independently, one may think of ways to improve the rule of thumb (25) in the chapter in order to increase the power of the test.

Bierens' procedure is of no direct help if the researcher is also interested in short-run dynamics. It can only serve for testing and estimating the long-run components of non-stationary multivariate time-series processes. It is therefore worth noting that there exists another alternative which requires as little *a priori* knowledge as Bierens' procedure but allows us to simultaneously estimate and test the parameterization of the long- and short-run dynamics. Dolado and Lütkepohl (1996) find that the dependence of the null distribution on the structure of the deterministic vector d_t vanishes if one is willing to add one more lag to the order of the true data-generating process. Although this implies inefficient estimates, only extensive Monte Carlo studies can answer the question as to the method that should be preferred in which situations.

M. DEISTLER AND M. WAGNER

This comment consists of two main parts: The first deals with general remarks on cointegration analysis, the second with the chapter by Bierens.

Cointegration analysis has become one of the most popular fields of modern econometrics. In the authors' opinion there are at least three reasons for this. The first is that many economic time series show apparent non-stationary features, such as trends in means and variances. It should be emphasized, however, that non-stationarities coming from unit roots are very special ones. Even in the setting of linear systems this is a highly non-generic case if one also allows for poles of the transfer-function at other places on the unit circle (e.g. seasonal integration and cointegration) and inside the unit circle (the explosive case). Clearly both stationary and integrated processes can serve only as approximate models for a certain time period; but also with this understanding, in a number of applications, models allowing for structural breaks or for slowly time-varying coefficients may be more appropriate for modelling non-stationarities.

The second and perhaps most important point is the following. In the past in econometric model building differenced data have often been used, which means that information concerning the relations at frequency zero is lost. In contrast in cointegration analysis, the primary emphasis is on relations at frequency zero, which in many cases carry the most important economic information, since they are related to steady-state equilibria described by static relations. Borrowing the notation from Bierens and setting $z_0 = 0$ we derive from equation (4) in the chapter

$$z_t = C(1)\frac{1}{1 - L}v_t + D(L)v_t \tag{1}$$

This may be interpreted as a factor model with non-stationary latent variables

$$C(1)\frac{1}{1 - L}v_t$$

(which are generated by a lower-dimensional factor process) and a stationary noise part $D(L)v_t$. Note that here latent process and noise are not orthogonal. As is well known, β is a cointegrating vector iff it is contained in the left kernel of $C(1)$. Since the stationary noise process is interpreted as negligibly small, the cointegrating vectors can be interpreted as the coefficients of a static equilibrium relation. Since the set of singular matrices is a thin subset of all square matrices, we see from equation (1) that the property of being cointegrated is highly non-generic among integrated processes. Thus in cointegration analysis rather special time-series models are considered, where the main emphasis is on the static equilibrium relations between non-stationary components. This special model structure is justified by economic arguments, but, on the other hand, seems to be a main reason why cointegration analysis is rarely used in other fields such as systems identification (in engineering) or signal processing.

There is also a third reason for the popularity of cointegration analysis. It opened a new field of activity for mathematically oriented econometricians, where, nevertheless, major components from probability theory such as functional central limit theorems were already available.

Major questions in cointegration analysis which are considered by Bierens are:

- Determination of the maximum number r of linearly independent cointegrating vectors
- Estimation of a basis for the left kernel of $C(1)$ (i.e. for the space of cointegrating vectors)
- Testing for linear restrictions on the cointegrating vectors
- The role of deterministic variables, such as constants or seasonal dummies. This point will be neglected in our comment for the sake of simplicity of presentation.

After a general introduction, in particular to the structure theory of cointegration models, Bierens describes Johansen's maximum likelihood approach to the problems mentioned above. Johansen's approach belongs to the most important contributions to econometrics in the last decade; it has, however, a limitation: The observed process has to be autoregressive (of course, not necessarily stationary)

$$a(L)z_t = \varepsilon_t \qquad (2)$$

where $a(L) = I - a_1 L - \ldots - a_p L^p$; $a_i \in \mathbb{R}^{q \times q}$.

Bierens considers a more general model class, namely unit root ARMA systems:

$$a(L)z_t = b(L)\varepsilon_t \qquad (3)$$

where $b(L)$ is a polynomial matrix. The case of an integration order higher than one is excluded.

It should be mentioned, however, that Johansen's procedure still has some nice properties if the data-generating process is ARMA and not AR. In Wagner (1994) the following has been obtained. If $(a(L), b(L))$ are left co-prime and $\det b(1) \neq 0$ holds, then the space of cointegrating vectors (of order one) is independent of $b(L)$ in equation (3) and using Johansen's procedure to estimate β still gives consistent estimates. Therefore in this sense Johansen's method for estimating β is still reasonable if the data-generating process is ARMA.

This does not hold, however, for estimation of γ and the other parameters. But also with Bierens' approach only β is estimated. At present the further properties of Johansen's estimate for β in the case of ARMA data-generating processes are investigated.

In Yap and Reinsel (1995) a theory for likelihood estimation and testing for Gaussian unit root ARMA systems is given. In particular they derive the asymptotic distribution of the likelihood ratio test for the number of cointegrating vectors. It turns out that this distribution is the same as in the AR case.

Bierens describes a procedure which is non-parametric in the sense that no order specification is required; Δz_t here is even not necessarily ARMA. The only requirement for Δz_t seems to be that it is regular with absolutely summable coefficients in the Wold decomposition. This procedure is based on certain weighted means of z_t and Δz_t. As in Johansen's approach the tests for the number of cointegrating vectors are based on a generalized eigenvalue problem.

There is a trade-off for this more general setting of Bierens, compared to Johansen's approach, in terms of higher computational load. An essential question in comparing Johansen's and Bierens' approach is the robustness of Johansen's procedure with respect to misspecifications.

One advantage of Johansen's approach is that in the same line γ and the Π_j in equation (1) in the chapter can be estimated. In particular often γ is important for further economic analysis, as it gives the loading weights for the error correction mechanism.

A further, more technical, point is that the optimal choice of the summation index m depends on r. Is it therefore necessary to repeat the procedure for the different dimensions of the cointegrating space, or does the procedure work sufficiently well also with non-optimal values of m? In Johansen's approach one only has to estimate once, the cointegrating rank can then be found, for example, by a sequential testing procedure.

REPLY

H.J. BIERENS

First, I would like to thank the discussants for their thoughtful comments. I agree with almost all their comments. The only exception is the minor last point raised by Manfred Deistler and Martin Wagner regarding the summation index m, which depends on the number r of cointegrating vectors. Admittedly, the non-parametric test has to be recomputed for each null hypothesis regarding the number r of cointegrating vectors. However, for the Swedish time series involved the two non-parametric tests (for $r = 0$ and $r = 1$) together took only 1 second on a 486 PC, which is less than the computing time of a single Johansen test with $q = 2$ and $p = 6$ on the same PC. In fact, it took me several hours to conduct all the Johansen tests reported in Tables 7.1–7.3 in the chapter. Therefore, the dependence of the summation index m on r is not a computational issue.

REFERENCES

Anderson, S.A., Brons, H.K. and Jensen, S.T. (1983) Distribution of eigenvalues in multivariate statistical analysis. *Annals of Statistics* **11**, 392–415.

Bierens, H.J. (1994) *Topics in Advanced Econometrics: Estimation, Testing, and Specification of Cross-Section and Time Series Models.* Cambridge University Press, Cambridge.

Bierens, H.J. (1997) Nonparametric cointegration analysis. *Journal of Econometrics* **77**, 379–404.

Bierens, H.J. and Guo, S. (1993) Testing stationarity and trend stationarity against the unit root hypothesis. *Econometric Reviews* **12**, 1–32.

Billingsley, P. (1968) *Convergence of Probability Measures.* John Wiley, New York.

Boswijk, H.P. (1994) Testing for an unstable root in conditional and structural error correction models. *Journal of Econometrics* **63**, 37–60.

Boswijk, H.P. (1995) Efficient inference on cointegrating parameters in structural error correction models. *Journal of Econometrics* **69**, 133–58.

Dickey, D.A. and Fuller, W.A. (1979) Distribution of the estimators for auto-regressive times series with a unit root. *Journal of the American Statistical Association* **74**, 427–31.

Dickey, D.A. and Fuller, W.A. (1981) Likelihood ratio statistics for auto-regressive time series with a unit root. *Econometrica* **49**, 1057–72.

Dolado, J.J. and Lütkepohl, H. (1996) Making Wald tests work for cointegrated VAR systems. *Economic Reviews* **15**, 369–86.

Engle, R.F. and Granger, C.W.J. (1987) Cointegration and error correction: representation, estimation, and testing. *Econometrica* **55**, 251–76.

Engle, R.F. and Yoo, S.B. (1987) Forecasting and testing in cointegrated systems. *Journal of Econometrics* **35**, 143–59.

Engle, R.F. and Yoo, S.B. (1991) Cointegrated economic time series: an overview with new results. In R.F. Engle and C.W.J. Granger (eds), *Long-Run Economic Relationships.* Oxford University Press, Oxford, pp. 237–66.

Friedman, M. (1957) *A Theory of the Consumption Function.* Princeton University Press, Princeton, NJ.

Fuller, W.A. (1976) *Introduction to Statistical Time Series.* John Wiley, New York.

Granger, C.W.J. (1981) Some properties of time series and their use in econometric model specification. *Journal of Econometrics* **16**, 121–30.

Hall, P. and Heyde, C.C. (1980) *Martingale Limit Theory and Its Applications.* Academic Press, San Diego.

Hamming, R.W. (1973) *Numerical Methods for Scientists and Engineers.* Dover Publications, New York.

Hansen, B.E. (1992) Tests for parameter instability in regressions with I(1) processes. *Journal of Business and Economic Statistics* **10**, 321–35.

Johansen, S. (1988) Statistical analysis of cointegrated vectors. *Journal of Economic Dynamics and Control* **12**, 231–54.

Johansen, S. (1991) Estimation and hypothesis testing of cointegrated vectors in Gaussian vector autoregressive models. *Econometrica* **59**, 1551–80.

Johansen, S. (1994) The role of the constant and linear terms in cointegration analysis of nonstationary variables. *Econometric Reviews* **13**, 205–29.

Johansen, S. and Juselius, K. (1990) Maximum likelihood estimation and inference on cointegration: with applications to the demand for money. *Oxford Bulletin of Economics and Statistics* **52**, 169–210.

Krantz, O. and Nilson, L. (1975) *Swedish National Product 1861-1970: New Aspects on Methods and Measurements*. G.W.K. Gleerup/Liber Läromedel, Lund.

Melander, E., Vredin, A. and Warne, A. (1992) Stochastic trends and economic fluctuations in a small open economy. *Journal of Applied Econometrics* **7**, 369–94.

Newey, W.K. and West, K.D. (1987) A simple positive definite heteroskedasticity and autocorrelation consistent covariance matrix. *Econometrica* **55**, 703–8.

Park, J.Y. (1990) Testing for unit root and cointegration by variable addition. *Advances in Econometrics* **8**, 107–33.

Perron, P. (1988) Trends and random walks in macroeconomic time series: further evidence from a new approach. *Journal of Economic Dynamics and Control* **12**, 297–332.

Perron, P. (1989) The Great Crash, the oil price shock and the unit root hypothesis. *Econometrica* **57**, 1361–1402.

Perron, P. (1990) Testing the unit root in a time series with a changing mean. *Journal of Business and Economic Statistics* **8**, 153–62.

Phillips, P.C.B. (1987) Time series regression with unit roots. *Econometrica* **55**, 277–302.

Phillips, P.C.B. (1991) Optimal inference in cointegrated systems. *Econometrica* **59**, 283–306.

Phillips, P.C.B. and Hansen, B. (1990) Statistical inference in instrumental variables regression with I(1) processes. *Review of Economic Studies* **57**, 99–125.

Phillips, P.C.B. and Ouliaris, S. (1990) Asymptotic properties of residual based tests for cointegration. *Econometrica* **58**, 165–93.

Phillips, P.C.B. and Perron, P. (1988) Testing for a unit root in time series regression. *Biometrika* **75**, 335–46.

Phillips, P.C.B. and Solo, V. (1992) Asymptotics for linear processes. *Annals of Statistics* **20**, 971–1001.

Said, S.E. and Dickey, D.A. (1984) Testing for unit roots in autoregressive-moving average of unknown order. *Biometrika* **71**, 599–607.

Sims, C.A., Stock, J.H. and Watson, M.W. (1990) Inference in linear time series models with some unit roots. *Econometrica* **58**, 113–44.

Stock, J.H. and Watson, M.W. (1988) Testing for common trends. *Journal of the American Statistical Association* **83**, 1097–1107.

Wagner, M. (1994) *Robustheitsuntersuchung des Cointegrationstests von Johansen*. Master Thesis (in German), University of Technology Vienna.

Yap, S.F. and Reinsel, G.C. (1995) Estimation and testing for unit roots in a partially nonstationary vector autoregressive moving average model. *Journal of the American Statistical Association* **90**, 253–67.

———— 8 ————

The Relationship Between Money and Prices: An Econometric Appraisal Based on Cointegration and Causality

M. FUNKE, S.G. HALL AND M. BEEBY

8.1 INTRODUCTION

This chapter surveys a body of work which we have been undertaking over the last few years that has both illustrated and extended some of the new methodologies which have grown around the broad area of multivariate cointegration. This work has focused on the well-trodden ground of the relationship between money, prices and income which has been at the heart of the monetarist/ Keynesian controversies for many years and which has also been an implicit part of many single-equation econometric studies dealing with money demand or price determination. The earlier work discussed here shows how the idea of causality (which is central to the monetarist/Keynesian debate) can be given an operational definition in a multivariate framework and that formal tests can then be adopted to test for the direction of long-run causality. The later work then recognizes that this causal structure may be a consequence of the institutional framework, hence it may vary both between economies and over time. Multivariate techniques can then attempt to detect these changes and guide us in selecting better institutional frameworks which may actually alter the structure of the economic system in a desirable way.

System Dynamics in Economic and Financial Models. Edited by C. Heij, J.M. Schumacher, B. Hanzon and C. Praagman © 1997 John Wiley & Sons Ltd

The main work to be covered here are Allen and Hall (1991), Hall and Milne (1994), Funke and Hall (1994) and Beeby, Hall and Funke (1995). This strand of work has all developed from the concept of p^*, which was first proposed by Hallman, Porter and Small (1989a, b, 1991), hereafter abbreviated as HPS, which was designed to analyse the long-run determination of the price level and which will be defined more precisely in Section 8.2.

This chapter is organized as follows. Section 8.2. outlines the basic ideas of the p^* analysis and the way it has been used in the past. Section 8.3 then outlines the basic statistical framework used in the multivariate cointegration literature; it also defines some basic concepts in causality and illustrates how very different causal structures can arise in very similar systems. Section 8.4 presents the empirical results for the UK and Section 8.5 the companion results for Germany. Section 8.6 then discusses the question of structural change and illustrates this with a combined model of the UK and Germany which seeks to test for a changing structure as the European Exchange Rate Mechanism (ERM) was formed. Section 8.7 draws some overall conclusions.

8.2 THE DERIVATION OF THE p^* MODEL AND COINTEGRATION

The quantity theory of money has attracted renewed interest in recent years following HPS's observations that short-run inflation dynamics may be influenced by the long-run price level. In their approach, differences between the long-run equilibrium price level and the actual price level were seen to feed back on to actual prices pushing them towards equilibrium. Other work testing and extending theirs has been conducted. The general concensus seems to be that it is most applicable to the larger, more closed economies. However, Kool and Tatom (1994) dispute this and argue that the standard p^* model simply needs to be augmented for open-economy, fixed exchange rate effects. For an application to the UK see Hannah and James (1989).

HPS base their analysis around the simple well-known quantity theory of money identity,

$$p = m + v - q \tag{1a}$$

where p is the logarithm of the price level, m the logarithm of money, v the logarithm of velocity, and q the logarithm of the level of real output. For notational simplicity we drop all time subscripts except where the dynamic structure becomes important. By a * superscript we denote a 'long-run' value so that according to equation (1a) by definition

$$p^* = m + v^* - q^* \tag{1b}$$

The critical step in the analysis comes in the way m, q^* and v^* are defined. Any set of variables may be selected which 'explain' the change in equilibrium money, output and velocity over time. It follows from equations (1a) and (1b) that, the closer (v^*, q^*) are to actual (v, q), the closer will p^* be to actual p. Given models for v^* and q^*, p^* follows from equation (1b). HPS follow a fairly conventional dynamic modelling procedure and use an error correction model (ECM, see Engle and Granger (1987) for a general discussion of ECM models), so that

$$\Delta p_t = a(p^*_{t-1} - p_{t-1}) + b(L)\Delta p_{t-1} + e_t \qquad (2)$$

Here $\Delta p_t = p_t - p_{t-1}$ is the rate of inflation, $0 < a < 1$, $b(L)$ is a lag polynomial so that $1 - Lb(L)$ is stable, and e_t is gaussian white noise.

Given the Granger representation theorem, a necessary condition for the above model to be a valid representation of the data is that p and p^* must form a cointegrating pair (see Engle and Granger (1987)). This is not in practice an important requirement, however, as the p^* approach allows the addition of extra variables to the model which explain the long-term movements of v and q. In the USA, the actual velocity for M2 (a broad monetary aggregate) shows no clear trend over recent decades and HPS take the simple average level of velocity as their measure of v^*. Other applications have used more elaborate models of velocity. Hannah and James (1989), for example, define v^* in the UK as the trend in actual velocity, allowing for a shift in the trend in 1974. It follows that, as long as v and v^*, and q and q^* are both cointegrated, then p and p^* will also be cointegrated. Testing the set of variables for cointegration is a test of the modeller's competence therefore but not a test of the validity of the p^* approach. The real question which must be answered is that of causality within the full set of variables under consideration.

Criticism of the p^* approach has been similar to that originally applied to the quantity theory, namely that the crucial question of causality is blurred: does money cause prices or do prices cause money? HPS's development of the p^* approach took place in standard single equation cointegration analysis (Engle and Granger (1987)), where questions of causality are difficult to answer. Using a multi-equation vector auto-regression (VAR) system of the type developed by Johansen (1988, 1991) allows the issue of causality to be treated much more explicitly. The next section will introduce loading weights, the long-run matrix and the cointegrating vectors (CVs). These definitions allow us to investigate how CVs enter the full system, making it straightforward to examine any causal links.

8.3 THE ECONOMIC AND STATISTICAL FRAMEWORK

8.3.1 Multivariate Cointegration

We assume that there are m endogenous variables Y and k strongly exogenous (Engle et al., (1983)) variables X, and we define $n = m + k$. We assume that the variables are related by

$$B(L)Y_t + C(L)X_t = u_t \tag{3}$$

$$D(L)\Delta X_t = \epsilon_t \tag{4}$$

where u_t, ϵ_t are conformably dimensioned vectors of gaussian white-noise processes with zero mean and constant variance. The complete system may be formulated as a structural vector error correction model

$$\begin{pmatrix} B^*(L) & C^*(L) \\ 0 & D(L) \end{pmatrix} \begin{pmatrix} \Delta Y_t \\ \Delta X_t \end{pmatrix} + \begin{pmatrix} B(1) & C(1) \\ 0 & 0 \end{pmatrix} \begin{pmatrix} Y_{t-1} \\ X_{t-1} \end{pmatrix} = \begin{pmatrix} u_t \\ \epsilon_t \end{pmatrix} \tag{5}$$

where a $*$ refers to matrices that are implicitly defined from equations (3) and (4). The relationships

$$B(1)Y_{t-1} = -C(1)X_{t-1} \tag{6}$$

may be regarded as the structural or target relations (in the sense of Davidson and Hall (1991)), that is, economically meaningful relationships which underlie the behaviour of the system. Assuming $B(0)$ is non-singular, the model may be rewritten as

$$\begin{pmatrix} B(0) & C(0) \\ 0 & I_k \end{pmatrix}^{-1} \left[\begin{pmatrix} B^*(L) & C^*(L) \\ 0 & D(L) \end{pmatrix} \begin{pmatrix} \Delta Y_t \\ \Delta X_t \end{pmatrix} + \begin{pmatrix} B(1) & C(1) \\ 0 & 0 \end{pmatrix} \begin{pmatrix} Y_{t-1} \\ X_{t-1} \end{pmatrix} \right]$$

$$= \begin{pmatrix} B(0) & C(0) \\ 0 & I_k \end{pmatrix}^{-1} \begin{pmatrix} u_t \\ \varepsilon_t \end{pmatrix} \tag{7}$$

We define the $n \times n$ long-run matrix as

$$\Pi = \begin{pmatrix} \Pi_1 & \Pi_2 \\ 0 & 0 \end{pmatrix} = \begin{pmatrix} B(0) & C(0) \\ 0 & I_k \end{pmatrix}^{-1} \begin{pmatrix} B(1) & C(1) \\ 0 & 0 \end{pmatrix} \tag{8}$$

where Π_1 is an $m \times m$ matrix and Π_2 an $m \times k$ matrix, and we define the dynamics as

$$\Gamma(L) = \begin{pmatrix} B(0) & C(0) \\ 0 & I_k \end{pmatrix}^{-1} \begin{pmatrix} B^*(L) & C^*(L) \\ 0 & D(L) \end{pmatrix} \tag{9}$$

The estimation methodology of Johansen (1988, 1991) rests on a decomposition of the long-run matrix that is restricted by the condition that Π is of deficient rank r. In our setting, r is the rank of the matrix $[B(1), C(1)]$ which is always smaller than n when $k > 0$. We write

$$\Pi = \alpha\beta' \tag{10}$$

with β the $n \times r$ matrix of cointegrating vectors and α the $n \times r$ matrix of loading weights. It is important to stress that in general the matrix of cointegrating vectors will not map on to the long-run target relationships in any simple way. This may be seen by noting that $\Pi = \alpha\beta' = \alpha H^{-1} H\beta'$ where H may be any $r \times r$ non-singular matrix. So, except in the special case where $r = 1$, the estimated cointegrating vectors may be linear combinations of the underlying target vectors. These target vectors may only be found by imposing suitable identifying restrictions on the system.

Let $Z = (Y', X')'$ denote the complete set of variables and let $e_t = (u'_t, \varepsilon'_t)'$. The foregoing equations (7)–(9) give the model in autoregressive form

$$\Gamma(L)\Delta Z_t + \Pi Z_{t-1} = \begin{pmatrix} B(0) & C(0) \\ 0 & I_k \end{pmatrix}^{-1} e_t \qquad (11)$$

There is also a moving average or common stochastic trend representation that can be derived by using the Smith–McMillan–Yoo generalized inverse (see Engle and Yoo (1991)), so that

$$\Delta Z_t = R(L)e_t = R(1)e_t + R^*(L)\Delta e_t \qquad (12)$$

where $R(L)$ and $R^*(L)$ are $n \times n$ polynomial matrices and the rank of $R(1)$ is $n - r$.

8.3.2 Granger Causality

In a system such as (5), Y does not Granger-cause X (Granger (1969)) because the parameter matrices are upper block triangular. The implication of this in equation (12), the stochastic trend representation, is that shocks to the Y equations (u_t) have no effect on X so that $R(L)$, $R(1)$ and $R^*(L)$ are upper block triangular. Formally, following Mosconi and Giannini (1992), Y does not Granger-cause X if in equation (11)

$$U'\Gamma(L)V = 0 \text{ and } U'\Pi V = 0 \qquad (13)$$

where $U = (0, I_k)'$ and $V = (I_m, 0)'$. These conditions are clearly satisfied for our model (7), (8), (9).

8.3.3 Weak Causality

Hall and Wickens (1993) argue that in many cases the condition involving only the long-run matrix may also be a useful definition of causality. They introduce the notion of long-run, or weak causality. Here X is said to be not weakly caused by Y if the long-run level of X is not affected by the level of Y, and, in particular, departures from the equilibrium between X and Y defined in the cointegrating vector will not affect X in the long run.

In what follows we assume that Π_1 has full rank m. This assumption rules out the so-called unstable case discussed in Davidson and Hall (1991). The assumption can easily be tested and seems not too restrictive in the case of reasonably small systems (see, for example, Granger and Lin (1993) for the bivariate case ($m = k = 1$)). Hall and Wickens (1993) show that, when Π_1 has full rank,

$$U'\Pi V = 0 \tag{14}$$

is a sufficient condition for weak causality. The intuition here is that as long as endogenous variables (Y) do not generate stochastic trends among themselves, the only long-run trends in the data will come from the exogenous variables (X) and hence the Y variables can have no long-run effect on the long-run values of the X variables. The test of weak causality thus becomes a test of zero restrictions in the Π matrix. This can be achieved through testing for zero restrictions in the α matrix using standard tests within the Johansen framework.

8.3.4 Examples of Causal Structures

Following the analysis of Davidson and Hall (1991) we may characterize some of the extreme positions of the monetarist and Keynesian debate on causality through sets of restrictions on the long-run coefficient matrix (10). If, for ease of exposition, we think of our whole model as a conditional sub-system consisting of three endogenous variables $Y = (m, p, q)'$ and a set of weakly exogenous processes X, then the long-run relations in terms of equation (8) may be written as,

$$(\Pi_1 \Pi_2)\begin{pmatrix} Y \\ X \end{pmatrix} = \begin{pmatrix} c_1 & 0 & 0 \\ 0 & c_2 & 0 \\ 0 & 0 & c_3 \end{pmatrix}\left[\tilde{\Pi}_1 \begin{pmatrix} m \\ p \\ q \end{pmatrix} + \tilde{\Pi}_2 X \right] \tag{15}$$

where the coefficients c_i are chosen so that $\tilde{\Pi}_1$ has units along the leading diagonal. This is merely to simplify the discussion of this matrix below. The $\tilde{\Pi}_1$ matrix is the key to our analysis because this determines the causality within the model.

As discussed in detail in Davidson and Hall (1991), (m, q, p) may be integrated processes either because some element of the exogenous driving processes (X) is integrated or because the $\tilde{\Pi}_1$ matrix has deficient rank. Various restrictions on this matrix may be seen as characterizing the various positions in the monetarist debate. For example, if

$$\tilde{\Pi}_1 = \begin{pmatrix} 1 & 0 & 0 \\ -1 & 1 & 1 \\ a_3 & -a_3 & 1 \end{pmatrix} \tag{16}$$

(with $a_3 \neq -1$), then this has the interpretation that money is driven by some exogenous process, prices follow money per unit of output and output is determined by the real money supply. This may be seen as a characterization of the extreme monetarist view. It has the implication that there is only one cointegrating vector involving (m, p, q) in the system which obeys the simple quantity theory restrictions and that this vector only appears in the price equation. The opposite extreme is given by

$$\tilde{\Pi}_1 = \begin{pmatrix} 1 & -1 & -1 \\ 0 & 1 & 0 \\ a_3 & -a_3 & 1 \end{pmatrix} \qquad (17)$$

(with $a_3 \neq -1$). In this case it is prices which are driven by some exogenous process and money follows in an entirely accommodating fashion. This may be seen as a characterization of the Keynesian view of price determination. Again the monetarist cointegrating vector involving (m, p, q) is present, but now it affects only money. As $\tilde{\Pi}_1$ has full rank there are three cointegrating vectors. Both of these examples fall within the scope of theorem 1 in Davidson and Hall (1991) and would be described as stable models; even though the variables are trended, the trend comes solely from the exogenous processes and the conditional model for Y given X is stable. If the quantity theory restriction drives both the price and the money equations, an assumption which would often be made in econometric models, then, for example,

$$\tilde{\Pi}_1 = \begin{pmatrix} 1 & -1 & -1 \\ -1 & 1 & 1 \\ a_3 & -a_3 & 1 \end{pmatrix} \qquad (18)$$

In this situation prices are marked up in line with the money stock and money is allowed to increase in line with prices. This will generate integrated processes even when the X variables take on fixed values so that the model is unstable in this sense.

Note that all three foregoing cases contain the quantity theory relationship between money, prices and output as cointegrating vector, so that even the Keynesian model (17) would still generate data in which the quantity theory relationship holds. This illustrates the point that demonstrating the validity of this relationship as a cointegrating vector proves nothing about the usefulness or otherwise of the money stock as an instrument of monetary policy.

It would require only a small departure from equation (18) to allow $\tilde{\Pi}_1$ to have full rank, for example,

$$\tilde{\Pi}_1 = \begin{pmatrix} 1 & -0.9 & -1 \\ -1 & 1 & 1 \\ a_3 & -a_3 & 1 \end{pmatrix} \qquad (19)$$

(with $a_3 \neq -1$). Then the money supply would not increase in a fully accommodating way for price rises and the system would not be inflation prone (although prices could still rise because of the X processes). For money to be effective we therefore require a feedback from money into prices as a minimum requirement. For a fully stable price system we also need the unit root in the price sector to be eliminated so that any remaining trend comes solely from exogenous processes.

It is possible to design a system which meets our definition of stability in other ways, for example because prices do not fully mark up increases in the money supply with

$$
\tilde{\Pi}_1 = \begin{pmatrix} 1 & -1 & -1 \\ -0.9 & 1 & 1 \\ \alpha_3 & -\alpha_3 & 1 \end{pmatrix} \tag{20}
$$

8.4 AN EMPIRICAL INVESTIGATION FOR THE UK

In this section we report on work of Hall and Milne (1994) on broad money M4 (which includes interest-bearing bank accounts as well as notes and coins and non-interest-bearing accounts) for the UK. As a starting point they took the study of Hall, Henry and Wilcox (1990) which demonstrated that a simple measure of velocity is non-stationary. They obtained a cointegrating set of variables by adding the logarithm of the ratio of financial wealth to Gross Domestic Product $(w - q)$, a dummy effect for competition and credit control (a change in the system of regulating the UK financial system), and a measure of the return in the equity market. In order to limit the dimension of the analysis and to put it more closely into the p^* framework, Hall and Milne (1994) assume that these variables are strongly exogenous and define them as part of the X vector in the above framework. We will focus on the three endogenous variables money, prices and output (m, p, q), and we will not report any results for the X variables.

Unrestricted estimation leads to the conclusion that there is one cointegration relation. The parameter estimates in this vector all have the correct sign and are very close to the expected value of $(1, -1, -1)$ for (m, p, q), the quantity theory, or p^*, restriction. Statistical tests confirm these coefficient restrictions.

It is of interest to see how this cointegrating vector gets loaded into the dynamic system, as this is related to weak causality. Table 8.1 gives the estimated loading parameters with the corresponding Wald test that they are in fact zero. This table demonstrates that the p^* cointegrating vector has no link with prices and that the main direction of long-run casuality flows into real income and into M4 money. So this result strongly argues that money does not cause prices but rather that prices cause money (M4). Departures from the cointegrating equilibrium relation also have predictive power for future changes in real income.

Table 8.1 The loading weights for the restricted model for the UK

	m	p	q
α	0.0834	−0.0132	−0.06
$W(1)$	13.68	0.29	6.53

Note: The Wald tests $[W(n)]$ for the α matrices are tests for the hypotheses that there are no cointegrating vectors in each equation and are asymptotically $\chi^2(n)$ variates.

8.5 THE ANALYSIS FOR GERMANY

Anecdotal accounts of the working of the German system would suggest that monetary factors play a much more important part in the economic system than they do in the UK. In this section we report on the work of Funke and Hall (1994) which investigated the p^* approach for Germany and found a very different causal structure from that for the UK.

Funke and Hall (1994) consider (m, p, q) and the logarithm of the wealth to output ratio $(w - q)$ as a potential cointegrating set of variables. Formal tests confirm at a 95% confidence level that there exist two cointegrating vectors among this set of variables. The parameter estimates in the first cointegrating vector are not very far from their *a priori* expected values $(1, -1, -1)$ for (m, p, q). However, the second cointegrating vector is not homogeneous and is hard to interpret. Table 8.2. gives details of how the variables get loaded into the system, together with Wald tests for the hypothesis that the loading weights are in fact zero.

Table 8.2 demonstrates that under the assumption of two distinct cointegrating vectors, all the equations are affected by at least one of these vectors. Under the assumption of one cointegrating relationship (which is not the most appropriate

Table 8.2 The loading weights for the unrestricted model for Germany

(a) Loading weights under the assumption of two distinct cointegrating vectors:

	m	p	q	$(w - q)$
α_{1i}	0.182	−0.131	0.210	0.47
α_{2i}	0.015	0.134	0.109	−0.152
$W(2)$	15.8	27.9	11.4	18.1

(b) Loading weights under the assumption of one cointegrating vector:

	m	p	q	$(w - q)$
α_{1i}	0.18	−0.13	0.21	0.47
$W(1)$	15.7	10.3	8.3	1.1

Note: see Table 8.1.

assumption but we consider this also as the second vector is only marginally significant), the Wald test for $(w - q)$ is insignificant, indicating that the second cointegrating vector is particularly important in driving $(w - q)$. The large difference in the size of the Wald tests for the assumptions of one and two cointegrating vectors for the price level suggests that the second vector is also important in determining prices. The tests are almost identical for money, however, and this suggests that the second vector does not enter the money equation.

The overall pattern of these results, as compared with those for the UK, is interesting in two respects. As in the UK, there is strong evidence of a relationship which is very close to the velocity relation. But in the case of Germany causality does indeed run from this relationship into prices as well as into money, so the casual linkages are quite different in Germany. The second feature which is distinctive to Germany is the probable presence of a second cointegrating vector, which is far from homogeneous. This means a rather different inflation performance of the system.

After analysing the unrestricted cointegration space, Funke and Hall (1994) then probe more deeply into the effect of this second cointegrating vector. For this purpose, the dominant effect of the velocity relationship in the system needs to be removed. This may be done by identifying the first cointegrating vector by restricting the coefficients to have the expected unit coefficients, constructing a variable representing this long-run relationship, and then including this variable in equation (7) as an extra stationary term in X. Estimation of the remaining cointegrating relationships is then carried out under the hypothesis that the velocity relationship is correct. Hypothesis tests on these vectors may be carried out in the usual way, conditional on the assumption that the velocity relationship is true. This technique effectively partials out the dominant velocity effect from the analysis.

This conditional estimation again reveals a cointegrating vector which is similar to the second vector found previously. The loading weights and the corresponding Wald tests in Table 8.3 tell an interesting story. This cointegrating vector has no causal link with money but operates strongly on prices. So this non-homogeneous effect is working on prices directly rather than on the stock of money. This suggests that the system could be operating in the way characterized by equation (20), so that the money stock is moved in an accommodating fashion but the system is stabilized through the response of the price system. A

Table 8.3 The loading weights for the conditional model for Germany

	m	p	q	$(w - q)$
α	−0.013	0.088	0.122	−.013
$W(1)$	0.14	9.3	5.0	18.4

Note: see Table 8.1

likelihood ratio test convincingly rejects the homogeneity restriction. By carrying out the analysis conditional on the existence of the velocity relationship, we obtain much more sensitive tests on the properties of the second cointegrating vector.

So we have established that the structure of causality in Germany is different from that of the UK. The German system is more complex with a simultaneous determination of money and prices and the velocity relationship having casual linkages with both money and prices. This is not, however, enough to stabilize the German inflation process. The stability seems to come from a second, non-homogeneous, relationship where prices are not fully marked up in line with money. There are, at least, two interpretations of this. One is that the implicit social contract between firms and unions in Germany tends to inherently stabilize the system. The other interpretation is that the Bundesbank is operating to stabilize prices but is not doing it strictly through the money supply. It might, for example, be operating directly on interest rates and thus affecting price determination directly. It is probably impossible to distinguish convincingly between these alternatives in an econometric framework without the imposition of considerable structural restrictions which may or may not be valid. We are, however, convinced that we have detected two significant ways in which Germany does differ from the UK, even if we are not able to uncover the fundamental cause of this difference.

8.6 AN ANALYSIS OF A CHANGING CAUSAL STRUCTURE

In this section we outline the work of Beeby, Hall and Funke (1995) which introduces the notion of changes in the long-run causal structure of an economic system without affecting the underlying structural cointegrating vectors. The aim is to discuss this issue in the context of the UK's entrance into the exchange rate mechanism (ERM) and to test if the process driving monetary growth in Germany has become increasingly important in determining the UK price level. It is the commonly held view that it has, though it is a view which so far is untested.

8.6.1 Structural Change and Cointegration

We extend the general statistical framework of Section 8.3 by allowing for changes in the causal structure, but not in the underlying cointegrating vectors. This involves changes in the loading weights α in equation (10) which govern the causality of the system. An important issue is the identification of the underlying structure (see Pesaran and Shin (1994)). The estimation problem may be dealt with in one of two ways. First, we could simply fix the cointegrating vectors at their estimates given by the Johansen procedure and investigate a changing structure in the loading matrix. Second, and we believe preferably, we could impose an identifying set of restrictions on the cointegrating vector so that they become estimates of the desired target relationships. This would allow us to interpret the cointegrating vectors in a structural way and to address structural changes in causality more convincingly.

We start from the structural system in equation (7) where the X variables are allowed to be cointegrated among themselves with a cointegrating matrix $D(1)$. If we impose a suitable set of normalizing and identifying restrictions, then the estimated cointegrating vectors will be estimates of the target relationships and

$$\Pi = \begin{pmatrix} \Pi_{11} & \Pi_{12} \\ 0 & \Pi_{22} \end{pmatrix} = \begin{pmatrix} \alpha_{11} & \alpha_{12} \\ 0 & \alpha_{22} \end{pmatrix} \begin{pmatrix} B(1) & C(1) \\ 0 & D(1) \end{pmatrix} \tag{21}$$

where the loading matrix is defined analogous to equations (8), (10) and (11). Different forms of structural change can then occur in the loading weights which would result in a different long-run matrix but with the same underlying cointegrating vectors. For example, if

$$\overline{\Pi} = \begin{pmatrix} \overline{\Pi}_{11} & \overline{\Pi}_{12} \\ \overline{\Pi}_{21} & \overline{\Pi}_{22} \end{pmatrix} = \begin{pmatrix} \alpha_{11} & \alpha_{12} \\ \alpha_{21} & \alpha_{22} \end{pmatrix} \begin{pmatrix} B(1) & C(1) \\ 0 & D(1) \end{pmatrix} \tag{22}$$

then the cointegrating vectors which in equation (21) affect only Y will now affect both Y and X. The long-run causal structure changes completely, Y having a long-term influence on X.

8.6.2 p^* Analysis with a Changing Structure

We now investigate a possible structural change due to the UK's entry into the ERM. We particularly wish to study the effects of German monetary growth on the UK price level, by including the cointegrating vector for German money demand into the UK price equation and investigating how its loading weight varies over time. One might expect that, given the UK's experiences with the ERM, German monetary growth would have some effect, though how much and over what period is not clear. We combine the models for the UK and Germany discussed above to produce a six-equation VAR made up of two three-equation sub-systems. These sub-systems are money, price and output equations for the UK and Germany:

$$\begin{bmatrix} \Delta m_t^{UK} \\ \Delta p_t^{UK} \\ \Delta q_t^{UK} \\ \Delta m_t^{G} \\ \Delta p_t^{G} \\ \Delta q_t^{G} \end{bmatrix} = A(L) \begin{bmatrix} \Delta m_t^{UK} \\ \Delta p_t^{UK} \\ \Delta q_t^{UK} \\ \Delta m_t^{G} \\ \Delta p_t^{G} \\ \Delta q_t^{G} \end{bmatrix} + \Pi \begin{bmatrix} m_{t-1}^{UK} \\ p_{t-1}^{UK} \\ q_{t-1}^{UK} \\ m_{t-1}^{G} \\ p_{t-1}^{G} \\ q_{t-1}^{G} \end{bmatrix} + \Psi DUM_t + \begin{bmatrix} e_{1t} \\ e_{2t} \\ e_{3t} \\ e_{4t} \\ e_{5t} \\ e_{6t} \end{bmatrix} \tag{23}$$

where, in terms of equation (11), $A(L) = I + \Gamma(L)$ and DUM_t is a vector containing the constant and dummies. We ignore for the moment the issue of whether any additional variables other than the six above need to be included to achieve cointegration.

Suppose we restrict the long-run matrix Π by assuming that a single cointegrating vector exists in both the UK and Germany for the entire sample period, but a new cointegrating vector appears in the UK equations for only a sub-sample of the data set, for example from the time of ERM membership. We also assume that the permanent cointegrating vectors contain only domestic variables. These assumptions lead to

$$\Pi = \alpha\beta' = \begin{bmatrix} \alpha_{11} & \alpha_{12} & \alpha_{13} \\ \alpha_{21} & \alpha_{22} & \alpha_{23} \\ \alpha_{31} & \alpha_{32} & \alpha_{33} \\ \alpha_{41} & \alpha_{42} & \alpha_{43} \\ \alpha_{51} & \alpha_{52} & \alpha_{53} \\ \alpha_{61} & \alpha_{62} & \alpha_{63} \end{bmatrix} \begin{bmatrix} \beta_{11} & \beta_{12} & \beta_{13} & 0 & 0 & 0 \\ 0 & 0 & 0 & \beta_{24} & \beta_{25} & \beta_{26} \\ \beta_{31} & \beta_{32} & \beta_{33} & \beta_{34} & \beta_{35} & \beta_{36} \end{bmatrix} \quad (24)$$

where the first column of the matrix β is the UK's CV, the second column is Germany's, and the third column is the new CV, a combination of the German and UK variables. With the UK's entry into the ERM, we investigate whether the loading weights, α_{i2}, α_{i3}, for $i = 1, 2, 3$, change from being zero to non-zero.

8.6.3 Results

The full system estimated in Beeby, Hall and Funke (1995) is slightly more complex than that outlined above in that a range of extra exogenous variables is needed to ensure cointegration. This basically conforms with the two studies on the UK and Germany discussed above. The full system which is estimated is of the form (23), with variables with lag one replaced by variables with lag four, and with the inclusion of dummies and exogenous variables and further dynamics. The matrix $\Pi = \alpha\beta'$ of equation (10) is restricted so that the cointegrating vectors are given by

$$\beta' \begin{pmatrix} Y_{t-4} \\ X_{t-4} \end{pmatrix}$$

with $Y_{t-4} = (m_{t-4}^{UK}, p_{t-4}^{UK}, q_{t-4}^{UK}, m_{t-4}^{G}, p_{t-4}^{G}, q_{t-4}^{G})'$ and

$$\beta' = \begin{pmatrix} 1 & -1 & -1 & 0 & 0 & 0 & * & 0 \\ 0 & 0 & 0 & 1 & -1 & -1 & 0 & * \\ 0 & 1 & 0 & \gamma & 1-\gamma & 0 & 0 & 0 \end{pmatrix} \quad (25)$$

where $*$ denotes coefficients corresponding to the exogenous variables specific for each country. The first column of β contains the CV estimated for the UK in

Section 8.4. Similarly, the second column is the CV for Germany from Section 8.5. In the third column of the matrix β is the new CV which may potentially have appeared as a result of the structural change. Since we are only interested in the long-run properties of the system, other terms, such as the dynamics or the dummies, are not relevant to the story, although they are, of course, included in the estimation.

A sequential estimation procedure was employed to test for the structural change in the loading weights. For example, the hypothesis that German monetary growth enters the UK price equation is tested by multiplying the German CV in the UK equations by a dummy variable. This dummy variable is then switched on for sub-samples of the data set, and we investigate for which sub-period the t-statistic for this variable is the largest. To make this testing procedure manageable, the German CV remained switched on until the end of the estimation period (1993 quarter four) regardless of its initial switching-on date. We tried each possible starting date given this fixed end date, with observations running from 1973 quarter two to 1993 quarter four. Of course, the German CV in the German equations, and the UK CV in the UK equations were included for the whole of the sample.

Our primary interest is in the effects of German monetary growth on prices in the UK. One might expect that with the UK's entry into the ERM, any such effects on UK inflation would become increasingly powerful, tapering off only with the UK's exit. It is difficult to have any firm *a priori* views when one should first expect to see these effects. They may enter into the UK's price equation prior to its official entry date because forward-looking wage bargainers and price setters negotiate contracts on the expectation of the UK government's imminent membership of the ERM. It may be that they regard the late 1980s policy of shadowing the Deutschmark both as a sign of the UK's commitment to price stability and as a statement of intent to join the ERM. Perhaps more likely is the view that any effects will only be observed after entry. The argument here is that the wage bargainers and price setters will wait for signs of the strength of the UK government's commitment to the ERM before they are willing to accept that the strictures of ERM membership will limit the propensity of the UK government to inflate. This hypothesis can be investigated by examining the structure of loading weight matrix α. For example, with $\Pi = \alpha\beta'$ and β' as in equation (25), α_{22} measures the strength with which the German money growth process enters the UK price equation. We are only interested in the t-statistic for the loading weight of the German CV in the UK price regression (we do not use the term 'significance' as these statistics are unlikely to have a standard 't' distribution). This is presented in Figure 8.1. The t-statistics for the loading weights of the same variable in the UK money and output equations are not shown as they show no distinct change or significant pattern.[1]

The interpretation of this figure is as follows. The value of the t-statistic in 1981 quarter 2, say, shows that if the German CV is switched on for the period

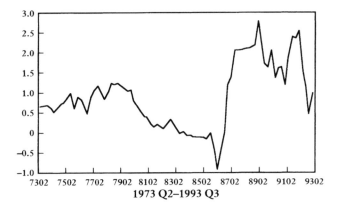

Figure 8.1   Plot of the t-statistic on Germany's CV in the UK's price equation

1981 quarter 2 until 1993 quarter 4, then it has a t-statistic of approximately 0.25 in the UK price equation. So, measured over this sub-sample of the data set, we can be reasonably certain that German monetary growth had no effect on the level of UK prices. During 1987, the period when the policy of shadowing the Deutschmark was introduced, the value of the t-statistic changes abruptly from being approximately zero, to above two. It remains significant until the end of 1992/beginning of 1993. Over this period the variable's coefficient is correctly (i.e. positively) signed, and exerts a reasonably strong influence. The coefficient's value of between 0.12 and 0.40 indicates that any increase in the German money supply above its long-run level will result, in the first instance, in a rise in UK prices of at least 12% of the increase. Entry into the ERM in September 1990 does not seem to have had any marked effect, though exit in September 1992 does lead to a large fall in the value of the t-statistic over the rest of the sample period. We repeated the experiment to check for a structural change in Germany but found no significant effects. There was also little evidence for the appearance of a new cointegrating vector in the system.

8.7 CONCLUSION

This chapter has summarized a broad strand of research on the relationship between money and prices and the causal nature of that relationship. We have shown that while countries may exhibit similar cointegrating vectors, the causal working of the system may be quite different. We investigated whether an individual country may change the working of its system through deliberate policy intervention, and we found some evidence that the UK price system was indeed influenced in the way one might expect during the period of membership of the ERM. This illustrates the power of the new system cointegration techniques to analyse much deeper questions about the working of economic systems than would have been possible with more traditional techniques.

ACKNOWLEDGEMENTS

Financial support from ESRC grant No. W116251003 is gratefully acknowledged. The first author is grateful to the German Research Council (Deutsche Forschungsge-meinschaft) for financial support under grant No. Fu 178/3-1.

ENDNOTE

1. Results from econometric estimations conducted for this chapter can be obtained from the authors upon request.

COMMENT

P.H.B.F. FRANSES

This chapter by Funke, Hall and Beeby (hereafter abbreviated as FHB) contains a wealth of material on the important relationship between money and prices. In this comment I focus on only one but very interesting part of their work. This concerns the analysis of long-run properties and short-run dynamics of money and price movements in and across Germany and the UK. The economic issue is whether the entrance of the UK into the Exchange Rate Mechanism (ERM) has established that monetary growth in Germany became important for the UK price level.

FHB put the economic question of a changing causality structure in an econometric framework, which in a simplified and stylized form looks like

$$\Delta_1 x_t = \alpha_t(x_{t-1} - \beta y_{t-1}) + \varepsilon_{1,t} \qquad (1)$$

$$\Delta_1 y_t = \gamma_t(x_{t-1} - \beta y_{t-1}) + \varepsilon_{2,t} \qquad (2)$$

where x_t and y_t are unit-root non-stationary time series variables that require the first differencing filter Δ_1 to become stationary, where $\varepsilon_{1,t}$ and $\varepsilon_{2,t}$ are standard white-noise processes, β is the cointegration parameter that reflects a long-run relation between the two variables, α_t and γ_t are the short-run adjustment parameters, where α_t and γ_t can take different values over time. FHB assume that

$$\alpha_t = 0 \qquad \text{when } t < \tau \qquad (3)$$

$$\alpha_t = \alpha \qquad \text{when } t \geq \tau$$

where in their case the break-date τ would lie around the entrance of the UK into the ERM. FHB fit a model like (1), and use recursive t-tests to analyse if and when α becomes significant, while it is assumed that the cointegration parameter β is non-zero and constant. In this comment I suggest two modifications of the procedure in FHB, which can be useful in practically relevant cases similar to the one studied by FHB.

Time-varying Adjustment

An important unknown parameter in the FHB approach is the break-date τ. Hence, the distribution of the t-test statistic used by FHB is complicated and probably not normal (as is assumed in FHB). Additionally, one may want to extend the FHB framework by allowing the rank of the cointegration matrix to vary over time. Quintos (1995) proposes statistical tests for τ and for the change in the rank of Π within the Johansen cointegration testing framework.

An alternative version of (1), which may be more easy to analyse since it does not require a search over possible values of τ, assumes that (3) becomes a continuous function such as

$$\alpha_t = \alpha\{1 + \exp(-\gamma(t - \tau^*))\}^{-1}, \qquad \gamma > 0 \qquad (4)$$

With (4), model (1) then becomes a so-called smooth transition error correction model, which extends in a sense the threshold error correction model proposed in Balke and Fomby (1996). The simulation results in Van Dijk and Franses (1996) show that, given short-run adjustment such as (4), the Johansen cointegration method yields unbiased estimates of the cointegration parameter β. In cases where α_t takes different values depending on, say, the business cycle states, one may consider Markov switching error correction models. Another so-called temporary cointegration model is given in Siklos and Granger (1996).

Time-varying Cointegration

A second more formal framework within which one may analyse changing causal structures concerns time-varying cointegration. A simple example is given by the model

$$\Delta_1 x_t = \alpha(x_{t-1} - \beta_t y_{t-1}) + \varepsilon_{1,t} \qquad (5)$$

where

$$\beta_t = 0 \qquad \text{where } t < \tau$$

$$\beta_t = \beta \qquad \text{where } t \geq \tau$$

This model extends the periodic cointegration model proposed in Boswijk and Franses (1995), where β_t can take different values in different seasons. Some diagnostic tests for versions of models such as (5) are proposed in Gregory and Hansen (1996) and Quintos and Phillips (1993). In the latter study, β_t is described by a random walk time series model. Of course, in specific cases one may also want to consider, e.g., $\beta_t = \beta + \gamma w_{t-1}$, where w_t is a certain variable, or $\beta_t = \beta + \gamma I[w_{t-1} > d]$, where d is some threshold. At present, the statistical analysis of the latter type of models has not yet been developed.

Concluding Remarks

The FHB chapter on changing causal structures in money and price relations shows that economically meaningful hypotheses can be formulated in terms of non-linear cointegration models. It can be expected that a statistical analysis as well as economic applications of such models will become important in the near future.

I thank Dick van Dijk for some helpful comments.

REPLY

M. FUNKE, S.G. HALL AND M. BEEBY

We are grateful to the helpful comments made above and we have no serious disagreement with them. It is perhaps important to appreciate that in this chapter we are going well beyond the limits fully understood by econometric theory. Hence there must be profound theoretical problems with formal testing in the context of structural change, sequential estimation and non-stationary data with many conintegrating vectors. We do not therefore interpret our results in a strict statistical way but we prefer to weigh the overall evidence and to suggest that, taken as a whole, the argument that we have found a sensible structural change is reasonably convincing. We are not basing this purely on the size of the formal t-statistic in Figure 8.1 but also on the timing of the sudden change and the dramatic nature of this change in terms of a complete change in sign. We are aware that these three factors cannot be given a joint formal interpretation, but in our view they are jointly convincing.

REFERENCES

Allen, C. and Hall, S.G. (1991) Money as a potential anchor for the price level: a critique of the p^* approach. *Economic Outlook* **15**, 45–9.

Balke, N.S. and Fomby, T.B. (1996) Threshold cointegration. Forthcoming in *International Economic Review*.

Beeby, M., Hall, S.G. and Funke, M. (1995) Long run causality and structural change: an application of p^* analysis to the UK's entry into the ERM. London Business School Discussion Paper No. 19–95.

Boswijk, H.P. and Franses, P.H. (1995) Periodic cointegration: representation and inference. *Review of Economics and Statistics* **77**, 436–54.

Davidson, J. and Hall, S.G. (1991) Cointegration in recursive systems. *The Economic Journal* **101**, 239–51.

Engle, R.F. and Granger, C.W.J. (1987) Cointegration and error correction: representation, estimation and testing. *Econometrica* **55**, 251–76.

Engle, R.F., Hendry, D.F. and Richard, J.F. (1983) Exogeneity. *Econometrica* **51**, 277–304.

Engle, R.F. and Yoo, S. (1991) Cointegrated economic time series: an overview with new results. R.F. Engle and C.W.J Granger (eds), *Long Run Economic Relationships: Readings in Cointegration*, Oxford University Press, Oxford.

Funke, M. and Hall, S.G. (1994) Is the Bundesbank different from other central banks? A study based on p^*. *Empirical Economics* **19**, 691–707.

Granger, C.W.J. (1969) Investigating causal relationships by econometric models and cross-spectral methods. *Econometrica* **37**, 424–38.

Granger, C.W.J. and Lin, Jin-Lung (1993) Causality in the long-run. Mimeo, University of San Diego.

Gregory, A.W. and Hansen, B.E. (1996) Residual-based tests for cointegration in models with regime shifts. *Journal of Econometrics* **70**, 99–126.

Hall, S.G., Henry, S.G.B. and Wilcox, J.B. (1990) The long run determination of the UK monetary aggregates. In S.G.B. Henry and K.D. Patterson, (eds), *Economic Modelling at the Bank of England*. Chapman and Hall, London.

Hall, S.G. and Milne, A. (1994) The relevance of p^* analysis to UK monetary policy. *Economic Journal* **104**, 597–603.

Hall, S.G. and Wickens, M. (1993) Causality in integrated systems. Centre for Economic Forecasting Discussion Paper, No. 27–93, London Business School.

Hallman, J.J., Porter, R.D. and Small, D.H. (1989a) M2 per unit of potential GNP as an anchor for the price level. *Federal Reserve Board Staff Paper*.

Hallman, J.J., Porter, R.D. and Small, D.H. (1989b) M2 per unit of potential GNP as an anchor for the price level. *Federal Reserve Bulletin*, April, 263–4.

Hallman, J.J., Porter, R.D. and Small, D.H. (1991) Is the price level tied to the M2 monetary aggregate in the long-run? *American Economic Review* September, **81**.

Hannah, S. and James, A. (1989) p^* as a monetary indicator for the UK. *NatWest Capital Markets Report*.

Hendry, D.F. (1979) Predictive failure and econometric modelling in macroeconomics: the transactions demand for money. In P. Ormerod (ed.), *Modelling the Economy*. Heineman Educational Books, London.

Johansen, S. (1988) Statistical analysis of cointegrating vectors. *Journal of Economic Dynamics and Control* **12**, 231–54.

Johansen, S. (1991) Estimation and hypothesis testing of cointegration vectors in Gaussian vector autoregression models. *Econometrica* **59**, 1551–80.

Kool, C.J.M. and Tatom, J.A. (1994) The p^* model in five small economies. *Federal Reserve Bank of St Louis*, May/June.

Mosconi, R. and Giannini, C. (1992) Non-causality in cointegrated systems: representation, estimation and testing. *Oxford Bulletin of Economics and Statistics* **54**, 399–417.

Pesaran, M.H. and Shin, Y. (1994) Long-run structural modelling. Department of Applied Economics Discussion Paper, University of Cambridge.

Quintos, C.E. (1995) Sustainability of the deficit process with structural shifts. *Journal of Business and Economic Statistics* **13**, 409–17.

Quintos, C.E. and Phillips, P.C.B. (1993) Parameter constancy in cointegrating regressions. *Empirical Economics* **18**, 675–706.

Reimers, H.-E. (1991) Comparison of tests for multivariate cointegration. Institut für Statistik und Ökonometrie, Kiel, discussion paper no. 58/1991.

Reinsel, G.C. and Ahn, S.K. (1988) Asymptotic distribution of the likelihood ratio test for cointegration in the nonstationary vector AR model. Technical Report, University of Wisconsin, Madison.

Siklos, P.L. and Granger, C.W.J. (1996) Temporary cointegration with an application to interest rate parity. Report, UCSD Department of Economics.

Spanos, A. (1986) *Statistical Foundations of Econometric Modelling*. Cambridge University Press, Cambridge.

Van Dijk, D. and Franses, P.H. (1996) Testing for threshold cointegration. Tinbergen Institute Report 96–78, Erasmus University Rotterdam.

9

Multivariate Structural Time Series Models

A.C. HARVEY AND S.J. KOOPMAN

9.1 INTRODUCTION

This chapter describes the ways in which multivariate structural time series models can be used to describe the features and properties of economic time series, thereby establishing a set of stylized facts. An introduction to these models can be found in Harvey (1989, Chapter 8). A new feature introduced here is the way in which we construct cyclical components which, although different for different series, have common parameters. Thus the cycles in the different series have similar properties; in particular, their movements are centred around the same period. This seems eminently reasonable if the cyclical movements all arise as a result of a common business cycle. As regards the trends themselves, constraints can be imposed so that there are fewer trends than series. The idea of imposing common trends is often a very natural one, for example when the series all have the same underlying source of growth. On the other hand, it is sometimes the case that economic theory suggests constraints arising from long-run cointe-grating relationships. Both interpretations are possible within our framework, the cointegration interpretation being based on a triangular representation similar to that in Phillips (1991).

Having established the stylized facts associated with a group of series, the next step may be to try to construct models which aim to capture the dynamic interactions between them. In some circumstances, such models may have advantages over the widely used vector autoregressive (VAR) representations. For example, if the data are well represented by slowly changing trends upon

System Dynamics in Economic and Financial Models. Edited by C. Heij, J.M. Schumacher, B. Hanzon and C. Praagman © 1997 John Wiley & Sons Ltd

which are superimposed short-term movements, the differenced observations will be almost non-invertible, leading to long lags, many parameters, and unit root and cointegration tests with poor properties. Multivariate structural time series models are designed to handle this kind of situation. Because trends are modelled explicitly, short-term dynamics can be captured by a low-order VAR. Co-integration appears when there are common trends as in Harvey and Stock (1988). Thus although structural time series models are a way of presenting stylized facts, they start to become behavioural models once we start making restrictions, introducing short-run dynamics and including exogenous variables in some of the equations.

The approach is illustrated with a number of applications. The models were fitted using the STAMP 5.0 package, described in Koopman *et al.* (1995). The power of a modern computer, coupled with the theoretical and computational advances described in Koopman (1993) and Koopman and Shephard (1992), allows even the extensive calculations required for a multivariate model to be carried out very quickly thereby opening the way to full data exploration. Graphical analysis of residuals, components and forecasts plays a key role.

9.2 UNIVARIATE STRUCTURAL TIME SERIES MODELS

A typical univariate structural time series model for economic data is

$$y_t = \mu_t + \gamma_t + \psi_t + \epsilon_t \qquad t = 1, \ldots, T \qquad \epsilon_t \sim NID(0, \sigma_\epsilon^2) \qquad (1)$$

where μ_t, γ_t and ψ_t are trend, seasonal and cyclical components, respectively. These components depend on disturbances which allow them to change over time rather than being deterministic. The disturbances are independent of each other and of the irregular component, ϵ_t. The definitions of the components are given below, but a full explanation of the underlying rationale can be found in Harvey (1989, Chapter 2).

The stochastic trend component is defined as

$$\mu_t = \mu_{t-1} + \beta_{t-1} + \eta_t \qquad \eta_t \sim NID(0, \sigma_\eta^2)$$
$$\beta_t = \beta_{t-1} + \zeta_t \qquad \zeta_t \sim NID(0, \sigma_\zeta^2)$$
$$(2)$$

where the level and slope disturbances, η_t and ζ_t, respectively, are mutually uncorrelated. When σ_ζ^2 is zero we have a *random walk plus drift*, and when σ_η^2 is zero as well a deterministic linear trend is obtained. A relatively *smooth trend*, related to a cubic spline, results when a zero value of σ_η^2 is coupled with a positive σ_ζ^2; Young (1984) calls this model an 'integrated random walk'.

The seasonal has the dummy variable form

$$\gamma_t = \gamma_{t-1} + \ldots + \gamma_{t-s+1} + \omega_t \qquad \omega_t \sim NID(0, \sigma_\omega^2) \qquad (3)$$

or the trigonometric form

$$\gamma_t = \sum_{j=1}^{[s/2]} \gamma_{j,t} \tag{4}$$

where each $\gamma_{j,t}$ is generated by

$$\begin{bmatrix} \gamma_{j,t} \\ \gamma_{j,t}^* \end{bmatrix} = \begin{bmatrix} \cos\lambda_j & \sin\lambda_j \\ -\sin\lambda_j & \cos\lambda_j \end{bmatrix} \begin{bmatrix} \gamma_{j,t-1} \\ \gamma_{j,t-1}^* \end{bmatrix} + \begin{bmatrix} \omega_{j,t} \\ \omega_{j,t}^* \end{bmatrix} \quad \begin{array}{l} j = 1, \ldots, [s/2] \\ t = 1, \ldots, T \end{array} \tag{5}$$

where $\lambda_j = 2\pi j/s$ is frequency, in radians, and $\omega_{j,t}$ and $\omega_{j,t}^*$ are two mutually uncorrelated white-noise disturbances with zero means and common variance σ_ω^2. For s even $[s/2] = s/2$, while for s odd, $[s/2] = (s-1)/2$. For s even, the component at $j = s/2$ collapses to

$$\gamma_{j,t} = \gamma_{j,t-1} \cos\lambda_j + \omega_{j,t} \quad j = s/2 \tag{6}$$

When the disturbances have zero variance, the dummy variable and trigonometric models give identical deterministic seasonal patterns.

The statistical specification of a cycle, ψ_t, is as follows:

$$\begin{bmatrix} \psi_t \\ \psi_t^* \end{bmatrix} = \rho \begin{bmatrix} \cos\lambda_c & \sin\lambda_c \\ -\sin\lambda_c & \cos\lambda_c \end{bmatrix} \begin{bmatrix} \psi_{t-1} \\ \psi_{t-1}^* \end{bmatrix} + \begin{bmatrix} \kappa_t \\ \kappa_t^* \end{bmatrix} \quad t = 1, \ldots, T \tag{7}$$

where λ_c is frequency, in radians, in the range $0 < \lambda_c < \pi$, κ_t and κ_t^* are two mutually uncorrelated white-noise disturbances with zero means and common variance σ_κ^2, and ρ is a *damping factor*. Note that the *period* is $2\pi/\lambda_c$. For some purposes it is useful to take the variance of ψ_t, rather than the variance of κ_t, as the unknown parameter. Then, since $\sigma_\kappa^2 = (1 - \rho^2)\sigma_\psi^2$, a deterministic cycle is obtained when $\rho = 1$; see Harvey and Streibel (1996).

9.3 MULTIVARIATE MODELS

9.3.1 Seemingly Unrelated Time Series Equations

Now consider a model for an $N \times 1$ vector of observations, $\mathbf{y}_t$, that is,

$$\mathbf{y}_t = \boldsymbol{\mu}_t + \boldsymbol{\gamma}_t + \boldsymbol{\psi}_t + \boldsymbol{\epsilon}_t \tag{8}$$

In the seemingly unrelated time series equations (SUTSE) model, each series is modelled as in the univariate case, but the disturbances may be correlated across series. Thus if $\boldsymbol{\epsilon}_t = (\epsilon_{1t}, \ldots, \epsilon_{Nt})'$ is the irregular disturbance,

$$\text{Var}(\boldsymbol{\epsilon}_t) = \boldsymbol{\Sigma}_\epsilon \tag{9}$$

The other disturbances similarly become vectors which have $N \times N$ covariance matrices. In the case of trigonometric seasonals there are two sets of $N \times 1$ vectors for each seasonal frequency such that

$$E(\omega_{it}\omega_{it}') = E(\omega_{it}^{*}\omega_{it}^{*\prime}) = \Sigma_{\omega}$$

$$E(\omega_{it}\omega_{it}^{*\prime}) = 0 \qquad i = 1, 2, \ldots, [s/2]$$

(10)

and all disturbances at different frequencies are independent.

9.3.2 Homogeneous Models

A SUTSE model is said to be homogeneous when the covariance matrices driving the disturbances are proportional to each other. For example, the homogeneity restriction for the multivariate local level model

$$\mathbf{y}_t = \boldsymbol{\mu}_t + \boldsymbol{\epsilon}_t \qquad \boldsymbol{\epsilon}_t \sim NID(\mathbf{0}, \boldsymbol{\Sigma}_{\epsilon})$$

$$\boldsymbol{\mu}_t = \boldsymbol{\mu}_{t-1} + \boldsymbol{\eta}_t \qquad \boldsymbol{\eta}_t \sim NID(\mathbf{0}, \boldsymbol{\Sigma}_{\eta})$$

(11)

where $\boldsymbol{\Sigma}_{\epsilon}$ and $\boldsymbol{\Sigma}_{\eta}$ are $N \times N$ covariance matrices is $\boldsymbol{\Sigma}_{\eta} = q_{\eta}\boldsymbol{\Sigma}_{\epsilon}$ where q_{η} is the signal-to-noise ratio. This means that all the series in $\mathbf{y}_t$ have the same dynamic properties, that is, the same autocorrelation function for the stationary form of the model. A homogeneous model is a rather special case but it is easy to estimate and because the signal-to-noise ratios are the same for all the series, they can be estimated with an N-fold gain in efficiency; see Harvey (1989, Chapter 8).

9.3.3 Similar Cycles

Cycles may be introduced into the model. We impose the constraint that ρ and λ are the same for the cycles in each series and set

$$E(\boldsymbol{\kappa}_t\boldsymbol{\kappa}_t') = E(\boldsymbol{\kappa}_t^{*}\boldsymbol{\kappa}_t^{*\prime}) = \boldsymbol{\Sigma}_{\kappa} \qquad E(\boldsymbol{\kappa}_t\boldsymbol{\kappa}_t^{*\prime}) = \mathbf{0} \qquad (12)$$

where $\boldsymbol{\kappa}_t$ and $\boldsymbol{\kappa}_t^{*}$ are $N \times 1$ vectors of the disturbances in equation (7) and $\boldsymbol{\Sigma}_{\kappa}$ is an $N \times N$ covariance matrix. The model allows the disturbances to be correlated across the series. Imposing the restriction that the damping factor and the frequency be the same in all series means that the cycles have the same properties, that is, the same ACF and spectrum. We call them *similar* cycles. The strength of a cycle in a particular series depends on the variance of its disturbance.

The dynamic interactions between the cycles are captured by the auto-covariance matrices of $\boldsymbol{\psi}_t$ which are given by

$$\boldsymbol{\Gamma}_{\psi}(\tau) = \{1/(1 - \rho^2)\}\rho^{\tau}\cos\lambda_c\tau\boldsymbol{\Sigma}_{\kappa} \qquad (13)$$

Hence the cross-correlation between the cycles in series i and series j at lag τ is given by

$$\rho_{ij}(\tau) = \{\rho^\tau \cos \lambda_c \tau\} \rho_{ij}(0) \qquad i, j = 1, \ldots, N \qquad (14)$$

Note that each $\rho_{ij}(0)$, for $i, j = 1, \ldots, N$, is equal to the corresponding element in the correlation matrix derived from the Σ_κ matrix.

The hypothesis of similar cycles can be tested by fitting the unrestricted model and carrying out an LR test. However, similar cycles are quite plausible on prior grounds and if the hypothesis is true there is a gain in efficiency from pooling the information in all the series. For example, in the special case when $\lambda_c = 0$ so that each cycle is an AR(1) process, and there are no other components so that ψ_t is observed directly, it can be shown that the asymptotic variance of the ML estimator of ρ is

$$\text{Avar}(\tilde{\rho}) = (1 - \rho^2)/TN \qquad (15)$$

which is N times smaller than the asymptotic variance of the ML estimator from a single series.

Similar cycles are not intended to capture any interactions between the series; indeed it is easy to show that the similar cycle component is Granger non-causal. Furthermore, aggregation of similar cycles leaves the properties unchanged.

9.3.4 Vector Autoregression (VAR)

A stationary VAR may be included in equation (8) as an alternative to, or even as well as, a cycle. Thus

$$\psi_t = \Phi_1 \psi_{t-1} + \ldots + \Phi_p \psi_{t-p} + \kappa_t \qquad \kappa_t \sim NID(0, \Sigma_\kappa) \qquad (16)$$

Within a numerical optimization procedure, the constraints on the matrices Σ_κ and Φ_i, for $i = 1, \ldots, p$, needed to keep a VAR(p) process stationary may be imposed by means of an algorithm given by Ansley and Kohn (1986).

Although a VAR(1) can produce cycles, it has different properties from the similar cycle model, in that in order to produce cycles the off-diagonal elements of Φ_i, for $i = 1, \ldots, p$, must be non-zero. This implies some kind of Granger causality. Thus a VAR of order at least two is needed to give similar dynamics to the similar cycle model. Of course, if there is Granger causality in ψ_t, the VAR(1) may give a better fit.

9.4 COMMON TRENDS AND COINTEGRATION

In a common factor model, some or all of the components are driven by disturbance vectors with less than N elements. Recognition of common factors yields models which may not only have an interesting interpretation but may also provide more efficient inferences and forecasts. In terms of a SUTSE model, the presence of common factors means that the covariance matrices of the relevant disturbances are less than full rank.

9.4.1 Common Levels

Consider the local level model (11) but suppose that the rank of $\boldsymbol{\Sigma}_\eta$ is $K < N$. The model then contains only K underlying level components. These common levels are a special case of what are called common trends in the econometric literature. With an appropriate ordering of the series the model may be written as

$$\mathbf{y}_t = \boldsymbol{\Theta}\boldsymbol{\mu}_t^\dagger + \boldsymbol{\mu}_\theta + \boldsymbol{\epsilon}_t \qquad \boldsymbol{\epsilon}_t \sim NID(\mathbf{0}, \boldsymbol{\Sigma}_\epsilon) \qquad (17)$$

$$\boldsymbol{\mu}_t^\dagger = \boldsymbol{\mu}_{t-1}^\dagger + \boldsymbol{\eta}_t^\dagger \qquad \boldsymbol{\eta}_t^\dagger \sim NID(\mathbf{0}, \boldsymbol{\Sigma}_\eta^\dagger) \qquad (18)$$

where $\boldsymbol{\mu}_t^\dagger$ and $\boldsymbol{\eta}_t^\dagger$ are $K \times 1$ vectors, $\boldsymbol{\Theta}$ is an $N \times K$ matrix of the form $\boldsymbol{\Theta} = (\mathbf{I}_K, \mathbf{B}')'$, $\boldsymbol{\Sigma}_\eta^\dagger$ is a $K \times K$ positive definite matrix and $\boldsymbol{\mu}_\theta$ is an $N \times 1$ vector in which the first K elements are zeroes and the last $N - K$ elements are contained in a vector $\overline{\boldsymbol{\mu}}$.

The model may also be written as

$$\mathbf{y}_t = \boldsymbol{\Theta}^*\boldsymbol{\mu}_t^* + \boldsymbol{\mu}_\theta + \boldsymbol{\epsilon}_t \qquad \boldsymbol{\epsilon}_t \sim NID(\mathbf{0}, \boldsymbol{\Sigma}_\epsilon) \qquad (19)$$

$$\boldsymbol{\mu}_t^* = \boldsymbol{\mu}_{t-1}^* + \boldsymbol{\eta}_t^* \qquad \boldsymbol{\eta}_t^* \sim NID(\mathbf{0}, \mathbf{I}) \qquad (20)$$

where $\boldsymbol{\mu}_t^* = (\boldsymbol{\Sigma}_\eta^\dagger)^{-1/2}\boldsymbol{\mu}_t^\dagger$ and $\boldsymbol{\Theta}^* = \boldsymbol{\Theta}(\boldsymbol{\Sigma}_\eta^\dagger)^{1/2}$ is a matrix of *factor loadings*. When there is more than one common factor, they are not unique. A factor rotation may give components with a more interesting interpretation; see Section 9.7.2.

9.4.2 Common Slopes

The multivariate local linear trend model is

$$\mathbf{y}_t = \boldsymbol{\mu}_t + \boldsymbol{\epsilon}_t \qquad \boldsymbol{\epsilon}_t \sim NID(\mathbf{0}, \boldsymbol{\Sigma}_\epsilon) \qquad (21)$$

$$\boldsymbol{\mu}_t = \boldsymbol{\mu}_{t-1} + \boldsymbol{\beta}_{t-1} + \boldsymbol{\eta}_t \qquad \boldsymbol{\eta}_t \sim NID(\mathbf{0}, \boldsymbol{\Sigma}_\eta) \qquad (22)$$

$$\boldsymbol{\beta}_t = \boldsymbol{\beta}_{t-1} + \boldsymbol{\zeta}_t \qquad \boldsymbol{\zeta}_t \sim NID(\mathbf{0}, \boldsymbol{\Sigma}_\zeta) \qquad (23)$$

We first consider the case where the covariance matrix of the slope disturbances is of rank K_β but the covariance matrix of levels is null ($\boldsymbol{\Sigma}_\eta = \mathbf{0}$) so that the estimated trends are relatively smooth. Following equation (17) above, the model may be reformulated as

$$\mathbf{y}_t = \boldsymbol{\Theta}\boldsymbol{\mu}_t^{\dagger\dagger} + \boldsymbol{\mu}_{\theta t} + \boldsymbol{\epsilon}_t \qquad \boldsymbol{\epsilon}_t \sim NID(\mathbf{0}, \boldsymbol{\Sigma}_\epsilon) \qquad (24)$$

$$\boldsymbol{\mu}_t^{\dagger\dagger} = \boldsymbol{\mu}_{t-1}^{\dagger\dagger} + \boldsymbol{\beta}_{t-1}^{\dagger\dagger} \qquad (25)$$

$$\boldsymbol{\beta}_t^{\dagger\dagger} = \boldsymbol{\beta}_{t-1}^{\dagger\dagger} + \boldsymbol{\zeta}_t^{\dagger\dagger} \qquad \boldsymbol{\zeta}_t^{\dagger\dagger} \sim NID(\mathbf{0}, \boldsymbol{\Sigma}_\zeta^{\dagger\dagger}) \qquad (26)$$

such that the first K_β elements in $\boldsymbol{\mu}_{\theta t}$ are zeroes and the remainder are contained in an $(N - K) \times 1$ vector $\bar{\boldsymbol{\mu}} + \bar{\boldsymbol{\beta}}t$. If $K_\beta = 1$ and we feel *a priori* that the series have exactly the same growth rate we set $\boldsymbol{\Theta}$ to a vector of ones and $\bar{\boldsymbol{\beta}} = \mathbf{0}$. In this case the trend components in the forecast functions are parallel.

In the general case when the level covariance matrix is of rank K_μ, one way of writing the model is

$$\mathbf{y}_t = \boldsymbol{\Theta}_\mu \boldsymbol{\mu}_t^\dagger + \boldsymbol{\Theta}_\beta \boldsymbol{\mu}_t^{\dagger\dagger} + \boldsymbol{\mu}_{\theta t} + \boldsymbol{\epsilon}_t \qquad \boldsymbol{\epsilon}_t \sim NID(\mathbf{0}, \boldsymbol{\Sigma}_\epsilon) \qquad (27)$$

where $\boldsymbol{\mu}_t^\dagger$ is a $K_\mu \times 1$ vector of random walks as in equation (17), $\boldsymbol{\mu}_t^{\dagger\dagger}$ is a $K_\beta \times 1$ vector of integrated random walks as in equation (26) and $\boldsymbol{\mu}_{\theta t}$ contains the appropriate number of constants and slopes. If $K_\mu = K_\beta$ and $\boldsymbol{\Theta}_\mu = \boldsymbol{\Theta}_\beta$, the slope can be incorporated into the level giving a single set of K_μ stochastic trends. If, in addition, $\boldsymbol{\Sigma}_\zeta^{\dagger\dagger}$ is proportional to $\boldsymbol{\Sigma}_\eta^\dagger$, the model is 'partially homogeneous' and the K_μ trends can be written with independent standardized disturbances for both level and slope, thereby generalizing equation (19).

9.4.3 Cointegration

The presence of common trends implies cointegration. Thus in the local level model, there exists $r = N - K$ cointegrating row vectors in an $r \times N$ matrix $\mathbf{A}$, such that $\mathbf{A}\mathbf{y}_t$ is stationary; see Engle and Granger (1987). This means that $\mathbf{A}\boldsymbol{\Theta} = \mathbf{0}$. Two questions then arise: can we estimate $\mathbf{A}$ from $\boldsymbol{\Theta}$ and can we estimate $\mathbf{A}$ directly?

Suppose equation (17) is partitioned into the first K and last r rows, that is

$$\mathbf{y}_{1t} = \boldsymbol{\mu}_t^\dagger + \boldsymbol{\epsilon}_{1t}$$
$$\mathbf{y}_{2t} = \mathbf{B}\boldsymbol{\mu}_t^\dagger + \bar{\boldsymbol{\mu}} + \boldsymbol{\epsilon}_{2t} \qquad t = 1, \ldots, T \qquad (28)$$

If the observations are transformed by pre-multiplying by an $N \times N$ matrix

$$\begin{bmatrix} \mathbf{I}_K & \mathbf{0} \\ \mathbf{A}_1 & \mathbf{A}_2 \end{bmatrix}$$

where $\mathbf{A} = (\mathbf{A}_1, \mathbf{A}_2)$, the first K equations in equation (28) remain the same while the last r become

$$\mathbf{A}_1 \mathbf{y}_{1t} + \mathbf{A}_2 \mathbf{y}_{2t} = \mathbf{A}_2 \bar{\boldsymbol{\mu}} + \mathbf{A}_1 \boldsymbol{\epsilon}_{1t} + \mathbf{A}_2 \boldsymbol{\epsilon}_{2t} \qquad t = 1, \ldots, T \qquad (29)$$

Now $\mathbf{A}_1$ and $\mathbf{A}_2$ should contain the same number of unknown parameters as $\mathbf{B}$ namely Kr. Further, if the likelihood of the transformed model is to be the same as the original, the determinant of the transforming matrix should be one. The simplest way of enforcing these restrictions is to set $\mathbf{A}_2 = \mathbf{I}_r$. Then the system becomes

$$\mathbf{y}_{1t} = \boldsymbol{\mu}_t^{\dagger} + \boldsymbol{\epsilon}_{1t}$$

$$\mathbf{y}_{2t} = \mathbf{B}\mathbf{y}_{1t} + \overline{\boldsymbol{\mu}} + \{\boldsymbol{\epsilon}_{2t} - \mathbf{B}\boldsymbol{\epsilon}_{1t}\}$$

(30)

because $\mathbf{A}_1 = -\mathbf{B}$. This is a special case of the triangular representation of a cointegration model analysed in Phillips (1991, 1994). With system estimation the t-statistics on elements of $\mathbf{B}$ can be treated as asymptotically normal.

The above triangular representation has the interpretation that the second set of equations are the cointegrating relationships, while the first set contain the common trends. Estimation of the common trends model (17) and the triangular cointegration model should, in principle, give the same results. However, the triangular system may be easier to estimate as the elements of $\mathbf{B}$ can be treated as the coefficients of explanatory variables.

The cointegrating equations should hopefully have some economic interpretation. The plausibility of the fitted model can then be assessed and tests on the coefficients can be carried out. If further restrictions can be placed on the $\mathbf{B}$ matrix, there is the possibility of gains in efficiency. Such restrictions are *overidentifying*. However, the transformation leading to equation (30) is arbitrary, and may not lend itself to an economic interpretation and hence to overidentifying restrictions. Returning to equation (29), we see that exact identifiability requires r^2 restrictions on $\mathbf{A}$ to bring the number of free parameters down to Kr. This requires r restrictions on each row of $\mathbf{A}$, including a normalizing constant. If the other $r - 1$ restrictions are achieved by setting elements to zero, this must be done in such a way that the square matrix of order $r - 1$, formed from the elements of the other rows of $\mathbf{A}$ in the same columns as the zeroes, is of full rank. This is exactly the same as the rank condition in a classical simultaneous equations model. (Setting $\mathbf{A}_2 = \mathbf{I}_r$ obviously satisfies this condition.) Further restrictions are overidentifying, and may be incorporated in to the common trends form by setting $\mathbf{B} = -\mathbf{A}_2^{-1}\mathbf{A}_1$.

The cointegrating interpretation continues to hold if the trends contain stochastic slopes. Thus, for example, with smooth trends the system is cointegrated of order $(2, 2)$, written $\mathrm{CI}(2, 2)$. The series are $\mathrm{I}(2)$ and there is a combination of them which is stationary; see Engle and Granger (1987). The triangular representation is as before but with the inclusion of a set of time trends in the cointegrating equations. More generally, with common levels and slopes it should be apparent from equation (27) that there are two sets of cointegrating vectors, one to annihilate the stochastic slopes, that is, with the property

$\mathbf{A}\boldsymbol{\Theta}_\beta = \mathbf{0}$, the other to remove the stochastic levels. If $\boldsymbol{\Theta}_\mu = \boldsymbol{\Theta}_\beta$ the two sets of cointegrating vectors are identical, because the stochastic levels and slopes are contained within the same set of trend components.

9.4.4 Illustrative Examples

Two simple trivariate examples may help to illustrate the relationship between the common trends and triangular representations. In both cases, it should be borne in mind that the stationary component would, in practice, be modelled by a more general process than white noise; see Section 9.5.

Balanced Growth

Suppose there is a single common trend in the logarithms of income, consumption and investment, so that $N = 3$, $r = 2$. Then $\boldsymbol{\Theta} = (1, \theta_1, \theta_2)'$. If there is balanced growth then $\theta_1 = \theta_2 = 1$. The common trend is associated with income and the two cointegrating equations correspond to the 'great ratios' of consumption and investment to income; see King *et al.* (1991). In other words,

$$\mathbf{A} = [-\mathbf{B} \quad \mathbf{I}_2] = \begin{bmatrix} -1 & 1 & 0 \\ -1 & 0 & 1 \end{bmatrix}$$

Money Demand

Economic theory on money demand suggests a cointegrating relationship between the logarithm of real money balances, the logarithm of real income and the nominal interest rate; that is, $N = 3$, $r = 1$. Thus $\mathbf{B}$ is a (1×2) row vector containing the coefficients of income and the interest rate, and the two stochastic trends can be associated with each of these variables. Some judgement as to how reasonable the estimates are can be made from economic considerations; at the minimum theory suggests what the signs should be.

If income follows a smooth trend rather then a random walk, the system may be written in the form (30), that is,

$$\begin{pmatrix} r_t \\ y_t \\ m_t \end{pmatrix} = \begin{pmatrix} 1 \\ 0 \\ \theta_r \end{pmatrix} \mu_r^\dagger + \begin{pmatrix} 0 \\ 1 \\ \theta_y \end{pmatrix} \mu_t^{\dagger\dagger} + \mu_{\theta t} + \epsilon_t$$

The cointegrating row vector $(-\theta_r, -\theta_y, 1)$ removes the stochastic slope and the stochastic level, giving a money demand equation with a stationary disturbance term (plus a deterministic constant and slope).

9.5 SEASONALS, CYCLES AND EXPLANATORY VARIABLES

9.5.1 Common Seasonals

Common factors in seasonality implies a reduction in the number of disturbances driving changes in the seasonal patterns. It does not imply any similarity in seasonal patterns unless the deterministic seasonal components outside the common seasonals are set to zero. Thus suppose, for simplicity, that the series contain only seasonals and irregular components. Then,

$$\mathbf{y}_t = \mathbf{\Theta}\boldsymbol{\gamma}_t^\dagger + \boldsymbol{\gamma}_{\theta t} + \boldsymbol{\epsilon}_t \qquad \boldsymbol{\epsilon}_t \sim NID(\mathbf{0}, \boldsymbol{\Sigma}_\epsilon) \tag{31}$$

where the last $N - K$ elements $\boldsymbol{\gamma}_{\theta t}$ contain fixed seasonal effects.

For trigonometric seasonals it is possible, in principle, to have different disturbance covariance matrices for each of the seasonal frequencies, thereby allowing common factors in some frequencies but not in others. This implies seasonal cointegration at different frequencies; see Hylleberg *et al.* (1990). However, full seasonal cointegration, that is, common factors at all frequencies, is straightforward in this framework.

9.5.2 Common Cycles

A model with common trends and common cycles could be written

$$\mathbf{y}_t = \mathbf{\Theta}_\mu \boldsymbol{\mu}_t + \boldsymbol{\mu}_\theta + \mathbf{\Theta}_\psi \boldsymbol{\psi}_t + \boldsymbol{\epsilon}_t \tag{32}$$

where $\mathbf{\Theta}_\psi$ is $N \times K$. It is not necessary to include a vector of constant terms corresponding to $\boldsymbol{\mu}_\theta$ for the level since the expectation of a cycle is zero.

It should be clear that *common cycles* embody much stronger restrictions than similar cycles. Thus with two series and one common cycle, one cycle would be proportional to the other. Common cycles are like the common feature cycles of Engle and Kozicki (1993).

9.5.3 Explanatory Variables

Explanatory variables and interventions may be included in multivariate models. Thus equation (8) generalizes to

$$\mathbf{y}_t = \boldsymbol{\mu}_t + \boldsymbol{\gamma}_t + \boldsymbol{\psi}_t + \sum_{\tau=1}^{r} \mathbf{\Phi}_\tau \mathbf{y}_{t-\tau} + \sum_{\tau=0}^{s} \mathbf{D}_\tau \mathbf{x}_{t-\tau} + \mathbf{\Lambda}\mathbf{w}_t + \boldsymbol{\epsilon}_t \qquad t = 1, \ldots, T \tag{33}$$

where $\mathbf{x}_t$ is a $K \times 1$ vector of explanatory variables and $\mathbf{w}_t$ is a $K^* \times 1$ vector of interventions. Elements in the parameters' matrices, $\boldsymbol{\Phi}$, $\mathbf{D}$ and $\boldsymbol{\Lambda}$ may be specified to be zero, thereby excluding certain variables from particular equations.

9.5.4 Common Trends and Other Components

If, in equation (33), only the trends contain common factors, a transformation similar to equation (30) can be applied. This yields

$$y_{1t} = \boldsymbol{\Theta}_1\boldsymbol{\mu}_t^\dagger + \boldsymbol{\gamma}_{1t} + \boldsymbol{\psi}_{1t} + \sum_{\tau=1}^{r}\boldsymbol{\Phi}_{1\tau}y_{t-\tau} + \sum_{\tau-0}^{s}\mathbf{D}_{1\tau}\mathbf{x}_{t-\tau} + \boldsymbol{\Lambda}_1\mathbf{w}_t + \boldsymbol{\epsilon}_{1t}$$

$$y_{2t} = \mathbf{B}y_{1t} + \boldsymbol{\gamma}_{2t}^* + \boldsymbol{\psi}_{2t}^* + \sum_{\tau=1}^{r}\boldsymbol{\Phi}_{2\tau}^*y_{t-\tau} + \sum_{\tau=0}^{s}\mathbf{D}_{2\tau}^*\mathbf{x}_{t-\tau} + \boldsymbol{\Lambda}_2^*\mathbf{w}_t + \boldsymbol{\epsilon}_{2t}^*$$

where $\boldsymbol{\gamma}_{2t}^* = \boldsymbol{\gamma}_{1t} - \mathbf{B}\boldsymbol{\gamma}_{2t}$, $\boldsymbol{\Phi}_{2\tau}^* = \boldsymbol{\Phi}_{1\tau} - \mathbf{B}\boldsymbol{\Phi}_{2\tau}$, and similarly for the other components and parameter matrices. Unless there are restrictions on these components and parameter matrices in the original formulation, there are no restrictions in the triangular form. In other words, the seasonals and cycles can be specified as before and estimated with the transformed parameters. This result does not hold if $\boldsymbol{\psi}_t$ is a VAR rather than a set of similar cycles.

9.6 A TESTBED EXAMPLE: MINKS AND MUSKRATS

The two series of showing the numbers of skins of minks and muskrats traded annually by the Hudson Bay Company in Canada from 1848 to 1909 have been studied extensively in the time series literature. As a result they provide a useful testbed for new techniques. There is a known prey–predator relationship between the two species and this gives rise to inter-linked cycles. Chan and Wallis (1978) carried out analysis and modelling within a multivariate ARMA framework. They first detrended by quadratic regression on both series. The approach adopted here fits trend components as part of the overall model.

First, a model was fitted with similar cycles in order to establish the joint stylized facts associated with the two series. The last three observations were omitted as they are somewhat atypical. The trends are relatively smooth, not unlike the quadratics fitted by Chan and Wallis. The smoothness arises because the level variances were constrained to be zero. The cycles have a period parameter of 10.3 years. Figure 9.1 shows the minks and muskrats series together with their trends, while Figure 9.2 plots the two cycles together. By shifting the plots of the cycles backwards and forwards it is found, after some experimentation, that the mink cycle leads the muskrat cycle by about three periods, the

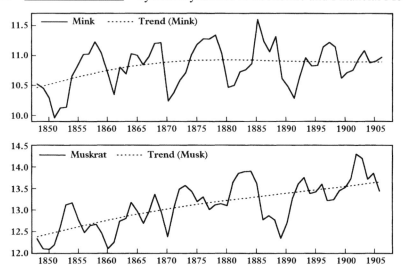

Figure 9.1   Mink and muskrat series with estimated trends

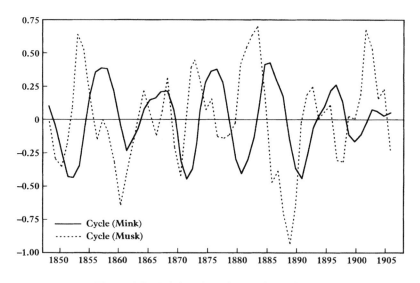

Figure 9.2   Mink and muskrat estimated cycles

correlation being 0.62. These results are consistent with the findings of Chan and Wallis (1978). It is interesting that the covariance matrix of the slope variance is singular, implying that the system is CI(2, 2).

Fitting a VAR(1) instead of similar cycles gave coefficients which were again

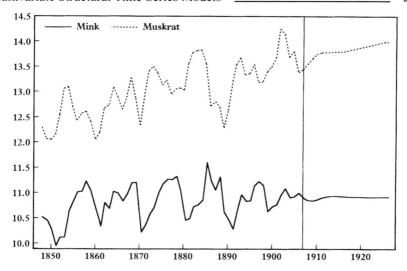

Figure 9.3 Mink and muskrat forecasts based on VAR(1) model

similar to those reported in Chan and Wallis. For example, the VAR coefficient matrix is estimated as

$$\mathbf{\Phi} = \begin{bmatrix} 0.573 & 0.282 \\ -0.685 & 0.659 \end{bmatrix}$$

The VAR model captures a simple behavioural system in which a rise in the population of muskrats is followed by a rise in the population of minks, and a subsequent fall in the population of muskrats. Figure 9.3 shows the forecasts for the VAR(1) model.

Although the original similar cycle model does not have a specification which can capture the dynamic interactions of the second model, it presents a robust set of stylized facts which provide a starting point for further analysis.

9.7 ECONOMIC APPLICATIONS

9.7.1 GNP and Investment

Harvey and Jaeger (1993) successfully fitted a plausible univariate structural time series model with trend and cycle components to US GNP. However, the likelihood function is quite flat, and the hyperparameters of the trend plus cycle model can be estimated more precisely by carrying out joint estimation with another series, such as investment. A bivariate model was originally estimated with level disturbance terms, but the associated covariance matrix was relatively small and found to be statistically insignificant when a LR test was carried out. The zero level variances result in quite smooth trends, as shown in Figure 9.4. The variance of the irregular component for GNP was estimated as zero. As in the mink–muskrat example the slope disturbances are perfectly correlated and so the system is CI(2, 2). Figure 9.5 shows the cycles in GNP and investment on the same graph.

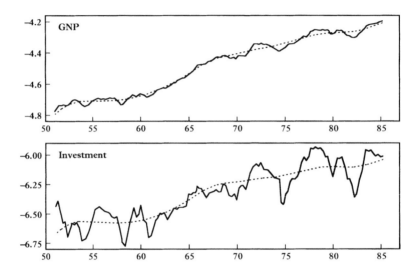

Figure 9.4   US GNP and Investment series with estimated trends

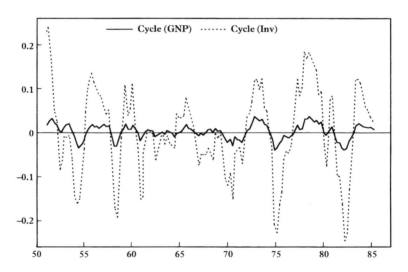

Figure 9.5   US GNP and Investment estimated cycles

9.7.2 Stochastic Volatility

Let y_t be a series such as stock returns or the difference of logged exchange rates. Such a series will normally be white noise. However, it may not be independent because of serial dependence in the variance. This may be modelled by

$$y_t = \sigma_t \varepsilon_t = \sigma \varepsilon_t \exp(h_t/2) \qquad \varepsilon_t \sim IID(0, 1) \qquad t = 1, \ldots, T \qquad (34)$$

where

$$h_{t+1} = \phi h_t + \eta_t \qquad \eta_t \sim NID(0, \sigma_\eta^2) \qquad |\phi| \leq 1 \qquad (35)$$

The term σ^2 is a scale factor, ϕ is the autoregressive parameter and η_t is a disturbance term which in the simplest model is uncorrelated with ε_t. This stochastic volatility (SV) model has two attractions relative to the popular GARCH class of models. The first is that it is the natural discrete time analogue of the continuous time model used in papers on option pricing, such as Hull and White (1987). The second is that its statistical properties are easy to determine. Maximum likelihood estimation can be carried out by computationally intensive simulation techniques such as Markov Chain Monte Carlo (MCMC) methods; see Shephard (1995) for a survey. A quasi-maximum likelihood (QML) procedure is not efficient but is relatively easy to apply. This method is based on transforming the observations to give:

$$\log y_t^2 = \kappa + h_t + \xi_t \qquad t = 1, \ldots, T \qquad (36)$$

where

$$\xi_t = \log \varepsilon_t^2 - E(\log \varepsilon_t^2) \qquad \text{and} \qquad \kappa = \log \sigma^2 + E(\log \varepsilon_t^2) \qquad (37)$$

The state space form provides the basis for QML estimation via the Kalman filter and also enables smoothed estimates of the variance component, h_t, to be constructed and predictions made. One attraction of the QML approach is that it can be applied without the assumption of a particular distribution for ε_t.

Harvey, Ruiz and Shephard (1994) use the QML approach to examine the volatility in the daily exchange rates of the US dollar against the British pound, the deutschmark, the Swiss franc and the yen. The multivariate model for the exchange data is based on the multivariate local level model (11) so each series is generated by a stochastic volatility model, with the volatility process following random walks. The disturbances in the different series are correlated with each other, the covariance matrices of the vectors $\boldsymbol{\epsilon}_t$ and $\boldsymbol{\eta}_t$ being denoted by $\boldsymbol{\Sigma}_\varepsilon$ and $\boldsymbol{\Sigma}_\eta$, respectively. If $\boldsymbol{\Sigma}_\eta$ is singular, there are common trends in volatility. On the basis of an examination of the principal components and eigenvalues of the estimate of $\boldsymbol{\Sigma}_\eta$, Harvey, Ruiz and Shephard (1994) decided that the number of common trends was two. A rotation of the common trends leads to a useful interpretation, namely that there is a world common trend in volatility, which together with another trend, which captures the difference between the yen and the three European currencies.

Another possibility to consider is whether there is any dynamic interaction between the various volatilities. For example, does the volatility in the deutschmark lead the volatility in the pound? One way of investigating such issues is to let the vector of volatilities, $\mathbf{h}_t$, follow a stationary VAR process.

9.7.3 Interest Rates

Figure 9.6 shows UK quarterly long- and short-term interest rates, as represented by the yield on 20-year gilts and the 91-day Treasury bill rate. The 'spread' between the two rates is an important variable in assessing theories of the term structure of interest rates; see Mills (1993, pp. 26–8, 225). After 1970 the series become considerably more volatile as the UK entered a period of relatively high inflation. We therefore first estimate the multivariate local level model (11) using data up to the end of 1970 only. The results show that the trends are perfectly correlated, while the cycle is present only in the short rate series, where it reduces to an AR(1) with coefficient 0.68. Thus the trend in the short series is just a linear function of the actual observations on the long series. The factor loading matrix shows that the common trend loads 0.27 on the long rate and 0.29 on the short (the same as the respective standard deviations of the level disturbance in the two series). If these loadings are taken to be the same, the multivariate model implies that the spread variable, i.e. $y_{1t} - y_{2t}$, is a stationary AR(1).

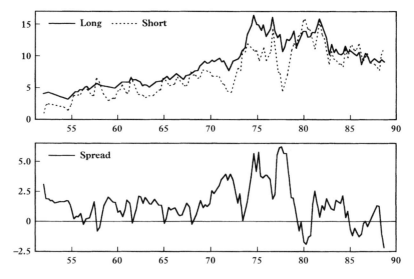

Figure 9.6 Long and short interest rate series and spread

Constructing a completely satisfactory model for the whole period is difficult. Given the nature of the data, it is perhaps not surprising that the model fitted to the earlier period fails the normality and heteroscedasticity tests. Nevertheless, it still provides an informative description of the data. The random walk trends are no longer perfectly correlated and a plot shows how in the 1980s they move so as to be much closer together. The cross-plot is also interesting in the way it shows a shift in the relationship.

9.8 DETRENDING

The common practice of detrending prior to any kind of analysis or modelling is not, in general, to be recommended. Nelson and Kang (1981) showed how fitting a linear trend to a non-stationary time series could result in spurious cycles, and more recently Harvey and Jaeger (1993) and King and Rebello (1993) have shown how similar effects can arise from the use of the more flexible Hodrick–Prescott detrending filter. The attraction of fitting a structural time series model is that the components are estimated simultaneously and so they are not distorted by any prior operations which may have been carried out.

The similar cycle model provides a reasonably robust model for the short-run component, but it embodies no interactions. In theory a more complex model, such as a VAR (p), may be fitted together with the trend, but this may not be easy in practice. It may therefore be necessary to contemplate the possibility of detrending the data, using either a univariate model with cycle or a multivariate model with a cycle and, possibly, common trend restrictions. A short-run model can then be fitted to the detrended series. (It may also be appropriate to remove seasonal components in a similar way). Once the short-run model has been estimated, its parameters may be inserted into a full structural time series model for forecasting purposes.

Although fitting a model to series detrended in this way has some practical appeal, it should be stressed that it will not give the same results as including a component with the same specification in a full model and estimating it simultaneously with the trend; see Harvey and Koopman (1992). In fact, as pointed out in Maravall (1993), the detrended series will be strictly non-invertible, so in theory an autoregressive approximation is impossible.

ACKNOWLEDGEMENTS

We would like to thank the ESRC for support under the grant 'Interrelationships in Economic Time Series', R000 23 5330.

COMMENTS

J.C. ENGWERDA, H. LÜTKEPOHL, P.C. YOUNG AND D.J. PEDREGAL

J.C. ENGWERDA

A well-known problem in empirical economics is the scarcity of data. To overcome this one is almost always forced to use models which contain, on the one hand, as few parameters as possible but, which are, on the other, still rich enough to explain the economic phenomena. This chapter addresses these issues. That is, how we can design models, which contain few parameters, that are still rich enough to describe stylized facts of economic time series.

The stylized facts the authors like to model are trends, seasonal components and cycles. To that end they consider the class of models that is described by time series y_t generated by:

$$y_t = \mu_t + \gamma_t + \psi_t + \epsilon_t \tag{1}$$

where μ is assumed to represent a stochastic trend, γ a seasonal component, ψ a cyclical component, and ϵ a pure stochastic component.

For univariate time series they assume that the stochastic trend is given by equation (2) in the chapter and the seasonal is either given by the dummy variable form (3) or by a sum of very specifically chosen base cycles, which modulo noise reduce to $\gamma_{j,t} = \alpha_j \cos(\lambda_j t) + \beta_j \sin(\lambda_j t)$ (equation (5)), where $\lambda_j = 2\pi j/s$, $j = 1, \ldots, [s/2]$ and s denotes the length of the seasonal period. Unfortunately no arguments are given why the authors like to call the dummy variable form a seasonal. Furthermore, they do not give a motivation for their choice of the base cycles, which is a pity since they play a basic role. In a similar way a cycle is assumed to be generated by equation (7). The question arises in this model formulation as to why the authors did not give a representation of the cycles of the form $\psi_t = \alpha \cos(\lambda_c t) + \beta \sin(\lambda_c t) + \kappa_t$, with κ_t some kind of noise.

The most simple extension to multivariate models is obtained by considering the case that each variable is generated as in the univariate case, but that the covariance matrices of the disturbance vectors are allowed to be non-diagonal the so-called SUTSE models. By assuming that in the SUTSE model all covariance matrices are proportional to each other we get the homogeneous models, and by assuming that for the cycles all damping factors and frequencies coincide we get SUTSE models containing similar cycles. The fact that trends, seasonals or cycles for different variables are proportional is modelled by replacing the variables μ_t, γ_t and ψ_t in equation (1) above by $\Theta_\mu \tilde{\mu}_t$, $\Theta_\gamma \tilde{\gamma}_t$ and $\Theta_\psi \tilde{\psi}_t$, respectively, where Θ_i is a full column rank matrix. In fact this assumption makes it possible to split up the multivariate system into a number of equations containing the common features and a set of equations which contain the cointegrating relationships. One point which remains somewhat unclear in this modelling is, for example, in formula (17) in the chapter, the role of μ_θ. It is unclear how the authors arrive at formula (17). It seems that the particular form the authors claim in this formula is not correct in general; for, consider

$$\Sigma_\eta = \begin{pmatrix} 0 & 0 \\ 0 & 1 \end{pmatrix}$$

in equation (11) in the chapter. It is unclear how for this particular choice of Σ_η equation (11) can be rewritten into equation (17) and (18) with the claimed specification of parameters. Probably, this flaw can be corrected by dropping the claimed structure in equations (17) and (18) for the constant vector μ_θ.

The advantages of this model approach are clear. First, it gives a systematic parsimonious framework to decompose time series into stochastic trend, seasonal and cyclical components. Second, due to its structure, it is statistically tractable.

Points which are not so clear at this moment are, for example, first, which kind of time series can be modelled this way. That is, does there not exist a broad class of time series which do not fit this model formulation? Second, it remains unclear how to deal with models containing a linear, or more generally an exponential, trend. Third, how parsimonious is this framework? That is, is it not possible to (approximately) model the same class of time series with a smaller number of parameters? Obviously, this point partly relates to the first point since first it has to be found which class of time series is attainable. A related point is how this relates to alternative approaches.

In conclusion, one might say that in this chapter a parsimonious framework is presented to describe stylized facts of economic time series, but that at this moment the limitations imposed by this approach are not clearly understood.

H. LÜTKEPOHL

The authors review the so-called structural time series model (STM) approach. Their point of departure is a model of the form

$$y_t = \mu_t + \gamma_t + \psi_t + \epsilon_t \tag{1}$$

where y_t is an observable variable or vector of variables, μ_t is a trend component representing long-term movements, γ_t represents a seasonal component, ψ_t is a cyclical component or perhaps an autoregressive part which represents cycles or short-term fluctuations and, finally, ϵ_t is a noise component. All components may be stochastic and μ_t, γ_t or ψ_t may also be specific deterministic functions. In this model the observed variables are decomposed in a sum of components associated with important features of economic variables such as trend, seasonal and irregular components. This is an attractive property of these models which is in line with classical components models and contrasts with other popular time series models such as VAR (vector autoregressive) type models. In the following I will compare the two rival model classes which are alternative and sometimes equivalent ways of representing the DGPs (data-generating processes) of univariate and multivariate time series.

When I speak of VAR type models I include vector autoregressive moving average (VARMA) processes, error correction models (ECMs) as well as EC–VARMA processes. Thus, a representative of this class has, for example, the form

$$A_0 \Delta y_t = v - \Pi y_{t-1} + A_1 \Delta y_{t-1} + \cdots + A_p \Delta y_{t-p} + M_0 u_t + \cdots + M_q u_{t-q}$$

$$(2)$$

where v is a vector of constants, u_t is a white-noise process, the A_j and M_i are coefficient matrices and Πy_{t-1} is the error correction term. If Π is a matrix of full rank the model is stationary whereas the variables are cointegrated if Π has a reduced rank. This is not the most general variant of a VAR type model which I have in mind but is just something the reader may hold on to in the following discussion. Possible generalizations include a u_t process with an ARCH structure, higher-order error correction terms, non-linear autoregressive models and inclusion of more general deterministic terms. Of course, in many applications $A_0 = M_0 = I$ and $q = 0$ are assumed so that the moving average term in equation (2) vanishes.

To assess the potential advantages and weaknesses of the STM and VAR type approaches it may be helpful to compare them in terms of their usefulness in performing the most important tasks of multiple time series analysis, namely forecasting and analysing the structure of a system of variables. The first step in carrying out both of these tasks is to specify and estimate a model. Therefore I will compare the two approaches in this respect first.

Model Specification and Estimation

Algorithms and computer programs are available for estimating both types of models. Hence, it seems that there is nothing much to choose between the two types of models with respect to the technical aspects of estimation once a specific candidate model has been specified. For VAR type models there is also a substantial amount of asymptotic theory available and even some small-sample results exist to assess the properties of the estimators and perform inference. From the chapter by Harvey and Koopman I understand that the situation is similar for STMs.

Harvey and Koopman do not say much about model specification and checking strategies for STMs. In contrast, specification and checking tools are well developed for VAR-type models. In particular, many tests against extensions of the basic linear model are available. For instance, VAR type models can be checked against seasonal models with periodically varying coefficients (see, for example, Lütkepohl (1991, Chapter 12)) or against ARCH components or various forms of non-linearities. These features can also be incorporated into VAR-type models if desired. I do not see how the STM approach can easily be extended in this direction. The stochastic volatility models presented in Section 9.7.2 of the chapter are still fairly restrictive relative to the flexible general non-linear and non-parametric ARCH variants discussed in the VAR-type literature. I wonder whether the same flexibility can be achieved in the STM approach. Clearly this flexibility is desirable nowadays where very long time series, especially for financial variables, are available which enable us to explore rather complex dynamic structures.

It is also not clear to me how easy it is to modify the specific assumptions for the trend and seasonal components which are considered by Harvey and Koopman. Is there software available that allows for other specifications as well, such as flexible non-linear trend functions as, for example, in Bierens (1996) and Granger, Inoue and Morin (1996)?

Another question that comes to mind is how the number of cointegrating relations or common trends is determined in the STM approach. If the same tests are used in both approaches, obviously, none can claim an advantage in this respect except perhaps that most of these tests are directly based on VAR-type models and, hence, the analysis remains within one model class if the latter are used.

Forecasting

Once a model has been specified and estimated it may be used for forecasting. It has been argued by a number of time series analysts that simple, parsimonious models tend to forecast better than complicated, heavily parameterized specifications. Hence, if STMs and VAR-type models represent the same DGP, the more parsimonious representation should be used. In their introduction to the chapter Harvey and Koopman argue that STMs may have advantages over VAR models in this respect in some situations. It seems to me, however, that the authors are referring to pure VAR models without allowance for moving-average terms. It is true that pure VAR models are by far the most popular multiple time series models in practice. On the other hand, estimation, specification and inference methods are available for VARMA processes as well, even for the case where the variables are cointegrated (see, for example, Lütkepohl (1991, Chapters 6–8) for the stationary case and Lütkepohl and Claessen (1996) for the cointegrated case). Thus, if MA terms are needed for a parsimonious representation, they can be used easily in VAR-type models.

An advantage of VAR-type models is that they represent a direct way of modelling the conditional expectation and, if desired, the conditional heteroscedasticity which is helpful in setting up forecast intervals. In contrast, STM analysis focuses on stylized factors and not on the forecasts directly. Although this is not necessarily a disadvantage for the resulting forecasts it may be a problem if features of a relationship other than the assumed stylized factors such as non-linearities are of importance.

Interpretation

The differences between the two competing approaches for multiple time series analysis may be greatest with respect to the interpretation of the models. If features such as business cycles are of interest which are sometimes thought of as common long-term cycles or trends these may be more directly captured by a STM analysis whereas they would have to be extracted indirectly from an ECM in the VAR approach. Still, it is not necessarily obvious in a particular situation which one of the two approaches is more suitable for finding a good representation of the DGP.

In this respect I am not sure that I find the illustrative examples in Section 9.4.4 of the chapter very convincing cases for the STM approach. Restrictions can be placed easily on the cointegration vectors in the ECM. It has the additional advantage that restrictions can be also imposed on the short-term dynamics which are an important component in the full dynamic relationship between the variables. Various kinds of impulse responses can be computed easily and constraints from economic theory may be placed on them. This, of course, is the issue dealt with under the heading of 'structural VAR modelling' (see Lütkepohl and Breitung (this volume, especially Section 10.2.2)). Moreover, tests for Granger-causality (between the variables and not some stylized factors) and exogeneity are easy to perform in the VAR framework. Toda and Yamamoto (1995) and Dolado and Lütkepohl (1996) show that asymptotic tests are available for the case of cointegrated variables despite the problems pointed out by Toda and Phillips (1993). These considerations are also of importance for the interest rate example discussed in Section 9.7.3. In analysing the term structure one may be interested in checking the expectations hypothesis by testing for Granger-causality (e.g. Lütkepohl and Reimers (1992)). It may also be worth noting that potential structural breaks as found by Harvey and Koopman can be handled relatively easily in these models. Hence, although there may be cases where it is more natural to think of the DGP of a multiple time series in terms of a sum of trend and cyclical components, it is my own experience that VAR type models are more easily interpretable in the light of economic theories and the restrictions implied by those theories are often relatively easy to impose or to test in the latter models.

Conclusion

In conclusion, I think that there is a case for STMs in certain situations where economic phenomena are of interest and Andrew Harvey and his colleagues have to be applauded for their efforts in pursuing the development of these models. To me, however, they are more natural in univariate time series analysis whereas I find VAR-type models usually easier to deal with in multiple time series analysis. This, of course, may be a matter of personal preferences and perhaps of habit persistence. The fact that most applied work in this context is based on VAR-type models indicates, however, that a majority of applied researchers and econometricians shares this habit which may be partly due to the simplicity of the basic model and the richness of the model class which can be extended easily to deal with various kinds of complications such as non-stationarity and non-linearity.

P.C. YOUNG AND D.J. PEDREGAL

The chapter proposes a multivariate structural time series (STS) approach as a logical extension of Andrew Harvey's previous univariate STS modelling approach. As usual, the extension from univariate to multivariate is not simple and many different possibilities are at hand. The main option selected in this case is the seemingly unrelated time series equations (SUTSE); or, in other words, the time series are related through the vector noise process. This is probably the most straightforward approach and it is very useful in terms of testing for common features among time series, as shown in the chapter (common trends, cycles, cointegration, etc.). But it is not necessarily the most interesting multivariable approach and the authors might like to comment on this. Indeed, as presented, the proposed method is more the joint estimation of components rather than a full multivariate modelling procedure. In this sense, there are some constraints that seem quite limiting: for example cyclical components have to be 'similar' (i.e. same period and damping factor) and, in STAMP, the only interactions among cyclical components that are possible are through VAR(1) processes. Again, the authors might like to comment a little more on these restrictions in the paper.

There is an understandable (and welcome to us) tendency in the chapter to constrain the estimation so that 'smooth' trends are obtained. This is achieved by constraining the variance of the first noise in the local linear trend (LLT) model to zero. The result is, of course, the integrated random walk (IRW) model which, as the authors point out, we advocated long ago as a model which helps to ensure the estimation of smooth trends (e.g. Jakeman and Young, (1979, 1984) and Young (1984)). It has been used as the default stochastic trend model in the microCAPTAIN software package for over 20 years and is a feature of all our papers on forecasting over the past decade (e.g. Young *et al.*, 1989). In the case of multivariate models, however, the choice of the IRW trend model instead of LLT seems important not only because of the enhanced degree of smoothness; it is also important in order to obtain reasonable results. For example, in the mink–muskrat case, multivariable ML estimation with unconstrained LLT (in STAMP) yields a smooth trend for the mink series but a much less smooth trend for the muskrat series, as shown in Figure 9.A.

This creates quite strange results, in the sense that the trend of the muskrat series does not look like a meaningful trend; and both the cycles (which are virtually deterministic with constant amplitude) and the irregular components are almost identical in both series. In effect, the stochastic aspects of the series have been driven to the trend and residual components, leaving small, almost deterministic cyclical components. This does not seem very reasonable for these series and is, presumably, the reason why the authors feel that IRW-constrained

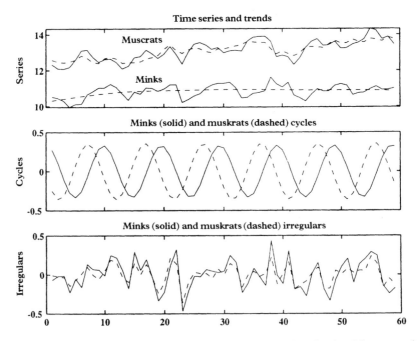

Figure 9.A STAMP results for the mink–muskrat example using local linear trends

estimation proves necessary. It is an effect caused by a combination of the less smooth properties of the LLT and the imposition of similar cycles. In general, as we have claimed for many years, IRW trend models often give more sensible results in practice and it is the unconstrained LLT model that should be used with great care. The authors might like to comment on this aspect of their analysis.

Nominally, the mink–muskrat example is a good one in relation to the topic of this paper: it is clearly multivariable, stochastic, and it is very well known. Having analysed the data ourselves, however, we feel that there are alternative multivariable models which make more sense and yield improved forecasting performance. We would merely comment that the authors' analysis is quite heavily constrained by STAMP (e.g. the restriction to a VAR(1) process when AIC identification suggests that the cyclical behaviour requires between VAR(3) and VAR(6) to fully explain the oscillatory movements). Two other small points in relation to the mink–muskrat example. First, it is not clear why the forecasts produced by the VAR model are provided rather than those produced by the multivariable structural model. Indeed, could not both have been provided on the same plot, together with standard error bounds? Second, and bearing on our discussion above, the current forecasts show that the estimated cycle model is heavily damped, tending to negate the usual predator–prey hypothesis of sustained cycles. Both our microCAPTAIN and Matlab analyses produce models which are not limited in this manner and, as we point out above, do a much better job at *ex-ante* forecasting the series within the sample, where evaluation of the forecasting performance is possible.

REPLIES

A.C. HARVEY AND S.J. KOOPMAN

J.C. Engwerda asks about the rationale of STMs. Space considerations require the treatment here to be brief and it is necessary to read an introductory paper, the early chapters in Harvey (1989) or the tutorials in Koopman *et al.* (1995) to appreciate the appeal of the approach. The point about the role of $\boldsymbol{\mu}_\theta$ is that if, in equation (11), an element of $\boldsymbol{\mu}_t$ is constant, then it is this constant which enters into $\bar{\boldsymbol{\mu}}$. A deterministic linear trend fits very nicely into the STM framework since, as noted below equation (2), it is a special case of the stochastic trend model; an exponential trend is obtained when working in logarithms. As regards parsimony, one of the main attractions of the STM approach for multivariate models is that it is likely to be very parsimonious compared with a VAR, since VARs may require a large number of lags when slowly evolving trends or seasonals are present.

H. Lütkepohl makes some very good points about the relative merits of structural time series models (STMs) and VARs. He lists a number of extensions that can be made to VARs which may be difficult to include within an unobserved components framework. For example, ARCH effects, which are formulated explicitly in terms of a predictive distribution, fit much more naturally into a VAR than a STM. Some progress has been made on estimating unobserved components models with ARCH effects, but the methods are approximate; see Harvey, Ruiz and Sentana (1992). Lütkepohl also mentions periodically seasonal effects, but here the STM approach may actually offer some advantages since the state-space form makes it is easy to allow coefficients to be different across different seasons. One could, of course, draw up a list of features which are more easily modelled by a VAR than an STM and vice versa. However, one of our main concerns about VARs is that their ease of estimation draws the econometrician into formulating models which do not necessarily have a useful economic interpretation, particularly with regard to dynamic effects.

Lütkepohl raises the issue of flexible trends. There is a link with the smooth trend ($\sigma_\eta^2 = 0$) used in STMs since this can be interpreted as a cubic spline when the model is set up in continuous time; see Wecker and Ansley (1983).

Another link is the time-varying splines used for hourly electricity data by Harvey and Koopman (1993) for capturing a weekly movement which changes over time.

The issue of testing for cointegration is clearly important in economics. The unobserved components approach leads one in the direction of testing the null of cointegration against the alternative of no cointegration; see, for example, Shin (1994) and Harris and Inder (1994). We believe this is more natural than taking the null hypothesis to be no cointegration as in autoregressive-based approaches. It may not be long before a viable procedure for testing for the number of cointegrating relationships, similar to that in Johansen (1988), but in the opposite direction, has been devised.

Lütkepohl argues that VARMA models may overcome some of the objections made regarding pure autoregressions. We have doubt as to whether VARMAs are viable in practice. MA parameters typically arise as a result of differencing non-stationary models and we believe it is much more natural, as well as being more parsimonious, to model the non-stationarity directly by stochastic trend components; see Harvey (1989, p. 432). The MA parameters in a multivariate model have no clear interpretation and hence reduction to a more parsimonious model is problematic.

Finally, on the general issue of the interpretation and ease of use of STMs and VARs, it must be remembered that a considerable amount of research has been put into the latter. Multivariate STMs are still in their infancy and with more applications, experience and theoretical development they become attractive even to those who are expert users of the VAR methodology.

We are grateful to P. Young and D. Pedregal for raising the issue of the smooth trend (IRW) specification. We have always been reluctant to impose smooth trends as a matter of course since there are many time series for which it is inappropriate. For example, many financial time series follow random walks and attempting to impose an underlying smooth trend on them would be totally misleading. Our preferred strategy is to fit the general local linear trend and then simplify to the smooth trend if the level variance is small. This is exactly what we did with the US GNP and investment series. However, we acknowledge that this does not always work and our approach is then to experiment by comparing the output from the smooth trend with that from other specifications, such as the random walk with drift. It was on this basis that we arrived at the smooth trend model for the mink–muskrat series and the analysis of Young and Pedregal makes it clear why we did.

Young and Pedregal are right to say that STAMP is limited at present in that if the stationary part is to be modelled by a VAR only a first-order process is permitted. We plan to extend this in the future. However, in a multivariate model a first-order process is not too restrictive in that it allows fairly rich dynamics. In the mink–muskrat example Chan and Wallis (1978) found a VAR(1) picked up the cycles very nicely and we find the same. Using a VAR(6), as Young and

Pedregal suggest, would introduce an extra twenty parameters into the model. While long VARs are often encountered in the literature on estimating non-stationary series, this is primarily because the lags are needed to pick up slowly changing trends; see our comments earlier. When the component is known to be stationary fewer lags are needed.

REFERENCES

Ansley, C.F. and Kohn, R. (1986) A note on reparameterizing a vector autoregressive moving average model to enforce stationarity. *Journal of Statistical Computation and Simulation* **24**, 99–106.

Bierens, H. (1996) Testing the unit root with drift hypothesis against nonlinear trend stationary, with an application to the US price level and interest rate. Forthcoming in *Journal of Econometrics*.

Chan, W.Y.T. and Wallis, K.F. (1978) Multiple time series modelling: another look at the mink-muskrat interactions. *Applied Statistics* **27**, 168–75.

Dolado, J.J. and Lütkepohl, H. (1996) Making Wald tests work for cointegrated VAR systems. *Econometric Reviews* **15**, 369–86.

Engle, R.F. and Granger, C.W.J. (1987) Co-integration and error correction: representation, estimation and testing. *Econometrica* **35**, 251–76.

Engle, R.F. and Kozicki, S. (1993) Testing for common features (with discussion). *Journal of Business and Economic Statistics* **11**, 369–95.

Granger, C.W.J., Inoue, T. and Morin, N. (1996) Non-linear stochastic trends. Forthcoming in *Journal of Econometrics*.

Harris, D. and Inder, B. (1994) A test of the null hypothesis of co-integration' in C. Hargreaves (ed.), *Non-stationary Time Series Analysis and Cointegration*. Oxford University Press, Oxford.

Harvey, A.C. (1989) Forecasting, Structural Time Series Models and the Kalman Filter. Cambridge University Press, Cambridge.

Harvey, A.C. and Jaeger, A. (1993) Detrending stylized facts and the business cycle. *Journal of Applied Econometrics* **8**, 231–47.

Harvey, A.C. and Koopman, S.J. (1992) Diagnostic checking of unobserved components time series models. *Journal of Business and Economic Statistics* **10**, 377–89.

Harvey, A.C. and Koopman, S.J. (1993) Forecasting hourly electricity demand using time-varying splines. *Journal of the American Statistical Association* **88**, 1228–36.

Harvey, A.C., Ruiz, E. and Sentana, E. (1992) Unobserved components time series models with ARCH disturbances. *Journal of Econometrics* **52**, 129–57.

Harvey, A.C., Ruiz, E. and Shephard, N. (1994) Multivariate stochastic variance models. *Review of Economic Studies* **61**, 247–64.

Harvey, A.C. and Stock, J.H. (1988) Continuous time autoregressive models with common stochastic trends. *Journal of Economic Dynamics and Control* **12**, 365–84.

Harvey, A.C. and Streibel, M. (1996) Tests for deterministic versus indeterministic cycles. LSE statistics research report, LSERR29.

Hull, J. and White, A. (1987), The pricing of options on assets with stochastic volatilities. *Journal of Finance* **42**, 281–300.

Hylleberg, S., Engle, R.F., Granger, C.W.J. and Yoo, B.S. (1990) Seasonal integration and co-integration. *Journal of Econometrics* **44**, 215–38.

Jakeman, A.J. and Young, P.C. (1979, 1984) Recursive filtering and the inversion of ill-posed causal problems. *Utilitas Math.* **25**, 351–76 (originally Report No. AS/R28/1979, Centre for Resource and Environmental Studies, Australian National University).

Johansen, S. (1988) Statistical analysis of co-integration vectors. *Journal of Economic Dynamics and Control* **12**, 131–54.

King, R.G., Plosser, C.I., Stock, J.H. and Watson, M.W. (1991) Stochastic trends and economic fluctuations. *American Economic Review* **81**, 819–40.

King, R.G. and Rebello, S.T. (1993) Low frequency filtering and real business cycles. *Journal of Economic Dynamics and Control* **17**, 207–31.

Koopman, S.J. (1993) Disturbance smoother for state space models. *Biometrika* **80**, 117–26.

Koopman, S.J. and Shephard, N. (1992) Exact score for time series models in state space form. *Biometrika* **79**, 823–6.

Koopman, S.J., Harvey, A.C. Doornik, J.A. and Shephard, N. (1995) *STAMP 5.0 Structural Time Series Analyser, Modeller and Predictor.* Chapman and Hall, London.

Lütkepohl, H. (1991), *Introduction to Multiple Time Series Analysis*, Springer-Verlag, Berlin.

Lütkepohl, H. and Claessen, H. (1996) Analysis of cointegrated VARMA processes. Forthcoming in *Journal of Econometrics*.

Lütkepohl, H. and Reimers, H.-E. (1992) Granger causality in cointegrated VAR processes: the case of the term structure. *Economics Letters* **40**, 263–8.

Maravall, A. (1993) Stochastic linear trends. *Journal of Econometrics* **56**, 5–37.

Mills, T.C. (1993) *Time Series Methods for Finance*. Cambridge University Press, Cambridge.

Nelson, C.R. and Kang, H. (1981) Spurious periodicity in inappropriately detrended time series. *Econometrica* **49**, 741–51.

Phillips, P.C.B. (1991) Optimal inference in cointegrated systems. *Econometrica* **59**, 283–306.

Phillips, P.C.B. (1994) Some exact distribution theory for maximum likelihood estimators of cointegrating coefficients in error correction models. *Econometrica* **62**, 73–93.

Shin, Y. (1994) A residual based test of the null of cointegration against the alternative of non cointegration. *Econometric Theory* **10**, 91–105.

Shephard, N. (1995) Statistical aspects of ARCH and stochastic volatility. In D.R. Cox, O.E. Barndorff-Nielson and D.V. Hinkley (eds), *Time Series Models in Econometrics, Finance and Other Fields*. Chapman and Hall, London, 1–63.

Toda, H. and Phillips, P.C.B. (1993) Vector autoregressions and causality. *Econometrica* **61**, 1367–94.

Toda, H. and Yamamoto, T. (1995) Statistical inference in vector autoregressions with possibly integrated processes. *Journal of Econometrics* **66**, 225–50.

Wecker, W.E. and Ansley, C.F. (1983), The signal extraction approach to nonlinear regression and spline smoothing, *Journal of the American Statistical Association* **78**, 81–9.

Young, P.C. (1984), *Recursive Estimation and Time Series Analysis*. Springer-Verlag, Berlin.

Young, P.C., Ng, C.N. and Armitage, P. (1989) Systems approach to recursive economic forecasting and seasonal adjustment. *Computers and Mathematics with Applications*, special issue on System Theoretic Methods in Economic Modelling **18**, 481–501.

10

Impulse Response Analysis of Vector Autoregressive Processes

H. LÜTKEPOHL AND J. BREITUNG

10.1 INTRODUCTION

More than fifty years ago the foundations were developed for analysing economic systems by simultaneous equations models. In the 1950s and 1960s the
development of computer technology and growing data availability resulted in a
corresponding increase in the size of these models. On the other hand, there was
a parallel growth in dissatisfaction with the performance of these models. In
particular, it was found that often simple, univariate time series models produced
more precise forecasts than some of the large-scale macroeconometric simultaneous equations models. The dissatisfaction with the state of macro models
resulted in a rethinking of econometric simultaneous equations modelling. In his
seminal critique Sims (1980) blamed the failure of macro models at least partly
on the 'incredible' identifying assumptions used in their construction. As an
alternative he advocated unrestricted reduced-form multivariate time series
models where all variables are *a priori* endogenous. Restrictions are imposed by
statistical tools. Since then vector autoregressive (VAR) models have become
standard instruments in the econometric toolkit.

Although these models are useful forecasting tools, their coefficients are
often not very informative about the relations between the variables of a
given system of interest. Therefore impulse responses and other quantities
derived from the VAR coefficients are frequently used in the interpretation of

System Dynamics in Economic and Financial Models. Edited by C. Heij, J.M. Schumacher,
B. Hanzon and C. Praagman © 1997 John Wiley & Sons Ltd

these models. It soon became apparent that these quantities may not be able to answer all questions of interest to economists if no identifying restrictions are imposed.

These problems became even more obvious with the advent of cointegration by Granger (1981) and Engle and Granger (1987). A set of trending non-stationary (integrated) variables are called cointegrated if a linear combination exists which is stationary. Such a linear combination is often regarded as an equilibrium or long-run relation. Hence the concept of cointegration results in a natural partition of a model in a long-run part and short term dynamics. The distinction between these parts raises further identification problems and questions of how to distinguish between the different features of a relationship. It is one main purpose of this chapter to make these issues more transparent.

In the next section the basic VAR framework will be established and impulse response analysis will be discussed. It is by now well documented even in the textbook literature (see e.g. Lütkepohl (1991), Hamilton (1994), Hendry (1995), Johansen (1995)). The statistical analysis of VAR models including estimation and inference is considered in Section 10.3. An example is given in Section 10.4 and conclusions follow in Section 10.5.

10.2 VECTOR AUTOREGRESSIVE MODELS

10.2.1 General Framework

Given a set of K time series variables $y_t = [y_{1t}, \ldots, y_{Kt}]'$, VAR models of the form

$$y_t = A_1 y_{t-1} + \ldots + A_p y_{t-p} + u_t \qquad (1)$$

provide a fairly general framework for the DGP (data-generation process) of the series. More precisely this model is called a VAR process of order p or a VAR(p) process. Here $u_t = [u_{1t}, \ldots, u_{Kt}]'$ is a zero mean independent white-noise process with non-singular, time invariant covariance matrix Σ_u and the A_i are $(K \times K)$ coefficient matrices. Obviously, process (1) is easy to use for forecasting purposes. On the other hand, it is not easy to determine the exact relations between the variables represented by it. For instance, the instantaneous relations are effectively summarized in the residual covariance matrix. Also the intertemporal relations are not immediately obvious from process (1). Below we will discuss possibilities to disentangle the structural information embodied in this model. There may also be deterministic terms such as polynomial trends or seasonal dummies in a model like (1). We have eliminated them here because they are not relevant for the issues of primary interest in the following.

Process (1) is stable if

$$\det(I_K - A_1 z - \ldots - A_p z^p) \neq 0 \quad \text{for } |z| \leq 1 \tag{2}$$

In that case it generates stationary time series with time invariant means, variances and covariance structure. It then also has a Wold moving average (MA) representation

$$y_t = \Phi_0 u_t + \Phi_1 u_{t-1} + \Phi_2 u_{t-2} + \cdots \tag{3}$$

where $\Phi_0 = I_K$ is the $(K \times K)$ identity matrix and the Φ_s can be computed recursively using

$$\Phi_s = \sum_{j=1}^{s} \Phi_{s-j} A_j, \qquad s = 1, 2, \ldots \tag{4}$$

(see Lütkepohl (1991, p. 18)). These quantities will be of importance in the following.

Many economic time series are not stationary, however. In particular, they have trends which can often be removed by differencing, that is, y_{kt} may not be stationary while $\Delta y_{kt} = y_{kt} - y_{k,t-1}$ is. Variables with this property are called integrated of order 1 ($I(1)$) because the trend can be removed by differencing them once. More generally, non-stationary variables which are stationary after differencing them d times are called $I(d)$. In particular, stationary variables are sometimes said to be $I(0)$. If there exists a linear combination of $I(d)$ variables which has a lower order of integration than the component series, the variables are called cointegrated. In particular, if some variables are $I(1)$ and a linear combination of them is $I(0)$, the variables are cointegrated. This is the case of foremost interest in the following.

A VAR process of type (1) may contain $I(d)$ variables if the determinant in equation (2) is allowed to have roots for $z = 1$ and all other roots are outside the complex unit circle. Suppose now for simplicity that all components of y_t are, at most, $I(1)$, that is, $y_{kt} \sim I(d)$, $d \leq 1$, for $k = 1, \ldots, K$. Subtracting y_{t-1} from both sides of (1) and rearranging terms gives the so-called error correction model (ECM) form of the process:

$$\Delta y_t = -\Pi y_{t-1} + D_1 \Delta y_{t-1} + \ldots + D_{p-1} \Delta y_{t-p+1} + u_t \tag{5}$$

where $\Pi = I_K - A_1 - \ldots - A_p$ and $D_i = -(A_{i+1} + \ldots + A_p)$ for $i = 1, \ldots, p - 1$. In this representation of the process all terms are stationary because Δy_t and u_t are stationary by assumption. Hence, although Πy_{t-1} contains the non-stationary levels y_{t-1}, it must also be stationary. In other words, Πy_{t-1} must contain the cointegrating relations of the system. Of course, it is also possible to obtain the A_j parameter matrices from the coefficients of the ECM as $A_1 = D_1 - \Pi + I_K$, $A_i = D_i - D_{i-1}$ for $i = 2, \ldots, p - 1$, and $A_p = -D_{p-1}$. The fact that $\det(I_K - A_1 z - \ldots - A_p z^p) = 0$ for $z = 1$ means, of course, that $\det(\Pi) = 0$ and hence Π is singular. Suppose $\text{rk}(\Pi) = r$. Then there exist r linearly independent cointegrating relations. Any $(K \times K)$ matrix of rank r can be written as a product of a $(K \times r)$ and an $(r \times K)$ matrix, hence $\Pi = BC$, where B is $(K \times r)$ and C is $(r \times K)$. Premultiplying a stationary vector by some matrix results again in a stationary process. Hence, premultiplying $\Pi y_{t-1} = BC y_{t-1}$ by $(B'B)^{-1}B'$ shows that Cy_{t-1} is stationary and, therefore, contains the cointegrating relations. Of course, B and C are not unique and consequently, there are many possible matrices C representing the linearly independent cointegrating relations which cannot be distinguished purely from the observed time series. In other words, there is an identification problem. Popular examples of identifying restrictions assume that the first part of C is an identity matrix, $C = [I_r: C_1]$, where C_1 is an $(r \times (K - r))$ matrix. This case has received some attention in the literature. For $r = 1$ it amounts to normalizing the coefficient of the first variable.

Model (5) includes as special cases stable, stationary processes for which $r = K$ and stable systems in first differences where $r = 0$. In both of these boundary cases no cointegration in the usual sense is present among the variables. Moreover, there are other cases where, strictly speaking, there is no cointegration although model (5) has a cointegrating rank strictly between 0 and K. For instance, if all variables but one are stationary then the cointegration rank is $K - 1$. Similarly, there could be $K - r$ unrelated non-stationary variables and r stationary components. Generally, in the matrix C there can be one row with a one and zeros elsewhere for each stationary variable in the system. Although in these cases there is no cointegration in the strict sense, it is convenient to include them all in the present framework because they do not require a special treatment in discussing estimation and model specification. Of course, the special properties of the variables have to be taken into account in the interpretation of a system. In Section 10.3 the statistical analysis of reduced form models like (1) and (5) is considered. Before we turn to that issue we will discuss problems related to the interpretation of VAR models.

10.2.2 Impulse Responses

In the stationary case the coefficients of the Wold representation (3) may be interpreted as impulse responses. The (i, j)th element of the matrix Φ_s, when treated as a function of s, traces out the expected response of $y_{i,t+s}$ to a unit change in y_{jt} holding constant all past values of y_t. Since the change in y_{it} given $\{y_{t-1}, y_{t-2}, \ldots\}$ is measured by the innovation u_{it}, the elements of Φ_s represent the impulse responses of the components of y_t with respect to the u_t innovations. Note that the existence of the infinite sum on the right-hand side of equation (3) requires that the $\Phi_s \to 0$ as $s \to \infty$. Consequently the effect of an impulse vanishes over time and is thus transitory. Since the u_t are the 1-step-ahead forecast errors these impulse responses are sometimes called forecast error impulse responses.

For non-stationary cointegrated processes the Φ_j impulse response matrices can be computed in the same way as in (4) although the Wold representation does not exist (see Lütkepohl (1991, Chapter 11)). In this case the Φ_j may not converge to zero as $j \to \infty$ and, hence, some shocks may have permanent effects. Assuming that all variables are $I(1)$, it is also possible to consider the stationary process Δy_t which has a Wold representation

$$\Delta y_t = \Xi_0 u_t + \Xi_1 u_{t-1} + \Xi_2 u_{t-2} + \cdots \tag{6}$$

where $\Xi_0 = I_K$ and $\Xi_j = \Phi_j - \Phi_{j-1}$ $(j = 1, 2, \ldots)$. The coefficients of this representation may be interpreted as impulse responses as well. Obviously,

$$\Phi_s = \sum_{j=0}^{s} \Xi_j \qquad s = 1, 2, \ldots \tag{7}$$

so that the Φ_s may be viewed as accumulated impulse responses of the representation in first differences.

In the early applications of Sargent (1978) and Sims (1980, 1981), the innovations of the VAR were orthogonalized using a Cholesky decomposition of the covariance matrix Σ_u. Let P be a lower triangular matrix such that $\Sigma_u = PP'$. Then, the orthogonalized shocks are given by $\varepsilon_t = P^{-1}u_t$. The reason for applying such an orthogonalization is that it may be problematic to consider the dynamic impact of the innovations in isolation when they are mutually correlated and, hence, in the actual system a shock of this type is not likely to occur in isolation.

Obviously, there is some degree of arbitrariness when constructing shocks in this manner. In general, choosing a different ordering of the variables in the vector y_t produces different shocks and, thus, the effects of the shock on the system depend on the way the variables are arranged in the vector y_t. To account for this difficulty, Sims (1981) recommends attempting various triangular ortho-gonalizations and checking whether the results are robust to the ordering of the variables. Furthermore: 'When results are sensitive to the ordering of the variables, one may make some progress by using a priori hypotheses about the structure' (Sims (1981, p. 288)). In this section we will address the question how prior information about the structure can be imposed to obtain what is now called a 'structural VAR'.

In recent years, different types of identifying restrictions were considered. For a comprehensive review of different approaches see e.g. Watson (1994). Most of the models encountered in empirical practice can be represented by a dynamic system of simultaneous equations

$$\Psi_0 y_t = \Psi_1 y_{t-1} + \cdots + \Psi_p y_{t-p} + v_t \tag{8}$$

where $v_t = R\varepsilon_t$ and ε_t is a $(K \times 1)$ vector of structural shocks with covariance matrix $E(\varepsilon_t \varepsilon_t') = \Sigma_\varepsilon$. Usually it is assumed that Σ_ε is a diagonal matrix so that the structural shocks are mutually uncorrelated.

The reduced form corresponding to the structural model (8) is a VAR as given in model (1) with $A_j = \Psi_0^{-1} \Psi_j$ $(j = 1, \ldots, p)$ and $\Psi_0^{-1} v_t = u_t$ so that

$$\Psi_0 u_t = R\varepsilon_t \qquad (9)$$

From this representation it is clear that a linear model is entertained to obtain structural shocks (ε_t) from the VAR innovations (u_t) such that ε_t is a vector of orthogonal shocks. Sims' triangular system is obviously a special case of such a class of structural models with $P = \Psi_0^{-1} R$. It is also clear that identifying restrictions are needed to obtain a unique structural representation. In the early literature, linear restrictions on Ψ_0 or R were used to identify the system. For illustration consider the simple IS-LM model discussed by Pagan (1995). Let q_t, i_t and m_t denote output, real money and an interest rate, respectively. The innovations of the corresponding VAR are denoted by $u_t = [u_t^q, u_t^i, u_t^m]'$. A structural model reflecting a traditional Keynesian view is

$$u_t^q = b_1 u_t^i + \varepsilon_t^{IS} \qquad \text{(IS curve)}$$

$$u_t^i = b_2 u_t^q + b_3 u_t^m + \varepsilon_t^{LM} \qquad \text{(inverse LM curve)}$$

$$u_t^m = \varepsilon_t^m \qquad \text{(money supply rule)}$$

where the structural shocks are assumed to be mutually uncorrelated. This model is a special case of (9) with

$$\Psi_0 = \begin{bmatrix} 1 & -b_1 & 0 \\ -b_2 & 1 & -b_3 \\ 0 & 0 & 1 \end{bmatrix}$$

and $R = I_3$.

In later work (Blanchard and Quah (1989), King et al. (1991), Gali (1992)), non-linear restrictions were introduced. To motivate the special non-linear restrictions we write the moving-average representation (6) as

$$\Delta y_t = \Theta_0 \varepsilon_t + \Theta_1 \varepsilon_{t-1} + \Theta_2 \varepsilon_{t-2} + \cdots \qquad (10)$$

where $\Theta_s = \Xi_s \Psi_0^{-1} R$ $(s = 0, 1, \ldots)$. The long-run impact of the structural shocks on y_t is given by

$$\lim_{n \to \infty} \frac{\partial y_{t+n}}{\partial \varepsilon_t'} = \lim_{n \to \infty} \Phi_n \Psi_0^{-1} R = \sum_{s=0}^{\infty} \Theta_s \equiv \overline{\Theta} \qquad (11)$$

If the shock ε_{jt} has a transitory effect on y_{it}, then the (i, j)th element of $\overline{\Theta}$ is zero. Accordingly, the restriction that ε_{jt} does not affect y_{it} in the long run amounts to the non-linear constraint

$$e_i' \overline{\Theta} e_j = e_i'(I + \Xi_1 + \Xi_2 + \cdots) \Psi_0^{-1} R e_j = 0 \tag{12}$$

where e_i (e_j) is the ith (jth) column of the identity matrix. Note that for a cointegrated system with rank r, the rank of the matrix $\overline{\Theta}$ is $n - r$ (e.g. Engle and Granger (1987)), i.e. there exist $n - r$ shocks with permanent effects.

Of course, in practice neither the VAR or ECM parameters nor the order p and cointegrating rank r are known. We will discuss estimation and order determination procedures next.

10.3 ESTIMATION AND SPECIFICATION OF VAR AND ECM FORMS

Estimation of the reduced form specifications (1) and (5) is straightforward if the order p and the cointegrating rank r are known. In practice this is almost certainly not true. Nevertheless, it is useful to discuss estimation issues first under this unrealistic but simplifying assumption and then consider the possibilities for determining p and r from data.

10.3.1 Estimation of the VAR Form

Based on data $y_1, \ldots, y_T$ and presample values $y_{-p+1}, \ldots, y_0$ the K equations of the VAR representation (1) may be estimated separately by LS (least squares). The resulting estimator can be written compactly by defining

$$Y = [y_1, \ldots, y_T] \qquad Z_{t-1} = \begin{bmatrix} y_{t-1} \\ \vdots \\ y_{t-p} \end{bmatrix} \qquad Z = [Z_0, \ldots, Z_{T-1}] \tag{13}$$

Then the LS estimator of $A = [A_1, \ldots, A_p]$ is

$$\hat{A} = [\hat{A}_1, \ldots, \hat{A}_p] = YZ'(ZZ')^{-1} \tag{14}$$

Under general conditions, the LS estimator $\hat{A}$ is consistent and asymptotically normally distributed,

$$\sqrt{T} \, \mathrm{vec}\, (\hat{A} - A) \xrightarrow{d} N(0, \Sigma_{\hat{A}}) \tag{15}$$

(see Park and Phillips (1988, 1989), Sims, Stock and Watson (1990), Lütkepohl (1991, Chapter 11)). Here vec denotes the column stacking operator which stacks the columns of a matrix in a column vector and $\xrightarrow{d}$ signifies convergence in distribution. The covariance matrix $\Sigma_{\hat{A}}$ can be estimated in the same way as for stationary processes. Thus, at first sight, it may appear as if there were no difference between the stationary and the presently considered non-stationary case where some variables may be integrated and cointegrated.

However, there is one important difference. Whereas in the stationary case $\Sigma_{\hat{A}}$ is non-singular, the same is no longer true for non-stationary processes. As a consequence, the t-, χ^2- and F-tests usually used for inference regarding the VAR parameters, may no longer be valid (see e.g. Toda and Phillips (1993)). In particular, in a univariate first-order AR model $y_t = \alpha y_{t-1} + u_t$ with unit root ($\alpha = 1$), the LS estimator $\hat{\alpha}$ of α has non-standard limiting behaviour. More precisely, $\sqrt{T}(\hat{\alpha} - \alpha)$ converges to zero, that is, the limiting distribution has zero variance, whereas $T(\hat{\alpha} - \alpha)$ has a non-normal limiting distribution. This result is well known from Dickey and Fuller (1979). Despite the general result there are a number of cases where no problems arise with the standard tests. For example, if the VAR order $p \geqslant 2$ or $r > 0$, the usual t-ratios remain asymptotically standard normal. Also, if all variables are $I(1)$ or $I(0)$ and if a null hypothesis is considered which does not restrict elements of each of the A_i the usual tests have their standard asymptotic properties (see Toda and Yamamoto (1995) and Dolado and Lütkepohl (1996)).

Generally, if the process is stationary, the LS estimator in equation (14) is identical to the maximum likelihood (ML) estimator if the white-noise process u_t is Gaussian (normally distributed) and the presample values are assumed to be fixed values. It is also possible to include deterministic terms such as polynomial trends in model (1). The necessary modifications for computing the estimators of the parameters of such a model are straightforward. Moreover, the asymptotic properties of the VAR coefficients remain essentially the same as in the case without deterministic terms.

The WN covariance matrix Σ_u may be estimated in the usual way as

$$\hat{\Sigma}_u = \frac{1}{T - Kp} \sum_{t=1}^{T} \hat{u}_t \hat{u}_t'$$

or

$$\tilde{\Sigma}_u = \frac{1}{T} \sum_{t=1}^{T} \hat{u}_t \hat{u}_t' \tag{16}$$

where $\hat{u}_t$ denotes the LS residuals, that is, $\hat{u}_t = y_t - \hat{A} Z_{t-1}$. Both estimators are consistent and asymptotically normally distributed, that is, $\sqrt{T}(\hat{\Sigma}_u - \Sigma_u)$ and $\sqrt{T}(\tilde{\Sigma}_u - \Sigma_u)$ have asymptotic normal distributions if sufficient moment conditions are imposed. Moreover, these terms are asymptotically independent of $\sqrt{T}(\hat{A} - A)$ (see Lütkepohl (1991) and Lütkepohl and Saikkonen (1997)). These properties are convenient in deriving asymptotic properties of impulse responses.

The previous analysis has the advantage that nothing much needs to be known about the trending and cointegration properties of the variables. On the other hand, it does not tell us much about these properties which are sometimes of foremost interest. Therefore we will now turn to the estimation of the ECM in equation (5). For that purpose we maintain the assumption that the cointegrating rank r is known in addition to the VAR order p.

10.3.2 Estimation of the ECM

In deriving an estimator for the parameters of model (5) we will use the following additional notation:

$$\Delta Y = [\Delta y_1, \ldots, \Delta y_T] \quad Y_{-1} = [y_0, \ldots, y_{T-1}] \quad X_{t-1} = \begin{bmatrix} \Delta y_{t-1} \\ \vdots \\ \Delta y_{t-p+1} \end{bmatrix}$$

$$X = [X_0, \ldots, X_{T-1}] \quad U = [u_1, \ldots, u_T] \quad D = [D_1, \ldots, D_{p-1}].$$

$$(17)$$

For $t = 1, \ldots, T$, the ECM (5) can now be written as

$$\Delta Y + \Pi Y_{-1} = DX + U \tag{18}$$

If Π were known the LS estimator of D would be

$$\hat{D} = (\Delta Y + \Pi Y_{-1})X'(XX')^{-1} \tag{19}$$

Substituting this estimator in (18) gives the multivariate regression model

$$\Delta YM = -\Pi Y_{-1}M + \hat{U}$$

where $M = I - X'(XX')^{-1}X$. Now an estimator $\hat{\Pi}$ of Π can be obtained by a reduced-rank regression or, equivalently, a canonical correlation analysis. Thereby the computation of the estimates is reduced to a straightforward eigenvalue problem. A feasible estimator of D is then obtained by replacing Π in (19) by $\hat{\Pi}$. If the process is normally distributed the estimators obtained in this way are in fact ML estimators (Johansen (1988, 1991)).

Under general assumptions the estimators of D and Π are consistent and asymptotically normal, say,

$$\sqrt{T} \text{ vec } ([\hat{D}_1, \ldots, \hat{D}_{p-1}] - [D_1, \ldots, D_{p-1}]) \xrightarrow{d} N(0, \Sigma_{\hat{D}}) \tag{20}$$

and

$$\sqrt{T} \text{ vec } (\hat{\Pi} - \Pi) \xrightarrow{d} N(0, \Sigma_{\hat{\Pi}}) \tag{21}$$

The asymptotic distribution of $\hat{D}$ is non-singular and, hence, standard inference may be used. In contrast, $\Sigma_{\hat{\Pi}}$ in (21) has rank Kr and is consequently singular if $r < K$. The reason is that Π involves the cointegrating relations which are estimated superconsistently with a convergence rate $O_p(T^{-1})$ rather than the usual $O_p(T^{-1/2})$ rate. Still, in order to estimate the separate matrices B and C consistently it is necessary that identifying restrictions are available. Without such restrictions only the product $BC = \Pi$ can be estimated consistently. It is perhaps interesting to note that an estimator of A can be computed via the estimates of Π and D. That estimator has the advantage of satisfying the cointegrating restrictions. However, its asymptotic distribution is the same as in (15) where no restrictions have been imposed.

If identifying restrictions are available for the cointegrating relations then other estimation possibilities are available. Suppose, for instance, that $C = [I_r: C_1]$ as in Section 10.2.1. With this restriction, model (5) may be estimated by LS without rank restriction ($r = K$) in a first step. Since B consists just of the first r columns of $\Pi = BC$ in this case, we use the first columns of $\hat{\Pi}$ as estimator $\hat{B}$ of B. In the second step an estimator of C_1 may then be obtained by applying a generalized LS approach to the last columns of $\hat{\Pi}$. In other words, denoting the last r columns of $\hat{\Pi}$ by $\hat{H}$, the estimator of C_1 is

$$\hat{C}_1 = -(\hat{B}'\tilde{\Sigma}_u^{-1}\hat{B})^{-1}\hat{B}'\tilde{\Sigma}_u^{-1}\hat{H} \tag{22}$$

where $\hat{\Sigma}_u$ is the residual covariance matrix estimator from (16) or equivalently from the unrestricted regression of model (5). The estimator $\hat{C}_1$ converges at the rate $O_p(T^{-1})$ (Saikkonen (1992)).

Occasionally all parameters of the cointegrating relations are known and also further restrictions on the B matrix may be available. In that case, ML or multivariate LS estimation may become particularly simple. An example will be given in Section 10.4.

The covariance matrix estimator $\hat{\Sigma}_u$ is again asymptotically independent of $\hat{C}_1$, $\hat{B}$ and $\hat{D}$. Its asymptotic distribution is the same as for the pure VAR form treated in the previous subsection.

10.3.3 Structural Form Estimation

The estimation of the general structural model (8) under rank restrictions and non-linear constraints requires some advanced computational methods and is not resolved completely. It is, however, possible to give simple solutions for some interesting special cases. Whenever the structural model is just identified, that is, there is a one-to-one relationship between the structural and the reduced-form parameters, the structural parameters can be derived by exploiting the relationship between both representations. In this case, estimates of the structural parameters are obtained directly from the estimated reduced form parameters. This approach is used in Blanchard and Quah (1989) and King *et al.* (1991).

In other applications (e.g. Bernanke (1986), Blanchard (1989)) it is possible to apply simple instrumental variable methods to obtain the structural parameters. For illustration, consider the IS–LM model presented in Section 10.2.2. Since the innovation u_t^m is uncorrelated with ε_t^{IS}, it is a valid instrument for estimating b_1 from the IS curve. This gives an estimate of ε_t^{IS}, which in turn can be used (together with u_t^m) to estimate b_2 and b_3.

10.3.4 Inference on Impulse Responses

The impulse responses considered in the previous section are non-linear functions of the coefficients of the VAR, ECM or structural forms of the DGP. Hence, they will usually be computed from estimated parameters and are therefore also estimated. It is desirable to know the properties of the resulting estimators for assessing the uncertainty associated with them. Because the model parameters have asymptotic normal distributions (see Sections 10.3.1–10.3.3) an obvious approach to inference for impulse responses is to determine their asymptotic distribution by considering the first-order Taylor approximation of the nonlinear functions defining the impulse responses.

Generally, assuming that the VAR, ECM or structural form parameters are collected in a vector β which is estimated by $\hat{\beta}$, we know from Sections 10.3.1–10.3.3 that

$$\sqrt{T}(\hat{\beta} - \beta) \xrightarrow{d} N(0, \Sigma_{\hat{\beta}}). \tag{23}$$

Then we have, under general conditions, for some vector function $\phi(\beta)$,

$$\sqrt{T}(\phi(\hat{\beta}) - \phi(\beta)) \xrightarrow{d} N(0, \Sigma_{\hat{\phi}}) \qquad \Sigma_{\hat{\phi}} = \frac{\partial \phi}{\partial \beta'} \Sigma_{\hat{\beta}} \frac{\partial \phi'}{\partial \beta} \tag{24}$$

where $\partial \phi / \partial \beta'$ denotes the matrix of first-order partial derivatives of ϕ with respect to β (see Serfling (1980) for the general result and Lütkepohl and Reimers (1992) or Lütkepohl (1991) for special cases of impulse response analysis). Generalizations of this result in the context of impulse response analysis are discussed by Lütkepohl and Poskitt (1996a), Lütkepohl and Saikkonen (1997) and Saikkonen and Lütkepohl (1995).

The result in (24) may be used for inference in the usual way if $\Sigma_{\hat{\phi}}$ is non-singular for all relevant vectors β. A minimum requirement for this condition to hold is that $\phi(\beta)$ has no more components than β. In impulse response analysis this condition is not trivially fulfilled because often many impulse responses are of interest. In that case tests of hypotheses involving all components of $\phi(\beta)$ may not have their standard asymptotic distributions. On the other hand, the asymptotic result in (24) is sometimes only used for setting up confidence intervals for individual impulse responses. In that case, problems may arise if some of the diagonal elements of $\Sigma_{\hat{\phi}}$ (some of the asymptotic variances of components of $\phi(\hat{\beta})$) are zero. Unfortunately, for impulse responses even this is possible in parts of the relevant parameter space (see Lütkepohl (1991, Section 3.7.1)). The reason is that impulse responses involve products of the β parameters. Hence, the first-order partial derivatives also contain parameters and not just fixed constants. If the parameters are potentially zero the same may be true for the partial derivatives and, hence, $\partial \phi / \partial \beta'$ may contain rows of zeros which imply zero diagonal elements of $\Sigma_{\hat{\phi}}$. In practice these problems are typically ignored although they can lead to distorted confidence intervals with actual confidence levels markedly different from the desired ones.

Another problem in this context is that of small-sample bias. It is known that the coefficient estimators $\hat{\beta}$ may be biased. The magnitude of the bias depends on the estimation procedure used, the properties of the actual DGP and the sample size. Of course, bias in $\hat{\beta}$ may result in a biased $\phi(\hat{\beta})$ estimator. Moreover, even if the bias in $\hat{\beta}$ is small it may be magnified by the non-linear function $\phi(\beta)$. More generally, the asymptotic distribution in (24) may not be a good indicator of the small-sample properties of $\phi(\hat{\beta})$. Therefore simulation-based methods such as the bootstrap are often used to assess the estimation uncertainty in the $\phi(\hat{\beta})$. One approach here is to estimate a model of forms (1) or (5), sample from the estimation residuals and generate many new artificial y_t series based on the estimated coefficients. From these artificial y_t series a large number of estimates $\hat{\beta}$ and $\phi(\hat{\beta})$ is then computed and the empirical distributions of these estimates is used for analysing the actual properties of the original estimators. Alternatively, instead of using the estimation residuals in generating artificial new series of y_ts one may sample from some prespecified distribution. In any case, it has been found by Griffiths and Lütkepohl (1989) and Kilian (1995) that without further adjustments simulation-based methods may give an unrealistic picture of the actual properties of the estimated impulse responses in small samples.

10.3.5 Determining the Autoregressive Order

There are a number of different possibilities for choosing the VAR order p of model (1) or the ECM (5). Because the cointegrating rank r is usually unknown when the choice of p is made, it is useful to focus on the VAR form (1). There are various model-selection criteria that can help in deciding on the VAR order. In using them, usually VAR(m) models with orders $m = 0, \ldots, p_{\max}$ are fitted and an estimator of the order p is chosen so as to optimize the preferred criterion.

Many of the criteria have the general form

$$Cr(m) = \log |\hat{\Sigma}_u(m)| + c_T \varphi(m) \tag{25}$$

where $|\cdot|$ denotes the determinant, log is the natural logarithm, $\hat{\Sigma}_u(m) = T^{-1}\sum_{t=1}^{T}\hat{u}_t\hat{u}_t'$ is the residual covariance matrix estimator for a model of order m, c_T is a sequence indexed by the sample size T, and $\varphi(m)$ is a function of the VAR order m such as the number of parameters estimated in a VAR(m) model. The first term on the right-hand side $(\log|\hat{\Sigma}_u(m)|)$ measures the fit of a model with order m. Since there is no correction for degrees of freedom in the covariance matrix estimator the log determinant decreases (or at least does not increase) when m increases. The last term in criterion (25), on the other hand, penalizes an increasing number of parameters which results from increasing the order. The VAR order is chosen such that both terms are balanced optimally. In other words, the estimator $\hat{p}$ of p is chosen to be the order which minimizes the criterion (25).

The criteria typically used in VAR analyses differ in the way they specify the penalty term model (25). Examples are

$$\text{AIC}(m) = \log|\hat{\Sigma}_u(m)| + \frac{2}{T}mK^2$$

(Akaike (1973, 1974)),

$$\text{HQ}(m) = \log|\hat{\Sigma}_u(m)| + \frac{2\log\log T}{T}mK^2$$

(Hannan and Quinn (1979), Quinn (1980)), and

$$\text{SC}(m) = \log|\hat{\Sigma}_u(m)| + \frac{\log T}{T}mK^2$$

(Schwarz (1978), Rissanen (1978)). In all three criteria $\varphi(m) = mK^2$ is the number of autoregressive parameters estimated in a VAR(m) model. The criteria differ in their choice of c_T. For AIC, $c_T = 2/T$, for HQ, $c_T = 2\log\log T/T$ and for SC, $c_T = \log T/T$. If the actual DGP has a finite VAR order and the maximum order $p_{\max}$ is larger than the true order, the AIC criterion asymptotically overestimates the order with positive probability whereas the last two criteria estimate the order consistently (plim $\hat{p} = p$ or $\hat{p} \to p$ a.s.) under quite general conditions. These results hold for stationary as well as non-stationary integrated and cointegrated processes. For more details and references see Lütkepohl (1991, Chapters 4 and 11).

Alternatively, sequential testing procedures may be employed in choosing the VAR order. In that case a series of hypotheses

$$H_0^{(1)}: p = p_{\max} - 1 \ (A_{p_{\max}} = 0) \quad \text{against} \quad H_1^{(1)}: p = p_{\max} \ (A_{p_{\max}} \neq 0)$$

$$H_0^{(2)}: p = p_{\max} - 2 \ (A_{p_{\max}-1} = 0) \quad \text{against} \quad H_1^{(2)}: p = p_{\max} - 1 \ (A_{p_{\max}-1} \neq 0)$$

$$\vdots \qquad\qquad\qquad\qquad \vdots$$

is tested with, say, likelihood ratio (LR) or Wald tests. The testing sequence terminates when the null hypothesis is rejected for the first time. The order specified in the previous null hypothesis is then chosen as an estimate for p.

A few issues may be worth noting regarding this procedure. First, some care has to be taken in specifying the maximum order and the significance levels of the individual tests. If a very large order p_{max} is used, a long sequence of tests may be necessary which will have an impact on the overall Type I error of the testing sequence, that is, the choice of p_{max} will have an impact on the probability of an erroneous selection of p. Second, in the individual tests only zero restrictions have to be checked. It can be shown that for this case the standard F- or χ^2-tests (e.g. LR or Wald tests) retain their usual asymptotic distributions under the null hypothesis (see again Lütkepohl (1991, Chapter 11)).

Of course, it may be possible that the true order is not finite, that is, the actual DGP is in fact a VAR process of infinite order. Some consequences of using these procedures in that case are discussed by Ng and Perron (1995) for univariate models.

In addition to using these procedures, the residuals are often checked for being white noise to reconfirm the model chosen. For instance, the residual autocorrelations can be used for that purpose.

10.3.6 Specifying the Cointegrating Rank

Assuming that the VAR order is known the cointegrating rank can also be determined by sequential testing procedures. Since under normality assumptions ML estimates are easy to compute for any given cointegrating rank r (see Section 10.3.2), LR tests are an obvious choice for this purpose. Such tests were indeed proposed by Johansen (1988, 1991) and are among the more popular tools for specifying the cointegrating rank of finite-order VAR systems. The following two possible testing sequences may be considered:

$$H_0^{(1)}: r = 0 \qquad \text{against} \qquad H_1^{(1)}: r > 0$$

$$H_0^{(2)}: r = 1 \qquad \text{against} \qquad H_1^{(2)}: r > 1$$

$$\vdots \qquad\qquad\qquad \vdots$$

$$H_0^{(K)}: r = K - 1 \qquad \text{against} \qquad H_1^{(K)}: r = K$$

The corresponding sequence of LR tests is known as the *trace test*. Alternatively the *maximum eigenvalue test* can be used which is based on the following sequence of hypotheses:

$$H_0^{(1)}: r = 0 \qquad \text{against} \qquad H_1^{(1)}: r = 1$$

$$H_0^{(2)}: r = 1 \qquad \text{against} \qquad H_1^{(2)}: r = 2$$

$$\vdots \qquad\qquad\qquad\qquad \vdots$$

$$H_0^{(K)}: r = K - 1 \qquad \text{against} \qquad H_1^{(K)}: r = K$$

In the first sequence each null hypothesis is tested against a model with no rank restriction at all while the alternative in the second sequence is a model with the next largest cointegrating rank. Both testing sequences terminate when the null hypothesis cannot be rejected for the first time. If the first null hypothesis, $H_0^{(1)}$, cannot be rejected, a VAR process in first differences is indicated. In turn, if all of the null hypotheses can be rejected, including $H_0^{(K)}$, the process is assumed to be stationary.

Several comments regarding these testing procedures are in order. First, the limiting distribution of the LR statistic under the null hypothesis is non-standard and, in particular, it is not χ^2 in general. It depends on the alternative, the difference $K - r$ and the trending properties of the DGP. More precisely, it depends on whether an intercept term is required in the model and whether it generates a deterministic trend or can be absorbed into the cointegrating relations. The asymptotic distributions of the LR statistics do not, however, depend on the short-term dynamics of the process (the D_i in (5)). The latter fact makes it possible to tabulate percentage points for the various different cases. This has been done by Johansen and Juselius (1990) and Osterwald-Lenum (1992). Yet another limiting distribution is obtained if a linear trend term is allowed in (5). The relevant percentage points for that case have been tabulated by Perron and Campbell (1993). Of course, in practice it may be difficult to know which case is relevant for a particular multiple time series of interest. In other words, it may be difficult to locate the correct table in a given situation. Still, the tests are used quite often in applied work.

Second, for univariate processes ($K = 1$) the testing sequences reduce to one test of $H_0: r = 0$ against $H_1: r = 1$. In other words, the null hypothesis is that the process is $I(1)$ which is tested against the alternative of stationarity. LR tests for this specific set of hypotheses were proposed by Dickey and Fuller (1979) and Fuller (1976). They are very popular in applied work and are known as Dickey–Fuller (DF) tests.

Third, the limiting distributions are not only valid for normally distributed (Gaussian) processes but also under much more general distributional assumptions even if the LR statistics computed under Gaussian assumptions are used. In that situation these tests are, of course, just pseudo LR tests. Saikkonen and Luukkonen (1997) show that some of the tests (based on finite-order VAR processes) remain asymptotically valid even if the true DGP has an infinite VAR order. This result is of interest because, for instance, in practice similar tests are usually applied to the univariate series or subsystems first to determine the order of integration for the individual variables or the cointegrating properties of a subset of variables. However, if the full system of variables is driven by a finite-order VAR process, then the generating process of the individual variables may be of infinite order autoregressive type (see Lütkepohl (1991, Section 6.6)). Hence, for the sake of consistency it is reassuring to know that the tests remain valid for this case. In fact, for the univariate case the validity of the DF tests in the infinite order autoregressive case has been shown by Said and Dickey (1984).

Fourth, although the asymptotic theory for the individual tests is well developed, choosing suitable significance levels may not be easy because the individual tests are not independent. This has to be taken into account in controlling the overall Type I error of the testing sequence.

Fifth, there is a notable difference between the asymptotic properties of the tests and their actual performance for samples of the size typically available in economics. This problem has been observed in several simulation studies (see e.g. Reimers (1992), Toda (1994, 1995)). Therefore, Ahn and Reinsel (1990) propose a small-sample modification of the tests. Also other tests for the cointegrating rank have been proposed. For a survey of some of them see Reimers (1992). However, their small-sample properties were found to be inferior to the LR tests in many situations.

As an alternative to the sequential testing procedures one may also use model-selection procedures for determining the cointegrating rank. Again it is possible to devise criteria which select the rank consistently. Moreover, the cointegrating rank and the VAR order may be chosen simultaneously rather than sequentially.

10.4 AN EMPIRICAL APPLICATION

In this section we discuss an empirical application of the framework considered in the previous sections. Following Blanchard and Quah (1989) we are interested in analysing the dynamic effects of demand and supply shocks. While Blanchard and Quah consider a VAR in output and unemployment, we will specify a VAR using the capacity utilization rate (CUR) instead of the unemployment rate. It was argued by Quah (1992, 1995) that in principle it should be possible to disentangle demand and supply shocks using any other variable instead of unemployment, provided it is stationary and has a dynamic interaction with output.

The variables are defined as follows. Output (q_t) is measured by the logarithm of quarterly US Gross Domestic Product. The quarterly values of the capacity utilization rate (c_t) are obtained by averaging the monthly observations. Since this variable is not available before 1967, the sample period ranges from 1967(i) through 1994(iv).[1] The time series are plotted in Figure 10.1.

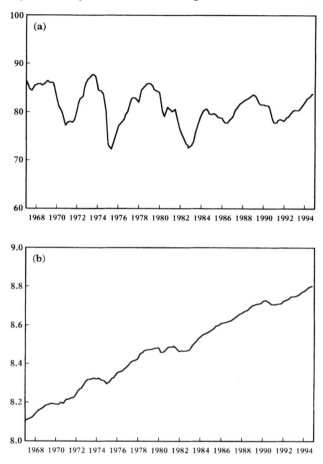

Figure 10.1   Plots of the time series. (a) Capacity Utilization Rate (CUR). (b) Log GNP in 1990 prices

We begin by choosing the VAR order p of the VAR process in levels, where a constant term is included in all equations. The values of several selection criteria for lag orders ranging from zero to eight are given in Table 10.1. It turns out that the SC and HQ criteria select a VAR(2), while the AIC criterion suggests a VAR(4) model. This result reflects the theoretical properties of the criteria. It is known (see e.g. Lütkepohl (1991, Section 4.3)) that among the criteria considered here, SC selects the most parsimonious specification whereas the AIC criterion chooses the largest order and asymptotically overestimates the true order, i.e. this criterion is not consistent. Since there is some residual autocorrelation left in the VAR(2) model we nevertheless decided to go with the order suggested by the AIC criterion.

Table 10.1   Model selection criteria

VAR order	AIC	HQ	SC
0	−0.0827	−0.0827	−0.0827
1	−0.9799	−0.9758	−0.9697
2	−1.0082	−0.9999*	−0.9878*
3	−1.0068	−0.9945	−0.9763
4	−1.0141*	−0.9976	−0.9734
5	−1.0083	−0.9877	−0.9575
6	−1.0052	−0.9805	−0.9442
7	−1.0065	−0.9777	−0.9353
8	−1.0081	−0.9751	−0.9267

Notes: For the definitions of AIC, HQ, and SC see Section 10.3.5. * indicates a minimum.

Based on a VAR(4) specification we performed LR tests for the cointegration rank. The results are shown in Table 10.2. As mentioned in Section 10.3.6, the asymptotic distribution of the LR statistic is non-standard in general and depends on whether or not there are deterministic trends in addition to the stochastic trends. Since these properties of the DGP are unknown we choose the maximum of the critical values for the different scenarios. Hence, our tests may be conservative. With this qualification the results suggest that there is a single cointegration relationship, that is, $r = 0$ is rejected while $r = 1$ is not. Furthermore, applying univariate Dickey–Fuller tests to check for unit roots in q_t and c_t, it appears that q_t is $I(1)$ while there is some evidence for c_t to be stationary ($I(0)$). Accordingly, the cointegration matrix should be a row vector of the form $C = [1, 0]$. This is confirmed by a LR test on the cointegrating space (cf. Johansen (1995, p.108f)). This test accepts the hypothesis that the cointegrating vector is (a multiple of) $C = [1, 0]$ while the cointegrating vector $C = [0, 1]$ is clearly rejected at a significance level of 0.05.

Table 10.2   Cointegration statistics

H_0	max EV	Crit. val.	TRACE	Crit. val.
$r = 0$	20.37	14.90	24.34	17.95
$r = 1$	3.97	8.18	3.97	8.18
	ADF	Crit. val.	LR	Crit. val.
q_t	3.21	3.45	15.52	3.84
c_t	4.49	2.89	0.03	3.84

Notes: max EV and TRACE denote Johansen's maximum eigenvalue and trace statistic, respectively. ADF indicates the augmented Dickey–Fuller statistics with two and three lagged differences for q_t and c_t, respectively. The augmentation lag is chosen with respect to the highest significant lagged difference. The test equations include a constant for c_t and a linear time trend for q_t. LR denotes the likelihood ratio statistic for hypothesis on the cointegration space. Crit. val. presents the critical values for a significance level of 0.05. The critical values for max EV and TRACE are taken from Osterwald-Lenum (1992, Table 1.1*).

Summing up, we found that $y_t^* = [c_t, \Delta q_t]'$ can be represented by a stationary VAR(4) model. Strictly, if $y_t = [c_t, q_t]'$ has a VAR(4) representation as suggested by the AIC criterion, then the representation for y_t^* implies that the coefficients attached to Δq_{t-4} are zero. However, as in Blanchard and Quah (1989) we will neglect such restrictions in what follows.

Having specified an appropriate VAR representation for the data we now consider different identification schemes to disentangle demand and supply shocks. First, we identify demand shocks as the innovations of the c_t equation. The supply shocks result from a Cholesky decomposition of the covariance matrix, i.e. Sims' triangular orthogonalization is applied. The resulting impulse response functions are depicted in Figure 10.2. The dashed lines indicate 95%

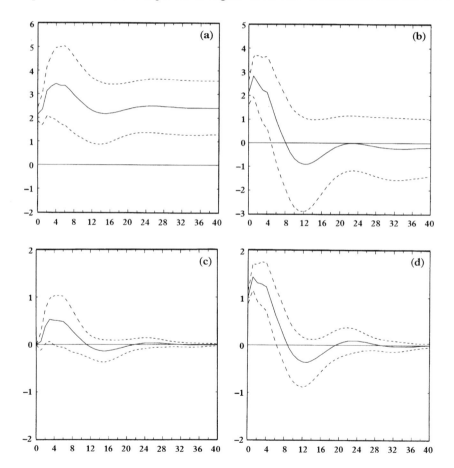

Figure 10.2 Impulse responses using the triangular identification. (a) Output response to supply shocks. (b) Output response to demand shocks. (c) CUR response to supply shocks. (d) CUR response to demand shocks

confidence intervals for the estimated responses. These confidence intervals are based on the asymptotic theory considered in Section 10.3.4 and were computed using the software package MulTi (Haase *et al.* (1992)).

To be consistent with the traditional view, we expect that the demand shock has a transitory impact on output whereas the supply shock is expected to have a permanent effect on output. This interpretation is supported by the estimated impulse response functions. The responses with respect to a supply shock are hump-shaped and converge to a limit that is significantly different from zero. On the other hand, the responses of the demand shock die out within four years and are insignificant for long horizons.

Next, we estimate a structural VAR as suggested by Blanchard and Quah (1989). Identification is achieved by assuming $\Psi_0 = I_2$ and restricting the upper-right element of the (2×2) matrix $\overline{\Theta}$ in equation (11) to zero, that is, the second shock in the vector ε_t in equation (9) is assumed to have a transitory impact on q_t. A convenient method to compute an estimate of the matrix R from the reduced form was suggested by Blanchard and Quah (1989). The impulse response function of y_t with respect to ε_t is then obtained from $\partial y_{t+n}/\partial \varepsilon_t' = \Phi_n R$, where the Φ_n can be computed using equation (4).

The responses to the permanent shock ε_{1t} and the transitory shock ε_{2t} are presented in Figure 10.3. The 95% confidence intervals are computed from 1000 Monte Carlo draws of the estimated model using normally distributed errors. It turns out that the shapes for the impulse response functions are very similar to those using the triangular identification (see Figure 10.2). The reason is that the matrix R in the Blanchard–Quah type structural model is estimated as

$$\hat{R} = \begin{bmatrix} 1.05 & -0.09 \\ 2.20 & 1.88 \end{bmatrix}$$

This matrix has approximately a triangular structure and, therefore, it is no surprise that both identification schemes produce similar results.

Comparing our results with those of Blanchard and Quah (1989) reveals that the general shapes of the impulse response functions for output are similar. However, the short-run effect of the demand shock to output is relatively more important in Blanchard and Quah's original specification.

10.5 CONCLUSIONS

During the last two decades VAR processes have become standard instruments for macroeconometric analyses. We have given a brief review of some important features and properties of these models including the case of cointegrated processes. We have also discussed estimation and specification of cointegrated VAR models and we have made the point that it may not be easy to infer the

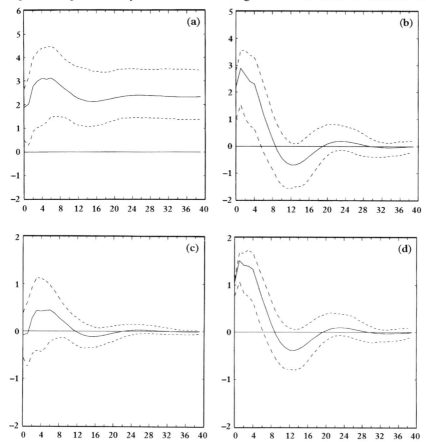

Figure 10.3   Impulse responses for the structural model. (a) Output reponse to supply shocks. (b) Output response to demand shocks. (c) CUR reponse to supply shocks. (d) CUR response to demand shocks

structure of the relationships between the variables involved from the VAR coefficients. Therefore impulse responses are often used for exhibiting important features of the relation between the variables. However, various different impulse responses may be computed from a given VAR model. To determine those which represent the actual reactions of the variables to shocks to the system requires identifying assumptions in addition to the information embodied in the data. In econometric analyses this additional structural information will usually come from economic theory.

As an example we have considered a system consisting of quarterly output and capital utilization data. It is demonstrated how structural information can be used in this case for identifying structural impulse responses.

ENDNOTE

1. The data for Gross Domestic Product are taken from the data bank of the St Louis Federal Reserve Bank (URL: http://www.stls.frb.org/fred) and the capacity utilization rate is taken from the MediaLogic data bank (URL: http://www.mlinet.com/mle).

COMMENT

P.C. YOUNG

The VAR model appears to be quite a good one for forecasting purposes but I am not so sure that it will always provide good impulse response information, unless used with a high enough VAR order. For instance, suppose that there is an underlying VAR process,

$$x_t = A_1 x_{t-1} + \ldots + A_p x_{t-p} + e_t$$

but x_t is measured in noise: i.e. $y_t = x_t + a_t$. In this 'errors-in-variables' situation, which might well be encountered in practice, the model in terms of the observable y_t vector is,

$$y_t = A_1 y_{t-1} + \ldots + A_p y_{t-p} + u_t$$

$$u_t = a_t - A_1 a_{t-1} - \ldots - A_p a_{t-p}$$

Since u_t is no longer white, the estimates of the model parameters and, therefore, the impulse responses, will be asymptotically biased if the 'correct' order p is used for estimation. The authors propose using the various order identification criteria, such as AIC, for specifying the estimation model order. Will this always provide a high enough order to purge the bias from the impulse responses and, even if it does, will not the estimated impulse responses be rather inefficiently estimated? Might it not be better to formulate the problem in state space terms? Alternatively, either low-order models could be estimated from the high-order estimated VAR model responses (Young and Wang, 1986); or the estimated high order model innovations could be used as an estimate of the random noise inputs and then these could be used as the inputs for input–output estimation of the low order model (Young, 1985). The authors might like to comment on this aspect of their analysis.

REPLY

H. LÜTKEPOHL AND J. BREITUNG

We thank Peter Young for his insightful comments on our chapter. We fully agree that occasionally the VAR model may not provide the most efficient way to summarize the information in a given multiple time series. VARMA (vector autoregressive moving average) and other model classes have been proposed as alternatives. They may be superior to pure VAR models in many situations. Inference techniques are also available for these alternative model classes and, hence, they may be useful for applied studies (e.g. Lütkepohl (1991, Chapters 6–8 and 13) or Lütkepohl and Poskitt (1996b)). The technical details for these models are more complicated than for pure VAR models, however. Therefore we have focused on the latter models in our introductory exposition. Also, VAR type models have been used predominantly in applied macroeconometric studies possibly because of their greater simplicity.

Macroeconomic time series are usually relatively short with about 100 quarterly observations, say. Therefore, the sample information is often too scarce to discriminate between a VAR model of relatively low order and a model from some other class. In that case the impulse responses of alternative, equally well-fitting models will often not differ much. Having non-sample information as in the errors-in-variables situation described by Young may, of course, result in noticeable differences. More generally, parameter restrictions of various sorts may be imposed on the statistical model for the DGP to improve the estimation precision.

To clarify our discussion it may be helpful to distinguish between non-sample information which helps to improve statistical inference in a given model and information which eases the interpretation. The first type reduces the potential model class, simplifies the model-selection process and/or improves the estimation precision by reducing the parameter space. The second type of non-sample information helps to interpret the evidence summarized in a statistical model of the DGP. In an econometric analysis the latter information is often at least as important as the former because it may give economic content to a statistical model and may allow us to study the implications of economic theories within a given statistical framework. As we have pointed out in our contribution, such information is often fairly easy to use within a VAR or ECM model (see our example) which may be another reason for the popularity of this model class.

REFERENCES

Ahn, S.K. and Reinsel, G.C. (1990) Estimation of partially nonstationary multivariate autoregressive models. *Journal of the American Statistical Association* **85**, 813–23.

Akaike, H. (1973) Information theory and an extension of the maximum likelihood principle, In: B.N. Petrov and F. Csáki (eds), *2nd International Symposium on Information Theory.* Académiai Kiadó, Budapest, 267–81.

Akaike, H. (1974) A new look at the statistical model identification, *IEEE Transactions on Automatic Control* **AC-19**, 716–23.

Bernanke, B. (1986) Alternative explanations of the money-income correlation, *Carnegie–Rochester Conference Series on Public Policy* **25**, 49–99.

Blanchard, O. (1989) A traditional interpretation of macroeconomic fluctuations. *American Economic Review* **79**, 1146–64.

Blanchard, O. and Quah, D. (1989) The dynamic effects of aggregate demand and supply disturbances. *American Economic Review* **79**, 655–73.

Dickey, D.A. and Fuller, W.A. (1979) Distribution of the estimators for autoregressive time series with a unit root. *Journal of the American Statistical Association* **74**, 427–31.

Dolado, J.J. and Lütkepohl, H. (1996) Making Wald tests work for cointegrated VAR systems. *Econometric Reviews*, **15**, 369–86.

Engle, R.F. and Granger, C.W.J. (1987) Co-integration and error correction: representation, estimation and testing. *Econometrica* **55**, 251–76.

Fuller, W.A. (1976) *Introduction to Statistical Time Series*, John Wiley, New York.

Gali, J. (1992) How well does the IS-LM model fit postwar U.S. data, *Quarterly Journal of Economics* **107**, 709–38.

Granger, C.W.J. (1981) Some properties of time series data and their use in econometric model specification. *Journal of Econometrics* **16**, 121–30.

Griffiths, W. and Lütkepohl, H. (1989) Confidence intervals for impulse responses from VAR models: a comparison of asymptotic theory and simulation approaches, Discussion Paper, University of New England, Armidale, Australia.

Haase, K., Lütkepohl, H., Claessen, H., Moryson, M. and Schneider, W. (1992) *MulTi: A Menu-Driven GAUSS Program for Multiple Time Series Analysis*, Universität Kiel, Kiel, Germany.

Hamilton, J.D. (1994) *Time Series Analysis.* Princeton University Press, Princeton.

Hannan, E.J. and Quinn, B.G. (1979) The determination of the order of an autoregression. *Journal of the Royal Statistical Society,* Series **B41**, 190–5.

Hendry, D.F. (1995) *Dynamic Econometrics.* Oxford University Press, Oxford.

Johansen, S. (1988) Statistical analysis of cointegration vectors. *Journal of Economic Dynamics and Control* **12**, 231–54.

Johansen, S. (1991) Estimation and hypothesis testing of cointegration vectors in Gaussian vector autoregressive models. *Econometrica* **59**, 1551–80.

Johansen, S. (1995) *Likelihood Based Inference in Cointegrated Vector Autoregressive Models.* Oxford University Press, Oxford.

Johansen, S. and Juselius, K. (1990) Maximum likelihood estimation and inference on cointegration—with applications to the demand for money. *Oxford Bulletin of Economics and Statistics* **52**, 169–210.

Kilian, L. (1995) Small-sample confidence intervals for impulse response functions. Discussion Paper, University of Pennsylvania, Department of Economics.

King, R.G., Plosser, C.I., Stock, J.H. and Watson, M.W. (1991) Stochastic trends and economic fluctuations. *American Economic Review* **81**, 819–40.

Lütkepohl, H. (1991) *Introduction to Multiple Time Series Analysis.* Springer-Verlag, Berlin.

Lütkepohl, H. and Poskitt, D.S. (1996a) Testing for causation using infinite order vector autoregressive processes. *Econometric Theory* **12**, 61–87.

Lütkepohl, H. and Poskitt, D.S. (1996b) Specification of echelon form VARMA models. *Journal of Business and Economic Statistics* **14**, 69–79.

Lütkepohl, H. and Reimers, H.-E. (1992) Impulse response analysis of cointegrated systems. *Journal of Economic Dynamics and Control* **16**, 53–78.

Lütkepohl, H. and Saikkonen, P. (1997) Impulse response analysis in infinite order cointegrated vector autoregressive processes. Forthcoming in *Journal of Econometrics.*

Ng, S. and Perron, P. (1995) Unit root tests in ARMA models with data-dependent methods for the selection of the truncation lag. *Journal of the American Statistical Association* **90**, 268–81.

Osterwald-Lenum, M. (1992) A note with fractiles of the asymptotic distribution of the maximum likelihood cointegration rank test statistics: four cases. *Oxford Bulletin of Economics and Statistics* **54**, 461–72.

Pagan, A. (1995) Three econometric methodologies: an update. In L. Oxley, D.A.R. George, C.J. Roberts and S. Sayer (eds), *Surveys in Econometrics.* Basil Blackwell, Oxford.

Park, J.Y. and Phillips, P.C.B. (1988) Statistical inference in regressions with integrated processes: Part 1. *Econometric Theory* **4**, 468–97.

Park, J.Y. and Phillips, P.C.B. (1989) Statistical inference in regressions with integrated processes: Part 2. *Econometric Theory* **5**, 95–131.

Perron, P. and Campbell, J.Y. (1993) A note on Johansen's cointegration procedure when trends are present. *Empirical Economics* **18**, 777–89.

Quah, D. (1992) The relative importance of permanent and transitory components: identification and some theoretical bounds. *Econometrica* **60**, 107–18.

Quah, D. (1995) Misinterpreting the dynamic effects of aggregate demand and supply disturbances. *Economics Letters* **49**, 247–50.

Quinn, B.G. (1980) Order determination for a multivariate autoregression. *Journal of the Royal Statistical Society*, Series **B42**, 182–5.

Reimers, H.-E. (1992) Comparisons of tests for multivariate cointegration. *Statistical Papers* **33**, 335–59.

Rissanen, J. (1978) Modeling by shortest data description. *Automatica* **14**, 465–71.

Said, S.E. and Dickey, D.A. (1984) Testing for unit roots in autoregressive-moving average models of unknown order. *Biometrika* **71**, 599–607.

Saikkonen, P. (1992) Estimation and testing of cointegrated systems by an autoregressive approximation. *Econometric Theory* **8**, 1–27.

Saikkonen, P. and Lütkepohl, H. (1995) Asymptotic inference on nonlinear functions of the coefficients of infinite order cointegrated VAR processes. Discussion Paper No. 66, SFB 373, Humboldt University Berlin.

Saikkonen, P. and Luukkonen, R. (1997) Testing cointegration in infinite order vector autoregressive processes. Forthcoming in *Journal of Econometrics.*

Sargent, T.J. (1978) Estimation of dynamic labor demand schedules under rational expectation. *Journal of Political Economy* **86**, 1009–44.

Schwarz, G. (1978) Estimating the dimension of a model. *Annals of Statistics* **6**, 461–4.

Serfling, R.J. (1980) *Approximation Theorems of Mathematical Statistics*, John Wiley, New York.

Sims, C.A. (1980) Macroeconomics and and reality. *Econometrica* **48**, 1–48.

Sims, C.A. (1981) An autoregressive index model for the U.S. 1948–1975. In J. Kmenta and J.B. Ramsey (eds), *Large-Scale Macro-Econometric Models*. North-Holland, Amsterdam, 283–327.

Sims, C.A., Stock, J.H. and Watson, M.W. (1990) Inference in linear time series models with some unit roots. *Econometrica* **58**, 113–144.

Toda, H.Y. (1994) Finite sample properties of likelihood ratio tests for cointegrating ranks when linear trends are present. *Review of Economics and Statistics* **76**, 66–79.

Toda, H.Y. (1995) Finite sample performance of likelihood ratio tests for cointegrating ranks in vector autoregressions. *Econometric Theory* **11**, 1015–32.

Toda, H.Y. and Phillips, P.C.B. (1993) Vector autoregressions and causality. *Econometrica* **61**, 1367–93.

Toda, H.Y. and Yamamoto, T. (1995) Statistical inference in vector autoregressions with possibly integrated processes. *Journal of Econometrics* **66**, 225–50.

Watson, M.W. (1994) Vector autoregressions and cointegration. In R.F. Engle and D.L. McFadden (eds), *Handbook of Econometrics*, Vol. IV. Elsevier, New York.

Young, P.C. (1985) Recursive identification, estimation and control. Chapter 8 in E.J. Hannan, P.R. Krishnaiah and M.M. Rao (eds), *Time Series in the Time Domain*. North-Holland, Amsterdam, 213–56.

Young, P.C. and Wang, C.L. (1986) Identification and estimation of multivariable dynamic systems. In J. O'Reilly (ed.), *Multivariable Control for Industrial Applications*. Peter Peregrinus: London, 244–79.

Data Transformations and Detrending in Econometrics

D.S.G. POLLOCK

11.1 INTRODUCTION

In econometric time series the trend is often the dominant feature. A trend resembles the trajectory of a massive, slow-moving, body which is barely disturbed by collisions with other, smaller, bodies which cross its path. Trends in economic time series are often due to demographic factors or to the gradual social and economic transformations which proceed regardless of the fluctuating levels of employment and prosperity.

Sometimes trends are due, instead, to an uncommon persistence of habit on the part of powerful economic agents. The growth in the supply of money provides a good example. In many countries, this is more or less constant in proportional terms when the seasonal fluctuations are ironed out. Economic trends of this sort can sometimes be stopped in their tracks.

One definition of a trend would exclude any motion which contains cycles, whether they be regular or irregular (see, for example, Tintner (1953, p. 189)). We shall not impose this restriction. According to our own criteria, a trend must be less volatile than the fluctuations which surround it; and it is expected to originate from a different source. If the trend and the fluctuations do share the same motive power, then, at least, they must be mediated through separate social or economic structures. Our definition of a trend is flexible enough to allow for a motion which is a fluctuation in one perspective to be regarded as a trend in another.

The justification of this definition rests upon a distinction which we shall draw between trend estimation and data smoothing. Data smoothing is a justifiable

System Dynamics in Economic and Financial Models. Edited by C. Heij, J.M. Schumacher, B. Hanzon and C. Praagman © 1997 John Wiley & Sons Ltd

activity even when a meaningful distinction cannot be drawn between the trend and the fluctuations.

Often, economists are far more interested in the delicate patterns of the fluctuations which are superimposed upon the trends than they are in the trends themselves. They may wish to set aside the trend only in order to see these patterns more clearly. However, even in this case, there are compelling statistical reasons for wishing to extract the trend.

According to most criteria of statistical estimation, the object in modelling the trajectory of a variable is to explain as much of its variance as possible. The trend, which may be a perfectly smooth and monotone motion, often contributes by far the largest proportion of the variance. Therefore, unless it is removed, the parameters of the model, whose purpose is to explain the patterns of the fluctuations, will be devoted needlessly to explaining the trend.

Recently, some renewed attention has been paid to the matter of trend estimation (see, for example, Beveridge and Nelson (1981), Burman (1980), Cogley and Nason (1995), Harvey and Jaeger (1993), King and Rebelo (1993), Kydland and Prescott (1990)); and various problems have arisen which have not been fully resolved. In the first place, it is often unclear where the trend ends and the fluctuations begin; and the desiderata for separating the two, if they are separable, have remained in dispute. In the second place, it has often proved difficult to extract the trend, even when it is a clearly defined entity.

The purpose of this chapter is to conduct a critical review of some of the methods which are available for obtaining estimates of the trend and of the detrended series. In the process we aim to throw some light on the desiderata for separating the trend from the fluctuations. We shall also attempt to refine some existing techniques of trend extraction and to develop some new ones.

In order to accomplish these ends, we shall need to pursue several topics in turn. First, we shall examine the effects of one of the principal tools of time-series modelling which is the difference operator. Next, we shall examine the model-based methods of trend extraction which have been devised within the context of ARIMA models. For this purpose, we will give a brief exposition of the technique of signal extraction. Finally, we will propose some enhanced methods of trend extraction which are independent of any model. We shall use the theme of signal extraction as an heuristic device for explaining the methods, albeit that some of them can also be derived by other means. The Appendix of the chapter is devoted to certain technical problems in implementing the filters which perform the operations of trend estimation and of detrending.

11.2 THE EFFECTS OF THE DIFFERENCING OPERATOR

Differencing is an effective way of removing the non-stationary components from a data sequence. Its use was recommended by Tintner (1940), one of the first of the modern econometricians, in his book *The Variate Difference Method*. Its continued widespread use for this purpose owes something to Tintner's influence.

One of the justifications which Tintner offered for the method of differencing is the fact that a sequence of ordinates of a polynomial of degree m, corresponding to equally spaced values of the argument, can be reduced to a constant by taking m differences. If the time trend which underlies the data resembles a polynomial function, then, according to Tintner, 'We can eliminate, or at least greatly reduce, the systematic part [i.e. the trend] by taking finite differences'.

Unfortunately, this is a false prescription. The appropriate way of removing a polynomial trend from a data sequence is, of course, to fit a polynomial function. By taking a sufficient number of differences of the data, one will succeed in removing the trend, but the effect will be much wider; and the other components of the data which will be affected are bound to contain information which is of interest to the economist. According to one analogy, taking differences is akin to throwing out the baby with the bath water.

The effect of the difference operator is shown in Figure 11.1. Here the curve labelled D represents the frequency-response function of the second-difference operator $\delta(L) = (I - L)^2$. This function indicates the factors by which the operator attenuates or amplifies the amplitudes of the sinusoidal components of any time series to which it is applied.

The relevance of this characterization of the effects of the operator can be recognized once it is understood that all stationary stochastic processes, and

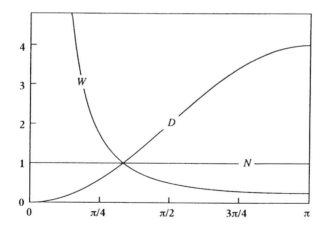

Figure 11.1 The frequency-response function, labelled D, of the second-order difference operator $(I - L)^2$, together with the power spectrum, labelled W, of a first-order random walk $y(t) = (I - L)^{-1}\varepsilon(t)$ where $\varepsilon(t)$ is a white-noise process. The power spectrum of $\varepsilon(t)$ is represented by the horizontal line labelled N

other processes besides, can be regarded as combinations of an indefinite number of sinusoidal components whose frequencies, denoted by ω, lie in the interval $[0, \pi]$, which is the range of the horizontal axis of the diagram.

The frequency-response function of a linear operator or filter $\psi(L)$ may be defined formally by the expression

$$|\psi(z)| = \sqrt{\psi(z)\psi(z^{-1})} \tag{1}$$

where $z = \exp\{i\omega\}$ stands for a complex exponential whose locus is the unit circle. Thus $|\psi(z)|$ denotes the modulus of the complex function $\psi(z)$.

A simple calculation shows that, in the case of the second-difference operator $\delta(L)$, the modulus is

$$|\delta(z)| = 2 - (z + z^{-1}) \tag{2}$$

On setting $z = \exp\{i\omega\}$, and using the identity $\frac{1}{2}(\exp\{i\omega\} + \{-i\omega\}) = \cos(\omega)$, this becomes

$$\delta(e^{i\omega}) = 2 - 2\cos(\omega) \tag{3}$$

Figure 11.1 shows that the (second) difference operator nullifies the component at zero frequency, which might be construed as a linear or a quadratic trend. This is the point which was emphasized by Tintner. However, it can be seen that the filter alters the relative amplitudes over the entire range of frequencies. At the upper end of the frequency range, it magnifies, by a factor of 4, the amplitude of the component with the frequency of π, which is the so-called Nyquist Frequency.

There is a further undesirable effect that accompanies the differencing operation which may be easily amended. This is the so-called phase effect whereby the transformed series suffers a time delay. Thus, for example, when two successive differencing operations are applied to a series of monthly observations, a time lag of one month is induced.

To understand how inappropriate the method of differencing can be as a means of removing a trend, one has only to consider applying it to a seasonally fluctuating series of sales figures. Not only will the relative sizes of the sales peaks be misrepresented, but also their timing will be altered by the uniform delay. Any sales organization which took the differenced figures at their face value would soon be bankrupt.

These matters can be illustrated by considering a monthly series on the sale of cars in the United States which is to be found in the text of Newbold and Bos (1990, p. 321). A subset of 120 observations is plotted in Figure 11.2. Figure 11.3 shows the residuals after a polynomial time trend of degree 8 has been extracted. Figure 11.4 shows the effect of applying the difference operator to the sales series. The phase effect of the difference filter is evident from the comparison of Figures 11.3 and 11.4.

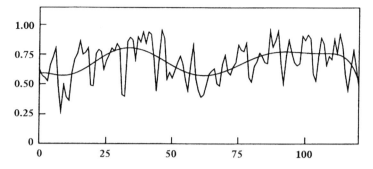

Figure 11.2 A series of 120 monthly observations on the number of cars sold in the United States from January 1960 to December 1970

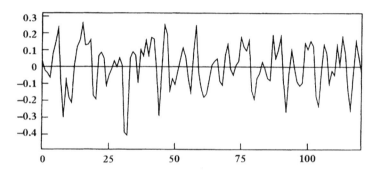

Figure 11.3 The residuals from fitting an eighth-degree polynomial to the data on car sales

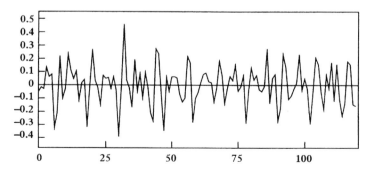

Figure 11.4 A series generated by applying the difference operator to the data on car sales

The phase effect of the difference filter may be eliminated by the simple expedient of shifting the affected series forwards in time. This possibility is due to the fact that the difference operator imposes the same time lag on all components regardless of their frequencies. With more complicated operators, such as those which are formed from the ratios of lag-operator polynomials, there are liable to be different time lags at different frequencies. In such cases, the phase effects can be removed by applying the operator again, but in reversed time.

Let $F = L^{-1}$ denote the inverse of the lag operator which can be described as the forwards-shift operator. The effect of this operator upon a sequence $z(t)$ is described by the equation $Fz(t) = z(t + 1)$. If the operator $\varphi(L) = \delta(L)/\gamma(L)$ induces a phase shift in the sequence $y(t)$, then this will be removed by applying the reversed-time operator $\varphi(F)$ to the transformed series $z(t) = \varphi(L)y(t)$. Thus $x(t)$ will suffer no phase effect if it is formed from $y(t)$ in two stages:

$$\text{(i)} \quad \gamma(L)z(t) = \delta(L)y(t) \qquad \text{(ii)} \quad \gamma(F)x(t) = \delta(F)z(t) \qquad (4)$$

The two equations above may be combined to give

$$x(t) = \varphi(F)\varphi(L)y(t) = \frac{\delta(F)\delta(L)}{\gamma(F)\gamma(L)}y(t) \qquad (5)$$

Here the combined operator $\psi(L) = \varphi(F)\varphi(L)$ may be described as a bidirectional filter.

11.3 ARIMA MODELS AND THE DIFFERENCING OPERATOR

Part of the reason why differencing continues to be a widely used data transformation is because it plays a central role in the methodology of Box and Jenkins (1976) by which ARIMA models are fitted to non-stationary time series. According to the prescription of Box and Jenkins, the first stage in building an ARIMA model should be to take as many differences of the original series as are needed to reduce it to stationarity. Thereafter, it is proposed that the differenced series should be treated in the same manner as a stationary series which has had no need of differencing.

The justification for this prescription is the belief that many trends in economic time series can be represented by random-walk processes of the sort which can be depicted by

$$y(t) = (I - L)^{-d}v(t) \qquad \text{or, equivalently,} \qquad (I - L)^d y(t) = v(t) \qquad (6)$$

wherein $v(t)$ represents a stationary stochastic process of the ARMA variety. In the simplest instance, $v(t)$ is a white-noise process which generates a sequence of independently and identically distributed random variables.

The effect of the difference operator upon $y(t)$ is no less drastic in the context of ARIMA modelling than in any other context. However, if the process generating $y(t)$ is indeed a species of random walk, then the use of the difference operator to reduce it to stationarity is undoubtedly called for. Nevertheless, the question arises of whether random walks are appropriate analogies for the types of time series which economists are likely to encounter.

One way of assessing the matter is to compare the power spectra of economic time series with the spectra which are generated by random walks. If a large and consistent disparity is evident, then doubt may be cast upon the appropriateness of random-walk models.

In Figure 11.1, the function labelled W represents the spectral density function, or power spectrum, of a first-order random walk $y(t)$ which is described by

$$y(t) = (I - L)^{-1}\varepsilon(t) \qquad \text{or, equivalently,} \qquad (I - L)y(t) = \varepsilon(t) \qquad (7)$$

wherein $\varepsilon(t)$ represents a white-noise process with a variance of $V\{\varepsilon(t)\} = 2\pi$. The function indicates the power which is attributable to the sinusoidal components of which the random walk is composed. An evident feature of this spectrum is that there is infinite power at zero frequency. This corresponds to the theoretical condition that the values generated by a random walk defined on an indefinite set of integers are unbounded.

The notion of power is synonymous with the notion of variance and, for a sinusoidal function, the variance is half the square of the amplitude. The white-noise process $\varepsilon(t)$, which is the motive force that drives the random walk, has a uniform distribution of power over the frequency interval $[0, \pi]$. Therefore the power spectrum of $y(t)$ is, in effect, the square of the frequency-response function of the operator $(I - L)^{-1}$ scaled by the variance, or power, of the process $\varepsilon(t)$.

Two comparisons are now in order. The first comparison is between the functions labelled D and W in Figure 11.1. The first of these, which has been used already to represent the frequency-response function of the second-difference operator $(I - L)^2$, can be taken now to represent the square of the frequency-response function of the operator $I - L$ which is effective in reducing the first-order random walk $y(t)$ to the white-noise sequence $\varepsilon(t)$. Thus, the result of multiplying the curve W by the curve D is to produce the horizontal straight line N which represents the power spectrum of the process $\varepsilon(t)$.

The second comparison is between the power spectrum of a typical economic time series and that of the first-order random walk. Figure 11.6 shows the periodogram of the full series of 288 monthly figures of US car sales which are plotted in Figure 11.5. The periodogram is the empirical counterpart of the power spectrum. This periodogram shows an accumulation of power in the frequency interval $[0, \pi/8]$ which corresponds to the trend in the data.

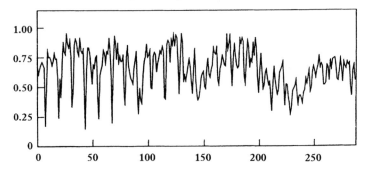

Figure 11.5   A series of 288 monthly observations on car sales

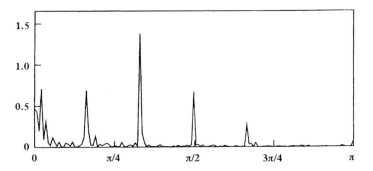

Figure 11.6   The periodogram of 288 observations on car sales

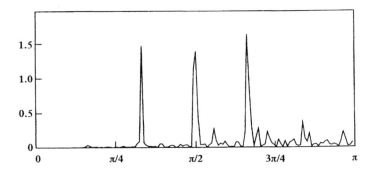

Figure 11.7   The periodogram of a sequence obtained by applying the second-differencing operator to the data on car sales

What is evident from this example, and from others like it, is that the periodograms of empirical series rarely show anything like the slew of power across the range of frequencies which is characteristic of a simple random walk. Therefore it appears that simple random walks provide inappropriate models for non-stationary economic time-series; and it needs to be explained why random walks feature so largely in econometric time-series modelling.

The resolution of the conundrum lies with the ARMA part of the ARIMA model which provides a model for the process $v(t)$ in equation (6). Thus, for example, if $v(t) = (I - \theta L)^d \varepsilon(t)$, where $\varepsilon(t)$ is white noise and θ is close to unity, then the equation will take the form

$$(I - L)^d y(t) = (I - \theta L)^d \varepsilon(t) \tag{8}$$

and the effect of the operator $(I - L)^d$, which induces the random walk, will be counteracted by that of the operator $(I - \theta L)^d$; and the power of the process will be largely confined to a neighbourhood of $\omega = 0$.

In devising a filter to eliminate the trend from an economic time series, one might take this lesson into account by using a modified difference operator of the form

$$\delta(L) = \left\{ \frac{(1 + \theta)^2}{4} \right\}^d \frac{(I - F)^d (I - L)^d}{(I - \theta F)^d (I - \theta L)^d} \tag{9}$$

As well as incorporating the parameter θ, which now serves to limit the effects of the difference operator, the filter has a bidirectional structure which eliminates the phase effect. The factor which precedes the operator on the right-hand side of equation (9) is to ensure that the frequency-response function attains the value of unity when $\omega = \pi$, which is when $z = -1$. Figure 11.8 shows the frequency-response function for the operator in the case where $d = 2$ and for various values of θ.

In the case of $d = 2$, the filter of equation (9) is very similar to the Hodrick–Prescott detrending filter which we shall examine later. It is apparent from Figure 11.8 that, even though the major effects of the modified filter are confined to the lower reaches of the frequency range, there is still a gradual transition between the effect of nullifying a frequency component, as happens at $\omega = 0$, and that of preserving it, as happens at $\omega = \pi$.

This can be a disadvantage in the case of time series whose periodogram shows a sharp distinction between those components which belong to the trend and those which belong to the fluctuations. It is arguable that such a distinction can be found in the periodogram of Figure 11.6 where the power is virtually zero in the vicinity of $\omega = \pi/8$. This is the point at which we should propose separating the trend from the fluctuations. The frequency of $\omega = \pi/6$, which corresponds to the fundamental frequency of an annual fluctuation, lies beyond the range of the frequencies which belong to the trend.

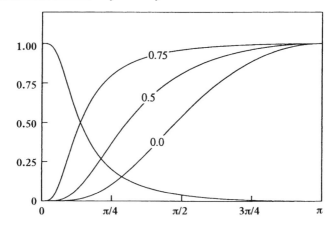

Figure 11.8 The frequency-response function of the modified difference operator of equation (9) when $d = 2$ for the values of $\theta = 0.0$, 0.5, 0.75, together with the complementary trend-estimation filter for the case of $\theta = 0.75$

The principal aim of the ensuing sections of this chapter is to discover the appropriate means of separating the trend and the fluctuations when a clear distinction is evident in the periodogram of the data.

11.4 TREND ESTIMATION BY SIGNAL EXTRACTION

A trend has only a tenuous existence within the context of an ARIMA model. In a conventional ARIMA model, a trend represents nothing more than the accumulation of fluctuations which are created by applying a filter to a white-noise sequence $\varepsilon(t)$ of independently and identically distributed random variables. If the trend and the fluctuations are due to the same motive force, which is the white-noise process, then it is meaningless to draw a distinction between them.

Faced with the insistence that the trend and the fluctuations are due to separate sources, an obvious recourse is to attribute a separate ARIMA model to each of them. In that case, the model which is generated by adding together the component ARIMA models is an ARIMA model itself.

Given that the ARIMA models for the structural components of a time series combine so seamlessly to form a reduced-form ARIMA model, it might seem like wasted effort to attempt to separate the combined series into its constituent parts. Thus, in the absence of any seams to show where the joins are to be found and where the cut is to be made, it is to be expected that whatever separation is achieved is liable to be a tentative and a doubtful one.

Econometricians have not been deterred by these difficulties, and they have developed a sophisticated methodology for separating an ARIMA model into its putative components. The methodology, which was originally proposed by Nerlove, Grether and Carvalho (1979), is based upon the techniques of signal extraction, of which accounts has been given by Whittle (1983) and by Harvey (1989). The methodology, as it applies to the problem of seasonal adjustment, has also been described by Maravall and Pierce (1987). We shall describe the signal-extraction technique briefly in the present section before examining its use in decomposing a seasonal ARIMA model into a trend component and a complementary component.

Let the observable sequence $y(t)$ be the sum of a trend component $\xi(t)$ and a residue $\eta(t)$ which are assumed to be statistically independent:

$$y(t) = \xi(t) + \eta(t) \tag{10}$$

The object is to infer the trajectory of the trend from the observations on $y(t)$ given a knowledge of the covariance structures of $\xi(t)$ and $\eta(t)$. The problem can be likened to one of signal extraction where $\xi(t)$ is the signal and $\eta(t)$ is the noise. However, the analogy may be misleading since, in the case of trend extraction, the residue contains information which is of primary interest whereas, in the usual case of signal extraction, the noise sequence is liable to be regarded as a nuisance which is to be discarded.

The estimate of $\xi(t)$, which is obtained by filtering $y(t)$, will be denoted by

$$x(t) = \psi(L)y(t) \tag{11}$$

Here $\psi(L) = \sum_j \psi_j L^j$ is a function of the lag operator L which may be a polynomial or a rational function. A single element of the sequence $x(t)$ from time t is denoted by $x_t = \sum_j \psi_j y_{t-j}$. When both succeeding and preceding values of $y(t)$ are available for the purpose of estimating the current value of $\xi(t)$, then $\psi(L)$ is liable to be a two-sided function containing both positive and negative powers L.

The coefficients of the filter $\psi(L)$ are estimated by invoking the minimum-mean-square-error criterion. The errors in question are the elements of the sequence $e(t) = \xi(t) - x(t)$. The principle of orthogonality, by which the criterion is fulfilled, indicates that the errors must be uncorrelated with the elements in the information set $\mathscr{I}_t = \{y_{t-k}; k = 0, \pm 1, \pm 2, \ldots\}$. Thus

$$0 = E\{y_{t-k}(\xi_t - x_t)\}$$

$$= E(y_{t-k}\xi_t) - \sum_j \psi_j E(y_{t-k}y_{t-j}) \tag{12}$$

$$= \gamma_k^{y\xi} - \sum_j \psi_j \gamma_{k-j}^{yy}$$

for all k. The equation may be expressed, in terms of the z-transform, as

$$\gamma^{y\xi}(z) = \psi(z)\gamma^{yy}(z) \tag{13}$$

where

$$\gamma^{yy}(z) = \gamma^{\xi\xi}(z) + \gamma^{\eta\eta}(z) \qquad \text{and} \qquad \gamma^{y\xi}(z) = \gamma^{\xi\xi}(z) \tag{14}$$

are respectively the autocovariance generating function of $y(t)$ and the cross-covariance generating function of $y(t)$ and $\xi(t)$. It follows that

$$\psi(z) = \frac{\gamma^{y\xi}(z)}{\gamma^{yy}(z)} = \frac{\gamma^{\xi\xi}(z)}{\gamma^{\xi\xi}(z) + \gamma^{\eta\eta}(z)} \tag{15}$$

Now, by setting $z = \exp\{i\omega\}$, one can derive the frequency-response function of the filter which is used in estimating the signal $\xi(t)$. The effect of the filter is to multiply each of the frequency components of $y(t)$ by the fraction of its variance which is attributable to the signal. The same principle applies to the estimation of the residual detrended component. The trend-elimination filter is just the complementary filter

$$1 - \psi(z) = \frac{\gamma^{\eta\eta}(z)}{\gamma^{\xi\xi}(z) + \gamma^{\eta\eta}(z)} \tag{16}$$

It has been shown by Cleveland and Tiao (1976) and, more recently, by Bell (1984) that these formulae apply equally to stationary ARMA processes and to non-stationary ARIMA processes.

11.5 MODEL-BASED METHODS OF TREND ESTIMATION

It has been argued that best way of separating the trend from the fluctuations is to model both of them at the same time within the framework provided by a structural ARIMA model which assigns separate parameters to the components. Some examples of detrending which follow this prescription are provided in the articles of Hillmer and Tiao (1982) and of Harvey and Jaeger (1993).

The focus of the two articles is slightly different. Whereas Hillmer and Tiao are concerned with extracting the hidden components from existing seasonal ARIMA models, Harvey and Jaeger specify the constituent parts of their models *ab initio* without placing any restriction upon the reduced-form model which results from adding the components together.

The estimates of the trend which result from these two approaches do not differ in any essential respects; and an adequate illustration is provided by the simplest of three seasonal models which have been examined by Hillmer and Tiao.

The model in question is specified by the equation

$$(I - L^s)y(t) = (I - \theta L^s)\varepsilon(t) \tag{17}$$

where s is the number of observations within the span of an annual cycle. The nature of the equation can be understood by considering first the case where $\theta = 0$. Then the value of $y(t)$ in any period of the year differs from the value in the same period of the previous year by the amount of a white-noise disturbance. The accumulation of such disturbances over the years will cause the seasonal value to follow a first-order random walk.

The elaboration of the model which introduces a nonzero value of θ has the same effect in limiting the random walk as it does in the analogous non-seasonal equation under (8). In the context of the seasonal model, it increases the concentration of the power of the process in the vicinities of the seasonal frequencies $\omega = 2\pi j/s; j = 1, \ldots, s/2$, thereby reducing the drift and regularising the cycles. In fact, equation (17) is nothing more than a battery of s separate equations in the form of (8).

The seasonal patterns which are typically exhibited by economic time series show a degree of persistence which is not found in the stochastic output generated by equation (17). There is no bound in the long run on the amplitude of the cycles generated by this equation. Also, there is a tendency for the phases of the cycles to drift without limit. If the latter were a feature of the monthly time series of consumer expenditures, for example, then we could not expect the annual boom in sales to occur at a definite time of year. In fact, it invariably occurs at Christmas time.

The virtue of equation (17) is not as a model of the processes generating the seasonal time series but as a device for forecasting the series. The forecasting rule which is implied by the equation when $\theta = 0$ is that the most recent set of s observations, which represent an annual cycle, should be taken as the pattern for all future years. In the case where $\theta \neq 0$, the pattern of the annual cycle which is to be extrapolated should be formed from a weighted average of all previous cycles, with θ as a discount factor which is applied repeatedly to the cycles as the years recede.

The autocovariance generating function of the model may be factorized into two partial fractions whose denominators contain, respectively, the trend operator $1 - z$ and the seasonal operator $S(z) = 1 + z + z^2 + \cdots + z^s$:

$$\gamma^{yy}(z) = \frac{(I - \theta z^s)(1 - \theta z^{-s})}{(1 - z^s)(1 - z^{-s})}$$

$$= \frac{A(z)}{(1 - z)(1 - z^{-1})} + \frac{B(z)}{S(z)S(z^{-1})}$$

(18)

To find the numerator $A(z)$, we multiply this equation throughout by the factor $(1 - z)(1 - z^{-1})$ and proceed to set $z = 1$. The result is

$$A(z) = \frac{1}{s^2}(1 - \theta)^2$$

(19)

Therefore the partial fraction associated with the trend is

$$\phi(z) = \frac{(1 - \theta)^2}{s^2(1 - z)(1 - z^{-1})} \tag{20}$$

This is the autocovariance generating function of a random-walk process. Setting $z = \exp\{i\omega\}$ in the function generates the pseudo spectral-density function of the process. The function $\phi(z)$ attains a minimum value of $(1 - \theta)^2/(4s^2)$ at the Nyquist frequency of $\omega = \pi$.

Consider a horizontal line drawn at this height over the interval $[0, \pi]$. The line represents the spectral density function of a white-noise component of variance $(1 - \theta)^2/(4s^2)$ which is an integral part of the trend component as it is currently defined. According to the principle of canonical factorization enunciated by Hillmer and Tiao (1982) and by Pierce (1979), this white-noise component should be subtracted from the trend component and attributed to the irregular component which is currently part of the residue. The subtraction of the white-noise component leads to a revised trend component of the form

$$\gamma^{\xi\xi}(z) = \frac{(1 - \theta)^2}{s^2(1 - z)(1 - z^{-1})} - \frac{(1 - \theta)^2}{4s^2}$$

$$= \frac{(1 - \theta)^2(1 + z)(1 + z^{-1})}{4s^2(1 - z)(1 - z^{-1})} \tag{21}$$

It follows that the filter which is appropriate to extracting the trend takes the form

$$\psi(z) = \frac{\gamma^{\xi\xi}(z)}{\gamma^{yy}(z)} = \frac{(1 - \theta)^2}{4s^2} \frac{(1 + z)S(z)S(z^{-1})(1 + z^{-1})}{(1 - \theta z^s)(1 - \theta z^{-s})} \tag{22}$$

Notice that, on setting $z = 1$, which is the same as setting $\omega = 0$ in $z = \exp\{i\omega\}$, we find that $\psi(1) = 1$. This indicates that the filter preserves intact the component of $y(t)$ with zero frequency. This is what we should expect of a filter designed to estimate the trend component.

The frequency-response function of the model-based trend-estimation filter with $s = 4$ is plotted in Figure 11.9 for various values of the parameter θ. For all values of the parameter, the function shows a very gradual transition between the effect of passing the components at the lowest frequencies and that of impeding those at the higher frequencies.

Thus the filter does not make a firm distinction between the components which belong to the trend and those which belong to the fluctuations. Its characteristics are attuned to those of an ARIMA model in which the frequency ranges of the two sets of components are bound to overlap substantially.

It is also notable that the frequency-response of the model-based filter is barely distinguishable from that of the filter which is complementary to the modified

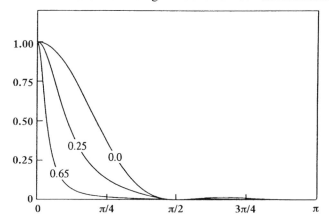

Figure 11.9 The frequency-response function of the model-based trend estimation filter of equation (22) when $s = 4$ for various values of θ

differencing filter of equation (9). The latter could well be used in place of the model-based filter.

The recommendation that trend estimation should be conducted only within the context of a structural ARIMA model is now in doubt. If there is a manifest distinction between the frequency domains of the trend and the fluctuations, then sharper tools are needed for separating the two.

11.6 TREND ESTIMATION BY HEURISTIC METHODS

The Hodrick–Prescott (H–P) (1980) filter is a heuristic or model-free method of data smoothing which is used widely by economists. The H–P filter closely resembles a classical smoothing device known as the Reinsch (1976) smoothing spline which has been used widely in industrial design. Both the filter and the spline are commonly derived by pursuing a criterion of curve fitting which balances the conflicting objectives of smoothness and goodness of fit. The parameter which regulates the trade-off between the objectives is known as the smoothing parameter.

With the appropriate choice of the smoothing parameter, the H–P filter is the optimal predictor of the trajectory of a discrete-time second-order random walk observed with error. The Reinsch spline, on the other hand, represents the optimal predictor of the trajectory of an integrated Wiener process of which the periodic observations are obscured by white-noise errors. This result, which appears to have been established first by Craven and Wahba (1979), has been used by Wecker and Ansley (1983) in deriving an algorithm for fitting the spline.

An integrated Wiener process is just the continuous-time analogue of a second-order random walk; and a sequence of equally-spaced (exact) observations of the process follows a discrete-time integrated moving-average IMA(2,1) process described by

$$(I - L)^2 \xi(t) = (1 + \mu L)\nu(t) \tag{23}$$

Here $\mu = 2 - \sqrt{3}$ and $V\{\nu(t)\} = \sigma_\nu^2$ are solutions of the equations

$$\frac{2}{3}\kappa = \sigma_\nu^2(1 + \mu^2), \qquad \text{and} \qquad \frac{\kappa}{6} = \sigma_\nu^2 \mu^2 \tag{24}$$

where κ is a scale parameter which affects only σ_ν^2.

The autocovariance generating function of the IMA(2,1) signal process $\xi(t)$ is

$$\gamma^{\xi\xi}(z) = \sigma_\nu^2 \frac{(1 + \mu z)(1 + \mu z^{-1})}{(1 - z)^2(1 - z^{-1})^2} \tag{25}$$

whilst that of the observable noise-corrupted process $y(t) = \xi(t) + \eta(t)$ is

$$\gamma^{yy}(z) = \frac{\sigma_\nu^2(1 - \mu z)(1 - \mu z^{-1}) + \sigma_\eta^2(1 - z)^2(1 - z^{-1})^2}{(1 - z)^2(1 - z^{-1})^2} \tag{26}$$

It follows that the formula for the signal-extraction filter is

$$\psi(z) = \frac{\gamma^{\xi\xi}(z)}{\gamma^{yy}(z)} = \frac{\sigma_\nu^2(1 + \mu z)(1 + \mu z^{-1})}{\sigma_\eta^2(1 - z)^2(1 - z^{-1})^2 + \sigma_\nu^2(1 + \mu z)(1 + \mu z^{-1})} \tag{27}$$

whereas the formula for the complementary 'detrending' filter is

$$1 - \psi(z) = \frac{\sigma_\eta^2(1 - z)^2(1 - z^{-1})^2}{\sigma_\eta^2(1 - z)^2(1 - z^{-1})^2 + \sigma_\nu^2(1 + \mu z)(1 + \mu z^{-1})} \tag{28}$$

The smoothing parameter is the ratio $\lambda = \sigma_\eta^2/\sigma_\nu^2$ of the variance of the error process $\eta(t)$ which obscures the observations and the variance of the process $\nu(t)$ which is the motive power of the signal.

It is interesting to discover that the filter in equation (27) is also optimal for the purpose of extracting the signal $\xi(t) = (1 + \mu L)\nu(t)$ from the sequence

$$q(t) = (1 + \mu L)\nu(t) + (I - L)^2 \eta(t) \tag{29}$$

Thus it is clear that, at least for time series defined over the entire domain of positive and negative integers, an optimal filter need not be tied to a single process.

Figure 11.10 displays the frequency-response of the filter associated with the Reinsch smoothing spline when the smoothing parameter takes various values. The H–P filter, which is obtained by setting $\mu = 0$, has a frequency-response

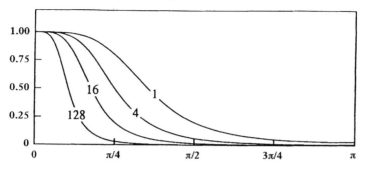

Figure 11.10 The frequency-response function of the Reinsch smoothing filter for various values of the smoothing parameter

function which is not perceptibly different from that of the spline; and it is unnecessary to plot them both.

The frequency response of the Reinsch filter has a sharper transition than that of the model-based filter which has been derived from equation (17). The difference is less pronounced when the Reinsch filter is compared with an alternative model-based filter which is derived from

$$(I - L)(I - L^s)y(t) = (I - \theta L^s)\varepsilon(t) \tag{30}$$

which incorporates the extra factor $(I - L)$ in the operator $(I - L)(I - L^s) = (I - L)^2 S(L)$ on the left-hand side. In that case, the trend component of the model follows a second-order random walk.

The Reinsch filter is one of the most widely used of smoothing devices. Its prevalence may be related to the fact that many of the human neurological mechanisms incorporate comparable smoothing devices. A good example is provided by the auditory mechanisms which succeed in attenuating high-frequency noise without leaving us wholly unaware of its presence.

Figure 11.11 displays the time plot of a frequency-modulated signal which is commonly known as a chirp, for the reason that the audible version resembles a bird noise. Figure 11.12 shows the same signal after it has been processed by the Reinsch filter. The presence of the high-frequency components can still be inferred from the time plot, but they no longer intrude noisily.

The attraction of a smoothing filter as a data-processing device in economics is much the same as in any other application. It assists us in assimilating the information by attenuating, but not completely eliminating, noisy and distracting detail. It seems, however, that a clear distinction should be made between data smoothing and trend estimation. If trend estimation is the objective, then a different filter is called for which is capable of selecting certain designated frequencies and rejecting others.

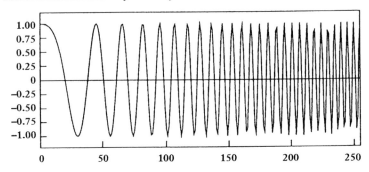

Figure 11.11 The time plot of the frequency-modulated signal known as a chirp

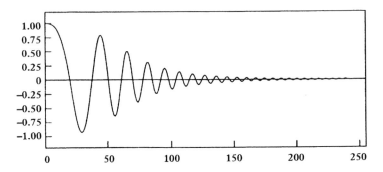

Figure 11.12 The chirp after it has been processed by the Reinsch smoothing filter

The H–P filter has virtually the same effect as the Reinsch filter. However, its use in estimating trends has been criticised recently by economists and econometricians (see, for example, Cogley and Nason (1995), Harvey and Jaeger (1993) and King and Rebelo (1993)). It has been suggested that the filter is liable to induce spurious cycles in the detrended data. This is not possible, since the gain of the filter $1 - \psi(z)$—which is the factor by which the amplitudes of the components are multiplied—never exceeds unity. The worst that the filter can do is to fail to remove from the data the types of motions which, in common opinion, should be attributed to the trend. This problem can arise from an inappropriate choice of the smoothing parameter; but it can also occur when the rate of transition in the frequency response is insufficiently rapid for the purpose of separating the trend from the fluctuations.

A family of filters with an enhanced rate of transition may be obtained by considering the artificial problem of estimating the signal sequence $\xi(t) = (I + \mu L)^n v(t)$ from the observable sequence

$$q(t) = (I + \mu L)^n v(t) + (I - \theta L)^n \eta(t) \tag{31}$$

The optimal filter for this purpose is given by the following formula:

$$\psi(z) = \frac{\sigma_\nu^2(1 + \mu z)^n(1 + \mu z^{-1})^n}{\sigma_\eta^2(1 - \theta z)^n(1 - \theta z^{-1})^n + \sigma_\nu^2(1 + \mu z)^n(1 + \mu z^{-1})^n} \tag{32}$$

The Hodrick–Prescott filter can be depicted as a special case of the filter above which comes from setting $n = 2$, $\mu = 0$ and $\theta = 1$. The family of filters which we propose for the purpose of extracting the trends from economic time series is obtained by setting $\mu = \theta = 1$. By raising the value of n, the sharpness of the transition can be increased. By varying the value of the smoothing parameter $\lambda = \sigma_\eta^2/\sigma_\nu^2$, the location of the midpoint of the transition, which is the nominal cut-off point, can be varied at will. The results may be described as square-wave filters.

A square-wave filter may be implemented using its bidirectional form

$$\psi(z) = \frac{\delta(z)\delta(z^{-1})}{\gamma(z)\gamma(z^{-1})} = \frac{(1 + z)^n(1 + z^{-1})^n}{\gamma(z)\gamma(z^{-1})} \tag{33}$$

This requires the isolation of the factors $\gamma(z)$ and $\gamma(z^{-1})$. One of the virtues of the filter is the ease with which analytic expressions may be found for the roots of these polynomial factors. The expressions are presented in the Appendix.

Figure 11.13 presents the frequency response of the square-wave filter. Figures 11.14, 11.15, and 11.16 show the effects of applying the filter to the problem of extracting the trend from the series on the number of cars sold in the USA. In this case, the cut-off point has been set at $\omega = \pi/8$. The effect of the filter

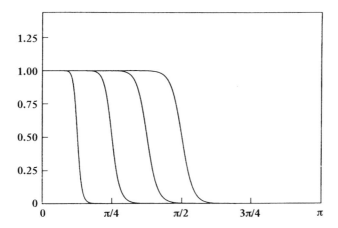

Figure 11.13 The frequency-response function of the square-wave trend-estimation filter for $n = 8$ with nominal cut-off points at $\omega = \pi/8, \pi/4, 3\pi/8$, and $\pi/2$

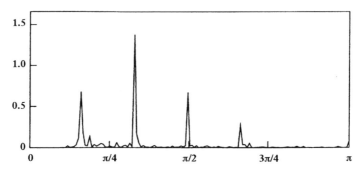

Figure 11.14 The periodogram of a sequence obtained by applying a highpass square-wave filter to the data on car sales

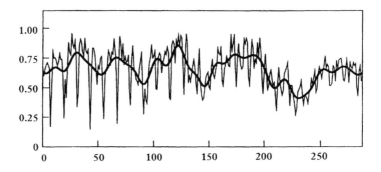

Figure 11.15 The trend of car sales estimated by applying a lowpass square-wave filter to the data

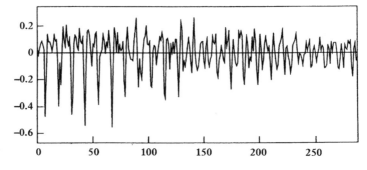

Figure 11.16 A detrended series obtained by applying a highpass square-wave filter to the data on car sales

may be judged by examining the periodogram of the detrended data plotted in Figure 11.14 and by comparing it with the periodogram in Figure 11.6 which is for the original series.

Is seems reasonable to suggest that the trend which is displayed in Figure 11.15 represents the underlying level of economic activity; and it would be interesting to discover whether it correlates at all closely with other trends extracted in the same way from comparable series spanning the same period. If similar motions were found to underlie other series, then the reality of this putative trend would be confirmed.

Some business-cycle analysts might wish to define a smoother trend in terms of a narrower range of frequencies. However, the square-wave filter enables any set of frequencies ranging from zero to a designated cut-off point to be selected; and therefore, in our contention, it represents an appropriate device for extracting a trend however it might be defined.

The cut by which the square-wave filter separates two ranges of frequencies can be made as sharp as is required by increasing the value of the parameter n which corresponds to the order of the filter. A low value of n will result in a filter whose frequency response shows a gradual transition in the vicinity of the cut-off frequency. Thus, with the appropriate choice of parameters, the square-wave filter will also serve the purpose of smoothing a data series in the manner of the Reinsch filter and the Hodrick–Prescott filter.

11.7 APPENDIX: IMPLEMENTING THE FILTERS

The bidirectional filters which are specified by the formula

$$\psi(z) = \frac{\delta(z)\delta(z^{-1})}{\gamma(z)\gamma(z^{-1})}$$

$$= \frac{\sigma_\nu^2(1 + \mu z)^n(1 + \mu z^{-1})^n}{\sigma_\nu^2(1 + \mu z)^n(1 + \mu z^{-1})^n + \sigma_\eta^2(1 - \theta z)^n(1 - \theta z^{-1})^n} \quad (A1)$$

can only be implemented by processing a data series in two passes in the manner represented in equation (4). In order to construct the constituent filters $\varphi(z) = \delta(z)/\gamma(z)$ and $\varphi(z^{-1}) = \delta(z^{-1})/\gamma(z^{-1})$ which are used in the forwards and backwards passes, it is necessary to factorize the numerator and the denominator of the filter.

There is no difficulty in factorizing the numerator. The denominator can be factorized using one of the iterative procedures which are used in finding the Cramér–Wold factorization of a Laurent polynomial. Alternatively, one may seek to isolate the roots of the denominator polynomial for the purpose of assigning them to one or other of the factors $\gamma(z)$ and $\gamma(z^{-1})$. The roots of $\gamma(z)\gamma(z^{-1}) = 0$ which fall outside the unit circle are assigned to $\gamma(z)$ whilst those which fall inside are assigned to $\gamma(z^{-1})$.

In general, it is impossible to find analytic expressions for the roots of polynomials of a degree in excess of four. However, in the present case, it is possible to find analytic expressions. When $\mu = \theta = 1$, which is the case of the square-wave filter, the expressions become reasonably tractable.

Consider the equation which is obtained by setting the denominator to zero:

$$\sigma_\nu^2 (1 + \mu z)^n (1 + \mu z^{-1})^n + \sigma_\eta^2 (1 - \theta z)^n (1 - \theta z^{-1})^n = 0 \tag{A2}$$

This can be rewritten in the form

$$\lambda + \left\{ \frac{(1 + \mu^2) + \mu(z + z^{-1})}{(1 + \theta^2) - \theta(z + z^{-1})} \right\}^n = 0 \tag{A3}$$

where $\lambda = \sigma_\eta^2 / \sigma_\nu^2$. Solving this for

$$s = \frac{(1 + \mu^2) + \mu(z + z^{-1})}{(1 + \theta^2) - \theta(z + z^{-1})} \tag{A4}$$

is a matter of finding the nth roots of $-\lambda$. These are given by

$$s = \lambda^{1/n} \exp\left\{ \frac{i\pi j}{n} \right\} \qquad j = 1, 3, 5, \ldots, 2n - 1 \tag{A5}$$

The roots correspond to n points equally spaced around the circumference of a circle of radius $\lambda^{1/n}$. The radii which join the points to the centre are separated by angles of $2\pi/n$, and one of them makes an angle of π/n with the horizontal real axis.

Equation (A4) may be rearranged to give the following quadratic equation in z:

$$(\mu + \theta s)z^2 + \{(1 + \mu^2) - (1 + \theta^2)s\}z + (\mu + \theta s) = 0 \tag{A6}$$

Given that the coefficients are complex-valued, this amounts to an ordinary polynomial equation of degree four which can be solved via the customary analytic formulae.

The case where $\mu = \theta = 1$ is more tractable. Then equation (A3) becomes

$$\lambda + \left(i \frac{1 + z}{1 - z} \right)^{2n} = 0 \tag{A7}$$

Solving this for

$$s = i \frac{1 + z}{1 - z} \tag{A8}$$

is a matter of finding the $2n$th roots of $-\lambda$. These are given by

$$s = \lambda^{1/(2n)} \exp\left\{ \frac{i\pi j}{2n} \right\} \qquad j = 1, 3, 5, \ldots, 4n - 1 \tag{A9}$$

Equation (A8) may now be rearranged to give

$$z = \frac{s - i}{s + i} = \frac{(ss^* - 1) - i(s^* + s)}{(ss^* + 1) + i(s^* - s)} \tag{A10}$$

The elements of this formula are

$$ss^* = \lambda^{1/n}$$

$$s + s^* = 2\lambda^{1/(2n)} \cos(\pi j / n) \tag{A11}$$

$$i(s - s^*) = 2\lambda^{1/(2n)} \sin(\pi j / n)$$

The values of z which lie inside the unit circle are the roots of $\gamma(z^{-1})$. Those which lie outside the unit circle are the roots of $\gamma(z)$.

In applying the filter to a finite data sequence, it is necessary to supply initial conditions for the recursions which are represented by equation (4). These are obtained by extrapolating the estimated trend at either end of the data period. At the start, a set of pre-sample values are obtained by fitting a polynomial trend to the data. After applying the filter $\delta(L)/\gamma(L)$ to the data in a forwards pass, the processed sequence is supplemented by a number of extrapolated post-sample values. These serve as initial conditions for the backwards pass which applies the filter $\delta(F)/\gamma(F)$ to the sequence generated by the forwards pass.

COMMENTS

I.J. STEYN AND M. OOMS

I.J. STEYN

Brief Summary of the Chapter

In this intriguing and occasionally disturbing chapter, the consequences of some very widely used 'detrending' procedures are examined, mostly in terms of their effect on the spectrum of the process under consideration. This effect is most conveniently summarized by the frequency-response function, which tells us which frequencies are attenuated or accentuated by a procedure.

By far the oldest and the best known of these procedures is the difference operator $(1 - L)^d$, and this is commonly justified by a line of thought that will haunt the rest of the story: the removal of non-stationarity is equivalent to 'detrending'. In fact, as we shall see, detrending *implies* removal of non-stationarity, not the other way around. The frequency-response function tells much of the story: the relative amplitudes of *all* frequencies are affected by differencing. In addition, a phase-shift occurs, a common effect of a data transformation, and the author shows a simple way of repairing this unwelcome side-effect.

The next group of detrending methods examined here are those inspired by an unobserved-components model: the observed variable y_t is assumed to consist of a 'trend' variable ξ_t and a 'non-trend' variable η_t, where I choose the name for the latter carefully to avoid stigmatizing it as 'noise', 'residual', etc. The author derives the filter needed to remove such a component for a number of possible model specifications, where it is worth noting that both the trend component and the non-trend component need to be fully specified in order for the optimal (least-squares) filter to be derived.

Finally, a number of heuristic methods are examined, such as the Hodrick–Prescott filter and the virtually identical Reinsch smoothing spline. Frequency-response functions are derived, as are the explicit formulae for the filters themselves. It is unsettling to note that again the effect of these filters goes far beyond a mere removal of low-frequency components, as high-frequency amplitudes are also affected. The author also proposes what he calls a square-wave filter, which affects low-frequency components not at all, and which removes high-frequency components completely. For reasons made explicit below, this filter is not only the author's favourite but mine as well.

Spotting a Trend

An irritating problem in this whole discussion is that a 'trend' is a very poorly defined concept, better described in terms of what it is not. The author's first paragraphs certainly imply that a trend should be a relatively smooth process, and we have already noted that it should be non-stationary, as stationary processes can only exhibit temporary 'trends' before they are inexorably driven towards their mean value. Trends are generally assumed to be non-cyclical, mostly to allow a decomposition of the observations into three components: trend, cycle and none of the above. If the cyclical aspects of the observations are not by themselves of interest, then the cyclical component may be absorbed into either a trend or a non-trend component. Note, incidentally, that the non-trend component should be stationary, and less smooth than the trend component.

Most importantly, from its very conception the 'trend' was seen as one *component* driving the observations, with cyclical and irregular components completing the picture. Even the univariate ARIMA model in which differencing is the weapon of choice for removing non-stationarity can be interpreted in this way, as every ARIMA(p, d, q) model can be written as the sum of an ARIMA(0, d, 0) model and a stationary component (although the two need not be driven by independent noise processes).

This also casts an interesting light on the 'smooth trend' versus 'fuzzy trend' debate. Some authors, such as Gersch and Kitagawa (1983) prefer to model the trend component as a pure ARIMA(0, d, 0) process, which is a smooth curve for $d > 1$, while others, e.g. Harvey (1989), allow a 'fuzzier' trend component such as an ARIMA(0, 2, 2) process. But such a 'fuzzy' trend can in its turn be represented as the sum of a smooth ARIMA(0, 2, 0) process and a 'fuzzy' stationary ARMA process. A smooth trend is therefore always attainable.

Smoothness implies low frequencies, and the author notes that any sensible definition of a trend should therefore include the stipulation that much of the power resides in the low frequencies. I would prefer to formalize this by stipulating that the spectrum of a trend be a monotonically decreasing function, with zero power at the Nyquist frequency.

An interesting alternative viewpoint which occasionally leads to the same procedures as outlined above is to assume that the trend is in fact a deterministic function of time. While the merits of such an assumption are questionable at best, it does lead to easily interpretable results, simple prediction functions and usually simple trend extraction procedures as well. Again, differencing does more than it is supposed to do in such a case: while it removes low-order polynomial trends it also mutilates the residuals. Extraction by regression also yields residuals—i.e. approximations of the true non-trend component rather than the actual non-trend component itself—but this is true of all the methods treated in this chapter.

Designing the Perfect Trend-trap

Our prey is now known to us. It is a relatively smooth process with most power in the lower frequencies. It will be hiding in a thicket of high-frequency processes, and many common detrending procedures succeed in capturing only part of the beast, and inflict distortions on innocent non-trend components to boot.

While this would appear to make trend extraction difficult if not impossible, there is in fact light at the end of the tunnel. In a comparison between deseasonalizing procedures, one can judge the relative merits of the two procedures through a variety of criteria. Of these, at least one should also be used when judging detrending procedures: the detrending procedure should ideally be *idempotent*: when applied to an already detrended series it should have no effect. In terms of the frequency-response function, this should only have values of 1 and 0, and in the light of the discussion above, it should have value 1 below some value ω_0 and 0 above it. And so we are immediately led to the square-wave filter introduced by the author at the end of the chapter, as this most closely conforms to this ideal. As for the choice of cut-off point, I would suggest that any cyclical components should be left intact, and this means that the cut-off point should lie below the frequency associated with a suspected cyclical component: $\pi/6$ for monthly data, $\pi/2$ for quarterly data. The obtained non-trend component can then be studied for any cyclical components it contains without any fear that these have been mutilated by the detrending procedure. Of course, for the capture of cyclical components we will again have to think very carefully about the ammunition we use, but that is another story.

M. OOMS

Pollock has written a clear survey of some univariate detrending methods in econometrics and applied economics. He largely deals with the subject as a matter of linear filter design for 'historical filtering' for covariance stationary monthly data. He advocates the use of an easy-to-compute high-pass 'square-wave' filter to estimate trends. This choice elicits his preferences in trend estimation.

Pollock's approach of detrending is not very 'econometric': It does not involve modelling economic data and it does not address the question of interpreting (statistical) relationships between economic variables. His purpose is to retain 'interesting fluctuations' while removing slow, structural movements 'originating from a different source' contained in 'the trend'. He prefers to evaluate his method graphically using frequency domain variance decompositions (see Figures 11.1, 11.6, 11.7, 11.8, 11.9, 11.10, 11.13, 11.14 in the chapter). A sound interpretation of these effects depends on the assumption of mean and covariance stationarity. However, stationarity seems to be an exceptional property for most economic time series, see the sales figures in Figure 11.5, where seasonal means clearly change over time. From an econometric point of view I support the model-based approaches of Sections 11.4 and 11.5 of the chapter. I think that the 'data-transformation' to stationarity and the identification and estimation of the (non-stationary) trend and seasonal component should be treated as two separate consecutive problems. I would like to complement Pollock's discussion of econometricians' methods by mentioning relationships with other common methods, including the Beveridge–Nelson decomposition and the Census X-11 detrending filter.

In economic research the goal is often to distinguish between long- and short-run movements. Correlations in short-run movements (dominated by business-cycle variations) of different variables are to be explained by economic theory. The short-run components are stationary and their changes are forecastable: when the cyclical component is high, one expects lower growth rates in the near future. Changes in the long-run component are largely unforecastable. Interpreting correlations between long-run movements is dangerous for statistical reasons. A statistical model which allows for non-stationary series is necessary to estimate and interpret relationships between components in an econometric way.

Pollock confines oneself in the theoretical part to discrete time (Gaussian) linear time series models without 'strong seasonality'. If series are strongly related it is often more natural to consider multivariate models for trends and cycles (see e.g. Stock and Watson (1988), Harvey (1989, Chapter 8)). The business cycle is a multivariate phenomenon by definition. I use the following simple univariate linear model to illustrate econometric issues in model selection and subsequent identification of seasonal and trend components. Suppose there are two observations per year:

$$(1 - L)^{d_1}(1 + L)^{d_2}(y(t) - \mu_1 - \mu_2(-1)^t - \beta t) = (1 - \theta_1 L)(1 + \theta_2 L)\epsilon(t)$$

In this model one has to select the 'orders of integration' d_1 at frequency 0 and d_2 at frequency π. If $d_1 = 0$ one obtains a deterministic model for the trend. For many economic series the 'stochastic trend' or 'unit root' $I(1)$ hypothesis, $d_1 = 1$, $\theta_1 \neq 1$, $\theta_2 \neq -1$, seems to be more reasonable than the 'deterministic trend' or 'short memory' $I(0)$ hypothesis, $d_1 = 0$. This implies that differencing the series often *is* a good idea. In that case the trend identification methods of Sections 11.4 and 11.5 apply. If $d_1 = 0$ one can simply use regression on a deterministic trend. In order to get a real 'long-run' trend one should not allow for too much flexibility in the deterministic part as illustrated in Figure 11.2 of the chapter. The econometric literature contains many statistical tests for $d_1 = 1$ and $d_1 = 0$, which can be used for explicit modelling rules. If the main goal of detrending is to avoid 'spurious cross-correlations' between detrended variables the danger of underestimating d_1 is most important. Since $d_1 = 1$ is often appropriate it is important to evaluate the result of frequency responses of detrending filters for economic series with an $I(1)$ process as input. Harvey and Jaeger (1993) derive that the H–P detrending filter *can* introduce 'spurious' cycles, because they consider the spectrum of a detrended *random walk*. In Section 11.6 Pollock discusses the effect of the filter on a *white-noise process*. He infers therefore that it does *not* lead to 'spurious' cycles.

The problem of selecting or estimating the coefficients d_2, μ_2 and θ_2 for the seasonal, i.c. frequency π ($e^{i\pi} = -1$) component, is analogous to the zero frequency problem. For many monthly data one may need to allow for different orders of integration at different seasonal frequencies. Figures 11.5 and 11.6 in the chapter seem to suggest zero-order integration at frequency $5\pi/6$ and positive order integration at frequencies $\pi/3$ and $\pi/2$. More generally, one can treat the question of seasonal data transformation and/or seasonal adjustment, i.e. the 'correction for seasonal trends', in exactly the same way as the zero-frequency detrending problem. The main purpose of seasonal adjustment is also to get a better view of 'business cycle fluctuations'. Figures 11.5, 11.6 and 11.14 in the chapter illustrate the issue of 'overwhelming seasonal variation' very clearly. Appropriate modelling is necessary to avoid statistically and economically spurious cross-correlations between variables due to omitted 'external' causes. In this case one could imagine changes in the way of registering the cars causing the permanent changes in the seasonal pattern of the sales.

Pollock only wants to 'identify' a trend if it manifests itself 'distinctly' from the 'fluctuations' in the frequency domain. In Figures 11.14–11.16 in the chapter he empirically identifies one trend-cycle component. The detrended series in Figure 11.16 is dominated by seasonal fluctuations. It is clear that one has to deal with seasonality to get a reasonably 'pure' cyclical component, which could be used to relate car sales to other economic variables.

Trend identification and estimation in the model-based approaches is more clearly defined. One first chooses a maximum order of integration for the series based on a (non-)stationarity test. The common assumption in the models is the (zero mean-)stationarity of the (short memory) cyclical/irregular component.

Identification differs across the methods. The structural time series modelling (STM) approach of Harvey (1989) and the widely used Beveridge–Nelson (BN) (1981) decomposition use the economically relevant aspect of long-run forecastability to identify the trend. The long run, i.e. the infinite-horizon, forecast of the cyclical component is assumed constant. Changes in the (filtered estimates of the) trend-component are therefore equal to changes in the long-run forecast of the series, see e.g. Watson (1986). These changes are often interpreted as 'permanent' shocks to the economic variables.

The canonical decomposition (CD), still applied by Gómez and Maravall (1994) is not forecast based. It uses a smoothness ('clean of noise') restriction for the systematic components. The canonical decomposition and the Beveridge–Nelson decomposition apply to a wide range of 'reduced-form' ARIMA models. They do not need very stringent simplifying 'overidentifying' assumptions like the STM approach. Finally STM and CD share the basic assumption of independence of innovations for the trend and the innovations for the cyclical component, which BN lacks. This independence does not hold for the *estimated* innovations, however (see Harvey and Koopman (1992)). The determination of the order of integration is crucial for all identification methods. The STM, BN and CD approaches provide 'optimal' estimation methods and statistical diagnostics which allow one to evaluate model adequacy, e.g. for multi-step forecasting.

If one has to detrend a very large number of series, the data-based modelling approach is not always feasible. Then one can use a simple smoother to estimate the trend. Widely used fixed smoothers are used in the H–P method of Section 11.6 and in the trend estimation part of the Census X-11 program (Shiskin *et al.* (1967)) for seasonal adjustment of quarterly data. Both procedures are implemented in many software packages like Eviews (QMS (1995)).

The coefficients of other simple smoothers depend on the data in a limited sense. They are meant for 'automatic detrending' of a wide range of 'typical' macroeconomic time series. Pollock's method falls into this category. The trend estimator of the monthly version of the Census X-11 procedure is another one. Just as one needs a good model for seasonal movements to efficiently estimate a trend one needs a good model for the trend in order to perform 'optimal' seasonal adjustment! The trend estimator is a (symmetric) Henderson Moving Average filter, which leaves second-order trends intact (see Laroque (1977)). One selects one out of three filters. The lag length of the filter depends on the variance ratio of the irregular (noise) and the trend-cycle component. High noise variance leads to a 'narrow-frequency-band' estimator for the trend, but not nearly as narrow as the H–P-filter (see Figure 11.A). This trend estimator seems to meet many of Pollock's demands. It is easy to compute. It is easily interpretable and it makes a clear distinction between trend/cycle and other fluctuations. Furthermore: its filter is pure MA, which means that historical trend estimates for a certain date do not change after 3–4 years as new observations for later dates become available.

Figure 11.A depicts the frequency response of the (linear part of the) 13- and 23-term Henderson trend estimator. It also shows the 13-term trend estimator of the Census procedure, where the seasonal adjustment already plays a crucial part

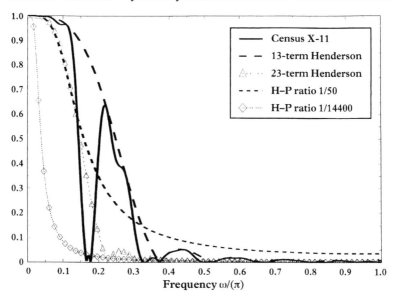

Figure 11.A Frequency response for trend-estimating filters: Henderson (13-term and 23-term), the corresponding filter of Census X-11 for monthly data and Hodrick–Prescott with smoothing parameters 1/14 400 and 1/50

(as it should for Pollock's car example). For comparison I included the H–P filter with smoothing parameters, $\lambda = \sigma_\eta^2 / \sigma_\nu^2$ (see equation (32) in the chapter), of 1/14 400 (standard for monthly data) and 1/50.

Let me conclude. For univariate analysis of a few series I would prefer a model-based approach where the method of detrending depends on some tests. I prefer data-based trend models forecasting with a forecasting interpretation. For a few closely related macro-series I would suggest a multivariate model-based approach. For many series I would suggest to use the standard Census-filter, since this automatically involves a lot of well-tested extras like trading-day corrections, and outlier resistance which are not yet implemented in the model-based approach. The new X-12 version implements useful ideas from the model-based approach like ARIMA (back)forecasting and outlier modelling. Knowledge about different types of detrending of economic time series should become more widespread. The consequences for use of detrended series in applied economics should be studied in more detail (see e.g. Watson (1986)).

REPLY

D.S.G. POLLOCK

The above two comments provide a good contrast. The first review, by Ivo Steyn, is a model of brevity and conciseness. It summarizes and reaffirms some of my contentions regarding the appropriate way of specifying a detrending filter. It also makes me wish that I had thought of such eloquent ways of stating the matter.

The second review, by Marius Ooms, asserts some of the opinions regarding the model-building approach to detrending which I have been calling into question; and so it provides me with the opportunity for restating my case. It also raises some technical matters in which I disagree with Ooms. I shall deal with these first. Thereafter, I shall take issue again with the model-building approach.

The first of the technical issues originates in Ooms' assertion that the treatment of the chapter is somehow limited to covariance-stationary processes, which carries the implication, if I understand him correctly, that the approach which he advocates is not limited in this way. Indeed, most people would agree that to talk of detrending a stationary process is a contradiction in terms; and, were Ooms correct in his aspersion, then the contents of the chapter would largely evaporate.

The idea that the account is confined to stationary processes may originate in a misinterpretation of the diagrams which represent the frequency responses of the various filters. These show the extent to which the filters amplify or attenuate cyclical components at all frequencies (measured in radians per period) ranging from the trend frequency of zero to the Nyquist frequency of π, which represents the maximum detectable frequency.

Of course, the diagrams show most clearly the effect which the filters have upon a signal with a uniform spectrum, of which a stationary white-noise process $\varepsilon(t)$, which has the spectral density function $f_\varepsilon = \sigma_\varepsilon^2/2\pi$, is a prime example. But this implies no restriction in the range of the signals to which the filters may be applied. (I should note in passing that the chirp signal of Figure 11.11 in the chapter also has a uniform spectrum.)

Consider some other process $y(t) = \mu(L)\varepsilon(t)$, where $\mu(L)$ is a rational operator which might contain roots or poles of unit modulus in its denominator. Then the spectrum or pseudo-spectrum of the process is given by

$$f_y(z) = \frac{\sigma_\varepsilon^2}{2\pi} \mu(z)\mu(z^{-1}) \qquad \text{where} \qquad z = e^{i\omega}$$

and, if $y(t)$ were passed through the filter $\psi(L)$, then the spectrum or pseudo-spectrum of the output $x(t) = \psi(L)y(t)$ would be given by

$$f_x(z) = \frac{\sigma_\varepsilon^2}{2\pi} \psi(z)\mu(z)\mu(z^{-1})\psi(z^{-1})$$

$$= \psi(z)\psi(z^{-1})f_y(z)$$

This will constitute a function which is analytic except at a finite number of singular points which correspond to the poles of $\mu(z)$ and $\psi(z)$ and of their conjugates $\mu(z^{-1})$ and $\psi(z^{-1})$. If none of the poles lie on the unit circle, then f_x will constitute a regular spectral-density function of the sort that pertains to a stationary process. We can guarantee that this is the case by ensuring that, whenever $\mu(z)$ has a unit pole, the filter function $\psi(z)$ has a corresponding zero which will serve to cancel the pole.

As an example, we may think of applying to a simple non-stationary random walk $y(t) = (I - L)^{-1}\varepsilon(t)$ the Hodrick–Prescott detrending filter which has the formula

$$\psi(L) = \frac{(I - L^{-1})^2(I - L)^2}{(I - L^{-1})^2(I - L)^2 + \lambda^{-1}I}$$

The resulting sequence $x(t)$ has the regular spectral density function which is labelled C in Figure 11.B. There are more (zero-frequency) unit zeros in the filter

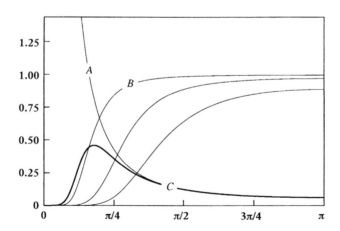

Figure 11.B   The effect of applying the Hodrick–Prescott filter to a random walk

than there are (zero-frequency) unit roots within the first-order random-walk process. Therefore the function C is zero-valued at the origin, which implies that the processed sequence $x(t)$ will be free of trend.

We might also note in passing that, contrary to an assertion in the comments, the low spectral peak in C, which corresponds to some degree of cyclicality in $x(t)$, is not due to the non-stationarity of the random walk. It is due, instead, to the peculiar profile, labelled B in the figure, of the frequency response of the filter. This filter allows some of the signal components to be transmitted when, perhaps, they should have been stopped or, at least, more firmly attenuated.

The highpass square-wave filter, which has been advocated in the chapter and which has the formula

$$\psi(L) = \frac{(I - L^{-1})^n(I - L)^n}{(I - L^{-1})^n(I - L)^n + \lambda^{-1}(I + L^{-1})^n(I + L)^n}$$

is appropriate to the detrending of non-stationary signals precisely because it nullifies the zero-frequency trend component. It achieves this effect by virtue of the difference operator $(I - L^{-1})^n(I - L)^n$ which is present in the numerator. The order of the operator is $2n$; and this is bound to be greater than the number of unit roots which a model builder might detect within an empirical econometric sequence. It follows that the square-wave filter is pre-eminently a device for reducing trended sequences to stationarity.

Ooms advocates a modelling procedure which begins by applying the difference operator alone to the sequence under investigation in what amounts to a preliminary detrending exercise. The argument of my chapter is that it is inappropriate to apply the difference operator in isolation because its effects encroach upon regions of the frequency range which are bound to contain information which has nothing to do with the trend and which may be of prime interest to the economists. The square-wave filter, which I recommend as a detrending device, is designed to avoid such problems.

The second of the technical issues raised in the review by Ooms concerns an old assertion that the Hodrick–Prescott detrending filter can introduce spurious cycles into the data which passes through it. My own assertion is that it cannot induce spurious cycles. At worst, it may fail to remove the sorts of motions which, in common opinion, should be attributed to the trend. It may be that the only issue here is a semantic one; but I think that it is important that, in this discussion, the key words should retain their exact meanings.

Perhaps it is best to describe the effect of the Hodrick–Prescott filter in terms of a simple physical analogy. The essential fact is that the gain of its frequency-response function never exceeds unity. This means that, seen as a physical device, its effect, at all frequencies, is either to preserve or to dissipate energy. In accordance with the normal meaning of the word 'filter', it blocks or holds back some of the components of the signal. It never amplifies any cycles and it never introduces any. If a cycle is seen in the processed data, then it must also be present to the same extent, or to a greater extent, in the original data; and it is wrong to describe such cycles as spurious.

Now let me talk of models. Economists and econometricians put great emphasis on these. I can understand why this should be so when I remember an ancient professor of economics who had been a young radical in the 1950s. He was imbued by the same spirit of modernism which gave rise to Tjalling Koopmans' (1947) tract entitled 'Measurement without theory' which pilloried business-cycle analysts who were content to examine the data without prejudice and without the aid of a formal model or an hypothesis.

Whenever one of the younger colleagues of this professor made an assertion about how the social world works or how it might be reformed, he would demand fiercely to know what their model was. The usual effect would be to cause a retreat, but occasionally the unrealistic assumptions upon which the assertions had been based would be revealed.

My reasons for disparaging the model-based approach to detrending is that I think that the underlying assumptions are unrealistic. Although unit-root stochastic processes do often provide good analogies for econometric sequences, such analogies can be carried too far. The pseudo-spectrum of the unit-root process, which is represented by A in Figure 11.B, is unlike anything which we observe in practice. This pseudo-spectrum manifests infinite power at zero frequency; and a substantial spread of power is to be found over the entire range of the frequencies.

If we were really faced with such an unbridled process, then we should have no alternative but to wield the crude difference operator. We should also have to reconcile ourselves to the fact that there is little chance of discerning fine detail in the midst of all the noise and fury which accompanies such a process.

In fact, the elements of non-stationarity which we find in econometric data are much tamer than an unbridled unit-root random-walk process. In some cases, they contain enough power in the low-frequency regions to evade the blocking effects of badly designed filters; and, when they do so, a more carefully designed detrending filter, such as the square-wave filter, is usually equal to the task of stopping them.

The disadvantage of the model-based approach to detrending, which takes unit-root non-stationarity for granted, is that it wields some blunt instruments which crush the very objects which it purports to investigate.

REFERENCES

Bell, W. (1984) Signal extraction for nonstationary time series. *The Annals of Statistics* **12**, 646–64.

Beveridge, S. and Nelson, C. (1981) A new approach to the decomposition of economic time series into permanent and transitory components with particular attention to measurement of the 'business cycle'. *Journal of Monetary Economics* **7**, 151–74.

Box, G.E.P. and Jenkins, G.M. (1976) *Time Series Analysis: Forecasting and Control*, revised edition. Holden-Day, San Francisco.

Burman, J.P. (1980) Seasonal adjustment by signal extraction. *Journal of the Royal Statistical Society, Series A* **143**, 321–37.

Cleveland, W.P. and Tiao, G. (1976) A model for the Census X-11 seasonal adjustment process. *Journal of the American Statistical Association* **71**, 581–7.

Cogley, T. and Nason, J.M. (1995) Effects of the Hodrick–Prescott filter on trend and difference stationary time series, implications for business cycle research. *Journal of Economic Dynamics and Control* **19**, 253–78.

Craven, P. and Wahba, G. (1979) Smoothing noisy data with spline functions. *Numerische Mathematik* **31**, 377–403.

Gersch, W. and Kitagawa, G. (1983) The prediction of time series with trends and seasonalities. *Journal of Business and Economic Statistics* **1**, 253–64.

Gómez, V. and Maravall, A. (1994) Estimation, prediction, and interpolation for nonstationary series with the Kalman filter. *Journal of the American Statistical Association* **89**, 611–24.

Harvey, A.C. (1989) *Forecasting, Structural Time Series Models and the Kalman Filter*. Cambridge University Press, Cambridge.

Harvey, A.C. and Jaeger, A. (1993) Detrending, stylized facts and the business cycle. *Journal of Applied Econometrics* **8**, 231–47.

Harvey, A.C. and Koopman, S.J. (1992) Diagnostic checking of unobserved components time series models. *Journal of Business and Economic Statistics* **10**, 377–89.

Hillmer, S.C. and Tiao, G.C. (1982) An ARIMA-model-based approach to seasonal adjustment. *Journal of the American Statistical Association* **77**, 63–70.

Hodrick, R. and Prescott, E. (1980) Post-war U.S. business cycles: an empirical investigation. Working Paper, Carnegie–Mellon University, Pittsburgh, Pennsylvania.

King, R.G. and Rebelo, S.G. (1993) Low frequency filtering and real business cycles. *Journal of Economic Dynamics and Control* **17**, 207–31.

Koopmans, T.C. (1947) Measurement without theory. *Review of Economics and Statistics* **29**, 161–79.

Kydland, F.E. and Prescott, C. (1990) Business cycles: real facts and a monetary myth. *Federal Reserve Bank of Minneapolis Quarterly Review* **14**, 3–18.

Laroque, G. (1977) Analyse d'une méthode de désaisonnalisation: le Programme X 11, du US Bureau of Census, Version Trimestrielle. *Annales de l'INSEE* **28**, 105–27.

Maravall, A. and Pierce, D.A. (1987) A prototypical seasonal adjustment model. *Journal of Time Series Analysis* **8**, 177–93.

Nerlove, M., Grether, D.M. and Carvalho, J.L. (1979) *Analysis of Economic Time Series*. Academic Press, New York.

Newbold, P. and Bos, T. (1990) *Introductory Business Forecasting*. South-Western Publishing Co., Cincinatti, OH.

Pierce, D.A. (1979) Signal extraction in nonstationary time series. *The Annals of Statistics* **6**, 1303–20.

QMS, Quantitative Micro Software (1995) *Eviews, Econometric Views for Windows and Macintosh*. Irvine, CA, 2.0 edn.

Reinsch, C.H. (1976) Smoothing by spline functions. *Numerische Mathematik* **10**, 177–83.

Shiskin, J., Young, A.H. and Musgrave, J.C. (1967) The X-11 variant of the Census method II Seasonal Adjustment Program. Technical Paper No. 15, Bureau of the Census, US Department of Commerce, US Government Printing Office., Washington, DC, USA.

Stock, J.H. and Watson, M.W. (1988) Testing for common trends. *Journal of the American Statistical Association* **83**, 1097–1107.

Tintner, G. (1940) *The Variate Difference Method*. John Wiley, Bloomington, IN.

Tintner, G. (1953) *Econometrics*. John Wiley, New York.

Watson, M.W. (1986) Univariate detrending methods with stochastic trends. *Journal of Monetary Economics* **18**, 49–75.

Wecker, W.P. and Ansley, C.F. (1983) The signal extraction approach to nonlinear regression and spline smoothing. *Journal of the American Statistical Association* **78**, 81–9.

Whittle, P. (1983) *Prediction and Regulation by Linear Least-Square Methods*, second revised edition, Basil Blackwell, Oxford.

Index

Index compiled by Kim Harris